First World War

and Army of Occupation

War Diary

France, Belgium and Germany

38 DIVISION
115 Infantry Brigade
South Wales Borderers
10th Battalion
4 December 1915 - 21 May 1919

WO95/2562/1

The Naval & Military Press Ltd
www.nmarchive.com
Published in association with The National Archives

Published by

The Naval & Military Press Ltd

Unit 10 Ridgewood Industrial Park,

Uckfield, East Sussex,

TN22 5QE England

Tel: +44 (0) 1825 749494

www.naval-military-press.com

www.nmarchive.com

This diary has been reprinted in facsimile from the original. Any imperfections are inevitably reproduced and the quality may fall short of modern type and cartographic standards.

Contents

Document type	Place/Title	Date From	Date To
Heading	WO95/2562/1 38 Divn 115 Inf. Brig. 10 Bn. South Wales Borderers 1915 Dec-1919 May		
Heading	38th Division 115th Infy Bde 10th Bn Sth Wales Bordrs Dec 1915-May 1919		
Miscellaneous			
Miscellaneous	A Form. Messages And Signals.		
Heading	10th S.W. Borderers Vol I Dec 1915 Jan 1916		
War Diary	Havre	04/12/1915	04/12/1915
War Diary	Aire	05/12/1915	05/12/1915
War Diary	Quernes	05/12/1915	20/12/1915
War Diary	Robecq	20/12/1915	27/12/1915
War Diary	Levantie	27/12/1915	04/01/1916
War Diary	Robecq.	04/01/1916	13/01/1916
War Diary	Pont De Hem	13/01/1916	25/01/1916
War Diary	Locon	26/01/1916	31/01/1916
Heading	10 SWB Vol 3 March 1916 Vol 3		
Heading	10th S.W. Borderers Vol:2		
War Diary	Croix Barbee	01/02/1916	16/02/1916
War Diary	Croix Barbee Croix Marmeuse	17/02/1916	17/02/1916
War Diary	Croix Marmuse	18/02/1916	18/02/1916
War Diary	Le Touret	19/02/1916	23/02/1916
War Diary	Trenches	24/02/1916	27/02/1916
War Diary	Festubert	28/02/1916	06/03/1916
War Diary	Le Touret	07/03/1916	10/03/1916
War Diary	Trenches	11/03/1916	14/03/1916
War Diary	Festubert	15/03/1916	15/03/1916
War Diary	Harisoirs	16/03/1916	22/03/1916
War Diary	Harisoir Gorre	23/03/1916	23/03/1916
War Diary	Gorre	24/03/1916	24/03/1916
War Diary	Trenches	25/03/1916	28/03/1916
War Diary	Givenchy	29/03/1916	01/04/1916
War Diary	Trenches	02/04/1916	05/04/1916
War Diary	Gorre	06/04/1916	08/04/1916
War Diary	Harisoir	09/04/1916	13/04/1916
War Diary	Harisoirs Estaires	14/04/1916	15/04/1916
War Diary	Trenches	16/04/1916	19/04/1916
War Diary	Laventie	20/04/1916	23/04/1916
War Diary	Trenches	24/04/1916	27/04/1916
War Diary	Laventie	28/04/1916	30/04/1916
War Diary	Merville X29.d.22	30/04/1916	09/05/1916
War Diary	Trenches Winchester House M.23.a 4.1	10/05/1916	13/05/1916
War Diary	Trenches	11/05/1916	13/05/1916
War Diary	Pont Du Hem M14b7	14/05/1916	14/05/1916
War Diary	Pont Du Hem	15/05/1916	17/05/1916
War Diary	Trenches Winchester House M.23.a.4.1	18/05/1916	18/05/1916
War Diary	Trenches	19/05/1916	21/05/1916
War Diary	Pont Du Hem	22/05/1916	22/05/1916
War Diary	Pont Du Hem M.14.b.7.5	23/05/1916	25/05/1916
War Diary	Merville X29d22	26/05/1916	27/05/1916
War Diary	Merville	28/05/1916	31/05/1916

War Diary	Merville K29d2.2	01/06/1916	05/06/1916
War Diary	Red. House	06/06/1916	10/06/1916
War Diary	Merville K29.d.22	11/06/1916	11/06/1916
War Diary	Robecq B.23.d.0.0	12/06/1916	13/06/1916
War Diary	Robecq B13d00	13/06/1916	14/06/1916
War Diary	Auchel	15/06/1916	15/06/1916
War Diary	Villers. Brulin V26d5.3	16/06/1916	26/06/1916
War Diary	Bonnieres Sht Lens II	27/06/1916	27/06/1916
War Diary	Gezaincourt Sht. Lens II	28/06/1916	30/06/1916
Heading	115th Inf. Bde. 38th Div. War Diary 10th Battn. The South Wales Borderers. July 1916		
War Diary	Toutencourt Sht. Lens II.	01/07/1916	01/07/1916
War Diary	Acheux Sht Lens.II.	02/07/1916	03/07/1916
War Diary	Buire-Sur-Ancre. Sht Amiens 17	04/07/1916	05/07/1916
War Diary	Mametz Sht Amiens 17	06/07/1916	06/07/1916
War Diary	Trenches	07/07/1916	08/07/1916
War Diary	Mametz Bivuouc Sht Amiens 17	09/07/1916	13/07/1916
War Diary	Couin Sht Lens II.	14/07/1916	14/07/1916
War Diary	Courcelles Au-Bois. Sht Lens II	15/07/1916	18/07/1916
War Diary	Trenches	19/07/1916	19/07/1916
War Diary	Trenches Sht Lens II	20/07/1916	20/07/1916
War Diary	Trenches	21/07/1916	22/07/1916
War Diary	Courcelles-Au-Bois.	23/07/1916	26/07/1916
War Diary	Trenches	27/07/1916	27/07/1916
War Diary	Colincamps Trenches Sheet Lens II	28/07/1916	28/07/1916
War Diary	Trenches	29/07/1916	29/07/1916
War Diary	Bus, Sht Lens.II.	30/07/1916	31/07/1916
War Diary	Millain Sht Hazebrouck 5A Belgium	01/08/1916	01/08/1916
War Diary	Millain.	02/08/1916	03/08/1916
War Diary	Bollezeele A24C5.3. Sht 27	04/08/1916	19/08/1916
War Diary	Trenches St Julien Map Ed3.d. No. 28. C.25.dF2.4	20/08/1916	23/08/1916
War Diary	Trenches St Julien. Map Ed3d No 28	24/08/1916	28/08/1916
War Diary	Trenches West Bank of Yser A25.d.12.4	29/08/1916	31/08/1916
War Diary	Trenches West Bank of Yser. C25. 1 1/24 St Julien ED3 No 28	01/09/1916	01/09/1916
War Diary	Front Line Trenches Ypres Salient	02/09/1916	05/09/1916
War Diary	Trenches West Bank of Yser. Extreme Left of British Line	06/09/1916	06/09/1916
War Diary	Front Line Trenches.	07/09/1916	10/09/1916
War Diary	Trenches West Bank of Yser. Extreme Left of British Line	11/09/1916	14/09/1916
War Diary	Left Sub-Sector on Ypres Salient.	15/09/1916	17/09/1916
War Diary	Camp. E. Belgium & France. Map A 30 a 43	18/09/1916	18/09/1916
War Diary	Camp. "E"	19/09/1916	20/09/1916
War Diary	Yser Canal C 25 d 1. 1/24	21/09/1916	21/09/1916
War Diary	Trenches Irish Farm Right Subsector Left Sector.	22/09/1916	25/09/1916
War Diary	E. Ban of Yser. St Julien Map. C25d1.1/2.4	26/09/1916	27/09/1916
War Diary	East. Bank Of Yser Canal St Julien Map C.25. 1/2.4	28/09/1916	30/09/1916
War Diary	Camp. "D" Bel. 9 France Map. 30. a 4.2	01/10/1916	03/10/1916
War Diary	East Bank Yser Canal St. Juliens Trench Map C25d 2, 1/2.6	04/10/1916	08/10/1916
War Diary	Irish. Farm. Front Line. St. Julien Map C 25d1.1/2.4	09/10/1916	11/10/1916
War Diary	C.25 d 2.1/2 C St. Julien Tr. Map. E. Bank of R. Yser	12/10/1916	15/10/1916
War Diary	C19c72 St Julien Tr. Map E. Bank of. Yser	16/10/1916	24/10/1916
War Diary	Camp E. A30.a.7.3	25/10/1916	29/10/1916

War Diary	C 25 d1,11/2 to 30/10/16 (Irish Farm) Front Line (Map S1 Julian)	30/10/1916	30/10/1916
War Diary	Irish Farm C25d1,1/2.4	31/10/1916	31/10/1916
War Diary	Camp P.	07/11/1916	09/11/1916
War Diary	Right Sub Sector St Julien Front Map b 25.d.1.1/2.4	10/11/1916	11/11/1916
War Diary	Ref St Julien Trench Map C25.d.11.2.4	01/11/1916	04/11/1916
War Diary	Camp P.	05/11/1916	06/11/1916
War Diary	Right Sub Sector St Julien Trench Map 25d 1 1/2.4	12/11/1916	15/11/1916
War Diary	Left Sub Sector Left Sector St Julien Trench Map C 25 C 7.2	16/11/1916	17/11/1916
War Diary	Right Sub Sector St Julien Trench Map b25.C72	18/11/1916	25/11/1916
War Diary	Camp D A 30a 42	26/11/1916	03/12/1916
Heading	Some of The Note in ?		
War Diary	Camp D A30.a.4.2	04/12/1916	08/12/1916
War Diary	Canal Bank C25d	09/12/1916	11/12/1916
War Diary	Camp D A.10.a.4.8	12/12/1916	12/12/1916
War Diary	Bluit Farm. Boisinghe Sector B10 C2.3	13/12/1916	13/12/1916
War Diary	Bluit Farm B10 C.2.3	14/12/1916	16/12/1916
War Diary	B10.C.2.3	17/12/1916	17/12/1916
War Diary	Front Line Chateau	18/12/1916	18/12/1916
War Diary	B.11.b.8.5	19/12/1916	19/12/1916
War Diary	Front Line Bouinghe Chateau B.11.b.8.5	20/12/1916	22/12/1916
War Diary	Blust Farm Support B10C2.3	23/12/1916	23/12/1916
War Diary	Boesinghe Sector Blust Farm B10C.2.3	26/12/1916	26/12/1916
War Diary	Front Line Boesinghe Chateau B11.b.8.5	27/12/1916	28/12/1916
War Diary	Boesinghe Chateau B11.b.8.5	29/12/1916	30/12/1916
War Diary	Bollezeele Sheet 27 A24. C.5.3	31/12/1916	14/01/1917
War Diary	Camp D A30a42	15/01/1917	15/01/1917
War Diary	Camp D A30a42 (28 N.W)	15/01/1917	16/01/1917
War Diary	Finebluet B.10.C.2.3 (28 NW)	16/01/1917	16/01/1917
War Diary	Finebluet B.10.C.2.3.	17/01/1917	20/01/1917
War Diary	Front Line B.11.b.5 (Boesinghe Chateau)	21/01/1917	23/01/1917
War Diary	Front Line 11.b.8.5	23/01/1917	24/01/1917
War Diary	Roussel Fm B13a2.6	25/01/1917	28/01/1917
War Diary	Machine Gun Farm 5.C.8.8	28/01/1917	29/01/1917
War Diary	Machine Gun Farm 28 N.W. F 5.c.8.8	29/01/1917	14/02/1917
War Diary	Bluet Farm. B.10.C.2.3	15/02/1917	18/02/1917
War Diary	Boesinghe Chateau B12.b.5	19/02/1917	22/02/1917
War Diary	X. Camp A 16 Central	23/02/1917	26/02/1917
War Diary	Bluet Farm B10 C.2.3	27/02/1917	02/03/1917
War Diary	Front Line	02/03/1917	02/03/1917
War Diary	Boesinghe Chateau B.11.b.8.5	03/03/1917	06/03/1917
War Diary	X Camp A 16 Central	07/03/1917	10/03/1917
War Diary	Bluet Farm B10 C.2.3	11/03/1917	14/03/1917
War Diary	Boesinghe Chateau B11.b.8.5	15/03/1917	18/03/1917
War Diary	X Camp A. 16. Central	19/03/1917	21/03/1917
War Diary	Canal Bank B24.b.9.4 Sheet. 28 N.W.2	22/03/1917	12/04/1917
War Diary	X Camp A16 Central	13/04/1917	19/04/1917
War Diary	Front Line Boesinghe Chateau B.11.6.8.5	20/04/1917	25/04/1917
War Diary	Bleuet Farm B.10.C.2.3	26/04/1917	01/05/1917
War Diary	Bollezeele Sheet 27 A.24.C.5.3	02/05/1917	16/05/1917
War Diary	Houtkerque Sheet 27 E.14.d.	16/05/1917	17/05/1917
War Diary	Camp Z F.25.d.8.1	17/05/1917	17/05/1917
War Diary	Camp Z Sheet 27 F.25.d.8.1	18/05/1917	18/05/1917
War Diary	Roussel Farm. Sheet 28. B.13.a.2.6	18/05/1917	31/05/1917

Operation(al) Order(s)	Operation Order No. 42 By Lieut Col. C.D. Harvey Commanding D.L.R.	28/05/1917	28/05/1917
Operation(al) Order(s)	March Orders For Operation Orders No. 42. By Lt. Col. C.D. Harvey Commanding 10th Bn. S.W.B.	28/05/1917	28/05/1917
War Diary	Roussel Farm Sheet 28 B.13.a.2.6	01/06/1917	12/06/1917
War Diary	Front Line (Boesinghe Chateau) B.11.b.8.5	13/06/1917	15/06/1917
War Diary	Coppernollehoek A.8.d.2.3	16/06/1917	17/06/1917
War Diary	De Wippe Cabaret A.10.b.6.4	18/06/1917	27/06/1917
War Diary	Caestre Sheet 27. W.3.a.4.5	27/06/1917	28/06/1917
War Diary	Laires 6.D. (Hazebrouck 5A)	28/06/1917	30/06/1917
War Diary	Laires Sheet Hazebrouck 5A 6.D.	01/07/1917	16/07/1917
War Diary	Molinghem Sheet Hazebrouck 5A. 5F	17/07/1917	17/07/1917
War Diary	Caestre Sheet Hazebrouck 5A. 3H.	18/07/1917	19/07/1917
War Diary	Walon Sheet 27 E16.A95	19/07/1917	20/07/1917
War Diary	Walon Sheet 27 E16 A95 Stoke Farm Sheet 27 F.5.C	21/07/1917	22/07/1917
War Diary	Stoke Farm (Sheet 27) F.5C.	22/07/1917	30/07/1917
War Diary	Camp G.A.16.a.	30/07/1917	31/07/1917
War Diary	(28) G Camp, Area	30/07/1917	00/08/1917
War Diary	Assembly Trenches Sht 28 B 2 M	31/07/1917	31/07/1917
War Diary	Kiel Cott	31/07/1917	31/07/1917
War Diary	Pilckhem & Iron Cross Ridges N of Ypres	01/08/1917	03/08/1917
War Diary	Pilckhem Ridge and Iron Cross Ridge	01/08/1917	02/08/1917
War Diary	Pilckhem Ridge	03/08/1917	05/08/1917
War Diary	Elverdinghe Chateau	05/08/1917	05/08/1917
War Diary	Stoke Farm Camp 27.F5.C.	05/08/1917	18/08/1917
War Diary	Candle Trench	19/08/1917	21/08/1917
War Diary	Au Bon Gite	22/08/1917	29/08/1917
War Diary	Canal Bank C.13C.1,1/2.8 (28.N.W)	30/08/1917	30/08/1917
War Diary	L.E. Lines B.22.d.7.7 (28 N.W.)	30/08/1917	31/08/1917
War Diary	L.2. B.22.d.7.7 (Sh. 28)	01/09/1917	04/09/1917
War Diary	L.2.B.22.d.7.7	04/09/1917	04/09/1917
War Diary	Canal Bank C.13.C.1.1/2.8	05/09/1917	09/09/1917
War Diary	Persia Camp (Sh 27) E.16.d.9.5	10/09/1917	12/09/1917
War Diary	Steenvoorde.	12/09/1917	13/09/1917
War Diary	Morbecque	13/09/1917	14/09/1917
War Diary	La Gorgue	14/09/1917	15/09/1917
War Diary	Waterlands South. B.20.d.8.9	15/09/1917	16/09/1917
War Diary	Front Line L'Epinette Sub Sector I.3.d.35.70	17/09/1917	17/09/1917
War Diary	L'Epinette Sub Sector I.3.d.35.70	17/09/1917	24/09/1917
War Diary	The Laundries Erquinghem H.5.a.4.7	25/09/1917	02/10/1917
War Diary	Front Line L'Epinette Sub-Sector I.3.d.35.70	03/10/1917	08/10/1917
War Diary	The Laundries Erquinghem H.5.a.4.7	09/10/1917	17/10/1917
War Diary	The Laundries Erquinghem	17/10/1917	18/10/1917
War Diary	Front Line L'Epinette Sub-Sector T.3.d.35.70	18/10/1917	27/10/1917
War Diary	Laundries Erquinghem H.5.a.4.7	28/10/1917	31/10/1917
Operation(al) Order(s)	Operation Orders No. A. by Major. E.T. Rees. M.C. Commanding Hangar.	13/10/1917	13/10/1917
Operation(al) Order(s)	Operation Orders No. 12a by Major E.T. Rees M.C., Commanding Hangar and Hasten.	18/10/1917	18/10/1917
War Diary	Laundries Erquinghem H.5.a.4.7	01/11/1917	04/11/1917
War Diary	Front Line L'Epinette. I.3.d.80.85	04/11/1917	16/11/1917
War Diary	Armentieres H.5.b.8.7	16/11/1917	22/11/1917
War Diary	Front Line L'Epinette 1.3.d.80.85	22/11/1917	28/11/1917
War Diary	Laundries Erquinghem H.5.a.4.7	29/11/1917	04/12/1917
War Diary	Front Line. L'Epinette I.3.d.80.85	04/12/1917	09/12/1917
War Diary	Front Line L'Epinette Subsector 1.3.80.85	10/12/1917	10/12/1917

War Diary	Works in Subdiary Lines From I.9.b.50.35 to C 28.a.80.30 Hqrs at H.5.6.8.7	11/12/1917	16/12/1917
War Diary	Front Line L'Epinette I.3.d.80.85	16/12/1917	19/12/1917
War Diary	Estaires. 36a/L.30.a.5.2	20/12/1917	21/12/1917
War Diary	Estaires. L.30.a.5.2	22/12/1917	03/01/1918
War Diary	Estaires	04/01/1918	04/01/1918
War Diary	Estaires L.30.a.5.2	05/01/1918	06/01/1918
War Diary	H.13.b.5.5	07/01/1918	07/01/1918
War Diary	36/Ref H.13.b.5.5	07/01/1918	07/01/1918
War Diary	H.13.B.5.5	08/01/1918	13/01/1918
War Diary	Estaires L.30.a.5.2	14/01/1918	15/01/1918
War Diary	Estaires	16/01/1918	12/02/1918
War Diary	Estaires H.4.d.8.8	13/02/1918	13/02/1918
War Diary	H.4.d.8.8	14/02/1918	15/02/1918
War Diary	H4d.8.8 120.b.9.5	15/02/1918	19/02/1918
War Diary		28/01/1918	28/01/1918
War Diary	Estaires	29/01/1918	31/01/1918
War Diary	H4.d88. I20b9.5	20/02/1918	28/02/1918
War Diary	Wez Macquart Sector I.20.a.68.70	01/03/1918	18/03/1918
War Diary	Wez Macquart Sector	19/03/1918	20/03/1918
War Diary	Wez Macquart Sector I.20.a.68.70	21/03/1918	29/03/1918
War Diary	Neuveau Monde.	30/03/1918	30/03/1918
War Diary	Haverskerque J.28.d (36a)	31/03/1918	31/03/1918
Heading	115th Inf. Bde. 38th Div. War Diary 10th Battn. The South Wales Borderers. April 1918		
War Diary	Haverskerque J.27.d (36a)	01/04/1918	01/04/1918
War Diary	Villers Bocage (Amiens 37 1.D)	02/04/1918	02/04/1918
War Diary	Hedauville P.34.a.t.c. (57d)	03/04/1918	04/04/1918
War Diary	Hedauville P.34.a.t.c.	04/04/1918	07/04/1918
War Diary	Toutencourt (Lens 11)	08/04/1918	10/04/1918
War Diary	Warloy-Baillon (Lens 11)	10/04/1918	16/04/1918
War Diary	V.21.C W.13.C.	17/04/1918	18/04/1918
War Diary	Bouzincourt W.13.a.3.7	19/04/1918	21/04/1918
War Diary	V.28.b Near Millencourt	21/04/1918	25/04/1918
War Diary	Front Line W.20.c.7.8 (Nr. Albert)	25/04/1918	26/04/1918
War Diary	Bouzincourt W.13.a.5.9	27/04/1918	30/04/1918
War Diary	Bouzincourt W.13.a.50.85	01/05/1918	01/05/1918
War Diary	W.7.C.5.1	01/05/1918	02/05/1918
War Diary	Bouzincourt W.7.C.5.1	03/05/1918	14/05/1918
War Diary	Nr. Senlis V.22.b.4.8	15/05/1918	20/05/1918
War Diary	Herissart T.10.d.2.4	20/05/1918	03/06/1918
War Diary	P.14.C	03/06/1918	03/06/1918
War Diary	Acheux Wood P.14.C.	04/06/1918	04/06/1918
War Diary	Q2.6.a9.2 Sht 57d.SE	05/06/1918	06/06/1918
War Diary	Q34 a.5.2. Sht 57d.SE	07/06/1918	10/06/1918
War Diary	Q31.b.90.90. Sht 57d.S.E.	11/06/1918	12/06/1918
War Diary	Q19.C.5.8 Sht 57d S.E	13/06/1918	27/06/1918
War Diary	Q28.a.7.7	28/06/1918	28/06/1918
War Diary	Q28.a.7.7. Sht 57d S.E.	29/06/1918	01/07/1918
War Diary	P21.d.50.70 Sheet 57d S.E.	02/07/1918	10/07/1918
War Diary	C28 Central Sheet 57d SE.	11/07/1918	11/07/1918
War Diary	P21.d.50.70 Sheet 57D.SE	06/07/1918	08/07/1918
War Diary	C.28 Central Sheet 57D S.E.	12/07/1918	18/07/1918
War Diary	T10.C.90.95 Sheet 57D.SW.	19/07/1918	29/07/1918
War Diary	P.7d.45.32 Sheet 57d.SE	30/07/1918	31/07/1918
War Diary	T.10.C.90.75 Sheet 57D SW	01/08/1918	05/08/1918

War Diary	V.12.C.40.05. Sheet 57D.SE.	06/08/1918	09/08/1918
War Diary	T.10.C.40.05 Sheet 57D.S.E.	10/08/1918	18/08/1918
War Diary	Q.34.a.1.3	19/08/1918	20/08/1918
War Diary	Bouzincourt	21/08/1918	24/08/1918
War Diary	Mametz	24/08/1918	24/08/1918
War Diary	Bazentin-Le-Petit	25/08/1918	26/08/1918
War Diary	Near Longuevalle	27/08/1918	30/08/1918
War Diary	Les Boeufs.	31/08/1918	31/08/1918
War Diary		23/08/1918	20/09/1918
War Diary	Lechelle	21/09/1918	30/09/1918
War Diary	Sorel-Le Grand V.24b.8.8 57C.S.E. 1/20000	01/10/1918	03/10/1918
War Diary	Lempire. E10 1 16. Sht. 62.C 1/40000	04/10/1918	04/10/1918
War Diary	Le Catelet-Naurey Line.	05/10/1918	05/10/1918
War Diary	Near Aubencheul-Aux-Bois. Approx T.19b. Sht. 57.B. S.W.	06/10/1918	08/10/1918
War Diary	Approx. U.13. Sht. 57.B.S.W	09/10/1918	09/10/1918
War Diary	Near Milancourt Approx. U.13. Sht 57 B. S.W.	10/10/1918	10/10/1918
War Diary	Clary O.17.Sht 57.B.S.W.	11/10/1918	12/10/1918
War Diary	Troisville. Sht 57 B. N.E.	13/10/1918	13/10/1918
War Diary	K 19.b.2.9. Sht. 57.B.	14/10/1918	18/10/1918
War Diary	Troisville Sht 57.B.	19/10/1918	21/10/1918
War Diary	K16.a.20.90 Sht 57.B.N.E	22/10/1918	22/10/1918
War Diary	Forest Sht 57.B.W.E.	23/10/1918	26/10/1918
War Diary	F.5.a.1.9. (51a N.E)	27/10/1918	29/10/1918
War Diary	Forest (Sheet 57b.NE.)	30/10/1918	02/11/1918
War Diary	F.6.C.1.3 (Sheet 51a NE)	03/11/1918	04/11/1918
War Diary	Englefontaine (Sheet 51a NE)	05/11/1918	06/11/1918
War Diary	Locquignol	07/11/1918	07/11/1918
War Diary	Aulnoye	08/11/1918	29/12/1918
War Diary	Englefontaine	30/12/1918	30/12/1918
War Diary	Inchy	31/12/1918	31/12/1918
War Diary	Glisy	01/01/1919	22/03/1919
War Diary	Blangy Tronville	23/03/1919	16/05/1919
War Diary	Havre	14/05/1919	21/05/1919

WO 95 2562//

38 DIVN

115 INF BRIG

10 BN. SOUTH WALES BORDERERS

1915 DEC - 1919 MAY

38TH DIVISION

115TH INFY BDE

10TH BN STH WALES BORDRS

DEC 1915-MAY 1919

Previous to the sentries opening fire the Sgt of No 1 Party had rushed up trench forward of the place where No 2 Party entered & finding no enemy, came back & rejoined parties.

Enemy started to bomb directly No 1 Party attacked & the grenade [illegible] during which time he sent up from his front line (half left of post) several Very lights which [illegible] into 2 red [illegible]. He also sent up one green Very light.

During the period of his bombing his barrage consisting of T.M's 77 mm & 4.2 H.V. also ~~[illegible]~~ heavier calibre on back areas opened.

The relief from 'D' Co. arrived at 11.50 pm. Each man of D Co. was given full directions by the officer & Sgt i/c of sentries. The mounting of sentries was completed by 12.5 am when A Coy withdrew to our lines.

"A" Form.

Army [illegible] 2121.
(In pads of 100.)

MESSAGES AND SIGNALS.

No. of Message..............

Prefix............Code..............m.	Words.	Charge.	This message is on a/c of:	Recd. at ....m.
Office of Origin and Service Instructions.	Sent		......................Service.	Date..................
....	At...............m.			From..................
....	To..................		....	
....	By..................		(Signature of "Franking Officer.")	By..................

TO

Sender's Number.	Day of Month.	In reply to Number.	AAA
*			

From

Place

Time

The above may be forwarded as now corrected. (Z)

..............................*Censor.* Signature of Addressor or person authorised to telegraph in his name.

* This line should be erased if not required.

(3796.) Wt. W492/M1647. 650,000 Pads. 5/17. H. W. & V., Ld. (E. 1187.)

10th S.W. Borderers

Vol I

Dec 1915
Jan 1916

38

Dec '15
May 19

10th Bn. South Wales Borderers. 1

Instructions regarding War Diaries and Intelligence Summaries are contained in F. S. Regs., Part II. and the Staff Manual respectively. Title Pages will be prepared in manuscript.

WAR DIARY
or
INTELLIGENCE SUMMARY
(Erase heading not required.)

Army Form C. 2118.

Place	Date	Hour	Summary of Events and Information	Remarks and references to Appendices
Havre	4/12/15	7am	Disembarked from "Empress Queen" after voyage from Southampton.	
do	-do-	8am	Arrived at Rest Camp, & remained till 5.30pm.	
do	-do-	5.30pm	Marched to Station to entrain.	
do	-do-	7.0pm	Left Havre by Train.	
Aire	5/12/15	7pm	Arrived at Aire & detrained.	
do	-do-	9pm	Marched from Aire to Quernes.	
Quernes	-do-	11pm	Arrived at Quernes & Bn. was immediately billeted	
Quernes	6/12/15		Battalion paraded & carried out Route March.	
-do-	7/12/15		Battalion carried out usual training.	
-do-	8/12/15		Battalion carried out usual training.	
-do-	9/12/15		Battalion carried out usual training.	
-do-	10/12/15		Battalion carried out usual training	

1875 Wt. W593/826 1,000,000 4/15 J.B.C. & A. A.D.S.S./Forms/C. 2118.

Army Form C. 2118 2

Instructions regarding War Diaries and Intelligence Summaries are contained in F. S. Regs., Part II. and the Staff Manual respectively. Title Pages will be prepared in manuscript.

WAR DIARY
or
INTELLIGENCE SUMMARY
(Erase heading not required.)

Place	Date	Hour	Summary of Events and Information	Remarks and references to Appendices
Quernes	11/12/15		Battalion carried out usual training	
Quernes	12/12/15		Battalion carried out usual training	
Quernes	13/12/15		Battalion carried out usual training	
Quernes	14/12/15		Battalion carried out usual training	
Quernes	15/12/15		Battalion carried out usual training	
Quernes	16/12/15		Battalion carried out usual training	
Quernes	17/12/15		Battalion carried out usual training	
Quernes	18/12/15		Battalion carried out usual training	
Quernes	19/12/15	9.0am	Battalion marched to Aire & lined a portion of the Route covered by Sir John French on his leaving the Command of the troops in France.	
Quernes	20/12/15	8.0am	Paraded & Marched from Aire to Robecq.	
Robecq	do	2 pm	Battalion arrived at Robecq & were immediately billeted	
Robecq	21/12/15		Battalion carried out usual training	

1875 Wt. W593/826 1,000,000 4/15 J.B.C. & A. A.D.S.S./Forms/C. 2118.

Instructions regarding War Diaries and Intelligence Summaries are contained in F. S. Regs., Part II. and the Staff Manual respectively. Title Pages will be prepared in manuscript.

WAR DIARY
or
INTELLIGENCE SUMMARY
(Erase heading not required.)

Army Form C. 2118 3

Place	Date	Hour	Summary of Events and Information	Remarks and references to Appendices
Robecq	22/12/15		Battalion carried out usual Training	
Robecq	23/12/15		Battalion carried out usual Training	
Robecq	24/12/15		Battalion carried out usual Training	
do	25/12/15		Christmas Day – Holiday	
do	26/12/15		Boxing Day – Holiday	
do	27/12/15	10 am	Battalion left Robecq by Motor Buses to be attached to the Guards Division for Instruction in Trench Warfare.	
Levantie		12:30 pm	Arrived with Guards Division in vicinity of La Gorgue & Levantie. Battalion was split up & attached to various Guards Battalions. The period in trenches was 48 hours & then 48 hours rest in billets.	
Levantie	28/12/15		With Guards Division in Trenches. No Casualties. Lt Col Sir Hamar Greenwood Bt M.P. relinquished command of the Battalion on taking up position on Staff of War Office, London. Major C.D. Harvey took over Command.	

1875 Wt. W593/826 1,000,000 4/15 J.B.C. & A. A.D.S.S./Forms/C. 2118.

Instructions regarding War Diaries and Intelligence Summaries are contained in F. S. Regs., Part II. and the Staff Manual respectively. Title Pages will be prepared in manuscript.

WAR DIARY
or
INTELLIGENCE SUMMARY
(Erase heading not required.)

Army Form C. 2118 4

Place	Date	Hour	Summary of Events and Information	Remarks and references to Appendices
Levantie rc	29/12/15		Battalion with Guards Division in Firing Line. Casualties. – 2 Men wounded. – 1 remained at Duty as only slightly wounded.	
do	30/12/15		Battalion with Guards Division in Firing Line. No Casualties	
do	31/12/15		Battalion with Guards Division in Firing Line. No Casualties	
do	1/1/16		Battalion with Guards Division in Firing Line. Casualties – 1 Killed in action.	
do	2/1/16		Battalion with Guards Division in Firing Line. No Casualties.	
do	3/1/16		Battalion with Guards Division in Firing Line. Casualties – 2 Wounded. 1 remained at Duty as only slightly wounded.	
do	4/1/16		Battalion with Guards Division.	
Robecq.		1 pm.	Left in Motor Buses for Robecq + returned to Billets there	

1875 Wt. W593/826 1,000,000 4/15 J.B.C. & A. A.D.S.S./Forms/C. 2118.

Army Form C. 2118

Instructions regarding War Diaries and Intelligence Summaries are contained in F. S. Regs., Part II. and the Staff Manual respectively. Title Pages will be prepared in manuscript.

WAR DIARY
or
INTELLIGENCE SUMMARY
(Erase heading not required.)

Place	Date	Hour	Summary of Events and Information	Remarks and references to Appendices
Robecq	5/1/16		Battalion carried out usual training.	
do	6/1/16		Battalion carried out usual training.	
do	7/1/16		Battalion carried out usual training.	
do	8/1/16		Battalion carried out usual training.	
do	9/1/16		Battalion carried out usual training.	
do	10/1/16		Battalion carried out usual training. G.O.C 11th Army Corps interviewed all Officers	
do	11/1/16		Battalion carried out usual training.	
do	12/1/16		Battalion carried out usual training	
do	13/1/16	7am	Battalion vacated billets at Robecq, marched to Pont de Hem.	
Pont de Hem	do	11.30am	Battalion arrived at Pont de Hem & immediately took over billets.	
Pont de Hem	14/1/16	4.30pm	Battalion paraded & marched to Trenches via Winchester House. Casualties. - 1 Killed & 2 Wounded.	

1875 Wt. W593/826 1,000,000 4/15 J.B.C. & A. A.D.S.S./Forms/C. 2118.

Army Form C. 2118 6

Instructions regarding War Diaries and Intelligence Summaries are contained in F. S. Regs., Part II. and the Staff Manual respectively. Title Pages will be prepared in manuscript.

WAR DIARY
or
INTELLIGENCE SUMMARY
(Erase heading not required.)

Place	Date	Hour	Summary of Events and Information	Remarks and references to Appendices
Pont du Hem	15/1/16		Battalion in Trenches. Quiet Day. Casualties - 1 Wounded.	
do	16/1/16		Battalion in Trenches until 6 pm when relieved by 11th S. W. B. Quiet Day - Casualties. - 1 Killed. Battalion returned to Billets at Pont du Hem	
do	17/1/16		Battalion in Rest at Pont du Hem.	
do	18/1/16		Battalion in Rest until 4 pm, when they marched off to relieve 11th Bn S. W. B in Trenches. Casualties - nil.	
do	19/1/16		Battalion in Trenches. Quiet Day. Casualties - 1 Wounded. artillery active at night.	
do	20/1/16		Battalion in Trenches until 5 pm when relieved by 11th Bn S. W. B. Quiet Day. Casualties - nil. Battalion Headquarters visited by HRH The Prince of Wales.	
do	21/1/16		Battalion in Rest at Pont-du Hem	
do	22/1/16		Battalion in Rest until 4 pm, when they marched off to relieve 11th Bn S. W. B. in Trenches. - Casualties - 1 Killed. 1 Wounded	
do	23/1/16		Battalion in Trenches. Quiet Day. Casualties. 1 Killed. Pte Farquharson died from wounds. Buried at Merville.	
do	24/1/16		Battalion in Trenches until 5 pm when relieved by 2nd Bn Coldstream Gds. Quiet Day. Casualties - 1 Killed. Returned to billets at Pont du Hem.	

1875 Wt. W593/826 1,000,000 4/15 J.B.C. & A. A.D.S.S./Forms/C. 2118.

7

Army Form C. 2118

WAR DIARY
or
INTELLIGENCE SUMMARY
(Erase heading not required.)

Instructions regarding War Diaries and Intelligence Summaries are contained in F. S. Regs., Part II. and the Staff Manual respectively. Title Pages will be prepared in manuscript.

Place	Date	Hour	Summary of Events and Information	Remarks and references to Appendices
Pont-du-Hem	25/1/16	10am	Battalion vacated billets at Pont-du-Hem & were relieved by 3rd Bn Coldstream Guards. Marched to Locon & entered billets there at 2 pm.	
Locon	26/1/16		Battalion had General Clean up & Kit Inspection	
do	27/1/16		Battalion carried on light training in Rest Billets.	
do	28/1/16		Battalion carried on light training in Rest Billets.	
do	29/1/16		Battalion carried on light training in Rest Billets.	
do	30/1/16		Battalion in Rest Billets. Inspected by Mr Lloyd George in vicinity of Locon.	at 2.30 pm
do	31/1/16		Battalion remained in Rest Billets until 4 pm. when it marched out of Locon to Croix Barbee. Arrived at Croix Barbee 7.30 pm. and took over Billets of 114th Inf. Bde.	
Croix Barbee	1/2/16		Battalion in Brigade Reserve Billets. Casualties:- 1 Wounded (20784 Pte Roberts. G.).	
Croix Barbee	2/2/16		Battalion in Brigade Reserve Billets. Casualties - nil.	
do	3/2/16		Battalion in Brigade Reserve Billets. Casualties (Working Party) - 1 Killed (23135 G. Jones) 2 Wounded (20881 Morden & 21436 Dutton)	

1875 Wt. W593/826 1,000,000 4/15 J.B.C. & A. A.D.S.S./Forms/C. 2118.

[illegible]
for O.C. 10 S.W.B.

2/10

10th S. W. Borderers

Vol: 2

10th Bn South Wales Borderers

Instructions regarding War Diaries and Intelligence Summaries are contained in F. S. Regs., Part II. and the Staff Manual respectively. Title Pages will be prepared in manuscript.

WAR DIARY
or
INTELLIGENCE SUMMARY
(Erase heading not required.)

February 1916.

Army Form C. 2118 8

Place	Date	Hour	Summary of Events and Information	Remarks and references to Appendices
Croix Barbee	1/2/16		Battalion in Brigade Reserve Billets. Casualties:- 1 Wounded (20784 Pte Roberts. G. - On Working Party).	
do	2/2/16		Battalion in Brigade Reserve Billets. Casualties:- Nil.	
do	3/2/16		Battalion in Brigade Reserve Billets. Casualties (Working Party):- 1 Killed (23135 Pte G. Jones). 2 Wounded. (20881 Pte Morden + 21436 Pte Dutton).	
do	4/2/16		Battalion in Brigade Reserve Billets until 7 p.m. when it relieved 11th Bn S.W.B. in Trenches.	
do	5/2/16		Battalion in Trenches. Fairly quiet day. Casualties. 1 Killed (20500 Sgt T. Joseph) + 1 Wounded (20756 Pte Pritchard).	
do	6/2/16		Battalion in Trenches. D Coy shelled heavily during Day. Casualties:- 3 killed. 12 Wounded.	
do	7/2/16		Battalion in Trenches. Fairly quiet day. Casualties:- 1 Killed (2/Lt W.H. Seager). 2 Wounded.	
do	8/2/16		Battalion in Trenches until 7 p.m when relieved by 11th Bn S.W.B. Casualties:- 1 Wounded. Fairly quiet day.	
do	9/2/16		Battalion in Brigade Reserve Billets.	

1875 Wt. W593/826 1,000,000 4/15 J.B.C. & A. A.D.S.S./Forms/C. 2118.

Instructions regarding War Diaries and Intelligence Summaries are contained in F. S. Regs., Part II. and the Staff Manual respectively. Title Pages will be prepared in manuscript.

WAR DIARY
or
INTELLIGENCE SUMMARY
(Erase heading not required.)

Army Form C. 2118

9

Place	Date	Hour	Summary of Events and Information	Remarks and references to Appendices
Croix Barbee	10/2/16		Battalion in Brigade Reserve Billets. Casualties:- Nil	
do	11/2/16		Battalion in Brigade Reserve Billets. Casualties:- 6 Wounded in Grenade Accident, which took place during Instruction.	
do	12/2/16		Battalion in Brigade Reserve Billets until 7 pm when it relieved 11th Bn S.W.B. in trenches. Casualties:- Nil.	
do	13/2/16		Battalion in Trenches. Fairly quiet day. Casualties:- nil.	
do	14/2/16		Battalion in Trenches. Fairly quiet day. Casualties:- nil. 2 Officers joined Unit. 2/Lts N.C. Yonge + D.R. Davies	
do	15/2/16		Battalion in Trenches. Fairly quiet day. Casualties:- 1 Killed (Sgt ~~Joseph~~ A.J. Smart) + 1 Wounded (21437 Pte A. Roberts).	
do	16/2/16		Battalion in Trenches until 7 pm when relieved by 11th Bn S.W.B. Fairly quiet day. Casualties:- Nil. Returned to Brigade Reserve Billets.	2 Offrs joined 2/Lts H.E. Davis M.J. Everton
do Croix Marmeuse	17/2/16		Battalion left Billets at Croix Barbee at 11 am + marched to billets at Croix Marmeuse; being relieved by 7th Bn N. Lancs. Arrived in Billets Croix Marmeuse at 2 pm.	

Instructions regarding War Diaries and Intelligence Summaries are contained in F. S. Regs., Part II. and the Staff Manual respectively. Title Pages will be prepared in manuscript.

WAR DIARY
or
INTELLIGENCE SUMMARY
(Erase heading not required.)

Army Form C. 2118 10

Place	Date	Hour	Summary of Events and Information	Remarks and references to Appendices
Croix Marmeuse	18/2/16		Battalion in Divisional Reserve Billets.	
Le Touret	19/2/16		Battalion marched out of billets at Croix Marmeuse at 10 am & marched to Brigade Reserve billets at Le Touret, arriving 1 pm.	
do	20/2/16		Battalion in Brigade Reserve. Had Gas alarm (false) at 9.45 pm. Casualties:- nil. 18th Lancs Fus (D Coy & HdQrs) attached to Battalion for Instruction, arrived 12 noon.	
do	21/2/16		Battalion in Brigade Reserve. Casualties nil.	
do	22/2/16		Battalion in Brigade Reserve. Casualties nil.	
do	23/2/16		Battalion in Brigade Reserve until 7 pm when it relieved 11th Bn S.W.B in left Sector. Casualties nil. 6 Cadets attached for Instn for 48 hours.	
Trenches	24/2/16		Battalion in Trenches. Quiet day. Casualties:- 3 Wounded	
do	25/2/16		Battalion in Trenches. Quiett day. Casualties:- nil.	
do	26/2/16		Battalion in Trenches. Quiet day. Casualties:- 2 Wounded.	
do	27/2/16		Battalion in Trenches until 7 pm when relieved by 11th Bn S.W.B. Quiet day. Casualties:- 2 wounded. Bn went into Reserve Billets at Festubert, where Coy of 18th Glos: were attached for instruction. Coy of Lancs Regt left Bn at 6 am.	

1875 Wt. W593/826 1,000,000 4/15 J.B.C. & A. A.D.S.S./Forms/C. 2118.

Army Form C. 2118 11

Instructions regarding War Diaries and Intelligence Summaries are contained in F. S. Regs., Part II. and the Staff Manual respectively. Title Pages will be prepared in manuscript.

WAR DIARY
or
INTELLIGENCE SUMMARY
(Erase heading not required.)

Place	Date	Hour	Summary of Events and Information	Remarks and references to Appendices
Festubert	28/2/16		Battalion in Brigade Reserve. Casualties nil.	
do	29/2/16		Battalion in Brigade Reserve. Enemy shelled billets at 2 pm. Casualties:- 1 Killed (Pte Whatley 20252) + 2 Wounded.	

E. G. Orford
Lt & Adjt.
for OC 10 S W B

1875 Wt. W593/826 1,000,000 4/15 J.B.C. & A. A.D.S.S./Forms/C. 2118.

Army Form C. 2118 12

WAR DIARY
or
INTELLIGENCE SUMMARY

Instructions regarding War Diaries and Intelligence Summaries are contained in F. S. Regs., Part II. and the Staff Manual respectively. Title Pages will be prepared in manuscript.

10th Bn South Wales Borderers *(Erase heading not required.)* March 1916.

Place	Date	Hour	Summary of Events and Information	Remarks and references to Appendices
Festubert	1/3/16		Battalion in Brigade Reserve. Casualties ~~nil~~. 1 Wounded.	
do	2/3/16		Battalion in Brigade Reserve until 7 pm when it relieved 11th S.W.B in Trenches. Casualties, nil.	
do	3/3/16.		Battalion in Trenches. Fairly quiet day. Casualties 2 killed (20939 Pte A.E. Smith & 20903 Pte W.J. Williams) 1 Wounded (20778 Pte P. Reardon).	
do	4/3/16		Battalion in Trenches. Fairly quiet day. Casualties ~~&~~ - 2 Wounded.	
do	5/3/16		Battalion in Trenches. Fairly quiet day. Casualties :- 2 Wounded.	
do	6/3/16		Battalion in Trenches until 7 pm when relieved by 11th Bn S.W.B. Fairly quiet day. Casualties 1 killed (20375 Pte S. Williams). Battalion ~~to~~ moved to Brigade Reserve at Le Touret.	
Le Touret	7/3/16		Battalion in Brigade Reserve. Gloucester Bn left at 9 am & 5th Bn of Sherwood Foresters arrive at 12 noon for Instruction. Casualties:- nil.	
do	8/3/16		Battalion in Brigade Reserve. Casualties :- nil.	
do	9/3/16		~~Battalion in Brigade Reserve. Casualties :- nil.~~	
do	10/3/16		Battalion in Brigade Reserve until 7 pm when relieved 11th S.W.B in Trenches - Casualties nil	

1875 Wt. W593/826 1,000,000 4/15 J.B.C. & A. A.D.S.S./Forms/C. 2118.

13

Instructions regarding War Diaries and Intelligence Summaries are contained in F. S. Regs., Part II. and the Staff Manual respectively. Title Pages will be prepared in manuscript.

WAR DIARY
or
INTELLIGENCE SUMMARY
(Erase heading not required.)

Army Form C. 2118

Place	Date	Hour	Summary of Events and Information	Remarks and references to Appendices
Trenches	11-3-16		Battalion in Trenches (Festubert). Quiet day. Casualties :- nil.	
do	12-3-16		Battalion in Trenches. Quiet day. Casualties :- nil.	
do	13-3-16		Battalion in Trenches. Quiet day. Casualties :- nil.	
do	14-3-16		Battalion in Trenches, until 7 pm when relieved by 11th Bn S.W.B. Quiet day. Casualties :- 1 Wounded. 15th Bn Sherwood Foresters left Bn at 7 am. Battalion went into support at Festubert.	
Festubert	15-3-16		Battalion in support at Festubert until 6 pm. Casualties :- 2 Wounded (at Duty). At 6.30 pm Battn relieved by 14th Bn R.W.F. & marched to Le Harisoirs. Arrived Le Harisoirs 10.30 pm (Brigade in Reserve) & took over billets.	
Harisoirs	16-3-16		Battalion at Harisoirs. Cleaned billets & equipment.	
do	17-3-16		Battalion at Harisoirs. (Brigade in Reserve). Carried on Training.	
do	18-3-16		Battalion at Harisoirs. (Brigade in Reserve). Carried on Training.	
do	19-3-16		Battalion at Harisoirs. (Brigade in Reserve). Carried on Training.	
do	20-3-16		Battalion at Harisoirs. (Brigade in Reserve). Carried on Training.	
do	21-3-16		Battalion at Harisoirs (Brigade in Reserve). Carried on Training.	
do	22-3-16		Battalion at Harisoirs (Brigade in Reserve). Carried on Training.	

1875 Wt. W593/826 1,000,000 4/15 J.B.C. & A. A.D.S.S./Forms/C. 2118.

Army Form C. 2118

14

Instructions regarding War Diaries and Intelligence Summaries are contained in F. S. Regs., Part II. and the Staff Manual respectively. Title Pages will be prepared in manuscript.

WAR DIARY
or
INTELLIGENCE SUMMARY
(Erase heading not required.)

Place	Date	Hour	Summary of Events and Information	Remarks and references to Appendices
Harisoir Gorre	23/3/16		Battalion left Brigade Reserve at Harisoir at 7 am + marched to Gorre (Battalion in Reserve) + took over billets. Casualties:- nil.	
Gorre	24/3/16		Battalion remained in Reserve at Gorre until 2 pm when it relieved 14th Bn Welsh Regt in Trenches (Givenchy). Casualties:- nil.	
Trenches	25/3/16		Battalion in Trenches. Quiet Day. Casualties:- 1 Wounded.	
do	26/3/16		Battalion in Trenches. Fairly Quiet Day. Casualties:- 1 Offr + 2 O.R. Wounded. (2/Lt H. E. Davis. Coy S.M. Clissold + Sgt Gill). 2/Lt A. J. Evans joined Bn.	
do	27/3/16		Battalion in Trenches. Quiet Day. Casualties:- nil. Draft of 13 men joined Battalion.	
do	28/3/16		Battalion in Trenches until 2 pm when it was relieved by 11th Bn S.W.B. Casualties:- nil. Bn proceeded to billets in support at Givenchy.	
Givenchy ~~do~~	29/3/16		Battalion in Support (Givenchy). Casualties:- 1 killed (23023 Pte Davies)	
do	30/3/16		Battalion in Support (Givenchy). Casualties:- nil.	
do	31/3/16		Battalion in Support (Givenchy). Casualties:- nil	

1875 Wt. W593/826 1,000,000 4/15 J.B.C. & A. A.D.S.S./Forms/C. 2118.

J. R. Ingledew
Lieut + Qmr
for
COMMANDg 10TH SERVICE BATTN.,
SOUTH WALES BORDERERS,
(1ST GWENT.)

10th Bn South Wales Borderers

Instructions regarding War Diaries and Intelligence Summaries are contained in F. S. Regs., Part II. and the Staff Manual respectively. Title Pages will be prepared in manuscript.

WAR DIARY
or
INTELLIGENCE SUMMARY
(Erase heading not required.)

XXXVIII

April 1916

Army Form C. 2118

10 SWB
Vol 4

Place	Date	Hour	Summary of Events and Information	Remarks and references to Appendices
Givenchy	1/4/16		Battalion in support (Givenchy) until 2 pm when it relieved 11th S.W.B. in trenches. Casualties :- ~~[illegible]~~ 1 Wounded.	E.7.0
Trenches	2/4/16		Battalion in Trenches. Casualties :- 3 Wounded.	E.7.0
do	3/4/16		Battalion in Trenches. Enemy blew up mine at 6 am. Casualties :- 7 Killed + 20 Wounded.	E.7.0
do	4/4/16		Battalion in Trenches. Casualties :- 2 Wounded.	E.7.0
do	5/4/16		Battalion in Trenches until 2 pm when relieved by 11 SWB. Casualty :- 1 Wounded. Battalion proceeded to Reserve billets at Gorre.	E.7.0
Gorre	6/4/16		Battalion in Brigade Reserve at Gorre. Casualties :- nil	E.7.0
do	7/4/16		Battalion in Brigade Reserve at Gorre. Casualties :- nil	E.7.0
do	8/4/16		Battalion in Brigade Reserve at Gorre until 10 am when relieved by 14th Bn R.W.F. Bn then marched to Harisoir (Brigade in Reserve) ~~[illegible]~~ took over billets from 14th Bn R.W.F.	E.7.0
Harisoir	9/4/16		Battalion at Harisoir. Drill + Training carried out.	E.7.0
do	10/4/16		Battalion at Harisoir. Inspected by General Munro, Commanding 1st Army	E.7.0
do	11/4/16		Battalion at Harisoir. Drill + Training carried out.	E.7.0

H. Wilkinson (?) Lt Col

1875 Wt. W593/826 1,000,000 4/15 J.B.C. & A. A.D.S.S./Forms/C. 2118.

Instructions regarding War Diaries and Intelligence Summaries are contained in F. S. Regs., Part II. and the Staff Manual respectively. Title Pages will be prepared in manuscript.

WAR DIARY
or
INTELLIGENCE SUMMARY
(Erase heading not required.)

Army Form C. 2118

Place	Date	Hour	Summary of Events and Information	Remarks and references to Appendices
Harisoirs	12/4/16		Battalion at Harisoir. Carried out Drill + Training.	E.7.O
do	13/4/16		Battalion at Harisoir. Carried out Drill + Training.	E.7.O.
do Estaires	14/4/16		Battalion left Harisoir at 8 am + marched to Estaires where Unit was billeted.	E.7.O.
do	15/4/16		Battalion in billet at Estaires until 6 pm when it marched to Trenches at Laventie + relieved 17th West Yorks Bn. Casualties :- nil.	E.7.O.
Trenches	16/4/16		Battalion in Trenches. Quiet day. Casualties :- 1 Killed + 5 Wounded.	E.7.O
do	17/4/16		Battalion in Trenches. Quiet day. Casualties :- 1 Accidentally wounded.	E.7.O
do	18/4/16		Battalion in Trenches. Quiet day. Casualties :- nil.	E.7.O
do	19/4/16		Battalion in Trenches until 7 pm when relieved by 11th Bn S.W.B. Fairly quiet day. Casualties :- 2 killed + 2 wounded (At Duty). Battn then proceeded to Billets at Laventie (Battn in Support).	E.7.O.
Laventie	20/4/16		Battalion in Reserve. Casualties :- nil.	E.7.O.
do	21/4/16		Battalion in Reserve. Casualties :- nil.	E.7.O.
do	22/4/16		Battalion in Reserve. Casualties :- nil.	E.7.O.

1875 Wt. W593/826 1,000,000 4/15 J.B.C. & A. A.D.S.S./Forms/C. 2118.

Army Form C. 2118

Instructions regarding War Diaries and Intelligence Summaries are contained in F. S. Regs., Part II. and the Staff Manual respectively. Title Pages will be prepared in manuscript.

WAR DIARY
or
INTELLIGENCE SUMMARY
(Erase heading not required.)

Place	Date	Hour	Summary of Events and Information	Remarks and references to Appendices
Laventie	23/4/16		Battalion in Reserve until 7.30 pm when it relieved 11th Bn S.W.B in Trenches. Casualties :- nil.	E.T.O.
Trenches	24/4/16		Battalion in Trenches. Quiet Day. Casualty :- 2/Lt W.W. Haggett, Wounded (afterwards Died).	E.T.O.
do	25/4/16		Battalion in Trenches. Quiet Day. Casualties :- nil. (Lt Ralph, Trench Mortar Battery, Wounded). Lt-Col S.J. Wilkinson D.S.O. took over Command of Battn.	E.T.O.
do	26/4/16		Battalion in Trenches. Quiet Day. Casualties :- 1 Wounded. 3 men killed & 1 wounded, attached to Mining Coy 19th Pioneer Bn.	E.T.O.
do	27/4/16		Battalion in Trenches until 7 pm, when they were relieved by the 11th SWB. Fairly quiet day. Casualties 1 Killed, 2 wounded. Battalion went to Laventie to Reserve Billets. 3 men (Thomas, Beach and Evans) awarded Military medals by G.O.C. in C	E.T.O.
Laventie	28/4/16		Battalion in Laventie. Various training executed. Casualty — 1 man wounded by "aeroplane shrapnel." At duty. Quiet day.	E.T.O.
do	29/4/16		Battalion at Laventie Usual training carried out.	E.T.O.

1875 Wt. W593/826 1,000,000 4/15 J.B.C. & A. A.D.S.S./Forms/C. 2118.

Army Form C. 2118

Instructions regarding War Diaries and Intelligence Summaries are contained in F. S. Regs., Part II. and the Staff Manual respectively. Title Pages will be prepared in manuscript.

WAR DIARY
or
INTELLIGENCE SUMMARY
(Erase heading not required.)

Place	Date	Hour	Summary of Events and Information	Remarks and references to Appendices
~~[illegible]~~ Laventie	30/4/16		Battalion was relieved at 1.30pm by 16th R.W.F. and marched to Billets at Merville. Casualties, 4 wounded (not previously reported) Pte Thomas, Beach, & Evans presented with Military Medal Ribbon by General Munro	E.H.O.
MERVILLE X29.d.2.2.	30/4/16	4pm		

[illegible] Wilkinson
Lieutenant Colonel
Commanding
10th Service Bn S.W. Borderers

1875 Wt. W593/826 1,000,000 4/15 J.B.C. & A. A.D.S.S./Forms/C. 2118.

XXXVIII

Instructions regarding War Diaries and Intelligence Summaries are contained in F. S. Regs., Part II. and the Staff Manual respectively. Title Pages will be prepared in manuscript.

WAR DIARY
or
INTELLIGENCE SUMMARY
(Erase heading not required.)

May 1916

Army Form C. 2118

10 S W B Vol 5

Place	Date	Hour	Summary of Events and Information	Remarks and references to Appendices
MERVILLE X19d22	1/5/16		Battalion in MERVILLE. Physical training + cleaning up of equipment occupied the larger portion of the morning. Cpls Hulbert Nicholas + Woodhouse delivered lecture on Anti Gas. Band played in Square from 5.0 to 6.30 pm.	G.Y.O.
-do-	2/5/16.		Battalion at MERVILLE. Usual training. Band played in Square 5-6.30 pm	G.Y.O.
-do-	3/5/16.		Battalion at MERVILLE. Usual training. Band played in Square 5-6.30 pm	G.Y.O.
-do-	4/5/16.		Battalion at MERVILLE. Carried out usual training.	G.Y.O.
-do-	5/5/16.		Battalion at MERVILLE. Carried out usual training	G.Y.O.
-do-	6/5/16		Battalion at MERVILLE. Carried out usual training. Interbattalion Sports with 17th RW7.	G.Y.O.
-do-	7/5/16		Battalion at MERVILLE. Carried out usual training.	G.Y.O.
-do-	8/5/16		Battalion at MERVILLE Carried out usual training	G.Y.O
-do-	9/5/16		Battalion at MERVILLE until 1.55 pm when it left for PONT-DU-HEM. Battalion marched straight into trenches.	G.Y.O.

1875 Wt. W593/826 1,000,000 4/15 J.B.C. & A. A.D.S.S./Forms/C. 2118.

Instructions regarding War Diaries and Intelligence Summaries are contained in F. S. Regs., Part II. and the Staff Manual respectively. Title Pages will be prepared in manuscript.

WAR DIARY
or
INTELLIGENCE SUMMARY
(Erase heading not required.)

Army Form C. 2118

Place	Date	Hour	Summary of Events and Information	Remarks and references to Appendices
Trenches Winchester House	10/5/16		Battalion in Trenches. Casualties:– 10/20497, Pte L Moore wounded	E.J. Offord
M.23.a.4. Trenches " "	11/5/16		Battalion in Trenches. Casualties:– nil	E.J.O.
Trenches " "	12/5/16		Battalion in Trenches. Casualties:– 10/21465 Sgt J Payne killed; 10/20262 Pte C Moore wounded	E.J.O.
Trenches " "	13/5/16		Battalion in Trenches until 9.30 pm when relieved by 11th SWB and marched to Reserve Billets at Pont du hem. Casualties Nil.	E.J.O.
Pont du Hem M14 b 7.	14/5/16		Battalion at PONT DU HEM. Carried out bathing, cleaning up and usual training. Casualties:– nil	E.J.O.
Pont du Hem	15/5/16		Battalion at PONT DU HEM. Carried out usual training. Casualties: 1 wounded – 10/23042, William.	E.J.O.
Pont du Hem	16/5/16		Battalion at PONT DU HEM. Carried out usual training. Casualties 1 wounded – 10/20598 Lloyd.	E.J.O.
Pont du Hem	17/5/16		Battalion at PONT DU HEM all day, and carried out relief of 11th SWB between 8 and 12 MN. Casualties – nil	E.J.O.
Trenches Winchester House M.23.a.4.1	18/5/16		Battalion in Trenches. Quiet day. Casualties, 70262, E.E. Jones, wounded, afterwards died. One accidentally wounded (Tudor)	E.J.O.

1875 Wt. W593/826 1,000,000 4/15 J.B.C. & A. A.D.S.S./Forms/C. 2118.

Instructions regarding War Diaries and Intelligence Summaries are contained in F. S. Regs., Part II. and the Staff Manual respectively. Title Pages will be prepared in manuscript.

WAR DIARY
or
INTELLIGENCE SUMMARY
(Erase heading not required.)

Army Form C. 2118

Place	Date	Hour	Summary of Events and Information	Remarks and references to Appendices
Trenches	19/5/16		Battalion in Trenches. Quiet day. Casualties:– nil	G.Y.O.
Trenches	20/5/16		Battalion in Trenches Quiet day Casualties:– nil	G.Y.O.
Trenches	21/5/16		Battalion in Trenches until 8 30pm when relieved by 11th SWB. Relief completed. casualties – nil	G.Y.O.
~~Trenches~~ Pont du Hem	22/5/16		Battalion in Reserve Billet at PONT DU HEM Usual fatigues and training. Casualties:– ~~nil~~ 20180 T Banks wounded	G.Y.O.
PONT DU HEM M14 b 7.5	23/5/16		Battalion in Reserve Billet at PONT DU HEM Usual fatigues and training Casualties:– 1 wounded ~~[illegible]~~ Pte Ll Davies (33116)	G.Y.O.
PONT·DU·HEM M14 b 7.5	24/5/16		Battalion in Reserve Billets at PONT. DU. HEM Usual fatigues and training. Casualties – nil.	G.Y.O.
PONT·DU·HEM M14 B 7.5	25/5/16		Battalion left PONT DU HEM at 9 am and marched to MERVILLE where they occupied previous billets	G.Y.O.
MERVILLE ~~K35.~~ X29d22	26/5/16		Battalion at MERVILLE. Usual training	G.Y.O.

1875 Wt. W593/826 1,000,000 4/15 J.B.C. & A. A.D.S.S./Forms/C. 2118.

Instructions regarding War Diaries and Intelligence Summaries are contained in F. S. Regs., Part II. and the Staff Manual respectively. Title Pages will be prepared in manuscript.

WAR DIARY
or
INTELLIGENCE SUMMARY
(Erase heading not required.)

Army Form C. 2118

Place	Date	Hour	Summary of Events and Information	Remarks and references to Appendices
MERVILLE X29d.22	27/5/16		Battalion at MERVILLE. Carried on usual training	G.Y.O.
MERVILLE	28/5/16		Battalion at MERVILLE. Carried on usual training	G.Y.O.
MERVILLE	29/5/16		Battalion at MERVILLE. Carried on usual training	G.Y.O.
MERVILLE	30/5/16		Battalion at MERVILLE Carried out usual training –	G.Y.O.
MERVILLE	31/5/16		Battalion at MERVILLE. Carried out usual training	G.Y.O.

C J Wilkinson Lieut Colonel
COMMANDG 10TH SERVICE BATTN., SOUTH WALES BORDERERS, (1ST GWENT.)

1875 Wt. W593/826 1,000,000 4/15 J.B.C. & A. A.D.S.S./Forms/C. 2118.

XXXVIII

Instructions regarding War Diaries and Intelligence Summaries are contained in F. S. Regs., Part II. and the Staff Manual respectively. Title Pages will be prepared in manuscript.

WAR DIARY
or
INTELLIGENCE SUMMARY
(Erase heading not required.)

Army Form C. 2118

10th SWB Vol 6 June

Place	Date	Hour	Summary of Events and Information	Remarks and references to Appendices
MERVILLE K29d22	1/6/16		Battalion at MERVILLE. Carried on usual Training	G.F.O
do	2/6/16		Battalion at MERVILLE. Carried on usual Training	G.F.O
do	3/6/16		Battalion at MERVILLE. Carried on usual Training	G.F.O
do	4/6/16		Battalion at MERVILLE Carried out usual Training	G.F.O
do	5/6/16		Battalion at MERVILLE until 4pm when marched off to relieve 10th Welsh Regiment in Left Sub-sector of FAUQUISSART Section. Relief completed about 10pm	G.F.O
RED HOUSE	6/6/16		Battalion in Trenches. Quiet day. Casualties:- ~~no~~ One killed two wounded. 10/21064 G Bishop killed, 10/ Cpl. H.J. Charles, 10/33036 ~~Wounded~~ Pte Smith wounded ~~2/4~~ 1/4 Ox & Bucks (LCoy) attached to Bn for instruction	G.F.O
RED HOUSE	7/6/16		Battalion in Trenches Quiet day Casualties - 20981 Godfrey Killed	G.F.O

1875 Wt. W593/826 1,000,000 4/15 J.B.C. & A. A.D.S.S./Forms/C. 2118.

Instructions regarding War Diaries and Intelligence Summaries are contained in F. S. Regs., Part II. and the Staff Manual respectively. Title Pages will be prepared in manuscript.

WAR DIARY
or
INTELLIGENCE SUMMARY

(Erase heading not required.)

Army Form C. 2118

10th SWB

Place	Date	Hour	Summary of Events and Information	Remarks and references to Appendices
RED HOUSE	8/6/16		Battalion in Trenches. Quiet day. Casualties	G.Y.O.
RED HOUSE	9/6/16		Battalion in Trenches. Quiet day. 2/4 Berks Regt One Company + HQrs attached for instruction. Casualties 2 wounded 10/20198 Cpl. Murtagh. 10/20531 Pte A Jones.	G.Y.O.
-do-	10/6/16		Battalion handed over to 2/4 Berks Regt @ 3.30 am and marched to LAVENTIE. Bivouacked for Breakfast and then marched to Billet K29.d.2.2 MERVILLE. Casualties:- nil	G.Y.O.
MERVILLE K29.d.22	11/6/16		Battalion at MERVILLE until 12 noon. Marched to billets at ROBECQ. 36A. B23 d.0.0.	G.Y.O.
ROBECQ B23d.0.0.	12/6/16		Battalion at ROBECQ. Usual Training carried out	G.Y.O.
ROBECQ B23.d.0.0	13/6/16		Battalion at ROBECQ. Usual Training carried out.	G.Y.O.

1875 Wt. W593/826 1,000,000 4/15 J.B.C. & A. A.D.S.S./Forms/C. 2118.

Army Form C. 2118

WAR DIARY
or
INTELLIGENCE SUMMARY
(Erase heading not required.)

Instructions regarding War Diaries and Intelligence Summaries are contained in F. S. Regs., Part II. and the Staff Manual respectively. Title Pages will be prepared in manuscript.

10th BN. SOUTH WALES BORDERERS

Place	Date	Hour	Summary of Events and Information	Remarks and references to Appendices
Robecq B13d00	14/6/16		Battalion at ROBECQ until 9 a.m. & marched to Billets at Auchel.	G.Y.O.
AUCHEL	15/6/16		Battalion at AUCHEL until 7 a.m. & marched to Billets at VILLERS BRULIN V26d53.	G.Y.O.
VILLERS. BRULIN V26d5.3	16/6/16	Sheet 36 B	Battalion at VILLERS BRULIN. Usual Training carried out.	G.Y.O.
do	17/6/16	"	Battalion at VILLERS BRULIN. Usual Training carried out	G.Y.O.
do	18/6/16	"	Battalion at VILLERS BRULIN. Usual Training carried out	G.Y.O.
do	19/6/16	"	Battalion at VILLERS BRULIN. Usual Training carried out.	G.Y.O.
do	20/6/16	"	Battalion at VILLERS BRULIN. Usual training carried out	G.Y.O.
do	21/6/16	"	Battalion at VILLERS BRULIN. Usual Training carried out.	G.Y.O.
do	22/6/16	"	Battalion at VILLERS BRULIN. Usual Training carried out.	G.Y.O.
do	23/6/16	"	Battalion at VILLERS BRULIN. Usual Training carried out.	G.Y.O.
do	24/6/16	"	Battalion at VILLERS BRULIN. Usual Training carried out.	G.Y.O.
do.	25/6/16	"	Battalion at VILLERS BRULIN. Usual Training carried out.	G.Y.O.

1875 Wt. W593/826 1,000,000 4/15 J.B.C. & A. A.D.S.S./Forms/C. 2118.

Instructions regarding War Diaries and Intelligence Summaries are contained in F. S. Regs., Part II. and the Staff Manual respectively. Title Pages will be prepared in manuscript.

WAR DIARY
or
INTELLIGENCE SUMMARY
(Erase heading not required.)

10th SWB

Army Form C. 2118

Place	Date	Hour	Summary of Events and Information	Remarks and references to Appendices
VILLERS BRULIN V26d5.3.	26/6/16		Battalion at VILLERS BRULIN. Bn. marched to BONNIERES Sht LENS II	J.J.O.
BONNIERES Sht LENS II	27/6/16		Battalion at BONNIERES. Bn marched to GEZAINCOURT. Sht LENS II	J.J.O.
GEZAINCOURT Sht. LENS II	28/6/16		Battalion at GEZAINCOURT Bn Rested.	J.J.O.
GEZAINCOURT Sht LENS II	29/6/16		Battalion at GEZAINCOURT. Usual training carried out	J.J.O.
GEZAINCOURT Sht LENS II.	30/6/16		Battalion at GEZAINCOURT. Bn. marched to TOUTENCOURT. Sht LENS II	J.J.O.

[signature]
Lt. Col Commdg
10th SWB

1875 Wt. W593/826 1,000,000 4/15 J.B.C. & A. A.D.S.S./Forms/C. 2118.

115th Inf.Bde.
38th Div.

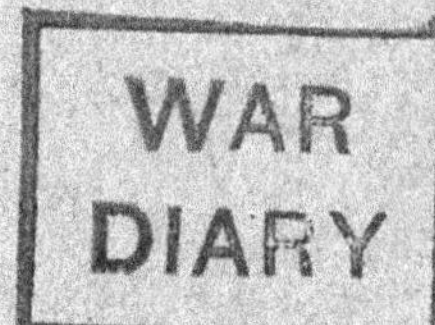

10th BATTN. THE SOUTH WALES BORDERERS.

J U L Y

1 9 1 6

Instructions regarding War Diaries and Intelligence Summaries are contained in F. S. Regs., Part II. and the Staff Manual respectively. Title Pages will be prepared in manuscript.

WAR DIARY
or
INTELLIGENCE SUMMARY
(Erase heading not required.)

Army Form C. 2118

Place	Date	Hour	Summary of Events and Information	Remarks and references to Appendices
Toutencourt Sht. LENS 11.	1.7.16.		Battalion at TOUTENCOURT. Battalion marched to Acheux. Sht LENS II	E.G.O.
Acheux Sht LENS. II.	2.7.16		Battalion at Acheux. Battalion carried out usual training. No 10/30111 L.Cpl. G. Broadhurst awarded Albert Medal 1st Class [illegible] in recognition of his Gallantry in saving life.	E.G.O.
Acheux Sht LENS II	3.7.16		Battalion at Acheux. Battalion marched to BUIRE-SUR-ANCRE. Sht AMIENS 17	E.G.O.
BUIRE-SUR-ANCRE. Sht AMIENS 17	4.7.16		Battalion at BUIRE-SUR-ANCRE. Battalion carried out usual training	E.G.O.
BUIRE-SUR ANCRE. Sht. [illegible] AMIENS 17	5.7.16		Battalion at BUIRE-SUR-ANCRE. Battalion marched to Bivouac situate between MAMETZ and CARNOY. Sht AMIENS 17.	E.G.O.
MAMETZ Sht AMIENS 17	6.7.16		Battalion at Bivouac & afterwards marched to Trenches as reserves to 16th Welch Regt & 11th S.W.B's attack on MAMETZ Wood	E.G.O.
TRENCHES	7.7.16		Battalion in Trenches in reserve to 16th WELCH REGT & 11th S W B's attack on MAMETZ Wood Casualties - 1 Officer (Lt. Col. S. J. Wilkinson D.S.O.) (Commanding Battn) Killed & 20 O.Rs. wounded & 2 killed.	E.G.O.
TRENCHES	8.7.16		Battalion in Trenches till 1 AM & returned to Bivouac between MAMETZ & CARNOY	E.G.O.

1875 Wt. W593/826 1,000,000 4/15 J.B.C. & A. A.D.S.S./Forms/C. 2118.

Instructions regarding War Diaries and Intelligence Summaries are contained in F. S. Regs., Part II. and the Staff Manual respectively. Title Pages will be prepared in manuscript.

WAR DIARY
or
INTELLIGENCE SUMMARY
(Erase heading not required.)

Army Form C. 2118

Place	Date	Hour	Summary of Events and Information	Remarks and references to Appendices
MAMETZ BIVOUAC Sht AMIENS 17	9/7/16		Battalion in Reserve at Bivouac	E.F.O.
MAMETZ BIVOUAC Sht AMIENS 17	10/7/16 + 11/7/16		Battalion at Bivouac until 12 noon when it departed for trenches to take part in attack on MAMETZ Wood by 38th Division. attack carried out, portion of wood captured. 3 Field Guns & 2 Heavy Guns taken by Bn & marked 10th S.W.B. Casualties Killed 2nd Lt M. J. Everton & 2nd Lt R. P. Taylor & 21 O Ranks. wounded Major C.D. Harvey, Capt Galsworthy (both at Duty) Lieuts Gill E & Parry R.B. 2nd Lts Davenport H.H. Davies D.J. Yorge H.S. Hillbourne H.E. & Williams H.C. & 120 Other Ranks. missing totals 6. D 10/20189 Pte Griffiths T. D 10/13170 Pte Lavender J.A. B 10/21472 Pte Bishop H. B 10/21329 Ewins D. B 10/20526 Pte Hughes F. B 10/20974 Pte Davies J. The Battalion suffered an intense bombardment during night of 11-12th of July 1916.	E.F.O.
MAMETZ WOOD Sht AMIENS 17	12/7/16		Battalion at MAMETZ Wood & returned to Bivouac at 9 A.m & stayed at Bivouac for the day.	E.F.O.
MAMETZ BIVOUAC Sht AMIENS 17	13/7/16		Battalion at MAMETZ BIVOUAC. Battn in Reserve E.F.O.	

1875 Wt. W593/826 1,000,000 4/15 J.B.C. & A. A.D.S.S./Forms/C. 2118.

Instructions regarding War Diaries and Intelligence Summaries are contained in F. S. Regs., Part II. and the Staff Manual respectively. Title Pages will be prepared in manuscript.

WAR DIARY
or
INTELLIGENCE SUMMARY
(Erase heading not required.)

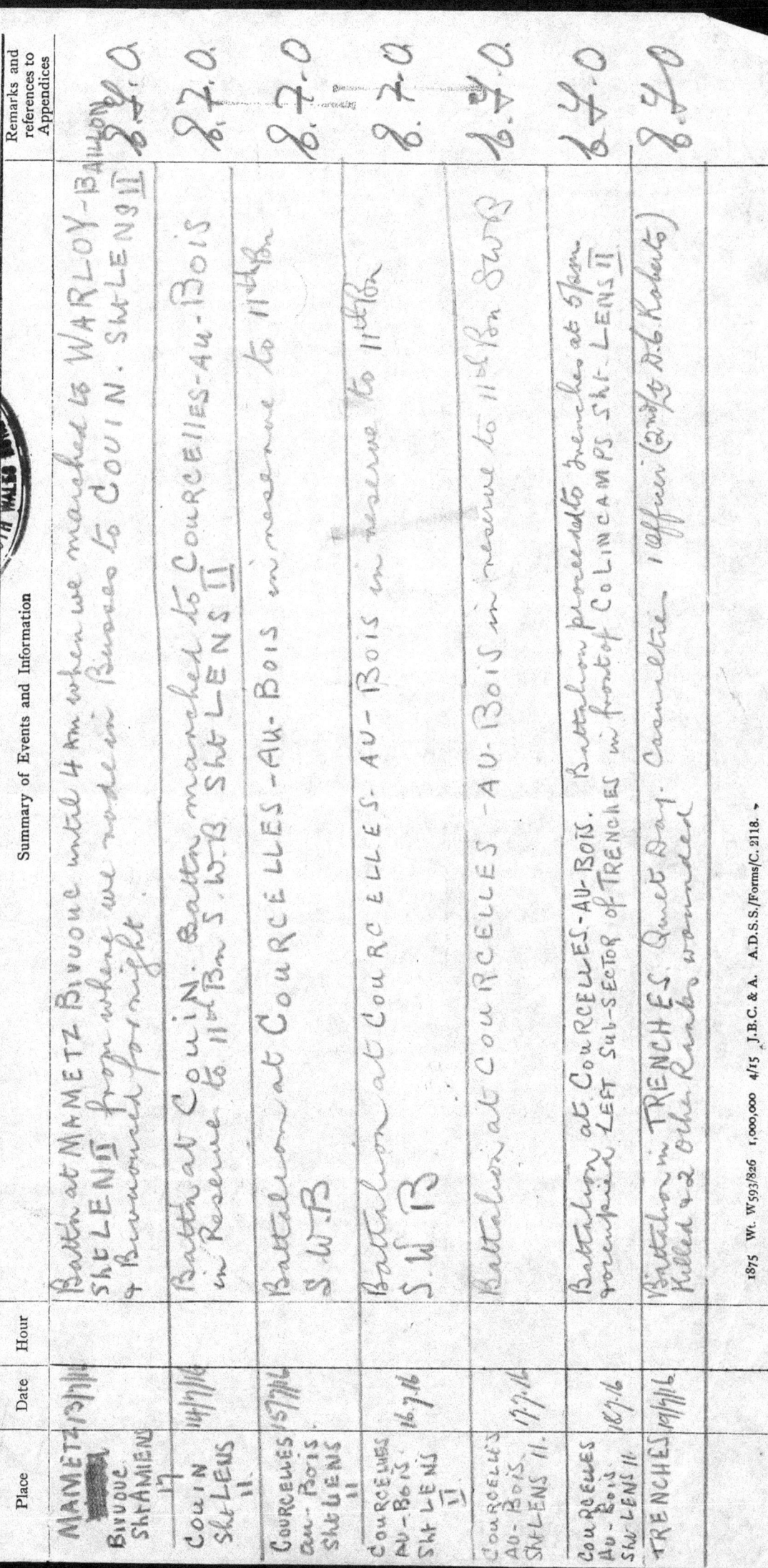

Army Form C. 2118

Place	Date	Hour	Summary of Events and Information	Remarks and references to Appendices
MAMETZ [illegible] BIVOUC ShtAMIENS 17	13/7/16		Battn at MAMETZ BIVOUC until 4 Am when we marched to WARLOY-BAILLON ShtLENS II from where we rode in Busses to COUIN. ShtLENS II & Bivouaced for night.	E.7.0
COUIN ShtLENS 11.	14/7/16		Battn at COUIN. Battn marched to COURCELLES-AU-BOIS in Reserve to 11th Bn S.W.B ShtLENS II	E.7.0.
COURCELLES au-Bois ShtLENS 11	15/7/16		Battalion at COURCELLES-AU-BOIS in reserve to 11th Bn S.W.B	E.7.0
COURCELLES AU-BOIS ShtLENS II	16.7.16		Battalion at COURCELLES-AU-BOIS in reserve to 11th Bn S.W.B	E.7.0
COURCELLES AU-BOIS ShtLENS 11.	17.7.16		Battalion at COURCELLES-AU-BOIS in reserve to 11th Bn SWB	E.7.0.
COURCELLES AU-BOIS ShtLENS 11.	18.7.16		Battalion at COURCELLES-AU-BOIS. Battalion proceeded to Trenches at 5pm & occupied LEFT SUB-SECTOR of TRENCHES in front of COLINCAMPS Sht. LENS II	E.7.0
TRENCHES	19/7/16		Battalion in TRENCHES. Quiet Day. Casualties 1 Officer (2nd Lt D.G. Roberts) Killed & 2 Other Ranks wounded	E.7.0

1875 Wt. W593/826 1,000,000 4/15 J.B.C. & A. A.D.S.S./Forms/C. 2118.

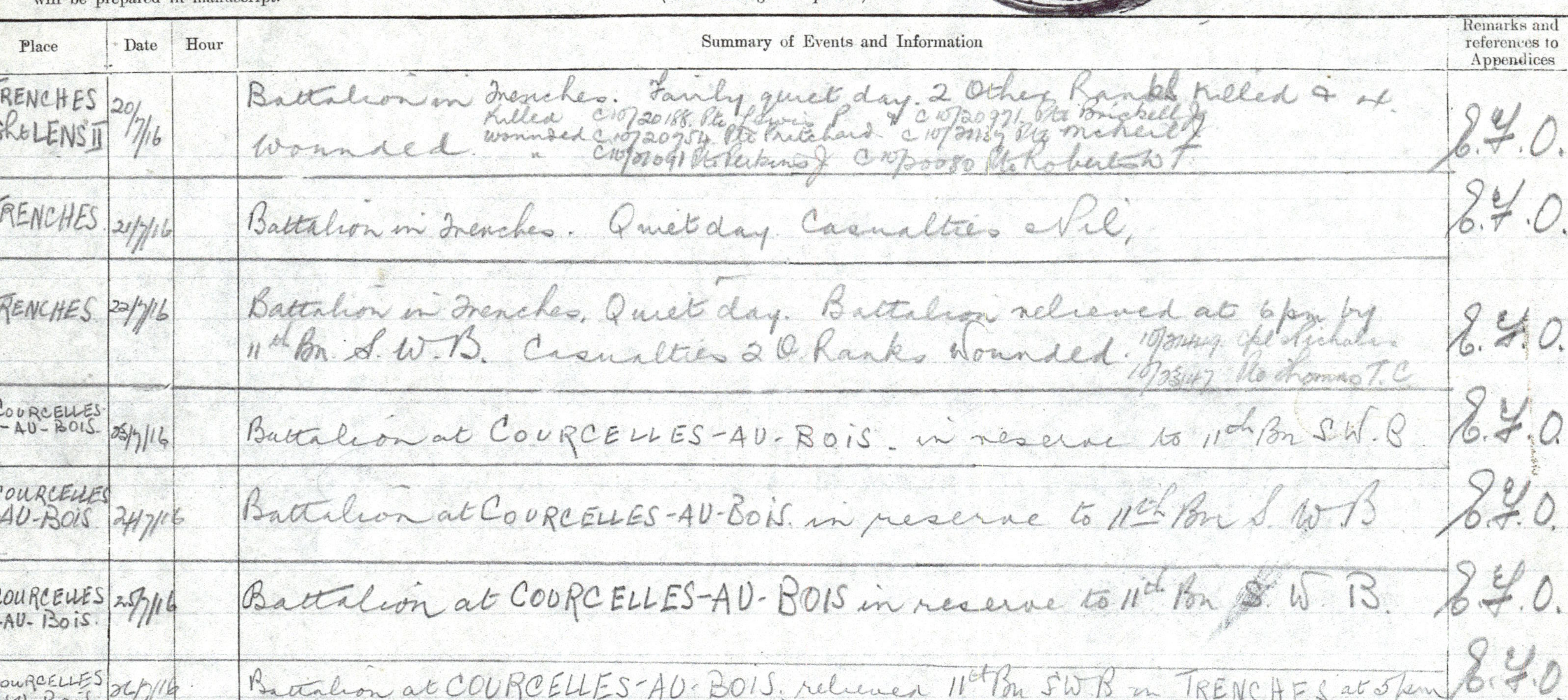

Instructions regarding War Diaries and Intelligence Summaries are contained in F. S. Regs., Part II. and the Staff Manual respectively. Title pages will be prepared in manuscript.

WAR DIARY
or
INTELLIGENCE SUMMARY.
(Erase heading not required.)

Army Form C. 2118.

Place	Date	Hour	Summary of Events and Information	Remarks and references to Appendices
TRENCHES S. of LENS II	20/7/16		Battalion in Trenches. Fairly quiet day. 2 Other Ranks killed & 4 wounded. Killed C10/20188 Pte Lewis P & C10/20971 Pte Brickell J; wounded C10/20754 Pte Pritchard, C10/21137 Pte Mitchell J, " C10/21091 Pte Perkins J, C10/20080 Pte Robertson W T.	E. F. O.
TRENCHES	21/7/16		Battalion in Trenches. Quiet day. Casualties = Nil.	E. F. O.
TRENCHES	22/7/16		Battalion in Trenches. Quiet day. Battalion relieved at 6pm by 11th Bn. S. W. B. Casualties 2 O. Ranks wounded. 10/21449 Cpl Nicholas, 10/23147 Pte Thomas T. C	E. F. O.
COURCELLES-AU-BOIS.	23/7/16		Battalion at COURCELLES-AU-BOIS. in reserve to 11th Bn S. W. B	E. F. O.
COURCELLES-AU-BOIS	24/7/16		Battalion at COURCELLES-AU-BOIS. in reserve to 11th Bn S. W. B	E. F. O.
COURCELLES-AU-BOIS.	25/7/16		Battalion at COURCELLES-AU-BOIS in reserve to 11th Bn S. W. B.	E. F. O.
COURCELLES-AU-BOIS.	26/7/16		Battalion at COURCELLES-AU-BOIS. relieved 11th Bn S W B in TRENCHES at 5pm	E. F. O.
TRENCHES ~~COURCELLES~~	27/7/16		Battalion in TRENCHES. Quiet day 1 Killed 10/21419 Pte Dobbs G	E. F. O.

T2134. Wt. W708—776. 500000. 4/15. Sir J. C. & S.

Instructions regarding War Diaries and Intelligence Summaries are contained in F. S. Regs., Part II. and the Staff Manual respectively. Title pages will be prepared in manuscript.

WAR DIARY
or
INTELLIGENCE SUMMARY.
(Erase heading not required.)

Army Form C. 2118.

Place	Date	Hour	Summary of Events and Information	Remarks and references to Appendices
COLINCAMPS TRENCHES Sht LENS II	28/7/16		Battalion in Trenches. Quiet day. Casualties 1 Killed + 1 Wounded 19008 Pte Pearce P. Killed 19/21088 Pte May T. Wounded	E.T.O.
TRENCHES	29/7/16		Battalion in Trenches. Bn. relieved at 7 am by 6th Ox & Bucks. Bn marched to Billets at ~~[illegible]~~ BUS. Sht LENS II	E.T.O.
BUS, Sht LENS. II	30/7/16 + 31/7/16		Battalion at BUS. Battalion marched to CANDAS Sht LENS II where Bn entrained for ST. OMER. Bn detrained at 2 am. 31/7/16 at ST. OMER + marched to Billets at MILLAIN. Sht. ~~[illegible]~~ ~~[illegible]~~ HAZEBROUCK 5A BELGIUM	E.T.O.

Edgar L. Orford
Lieut & Adjt
for Major Commanding
10th S Batt. S.W. Borderers

Instructions regarding War Diaries and Intelligence Summaries are contained in F. S. Regs., Part II, and the Staff Manual respectively. Title pages will be prepared in manuscript.

WAR DIARY
or
INTELLIGENCE SUMMARY.
(Erase heading not required.)

Army Form C. 2118.

Vol 8

Place	Date	Hour	Summary of Events and Information	Remarks and references to Appendices
MILLAIN Sht HAZEBROUCK 5A BELGIUM	1/8/16		Battalion at MILLAIN. Battalion carried out usual training.	E.T.O.
MILLAIN	2/8/16		Battalion at MILLAIN. Battalion carried out usual training.	E.T.O.
MILLAIN.	3/8/16		Battalion at MILLAIN. Battalion marched to B[illegible] at BOLLEZEELE. Sht 27 - A 24 c.5.3.	E.T.O.
BOLLEZEELE A24c5.3 Sht 27	4/8/16		Battalion at BOLLEZEELE. Bn carried out usual training	E.T.O.
BOLLEZEELE A24c5.3 Sht 27.	5/8/16		Battalion at BOLLEZEELE. Bn carried out usual training	E.T.O.
BOLLEZEELE A24c5.3 Sht 27	6/8/16		Battalion at BOLLEZEELE. Divine services & Kit inspections.	E.T.O.

Instructions regarding War Diaries and Intelligence Summaries are contained in F. S. Regs., Part II. and the Staff Manual respectively. Title pages will be prepared in manuscript.

WAR DIARY
or
INTELLIGENCE SUMMARY.
(Erase heading not required.)

SERVICE BATTALION (1st GWENT) 1. SEP. 1916 SOUTH WALES BORDERERS

Army Form C. 2118.

Place	Date	Hour	Summary of Events and Information	Remarks and references to Appendices
~~BOLLEZEELE~~ Sht 27. A24c53.	~~MONDAY~~ 7.8.16		Battalion at BOLLEZEELE. Battalion inspected by [illegible] H. J. Evans. 115th Infantry Brigade.	G. T. O.
BOLLEZEELE Sht 27 A24c53.	Tuesday 8/8/16		Battalion at BOLLEZEELE. Battalion carried out usual training.	G. T. O.
BOLLEZEELE Sht 27 A24c53.	WEDNESDAY 9/8/16		Battalion at BOLLEZEELE. Battalion carried out usual training in Bayonet Fighting, Musketry &c.	G. T. O.
BOLLEZEELE Sht 27. A24c53.	Thursday 10/8/16		Battalion at BOLLEZEELE. Battalion carried out usual training in Bayonet, Fighting, Musketry &c.	G. T. O.
BOLLEZEELE Sht 27. A24c53.	FRIDAY 11/8/16		Battalion at BOLLEZEELE. Battalion carried out usual training in Bayonet fighting, Musketry &c. & proceeded by Companies to ZEGGARS-CAPPEL for Bathing.	G. T. O.

T2134. Wt. W708—776. 500000. 4/15. Sir J. C. & S.

Instructions regarding War Diaries and Intelligence Summaries are contained in F. S. Regs., Part II. and the Staff Manual respectively. Title pages will be prepared in manuscript.

WAR DIARY
or
INTELLIGENCE SUMMARY.
(Erase heading not required.)

Army Form C. 2118.

Place	Date	Hour	Summary of Events and Information	Remarks and references to Appendices
[BOLL]EZEELE 27 4 c. 5. 3.	Saturday 12/8/16		Battalion at BOLLEZEELE. Battalion carried out usual training consisting of Battalion Drill, Physical Exercises & Bayonet fighting & Bomb & Rifle Grenade throwing.	E.G.O.
[BOL]LEZEELE 27 4 c. 5. 3.	Sunday 13/8/16		Battalion at BOLLEZEELE. Divine Services & Kit inspections.	E.G.O.
[BO]LLEZEELE 27 4 c. 5. 3.	Monday 14/8/16		Battalion at BOLLEZEELE. Route March, Physical Training &c carried out.	E.G.O.
[BOLL]EZEELE 27 4 c. 5. 3.	Tuesday 15/8/16		Battalion at BOLLEZEELE. 11 mile Route March, Bombing, Lectures, Bayonet fighting as day's "Programme of work."	E.G.O.
[B]OLLEZEELE 27 4 c. 5. 3.	Wednesday 16/8/16		Battalion at BOLLEZEELE. Musketry, Bayonet fighting, Lectures &c carried out. Tactical Exercise for Officers	E.G.O.
[BOLL]EZEELE 27 4 c. 5. 3.	Thursday 17/8/16		Battalion at BOLLEZEELE. Physical training, Musketry, Lectures, Bombing, Bayonet fighting, Artillery attack formations & practice over trenches carried out.	E.G.O.

T2134. Wt. W708—776. 500000. 4/15. Sir J. C. & S.

Instructions regarding War Diaries and Intelligence Summaries are contained in F. S. Regs., Part II. and the Staff Manual respectively. Title Pages will be prepared in manuscript.

WAR DIARY
or
INTELLIGENCE SUMMARY
(Erase heading not required.)

Army Form C. 2118

SERVICE BATTALION (1st GWENT) 1 SEP. 1916 SOUTH WALES BORDERERS

Place	Date	Hour	Summary of Events and Information	Remarks and references to Appendices
BOLLEZEELE Sht 27. A.24.c.5.3.	FRIDAY 18/8/16		Battalion at BOLLEZEELE. Physical Training, Bomb throwing musketry &c carried out as day's work.	R.F.O.
BOLLEZEELE Sht 27. A.24.C.5.3.	SATURDAY 19/8/16.		Battalion at BOLLEZEELE. Battalion entrained for Poperinghe. where they detrained & rested in Billets for 5 hours. Bn afterwards entrained for trenches to be in support to 11th Bn S.W.B. Relieved 2nd ESSEX Bn.	R.F.O.
TRENCHES. St JULIEN MAP Ed 3d. No 28. C.25.d.1/2.4.	Sunday 20/8/16		Battalion in TRENCHES. Battalion acting as Supports to 11th Bn S.W.B. on WEST BANK of RIVER YSER.	R.F.O.
TRENCHES as above	MONDAY 21/8/16.		Battalion in TRENCHES. Battalion acting as Supports to 11th Bn S.W.B. on WEST BANK of RIVER YSER. Casualties. 1 O.Rk. wounded. 20224 Pte Maddock	R.F.O.
TRENCHES as above	Tuesday 22/8/16		Battalion in TRENCHES Battalion acting as Supports to 11th Bn S.W.B. on WEST BANK of RIVER YSER.	R.F.O.
TRENCHES as above	WEDNESDAY 23/8/16		Battalion in TRENCHES. Battalion relieved 11th S.W.B. in FRONT LINE. Casualties Nil.	R.F.O.

1875 Wt. W593/826 1,000,000 4/15 J.B.C. & A. A.D.S.S./Forms/C. 2118.

Instructions regarding War Diaries and Intelligence Summaries are contained in F. S. Regs., Part II. and the Staff Manual respectively. Title pages will be prepared in manuscript.

WAR DIARY
or
INTELLIGENCE SUMMARY.
(Erase heading not required.)

Army Form C. 2118.

Place	Date	Hour	Summary of Events and Information	Remarks and references to Appendices
TRENCHES ST JULIEN. N. Ed 2d 10.2	24/8/16		Battalion in TRENCHES Casualties Nil.	G.T.O.
do.	25/8/16		Battalion in TRENCHES. Casualties Nil.	G.T.O.
do	26/8/16		Battalion in TRENCHES Casualties Nil. Bn inspected in TRENCHES. by Lt Gen Sir Aylmer Hunter Weston Comdg VIII Corps	G.T.O.
do	27/8/16		Battalion in TRENCHES. casualties 10. Rs. 1 Killed 9 H. wounded. Killed B10/20587. Pte. Rose H. Wounded. B10/21112 L/Cpl Veron B10/21304. Pte Dennis B10/21209 Pte. Holmes F. B10/21255. Pte Evans C.W.	G.T.O. G.T.O.
do.	28/8/16		Battalion in TRENCHES. Bn relieved by 11th Bn. S.W.B. Casualties Nil	G.T.O.
TRENCHES West Bank of YSER. C.25.d.1.x.4	29/8/16		Battalion in TRENCHES. Fatigues & Gas helmet Drill carried out.	G.T.O.

T2134. Wt. W708—776. 500000. 4/15. Sir J. C. & S.

Instructions regarding War Diaries and Intelligence Summaries are contained in F. S. Regs., Part II. and the Staff Manual respectively. Title pages will be prepared in manuscript.

WAR DIARY
or
INTELLIGENCE SUMMARY.
(Erase heading not required.)

Army Form C. 2118.

Place	Date	Hour	Summary of Events and Information	Remarks and references to Appendices
TRENCHES WEST BANK of YSER. C.25.d.1.3.4	30/8/16		Battalion in TRENCHES. Fatigues & Gas Helmet Drill carried out.	[illegible]
do	31/8/16		Battalion in TRENCHES. Fatigues &c carried out.	[illegible]

W. H. Gwyer
Lieutenant Colonel
Commanding 10th SWB

T2134. Wt. W708—776. 500000. 4/15. Sir J. C. & S.

Instructions regarding War Diaries and Intelligence Summaries are contained in F. S. Regs., Part II. and the Staff Manual respectively. Title pages will be prepared in manuscript.

WAR DIARY
or
INTELLIGENCE SUMMARY.
(Erase heading not required.)

10 S W B

Army Form C. 2118.

Vol 9

Place	Date	Hour	Summary of Events and Information	Remarks and references to Appendices
TRENCHES WEST BANK of YSER C25 d 1.4 ST JULIEN ED3 no 28	1/9/16		Battalion in TRENCHES. Battalion carried out fatigues when in Reserve to 11th Bn S.W.B. Battalion relieved 11th S.W.B. in FRONT LINE. Casualty 10/2168 Pte Preece R. (S.S)	E.J.O.
FRONTLINE TRENCHES YPRES SALIENT	2/9/16		Battalion in TRENCHES. Quiet day. Casualties Nil	E.J.O.
do	3/9/16		Battalion in TRENCHES. Quiet day. Casualty 10/20388 Pte Peeke J.W. wounded	E.J.O.
do	4/9/16		Battalion in TRENCHES. Quiet day. Battalion was relieved by 11th S.W.B. & then proceeded to TRENCHES on WEST BANK of YSER.	E.J.O.
do	5/9/16		Battalion in TRENCHES. Battalion relieved 16th Bn R.W.F. in LEFT SUB-SECTOR of British Line in Ypres Salient in Reserve to 15th Bn. R.W.F.	E.J.O.

T2134. Wt. W708—776. 500000. 4/15. Sir J. C. & S.

Instructions regarding War Diaries and Intelligence Summaries are contained in F. S. Regs., Part II. and the Staff Manual respectively. Title pages will be prepared in manuscript.

WAR DIARY
or
INTELLIGENCE SUMMARY.
(Erase heading not required.)

Army Form C. 2118.

Place	Date	Hour	Summary of Events and Information	Remarks and references to Appendices
TRENCHES WEST BANK of YSER. EXTREME LEFT of BRITISH LINE	6/9/16		Battalion in Reserve to 15th Bn. R. W. F. Battalion Relieved 15th Bn. R. W. F. in FRONT LINE. Casualties Nil	[illegible]
FRONT LINE TRENCHES	7/9/16		Battalion in Front Line TRENCHES. Quiet day Casualties Nil	[illegible]
do	8/9/16		Battalion in FRONT LINE TRENCHES. Quiet day Casualties 3 O.Rs wounded 17/30072 Pte H. Jones 17/20400 L/Cpl Morgan D. 17/21727 Pte McDonald	[illegible]
do	9/9/16		Battalion in FRONTLINE TRENCHES. Quiet day with exception of D Coy who were subject to a bombardment by enemy artillery. Casualties. Casualties - 9 O Ranks Wounded. 20034. Sgt. Collier B. 20785 Pte Griffiths R. M. 21791. Pte Davies O. 20719. Pte Whatley. 20738. Pte Whitcombe 21143. Pte Griffiths J. 21009. Pte Bethel S. + Pte Yonge.	[illegible]
do	10/9/16		Battalion in FRONT TRENCHES. Quiet day. Battalion Relieved by 11 S.W.B. & proceeded to Support Billets on WEST of CANAL BANK. Casualties Nil	[illegible]

Instructions regarding War Diaries and Intelligence Summaries are contained in F. S. Regs., Part II. and the Staff Manual respectively. Title pages will be prepared in manuscript.

WAR DIARY
or
INTELLIGENCE SUMMARY.
(Erase heading not required.)

Army Form C. 2118.

Place	Date	Hour	Summary of Events and Information	Remarks and references to Appendices
TRENCHES WEST BANK of YSER. EXTREME LEFT of BRITISH LINE	11/9/16		Battalion in Support to 11th Bn. S.W.B. Fatigues &c carried out. Casualties Nil	E.7.O
do	12/9/16		Battalion in Support to 11th Bn S.W.B. Usual fatigues carried out. Casualties Nil	E.7.O.
do	13/9/16		Battalion in Support to 11th Bn. S.W.B. Usual Fatigues carried out. Casualties Nil	E.7.O
do	14/9/16		Battalion in Support. Battalion relieved 11th Bn S.W.B. in LEFT-SUBSECTOR of British Line. Casualties Nil	[illegible]
LEFT SUB-SECTOR on YPRES Salient.	15/9/16		Battalion in FRONT LINE. Enemy's trenches severely Bombarded by our artillery & much damage done. Retaliation comparatively weak. Casualties. 4 O.Ranks wounded (3 ss. & remaining at Duty.)	[illegible]

T2134. Wt. W708–776. 500000. 4/15. Sir J. C. & S.

Instructions regarding War Diaries and Intelligence Summaries are contained in F. S. Regs., Part II. and the Staff Manual respectively. Title pages will be prepared in manuscript.

WAR DIARY
or
INTELLIGENCE SUMMARY.
(Erase heading not required.)

Army Form C. 2118.

Place	Date	Hour	Summary of Events and Information	Remarks and references to Appendices
LEFT SUB-SECTOR on YPRES SALIENT	16/9/16		Battalion in FRONT LINE TRENCHES. Quiet day. Casualties 3 wounded (OR) 1 suffering from SS.	[initials]
do	17/9/16		Battalion in Front Line TRENCHES. Casualty 1 O Rank wounded. Battalion relieved by 15th Bn. R.W.F. & afterwards marched to BILLETS at CAMP "E".	[initials]
CAMP "E" Belgium & France Map A 30 a 4 3	18/9/16		Battalion carried out Training Programme viz:- Physical Drill, Musketry, Bayonet fighting. Specialists under their own Officers.	[initials]
CAMP "E"	19/9/16		Battalion carried out Training Programme:- Bombing by Special Raiding Party, Bayonet fighting & Musketry.	[initials]
CAMP "E" S	20/9/16		Battalion relieved 11th Bn S.W.B. on E. BANK of YSER CANAL ~~[illegible]~~ C 25 d 1½ 4	[initials]
YSER CANAL C 25 d 1½ 4	21/9/16		Battalion relieved 13 Bn WELCH REGT in RIGHT Sub-SECTOR of 38th Div Bn Hqrs. IRISH FARM. St JULIEN TRENH MAP.	[initials]

Instructions regarding War Diaries and Intelligence Summaries are contained in F. S. Regs., Part II. and the Staff Manual respectively. Title pages will be prepared in manuscript.

WAR DIARY
or
INTELLIGENCE SUMMARY.
(Erase heading not required.)

Army Form C. 2118.

Place	Date	Hour	Summary of Events and Information	Remarks and references to Appendices
TRENCHES IRISH FARM RIGHT Subsector LEFT SECTOR	22/9/16		Battalion in Front Line Trenches. Very quiet day & casualties nil	[initials]
do.	23/9/16		Battalion in Front Line Trenches. Casualties nil & very quiet day	[initials]
do.	24/9/16		Battalion in Front Line Trenches Casualties nil & extremely quiet day.	[initials]
do	25/9/16		Battalion in Front Line Trenches. quiet day. Casualties 1 O.Rank Killed & 1 O.R. wounded. at 8pm Battalion was relieved by 13th Welch Regt & proceeded to E. BANK of RIVER YSER. St Julien MAP REF. C 25. d 1½. 4.	[initials]
E. BANK of YSER. St Julien MAP. C 25 d 1½ 4	26/9/16		Battalion in Support to 13th Welch Regt, fatigues carried out. Casualties nil.	[initials]
do	27/9/16		Battalion in Support to 13th Welch Regt fatigues carried out. Casualties nil	[initials]

Instructions regarding War Diaries and Intelligence Summaries are contained in F. S. Regs., Part II. and the Staff Manual respectively. Title pages will be prepared in manuscript.

WAR DIARY
or
INTELLIGENCE SUMMARY.
(Erase heading not required.)

Army Form C. 2118.

Place	Date	Hour	Summary of Events and Information	Remarks and references to Appendices
EAST BANK OF YSER CANAL ST JULIEN MAP C.25.d.1.7.4	28/9/16		Battalion in Support to 13th WELCH Regt. casualties 1 OR wounded. Bn relieved by 17th R.W.F. & then marched to Camp D. MAP REF. BELGIUM & FRANCE MAP. A.30.a.4.2.	[initials]
do	29/9/16		Battalion in Camp D. General clean up & kit inspections.	[initials]
do	30/9/16		Battalion in Camp D. Usual training carried out	[initials]

[signature] Lt Col Commanding 10th SWB

T2134. Wt. W708—776. 500000. 4/15. Sir J. C. & S.

Army Form C. 2118.

1 Vol 10

WAR DIARY
or
INTELLIGENCE SUMMARY.
(Erase heading not required.)

Instructions regarding War Diaries and Intelligence Summaries are contained in F. S. Regs., Part II. and the Staff Manual respectively. Title pages will be prepared in manuscript.

Place	Date	Hour	Summary of Events and Information	Remarks and references to Appendices
CAMP "D" BEL. 9 FRANCE MAP. Δ 30.a.4.2.	1/10/16		Battalion at CAMP "D" Usual training carried out, & Church Services.	G.T.O.
do.	2/10/16		Battalion at CAMP "D" Usual training & fatigues carried out.	G.T.O.
do.	3/10/16		Battalion at CAMP "D". Battalion relieved 11th Bn. S.W.B. in the evening on E. Side of RIVER YSER. Bn HQrs at C25d 2½.6 St Julien TRENCH MAP.	G.T.O.
EAST BANK of YSER Canal ST. JULIENS TRENCH MAP. C25d 2½.6	4/10/16		Battalion in Support to 11th S.W.B. on RIGHT Subsector of Right Sector. Usual fatigues. Nothing of Importance to report.	G.T.O.
do	5/10/16		Battalion in Support to 11th S.W.B. Usual fatigues carried out.	G.T.O.

T2134. Wt. W708–776. 500000. 4/15. Sir J. C. & S.

Instructions regarding War Diaries and Intelligence Summaries are contained in F. S. Regs., Part II. and the Staff Manual respectively. Title pages will be prepared in manuscript.

WAR DIARY
or
INTELLIGENCE SUMMARY.
(Erase heading not required.)

Army Form C. 2118.

II

Place	Date	Hour	Summary of Events and Information	Remarks and references to Appendices
E. BANK of R. YSER. ST JULIEN IK MAP C25d2.2	6/10/16		Battalion in Support to 11th S.W.B. usual fatigues carried out. at about 9 pm. a Fighting Patrol of 1 Officer & 10. O.Rs under Capt. G. F. H. Charlton entered Enemy Sap No. 9. & killed the Garrison of 6. men. After obtaining necessary identifications the order to withdraw was given owing to large enemy reinforcements. After withdrawing for a few hundred yards it was noticed that Capt. Charlton & 19/23016 Pte D. Sparswick had been left behind. Despite terrific Machine Gun Fire 2nd Lt T. T. Taylor & 19/20400 Sgt P. F. Evans proceeded again to the Sap with the intention of looking for Capt Charlton & Pte Sparswick. Capt Charlton was seen on a stretcher carried by 4 Germans following which were another 8 Huns. Pte Sparswick was not seen. Under these circumstances 2nd Lt. Taylor & Sgt Evans again withdrew, during which the former was wounded. The skill with which this small raid was carried gained the compliments of the Divisional & Corps	JFA

T2134. Wt. W708—776. 500000. 4/15. Sir J. C. & S.

Instructions regarding War Diaries and Intelligence Summaries are contained in F. S. Regs., Part II. and the Staff Manual respectively. Title pages will be prepared in manuscript.

WAR DIARY
or
INTELLIGENCE SUMMARY.
(Erase heading not required.)

Army Form C. 2118.

III

Place	Date	Hour	Summary of Events and Information	Remarks and references to Appendices
E. Bank of YSER St. LIEN TR. IA D. 35.d 2½.6	6/10/16		Commanders. For their excellent work in the Raid 2nd Lt. T. T. Taylor & 17/30460 Sgt. P. F. Evans were awarded the MILITARY CROSS & MILITARY MEDAL respectively. Our Casualties were:- Capt. G. J. H. Charlton Missing & Wounded, 17/3064 Pte. Spanswick D. Missing. 2nd Lt T. T. Taylor wounded & Sgt. R Edwards wounded.	
do	7/10/16		Battalion in Support to 11th S.W.B. Usual fatigues & Casualties nil	[illegible]
do	8/10/16		Battn in Support to ~~reached~~ 11th S.W.B. in RIGHT Sub-sector of RIGHT SECTOR. Casualties nil	[illegible]
RISH FARM FRONTLINE. T. Julien 35 d 1½.4	9/10/16		Battalion in FRONT LINE. Quiet day & Casualties nil.	[illegible]
do	10/10/16		Battalion in FRONT LINE. Enemy Artillery pretty active. Our casualties 3. O Ranks Killed & 5 wounded (3 of latter at Duty).	[illegible]

T2134. Wt. W708—776. 500000. 4/15. Sir J. C. & S.

Instructions regarding War Diaries and Intelligence Summaries are contained in F. S. Regs., Part II. and the Staff Manual respectively. Title pages will be prepared in manuscript.

WAR DIARY
or
INTELLIGENCE SUMMARY.
(Erase heading not required.)

Army Form C. 2118.

IV

Place	Date	Hour	Summary of Events and Information	Remarks and references to Appendices
IRISH FARM. FRONT LINE. ST. Julien MAP C 25 a 1.2.4	11/10/16		Battalion in FRONT LINE. Quiet day & Casualties nil. Battn was relieved by 11 S.W.B. in the evening & then proceeded to Billets on E. BANK of R. YSER	J.F.O.
C.25 d 2.1. ST. Julien TR. MAP. E. BANK of R. YSER	12/10/16		Battalion in Support to 11 S.W.B. General clean up. Casualties nil	J.F.O.
do.	13/10/16		Battalion in Support to 11th S.W.B. Usual Fatigues. Casualties nil	J.F.O.
do.	14/10/16		Battalion Relieved 15 Bn R.W.F. on Support line. ST. JULIEN. Casualties nil. C.19.c 7.2. took over Front Line. LEFT SUBSECTOR ~~RIGHT~~ LEFT SECTOR.	J.F.O.
	15/10/16		Battalion ~~in~~ relieved 16th R.W.F. Front Line. Enemy artillery quite active. Casualties 1. 17807 Sgt. T. Mcphee. wounded. ~~very extensive damage done by artillery~~	J.F.O.

T2134. Wt. W708—776. 500000. 4/15. Sir J. C. & S.

Instructions regarding War Diaries and Intelligence Summaries are contained in F. S. Regs., Part II. and the Staff Manual respectively. Title pages will be prepared in manuscript.

WAR DIARY
or
INTELLIGENCE SUMMARY.
(Erase heading not required.)

Army Form C. 2118.

Place	Date	Hour	Summary of Events and Information	Remarks and references to Appendices
C.19 F 72 St Julien TR. MAP F. BANK / R. YSER	16/10/16		Battalion in Front Line. Hostile Artillery Activity. Casualties 4 / 20866 Pte E. J. Williams. killed. R.S.M. G. Lockie wounded. and two other ranks. Front line slightly damaged.	E.T.O.
do.	17/10/16		Battalion in Front Line. Minenwerfer activity. Front line slightly damaged. Casualties nil.	E.T.O.
do	18/10/16		Battalion in Front Line. Quiet day. Casualties Nil.	E.T.O.
do.	19/10/16		Battalion in Front Line. Quiet day. Casualties Nil	E.T.O.
do.	20/10/16.		Battalion in Front Line. Quiet day. Casualties Nil. Battalion relieved by 11th S.W.B. Returned to Canal Bank in support to 11th S.W.B.	E.T.O.
do	21/10/16		Battalion in Support to 11th S.W.B. Usual fatigues. Casualties Nil.	E.T.O.

T2134. Wt. W708—776. 500000. 4/15. Sir J. C. & S.

Instructions regarding War Diaries and Intelligence Summaries are contained in F. S. Regs., Part II. and the Staff Manual respectively. Title pages will be prepared in manuscript.

WAR DIARY
or
INTELLIGENCE SUMMARY.
(Erase heading not required.)

Army Form C. 2118.

Place	Date	Hour	Summary of Events and Information	Remarks and references to Appendices
19 NC 72 St Julien ... inch Map ... Bank of ... River Yser	22/10/16.		Battalion in Support to 11th S. W. B. Usual fatigues. Casualty 7/20716 A. R. S. M. Bowden G. wounded.	G. F. O.
do	23/10/16		Battalion in Support to 11th S. W. B. Usual fatigues. Casualties Nil.	G. F. O.
do.	24/10/16		Battalion in Support to 11th S. W. B. Battalion relieved by 15th Bn R. W. F. Casualties nil. Marched to Camp E Map reference Belgium & France Map A 30 a 4 2	G. F. O.
Camp E A 30 a 7.3	25/10/16		Battalion at Camp E. Inspection of kit by O.C.O. Usual training carried out.	G. F. O.
Camp E. A 30 a 7.3	26/10/16		Battalion at Camp E. Usual training programme carried out. Cable Burying fatigue	G. F. O.

T2134. Wt. W708—776. 500000. 4/15. Sir J. C. & S.

Instructions regarding War Diaries and Intelligence Summaries are contained in F. S. Regs., Part II. and the Staff Manual respectively. Title pages will be prepared in manuscript.

~~WAR DIARY~~ or INTELLIGENCE SUMMARY.

(*Erase heading not required.*)

Army Form C. 2118.

VII

Place	Date	Hour	Summary of Events and Information	Remarks and references to Appendices
Camp E A 30. a. 7. 3	27/10/16		Battalion at Camp E. Usual training programme carried out.	[illegible initials]
Camp E A 30 a 7 3	28/10/16		Battalion at Camp E. Usual training programme carried out	
Camp E A 30 a 7 3	29/10/16		Battalion at Camp E. Church Parades	
C 25 d 1½ [illegible] (IRISH FARM) Front Line (Map St Julian)	30/10/16		Battalion at Camp E until evening. Marched to Bra[illegible] entrained, detraining at The Asylum, Ypres, after[illegible] marching to front Line, relieving 13th Battalion Welsh Regiment (114 Brigade) in the right sub-se[illegible] right sector. Relief carried out satisfactorily [illegible] somewhat difficult circumstances, the climat[illegible] conditions being very adverse, and trenc[illegible] accordingly in an ~~atrocious~~ bad state.	[illegible initials]

T2134. Wt. W708—776. 500000. 4/15. Sir J. C. & S.

Instructions regarding War Diaries and Intelligence Summaries are contained in F. S. Regs., Part II. and the Staff Manual respectively. Title pages will be prepared in manuscript.

WAR DIARY
or
INTELLIGENCE SUMMARY.
(Erase heading not required.)

Army Form C. 2118.

VIII

Place	Date	Hour	Summary of Events and Information	Remarks and references to Appendices
[illegible] FARM C25a1½.4	31/10 1915		Battalion in Front Line. Casualties - nil	[illegible]
			Edgar. L. Offord Captain Adjt. for Lieutenant Colonel Commanding 10th Bn S Wales Borderers	

Instructions regarding War Diaries and Intelligence Summaries are contained in F. S. Regs., Part II. and the Staff Manual respectively. Title pages will be prepared in manuscript.

WAR DIARY
or
INTELLIGENCE SUMMARY.
(Erase heading not required.)

Army Form C. 2118.

Place	Date	Hour	Summary of Events and Information	Remarks and references to Appendices
Camp P.	7/11/16		Battalion in Camp P. Usual training programme carried out Musketry & Bayonet fighting. G.O.C. inspected Camp, Huts etc.	G.F.O.
	8/11/16		Battalion in Camp P. Usual training programme carried out. Usual fatigues on cable burying	G.F.O.
	9/11/16		Battalion in Camp P. Usual training. Inspection of huts by C.O. At 3.15 p.m. Battalion marched to Peselhoek entraining for the Asylum, Ypres. Detrained and marched into trenches at right sub-sector right sector, relieving 11th Batt. S.W.B.	G.F.O.
Right sub sector [illegible] Trench Map 28.d.1½.4	10/11/16		Battalion in Front Line. Quiet day. Casualties Nil.	G.F.O.
	11/11/16		Battalion in Front Line. Quiet day. Casualties Nil.	G.F.O.

10th S.W.B.

Army Form C. 2118.

Vol XI

Instructions regarding War Diaries and Intelligence Summaries are contained in F. S. Regs., Part II. and the Staff Manual respectively. Title pages will be prepared in manuscript.

WAR DIARY
or
INTELLIGENCE SUMMARY.
(*Erase heading not required.*)

Place	Date	Hour	Summary of Events and Information	Remarks and references to Appendices
Ref St Julian Trench Map C 25.d 4½.2½	1/11/16		Battalion in Front Line. Quiet day. Casualties Nil.	J.F.O.
	2/11/16		Battalion in Front Line. Quiet day. Casualties Nil	J.F.O.
	3/11/16		Battalion in Front Line. Quiet day. Casualties Nil	J.F.O.
	4/11/16		Battalion in Front Line. Quiet day. Casualties Nil. Battalion relieved by 11th Batt S.W.B. and marched to the Asylum, Ypres where ~~it~~ entrained for Poselhoek. Detrained and marched to Camp P.	J.F.O.
Camp P.	5/11/16		Battalion at Camp P. General Clean up and Kit Inspection by C.O. ~~Divine Service at Cornish Hall.~~	J.F.O.
	6/11/16		Battalion at Camp P. Kit Inspection by C.O. Usual fatigues carried out.	J.F.O.

T2134. Wt. W708—776. 500000. 4/15. Sir J. C. & S.

Instructions regarding War Diaries and Intelligence Summaries are contained in F. S. Regs., Part II. and the Staff Manual respectively. Title pages will be prepared in manuscript.

WAR DIARY
or
INTELLIGENCE SUMMARY.
(Erase heading not required.)

Army Form C. 2118.

Place	Date	Hour	Summary of Events and Information	Remarks and references to Appendices
Right Sub Sector St Julien Trench C.5d 1½ 4	12/1/16		Battalion in Front line. Quiet day. Casualty Sgt Woodhouse W/d (at duty)	J.T.O.
	13/1/16		Battalion in Front line. Enemy artillery somewhat active. Casualties nil.	J.T.O.
	14/1/16		Battalion in Front line. Quiet day. Casualties nil.	
	15/1/16		Battalion in Front line. Very quiet day. Casualty 7 wd Cpl Warrener W/d. Battalion relieved by 12th R.W.F. and proceeded to left sub-sector and relieved 16th R.W.F. in support.	J.T.O.
Left sub sector St Julien Trench C25 a 4 2	16/1/16		Battalion in support to 11th Batt S.W.B. Usual fatigues carried out. Casualties nil.	J.T.O.
	17/1/16		Battalion in support to 11th Batt. S.W.B. Usual fatigues carried out. Casualties nil.	J.T.O.

Instructions regarding War Diaries and Intelligence Summaries are contained in F. S. Regs., Part II. and the Staff Manual respectively. Title pages will be prepared in manuscript.

WAR DIARY
or
INTELLIGENCE SUMMARY.
(Erase heading not required.)

Army Form C. 2118.

Place	Date.	Hour	Summary of Events and Information	Remarks and references to Appendices
Right Sub Sector St Julien Ylvs: at Map C25: C7 2 ~~[illegible]~~	18/11/16		Battalion in support to 11th Batt. S.W.B. Usual fatigues carried out. Casualties Nil.	J.F.O
	19/11/16		Battalion in support to 11th Batt. S.W.B. Battalion relieved 11th S.W.B in Front Line trenches. Relief completed at 9.30. Casualties nil.	J.F.O.
	20/11/16		Battalion in front line. Our artillery active during day and early part of the night. Enemy line somewhat damaged. Very little retaliation. Casualties Nil.	J.F.O
	21/11/16		Battalion in front line. Patrol left our line to ~~recc~~ reconnoitre No Mans Land and to deal with any enemy patrols met on the way. Reached enemy barbed wire and while looking for a breach in same were seen by enemy sentries, who opened fire on them. Patrol withdrew ~~retired~~ to our line, ~~[illegible]~~ one man slightly wounded, was found to be missing. Casualty 42193 Pte Vowles E. Wounded & missing.	J.F.O

T2134. Wt. W708—776. 500000. 4/15. Sir J. C. & S.

Instructions regarding War Diaries and Intelligence Summaries are contained in F. S. Regs., Part II. and the Staff Manual respectively. Title pages will be prepared in manuscript.

WAR DIARY
or
INTELLIGENCE SUMMARY.
(Erase heading not required.)

Army Form C. 2118.

Place	Date	Hour	Summary of Events and Information	Remarks and references to Appendices
Left sub sector Left sector St Julien Trench Map C 25 c 72	22/11/16		Battalion in Front Line. Quiet day. Casualty L. Sgt. Patrick S. wounded [illegible]	E. F. O.
	23/11/16		Battalion in Front Line. During night enemy patrol attempted to bomb one of our saps but were easily repulsed. Casualty one O.R. Pte. J. H. Adams w[ounded]. Battalion relieved by 11th Batt. S.W.B. and proceeded to Canal Bank in support	E. F. O.
	24/11/16		Battalion in Support to 11th Batt. S.W.B. Usual fatigues carried out. Casualties Nil.	E. F. O.
	25/11/16		Battalion in support to 11th Batt. S.W.B. Usual fatigues carried out. Battalion relieved by 16th Batt. R.W.F. and marched to D. Camp to Divisional Reserve	E. F. O.
Camp D [illegible] a 42	26/11/16		Battalion at Camp D. Usual training programme carried out. Usual night fatigue, cable carrying	E. F. O.

T2134. Wt. W708—776. 500000. 4/15. Sir J. C. & S.

Instructions regarding War Diaries and Intelligence Summaries are contained in F. S. Regs., Part II. and the Staff Manual respectively. Title pages will be prepared in manuscript.

WAR DIARY
or
INTELLIGENCE SUMMARY.
(Erase heading not required.)

Army Form C. 2118.

Place	Date	Hour	Summary of Events and Information	Remarks and references to Appendices
Camp D A30 a 4 2	27/11/16		Battalion at Camp D. Inspection of kit by C.O. and usual training programme. Usual night fatigues carried out.	E.J.O.
"	28/11/16		Battalion at Camp D. Usual training programme carried out. Usual night fatigues	E.J.O.
	29/11/16		Battalion at Camp D. Usual training programme. Usual night fatigues. cable burying	E.J.O.
	30/11/16		Battalion at Camp D. Inspection of 115th Bde. by Lieut-General Sir Aylmer Hunter-Weston. K.C.B. D.S.O., Commdg VIII Corps. Commented favourably on the appearance of the men. Usual night ~~fatigues~~ working parties	E.J.O.

J.H. [illegible] Major
for Lt Col
Commanding 10th Batt S.W.B.

T2134. Wt. W708—776. 500000. 4/15. Sir J. C. & S.

Instructions regarding War Diaries and Intelligence Summaries are contained in F. S. Regs., Part II. and the Staff Manual respectively. Title pages will be prepared in manuscript.

WAR DIARY
or
INTELLIGENCE SUMMARY.
(Erase heading not required.)

10 S W Borderers

Army Form C. 2118.

Vol 12

Place	Date	Hour	Summary of Events and Information	Remarks and references to Appendices
Camp Armagh Dec 1916	4/12/16		Physical Training B. C. D. Coys. A Coy Musketry [illegible] central. Brigade Bombing class 1 Off 20 O.R. Band [illegible] 2 [illegible] p.m. [illegible] Found 5 Off 170 O.R. for R.E. cable burying party	[illegible]
	5/12/16		A Battalion at Camp D. Liason between Infantry & Aeroplane (signallers) A 24 C A 23 C.d. Physical Training. Bayonet Fighting B. C. D. Coys. Wiring practice. Musketry & Bayonet Fighting A Coy. Brigade Bombing Course 20 men. Brigade Engineering Class. Lewis Gun Instruction. Inspection of huts by C.O. Cable burying fatigue at night	[illegible]
	6/12/16		Battalion at Camp D. Divine Service 9.15 a.m. Hair Cutting. Cleaning of Equipment & Huts. Inspection of Huts. Box respirator drill. Band played programme of music at 4 p.m. R.E. fatigue party cable burying 4.15 p.m. Regimental Exercises. Reconnaissance by Officers.	[illegible]

T2134. Wt. W708—776. 500000. 4/15. Sir J. C. & S.

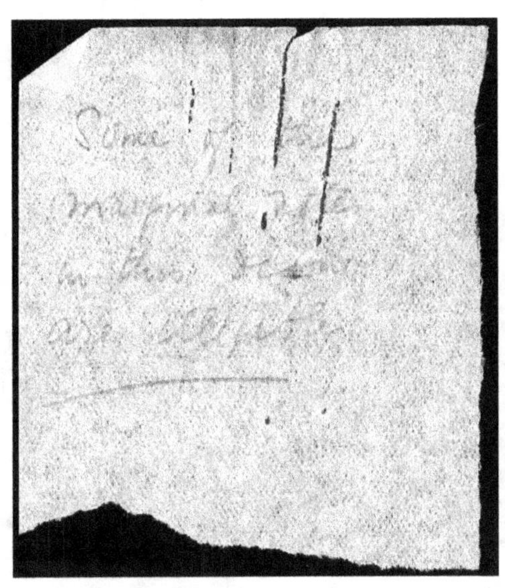

Instructions regarding War Diaries and Intelligence Summaries are contained in F. S. Regs., Part II. and the Staff Manual respectively. Title pages will be prepared in manuscript.

WAR DIARY
or
INTELLIGENCE SUMMARY.
(Erase heading not required.)

Army Form C. 2118.

Place	Date	Hour	Summary of Events and Information	Remarks and references to Appendices
[illegible] D				
[illegible]	7/12/16		Battalion at Camp D. Physical Training. Box Respirator Drill. Instruction in Lewis Gun by Lewis Gun Sergeant. Signaller's instruction under Signalling Officer. Inspection of Kits. General clean up and packing up before proceeding to Front Line. Battalion left Camp D at 4.30pm and marched to Brandhoek and entrained for The Asylum Ypres. It detrained and marched to front line trenches on right ~~[illegible]~~ Hill Top Section. Relief ~~carried out~~ of 13th Batt Welsh Regt. carried out satisfactorily despite adverse conditions. Casualty one 22337 Pte R Davies W. Ya.	[illegible]
			16th Welsh on left 166 Infantry Brigade on right	Hank? Hill Top [illegible]
	7/12/16		Battalion in Front Line. Quiet day. Patrol of 1 Off. and 10 O.R. left our line at 12. Object - To sweep No Mans Land and deal with any ~~hostil~~ hostile patrols met with. Going - ground rather soft. Result - Patrol swept ground but did not encounter any enemy patrol. Returned at 1.30 am	[illegible]

T2134. Wt. W708—776. 500000. 4/15. Sir J. C. & S.

Instructions regarding War Diaries and Intelligence Summaries are contained in F. S. Regs., Part II. and the Staff Manual respectively. Title pages will be prepared in manuscript.

WAR DIARY
or
INTELLIGENCE SUMMARY.
(Erase heading not required.)

Army Form C. 2118.

Place	Date	Hour	Summary of Events and Information	Remarks and references to Appendices
[illegible]	[illegible] a.m.		Patrol of 1 Off. & 3 O.R. left our line at 12 midnight 5-6th. Point of exit. C.21 c.8.4 (Forward Sap) Object of Patrol. To discover whether Sap 10 is occupied, also Sap 11. To look for gap in the wire. Result. Discovered that Sap 10 was occupied. Enemy wire strong. Sap 11 occupied. "Going" in No Mans Land & Rather wet. Time of Re-entry at C 21 c 8.4. 1.5 am. Casualties Nil.	
"	6/10/16		Battalion in Front Line. Very quiet day.	
		1.10 a.m.	Patrol of 1 Off and 10 O.R. left our line at C 21 c 9.4 at 1.10 am. Object. To sweep No Mans land and deal with any enemy patrol encountered. Result:- Sought the ground but no hostile patrols met with. Going:- Soft owing to recent rains. Grass long. Shell holes plentiful.	
		2.35	Point and time of Re-entry C.22.c.4.7 at 2.35 a.m. Casualties Nil. Our Artillery rather active in afternoon. Canadian Dug outs Shrapnelled.	

T2134. Wt. W708—776. 500000. 4/15. Sir J. C. & S.

Instructions regarding War Diaries and Intelligence Summaries are contained in F. S. Regs., Part II. and the Staff Manual respectively. Title pages will be prepared in manuscript.

WAR DIARY
or
INTELLIGENCE SUMMARY.
(Erase heading not required.)

Army Form C. 2118.

Place	Date	Hour	Summary of Events and Information	Remarks and references to Appendices
	7/2/16		Battalion in Front Line. Enemy Artillery active.	
		12.10 a.m.	Patrol of 2 Offs. + 19 O.R. left our line at C.21 a. 8.8½. Object:- To sweep No Man's Land and deal with any enemy patrol encountered. Result:- No patrol encountered. Going fairly good but rather wet. Withdrew at 12.45 a.m. Re entered at C.21.b.8.4 at 1.5 a.m. Casualties Nil.	[illegible]
	8/2/16		Battalion in Front Line. Very quiet day. Battalion was relieved by 11th Batt S.W.B. and marched to support line on Canal Bank. Casualties Nil.	[illegible]
[illegible]	9/2/16		Battalion in Support to 11th S.W.B. Box respirator drill carried out. Usual fatigues carried out - Wiring, repairing & carrying party. Casualties nil.	[illegible]

T2134. Wt. W708—776. 500000. 4/15. Sir J. C. & S.

Instructions regarding War Diaries and Intelligence Summaries are contained in F. S. Regs., Part II. and the Staff Manual respectively. Title pages will be prepared in manuscript.

WAR DIARY

or

INTELLIGENCE SUMMARY.

(Erase heading not required.)

Army Form C. 2118.

Place	Date	Hour	Summary of Events and Information	Remarks and references to Appendices
Canal Bank [illegible] I.15.d.2.6	[illegible]/12/16		Battalion in support to 11th S.W.B. Testing of Box Respirators. Usual fatigues — wiring, repairing line. Carrying party. [illegible] nil.	[illegible]
	[illegible]/12/16		Battalion in support to 11th S.W.B. [illegible] relieved by 13th [illegible] and marched to Camp D [illegible].	[illegible]
Camp D A.30.[illegible]	[illegible]/12/16		Battalion in Camp D. [illegible] [illegible] [illegible] Battalion left Camp at 4.30 p.m. and marched to reserve billets in Boesinghe section, in reserve to 16th Batt Welsh Regt. Casualties nil.	[illegible]
Bluet Farm Boesinghe Sector B.10.c.2.3	7/12/16		Battalion in reserve to 16th Welsh Regt. Reconnaissance of front area by officers and N.C.O.s. Box respirator drill. Fatigue party of 1 off 40 O.R. furnished for work in front line. Casualties nil.	[illegible]

T2134. Wt. W708—776. 500000. 4/15. Sir J. C. & S.

Army Form C. 2118

Instructions regarding War Diaries and Intelligence Summaries are contained in F. S. Regs., Part II. and the Staff Manual respectively. Title Pages will be prepared in manuscript.

WAR DIARY
or
INTELLIGENCE SUMMARY
(Erase heading not required.)

Place	Date	Hour	Summary of Events and Information	Remarks and references to Appendices
Bluet Wood B10 C23	4/7/16		Battalion in Reserve to 16th Welsh Regt. Box respirator and gas helmet drill. Elementary Lewis Gun Class under Lewis Gun sergeant. Signalling class under Signalling Sergeant. Demonstration of Armstrong carrier. Fatigue party of 3 Off and 80 O.R. furnished for Battalion in line. Casualties Nil.	B.T.O.
"	5/7/16		Battalion in Reserve to 16th Welsh Regt. Box respirators drill. Inspection of dug-outs by C.O. Inspection of equipment. Elementary Lewis Gun Class. Signalling class under Signalling Sergeant. Demonstration of Armstrong carrier. Fatigues of 2 Off and 80 O.R. furnished for Battalions in line. Casualties Nil.	B.T.O.
"	6/7/16		Battalion in Reserve to 16th Welsh Regt. Physical drill for ½ hour. Inspection of kit of Headquarters Coy. by C.O. Musketry drill. Fatigue party of 4 Off and 180 O.R. furnished for Battalion in line. Casualties Nil.	B.T.O.

1875 Wt. W593/826 1,000,000 4/15 J.B.C. & A. A.D.S.S./Forms/C. 2118.

Instructions regarding War Diaries and Intelligence Summaries are contained in F. S. Regs., Part II. and the Staff Manual respectively. Title pages will be prepared in manuscript.

WAR DIARY
or
INTELLIGENCE SUMMARY.
(Erase heading not required.)

Army Form C. 2118.

Place	Date	Hour	Summary of Events and Information	Remarks and references to Appendices
Elverdinghe [illegible] [illegible] B.10 C.23	[illegible]/16		Battalion in Reserve to 16th Welsh Regt. Physical drill. [illegible]. General clean up and packing preparatory to moving into front area. Battalion relieved by 17th Bn. R.W.F. and marched to front area. Relief carried out satisfactorily. Casualties Nil.	[illegible]
Elverdinghe [illegible] Chateau	[illegible]/16		Battalion in Front Line. Hostile artillery active during forenoon. Work – Repairing front line and [illegible] with Concertinas. Casualties 2 O.R. 72142 Pte Selvage J. W/a 15/12/16 at duty. 24191 Pte Smith R.O. w/a.	[illegible]
B.11.b.8.5.	[illegible]/16		Battalion in Front Line. Hostile minenwerfer activity during day. Enemy bombed the canal during the night. Work – Repair of front line & Communication trench. Wiring on slope of Canal Bank. Casualties 2 O.R. 42168 Pte Preece R. w/a. 72199 Cpl. Morgan S.J. w/a.	[illegible]

T2134. Wt. W708—776. 500000. 4/15. Sir J. C. & S.

Instructions regarding War Diaries and Intelligence Summaries are contained in F. S. Regs., Part II. and the Staff Manual respectively. Title pages will be prepared in manuscript.

WAR DIARY
or
INTELLIGENCE SUMMARY.
(Erase heading not required.)

Army Form C. 2118.

Place	Date	Hour	Summary of Events and Information	Remarks and references to Appendices
Front Line Boesinghe Chateau B.11.c.8.5.	20/12/16		Battalion in front line. Enemy's artillery and minenwerfers extremely active against front & support lines and communication trenches. Work. Repair of trenches. Erection of dug-outs. Casualties 2 O.R. 42194 Pte Brown J.J. w/d. 42269 Pte Morgan H.J. w/d.	E.Y.O.
"	21/12/16.		Battalion in front line. Quiet day. Work—repair of front line & fire-steps. Our artillery registered on enemy's front and support line and communication trench. Casualties Nil.	E.Y.O.
"	22/12/16.		Battalion in front line. Enemy artillery and minenwerfers extremely active on our front and support lines and communication trenches. Snipers less active during day. Work repair of front line and [illegible] communication trench, [illegible] up 4 [illegible]. Casualties Nil. Battalion was relieved by 17th K.L.R. and marched to support line at Blue? Farm	E.Y.O.

T2134. Wt. W708—776. 500000. 4/15. Sir J. C. & S.

Instructions regarding War Diaries and Intelligence Summaries are contained in F. S. Regs., Part II. and the Staff Manual respectively. Title pages will be prepared in manuscript.

WAR DIARY
or
INTELLIGENCE SUMMARY.
(Erase heading not required.)

Army Form C. 2118.

Place	Date	Hour	Summary of Events and Information	Remarks and references to Appendices
Black Farm Support Line Dec 23	23/12/16		Battalion in Support to 17th R.W.F. Enemy artillery active. Fatigue parties of 2 off and 110 O.R. furnished for Battalion in Front line. Box respirators drill. Inspection of equipment. Church Parade. Work carried out clearing communication trench in the neighbourhood by two men per Coy. Casualties Nil.	[illegible]
	24/12/16		Battalion in Support to 17th R.W.F. Inspection of equipment rifles and bayonets. Box respirator drill. Fatigue parties of 2 Off and 80 O.R. furnished for Battalion in the line. Casualties Nil.	[illegible]
	25/12/16		Battalion in Support to 17th R.W.F. Church parade at Battalion Headquarters. Fatigue parties of 2 Off and 80 O.R. furnished for Battalion in line. Enemy artillery shelled support lines [illegible]. Casualties Nil.	[illegible]

Instructions regarding War Diaries and Intelligence Summaries are contained in F. S. Regs., Part II. and the Staff Manual respectively. Title pages will be prepared in manuscript.

WAR DIARY
or
INTELLIGENCE SUMMARY.
(Erase heading not required.)

Army Form C. 2118.

Place	Date	Hour	Summary of Events and Information	Remarks and references to Appendices
Boesinghe Sector Canal Bank B10 C.2.5	26/12/16		Battalion in support to 17th R.W.F. Box respirator drill. Bathing for Headquarters Coy. General clean up and packing before proceeding to front area. Battalion relieved 9th Batt R.W.F. in front area. Relief carried out satisfactorily and completed at 8 p.m. Casualties Nil.	[illegible] (Hanks)
Front line Boesinghe Sector B11 b.8.5	27/12/16		Battalion in front line. Enemy artillery shelled front & support lines. Silenced by our retaliation. Work: Putting out concertina wire and knife rests. Making concertinas. Cutting timber for knife rests. Snipers active. Casualties Nil.	[illegible]
	28/12/16		Battalion in front line. Quiet day. Work: Wiring [illegible] front line. Completing dug-out at Battalion Hqrs. Enemy snipers active [illegible]. Casualties Nil.	[illegible]

T2134. Wt. W708–776. 500000. 4/15. Sir J. C. & S.

Instructions regarding War Diaries and Intelligence Summaries are contained in F. S. Regs., Part II. and the Staff Manual respectively. Title pages will be prepared in manuscript.

WAR DIARY
or
INTELLIGENCE SUMMARY.
(Erase heading not required.)

Army Form C. 2118.

Place	Date	Hour	Summary of Events and Information	Remarks and references to Appendices
Boesinghe Sector C.14.b.8.5	29/12/16		Battalion in front line. Enemy minenwerfer somewhat active, his snipers active during afternoon. Work: improving of front and support lines. Relaying trench boards. Completing dug-out at Battn. Hqrs. Casualties nil.	J.J.O.
	30/12/16		Battalion in front line. Quiet day. Work: improving front line. Cleaning Bombs. Completing dug-out at Battn. Hqrs. Battalion was relieved by 11th Battn. Royal Sussex Regt. Relief started at 4.30 p.m. and completed by 8 p.m. Battalion marched to Cheese Market Poperinghe and entrained for Bollezeele. Arrived at Bollezeele 2 a.m. 31/12/16 and marched to billets. Casualties nil.	J.J.O.
Bollezeele Sheet 27 A.29.c.5.3.	31/12/16		Battalion at Bollezeele. A General clean up and inspection by Coy. Commanders.	J.J.O.

[illegible] Lt.-Col.
Commanding 10th B.

T2134. Wt. W708—776. 500000. 4/15. Sir J. C. & S.

Instructions regarding War Diaries and Intelligence Summaries are contained in F. S. Regs., Part II. and the Staff Manual respectively. Title pages will be prepared in manuscript.

WAR DIARY
or
INTELLIGENCE SUMMARY.
(Erase heading not required.)

Army Form C. 2118.

115/38

Vol 13

Place	Date	Hour	Summary of Events and Information	Remarks and references to Appendices
Bollezeele Sheet 27 A24.C.5.3	1/1/17		Battalion at Bollezeele. Usual training:- Cleaning parade 7 to 7.45 a.m. Physical training & Bayonet Fighting 8.45-9.45. Company drill & arm drill 9.45-10.45. Musketry 11.0 a.m.-12.0 a.m. Wiring 12.0 am-1 p.m. Kit inspections 2.15 p.m.-3.15	840
"	2/1/17		Battalion at Bollezeele. Usual training:- Cleaning parade 7 to 7.45 a.m. Physical & Saluting drill 8.45-9.45. Company & Arm drill 9.45-10.45. Extended order drill 11.0 a.m.-12.0 noon. Rapid wiring 12 noon-1 p.m. Extension of working parties 2.15 p.m.-3.15 p.m. ~~[illegible]~~ Working party 1 off & 50 O.R. furnished for filling in trenches	840
"	3/1/17		Battalion at Bollezeele. Usual training:- Physical training & Coy. drill 8.45-9.45. Musketry 9.45 a.m.-10.45 a.m. Throwing bombs. Extensions from different formations, 11 a.m.-12 noon. Rapid wiring - Bayonet Fighting 12 noon-1 p.m. Lecture on Sanitation. Musketry at Range 2.15 p.m.-3.30 p.m. Lewis Gun instruction under Lewis Gun officer. Officers Tactical Exercise.	840

Instructions regarding War Diaries and Intelligence Summaries are contained in F. S. Regs., Part II. and the Staff Manual respectively. Title pages will be prepared in manuscript.

WAR DIARY
or
INTELLIGENCE SUMMARY.
(*Erase heading not required.*)

Army Form C. 2118.

Place	Date	Hour	Summary of Events and Information	Remarks and references to Appendices
Bollezeele Sheet 27 A24 C.5.3.	4/1/17		Battalion at Bollezeele. Usual training. Battalion marched to training area near Merckeghem. Lewis Gun instruction. Rapid entrenching, clearing enemy trenches and flanks, rapid wiring, bombing and Bayonet Fighting. Battalion returned at 12.30 p.m. Inter company football matches 2.0 p.m., 2.[illegible] p.m. The foll. awards appear in	J.W.G.O. New Year
		List	1/Major C. T. Rees - Military Cross. 7/20407 Sgt R. Edwards & 7/20408 Sgt W. J. Williams D.C.M.	
"	5/1/17	8.45-9.45	Battalion at Bollezeele. Usual training. Handling of Bombs and practising a charge 8.45-9.45. Musketry and Bayonet	
		9.30-12.30	Fighting. Lewis Gun instruction under Lewis Gun Officer.	J.W.G.O.
		2.30 p.m.	Battalion cross country run. Inspection of feet & hands 12.30 p.m. Officers of C & D Companies - Tactical exercise 2.15 p.m. - 3.45 p.m. Died of sickness D Coy Sgt James G.G. 7/21362	
"	6/1/17		Battalion at Bollezeele. Usual training. - Battalion marched to training area. Bombing, Bayonet Fighting, Rapid wiring, Digging; Lewis Gun instruction under Lewis Gun Officer. Final Inter-Company football match 2.45 p.m. Tug of war competition 2.15 p.m. Battalion Christmas dinner at 5 p.m. in [illegible] Hall.	J.W.G.O.

T2134. Wt. W708—776. 500000. 4/15. Sir J. C. & S.

Army Form C. 2118.

Instructions regarding War Diaries and Intelligence Summaries are contained in F. S. Regs., Part II. and the Staff Manual respectively. Title pages will be prepared in manuscript.

WAR DIARY
or
INTELLIGENCE SUMMARY.
(Erase heading not required.)

Place	Date	Hour	Summary of Events and Information	Remarks and references to Appendices
Bollezeele Sht 27 [illegible] 24. C.5.3	7/1/17		Battalion at Bollezeele. Church parade. C. E. 10 a.m. Non Con 11 a.m. R. C. 11.15 a.m. Inspection of box respirators and instructions by Divisional Gas expert	G.T.O.
	8/1/17	8.45 a.m.	Battalion at Bollezeele. Usual training. Cleaning parade 7.0 a.m.–7.45 Battalion Drill – Artillery Formation – Outpost drill – Inter coy bayonet fighting competition. – Wiring competition – Inter coy. Cross country run 2.30 p.m.–[illegible]30 p.m. [illegible] by [illegible] Boxing Competition.	G.T.O.
	9/1/17	9 a.m. 2.30 p.m.	Battalion at Bollezeele. Usual training. Cleaning parade [illegible] Battalion Route march with Band & Drums. Returned at 12.30 p.m. C Coy Cross Country team competed in Brigade Competition & succeeded in gaining first place.	G.T.O.

Instructions regarding War Diaries and Intelligence Summaries are contained in F. S. Regs., Part II. and the Staff Manual respectively. Title pages will be prepared in manuscript.

WAR DIARY
or
INTELLIGENCE SUMMARY.
(Erase heading not required.)

Army Form C. 2118.

Place	Date	Hour	Summary of Events and Information	Remarks and references to Appendices
Bollezeele Sheet 27 A24.c.5.3	10/1/17		Battalion at Bollezeele. Wet Morning. Battalion paraded in mass at 9.0 a.m. for Battalion drill. [illegible] of [illegible] and extending [illegible] drill 9.45 a.m. - 10.30 a.m. The following officers & N.C.O. are mentioned in Despatches in Supplement to London Gazette dated 4/1/17 Lt Colonel Harvey C.B. 12024. Sgt Woodall S.J. Battalion paraded at 12.45 p.m. Marched to training ground at Merckeghem for Brigade exercise. Parade dismissed owing to inclement wet weather.	[illegible]
"	11/1/17	9.0 a.m.	Battalion at Bollezeele. Fine Morning. Cleaning Parade 7.0 - 7.45 a.m. Battalion paraded in mass for Battalion Drill. - Musketry training Recognition of targets - Rapid loading and firing. Packing and Bayonet Fighting. Musketry 2.30 p.m. - 4 p.m. on 30 yards range. 2.30 p.m. - 3.30 p.m. Kit Inspection for C & D Coys. Football match A Coy. v Bde. H Qrs.	[illegible]

T2134. Wt. W708—776. 500000. 4/15. Sir J. C. & S.

Instructions regarding War Diaries and Intelligence Summaries are contained in F. S. Regs., Part II. and the Staff Manual respectively. Title pages will be prepared in manuscript.

WAR DIARY
or
INTELLIGENCE SUMMARY.
(Erase heading not required.)

Army Form C. 2118.

Place	Date	Hour	Summary of Events and Information	Remarks and references to Appendices
Bollezeele Sheet 27 [illegible]	12/1/17		Battalion at Bollezeele. Usual training. Cleaning parade 9.0–[illegible]	
		9am	Battalion paraded in Mass for battalion drill.	
		10.30am	Officers Commanding Coys. medically inspected their companies.	
		12.30pm	Battalion marched to Battalion Training Ground at Merckeghem for Brigade scheme but owing to bad weather parade was dismissed.	[illegible]
"	13/1/17		Battalion at Bollezeele. Usual training. Cleaning parade 9.0–[illegible]. Owing to inclement weather the battalion did not parade in Battalion Mass. Lectures held in Company billets instead.	[illegible]
	14/1/17	9.30am	Battalion left Bollezeele & entrained in 2 trains one [illegible] 9.30, the other at 9.38. Detrained at Poperinghe about 1pm and marched to Camp D.	[illegible]
			C.O. (Lt Col Harvey) proceeded to 2nd Army Course for C.Os.	
Camp D [illegible]	15/1/17		Battalion at D Camp. Cleaning up. Battalion Drill. Box Respirator Drill and Physical Training in morning	

T2134. Wt. W708—776. 500000. 4/15. Sir J. C. & S.

Instructions regarding War Diaries and Intelligence Summaries are contained in F. S. Regs., Part II. and the Staff Manual respectively. Title pages will be prepared in manuscript.

WAR DIARY
or
INTELLIGENCE SUMMARY.
(Erase heading not required.)

Army Form C. 2118.

Place	Date	Hour	Summary of Events and Information	Remarks and references to Appendices
Camp D I 30 a 4.7 (28 N.W.)	15/1/17	P.M. 2.30	C.O. Inspected huts in afternoon.	
		3.0	Bayonet Fighting performed during the afternoon.	J.G.O.
"	16/1/17	am	Battalion at Camp D. Normal Training carried	
		9.30	out. Physical Drill 9.30am to 10 am, Battalion	
		10.0	Drill 10 am to 10.45 am, Bayonet Fighting	
		11.0	11 am to 11.45 am Box Respirator Drill	
		11.45	11.45 am to 12.15 pm. C.O. inspected huts in the morning.	
Fme Bluet B.10.c.23. (36 N.W.)	"	pm 3.15	Battalion paraded 3.15 pm and left D Camp, marching to Fme Bluet (Support Bulech, Left Sector, Left Division) in Support to 16th Welch Regiment. Relieved 14th Bn Hants Regt.	J.G.O.
Fme Bluet B 10 c 23	17/1/17		Battalion in Support. Training carried out as far as fatigues re would allow. Company	J.G.O.

Army Form C. 2118.

Instructions regarding War Diaries and Intelligence Summaries are contained in F. S. Regs., Part II. and the Staff Manual respectively. Title pages will be prepared in manuscript.

WAR DIARY
or
INTELLIGENCE SUMMARY.
(Erase heading not required.)

Place	Date	Hour	Summary of Events and Information	Remarks and references to Appendices
Fme Blud B10c 2.3	17.1.17	AM	Commanders inspected clothing, rifles, equipment, Box Respirators and Gas Helmets. Box Respirator Drill carried out under Company arrangements. Commanding Officer inspected	
		11am	Company Guards & Billets at 11 am.	J.G.D.
Fme Blud B10c 2.3	18.1.17	AM	Battalion in Support. Parades were ordered under Company Commanders, for inspection of rifles and Box Respirator Drill. Commanding Officer inspected Headquarter Company & Billets 10.30	
		10.30am	am	J.G.D.
	19.1.17	AM.	Battalion in Support. Parades ordered under Company Commanders for inspection of rifles and Box Respirators. Medical Officer inspected men of A B & C Companies in Billets between 10am & 11am.	J.G.D.

T2134. Wt. W708—776. 500000. 4/15. Sir J. C. & S.

Instructions regarding War Diaries and Intelligence Summaries are contained in F. S. Regs., Part II. and the Staff Manual respectively. Title pages will be prepared in manuscript.

WAR DIARY
or
INTELLIGENCE SUMMARY.
(Erase heading not required.)

Army Form C. 2118.

Place	Date	Hour	Summary of Events and Information	Remarks and references to Appendices
Line Bluff B10c.2.3.	19 20/1/17		Battalion in Support. Company Commanders arranged inspections of rifles and bayonets, and Box Respirator Drill Battalion relieved 16th Welch Regiment in Front Line commencing 4.30 pm. Casualties - NIL. CO (Lt Col Harvey) Returned from 2nd Army Course for COs	J.G.D.
Front Line B.11.b.8.5 (Boesinghe Chateau)	21/1/17		Battalion in Front Line. Right Company (A Coy) in touch with A Coy 16th Battn. RWF. Left Company (C Coy) connected with 1st Company of 21st Regiment of Infantry (Belgian Army). Casualties - NIL. Enemy artillery fairly quiet but ours retaliated for hostile activity of yesterday. Our lines were shelled a little in the morning, much attention being paid to the Village Street + Bridge Street.	J.G.D.
	22/1/17		Battalion in Front Line. Companies on flanks unchanged	J.G.D.

T2134. Wt. W708—776. 500000. 4/15. Sir J. C. & S.

Instructions regarding War Diaries and Intelligence Summaries are contained in F. S. Regs., Part II. and the Staff Manual respectively. Title pages will be prepared in manuscript.

WAR DIARY
or
INTELLIGENCE SUMMARY.
(Erase heading not required.)

Army Form C. 2118.

Place	Date	Hour	Summary of Events and Information	Remarks and references to Appendices
Front line 3.11.b.9.5 Boesinghe Chateau	22/1/17		Enemy shelled at intervals during the day chiefly round Chateau and Boesinghe Ry Station. Work on Front Line under R.E. clearing and revetting Bridge Street. New kitchen erected at Centre Company Hdqrs. 110 RE concertina wires put out. Our artillery replied effectively to Hun hostile activity. Casualties Nil.	J.G.D.
"	23/1/17		Battalion in Front Line. Enemy shelled Headquarters and surroundings vigorously during the day without inflicting any material damage. Our Artillery returned the compliment retaliation being quickly forthcoming when asked for. Our aeroplanes very active the weather being admirably suited for aerial observation. Battalion besides work under R.E. commenced	J.G.D.

T2134. Wt. W708—776. 500000. 4/15. Sir J. C. & S.

Instructions regarding War Diaries and Intelligence Summaries are contained in F. S. Regs., Part II. and the Staff Manual respectively. Title pages will be prepared in manuscript.

WAR DIARY
or
INTELLIGENCE SUMMARY.
(*Erase heading not required.*)

Army Form C. 2118.

Place	Date	Hour	Summary of Events and Information	Remarks and references to Appendices
Front Line 11f.8.5	23.1.17		clearing Tunnel to MG Emplacement under Railway Bridge. Units on flanks unchanged. Casualties nil.	[illegible]
"	24.1.17		Battalion in Front Line. Units on flanks unchanged. Enemy heavily shelled front Line and Village Street. Cookhouse at A Co and Officers quarters C Co blown up. Casualties one OR wounded (remained at duty) 2 Camouflages rendered serviceable. Repaired tunnel until blown in by hostile ~~activity~~ artillery. 30 concertina wires put out. Observers report some gas shells amongst the others sent by enemy. Report not however confirmed. Battalion relieved 4.45pm by 16th Battalion	[illegible]

T2134. Wt. W708–776. 500000. 4/15. Sir J. C. & S.

Instructions regarding War Diaries and Intelligence Summaries are contained in F. S. Regs., Part II. and the Staff Manual respectively. Title pages will be prepared in manuscript.

WAR DIARY
or
INTELLIGENCE SUMMARY.
(*Erase heading not required.*)

Army Form C. 2118.

Place	Date	Hour	Summary of Events and Information	Remarks and references to Appendices
	24.1.17	5pm	Welch Regiment, and marched to Camp at B.13.a.2.6. ~~Erax~~	J.G.D.
Roussell Farm B.13.a.2.6	25.1.17		Battalion in Brigade Support. Cleaning parade arranged, afterwards cancelled on account of fatigue parties 300 O.R. being required. Casualties nil	J.G.D.
"	26.1.17		Battalion in Brigade Reserve fatigue parties of 300 Other Ranks again sent out. Casualties nil.	J.G.D.
	27.1.17		Battalion in Roussell Farm. Fatigue parties 9 officers 300 Other Ranks furnished for Railway Construction work Casualties nil.	

T2134. Wt. W708–776. 500000. 4/15. Sir J. C. & S.

Instructions regarding War Diaries and Intelligence Summaries are contained in F. S. Regs., Part II. and the Staff Manual respectively. Title pages will be prepared in manuscript.

WAR DIARY
or
INTELLIGENCE SUMMARY.
(Erase heading not required.)

Army Form C. 2118.

Place	Date	Hour	Summary of Events and Information	Remarks and references to Appendices
[illegible] 13 A [illegible]	28.1.17		Battalion at Roussell Farm. Usual Fatigue party of 9 officers 300 other ranks furnished evening early.	
[illegible] GUN FARM [illegible] 5 C 8 8		3.30 pm	Battalion left Roussell Farm 3.30 pm and marched to Elverdinghe where they relieved the 17th R.W.F. in Elverdinghe Defences, with Headquarters at MACHINE GUN FARM. (28 NW. H. 5. c. 8.8) Relief completed without casualties notwithstanding unusual activity on the part of Hun. Artillery, which held the ~~[illegible]~~ relief up a little. Relief was completed about 8 pm.	[illegible]
[illegible] FARM c 8 8	29.1.17		Battalion at Machine Gun Farm. Companies carried on independently combining normal training with work on the Defences.	[illegible]

T2134. Wt. W708–776. 500000. 4/15. Sir J. C. & S.

Instructions regarding War Diaries and Intelligence Summaries are contained in F. S. Regs., Part II. and the Staff Manual respectively. Title pages will be prepared in manuscript.

WAR DIARY
or
INTELLIGENCE SUMMARY.
(Erase heading not required.)

Army Form C. 2118.

Place	Date	Hour	Summary of Events and Information	Remarks and references to Appendices
MACHINE GUN FME. 28 NW) H.5.C.8.8	29.1.17		During the night Alarm was raised on account of Boche activity on the Belgian Front. No detailed particulars were immediately forthcoming. Battalion "Stood to" & manned the Elverdinghe Defences from approximately 2 am to 3.30 am, after which "Stand down" was received.	[illegible initials]
MACHINE GUN FARM 28 NW) H.5.C.8.8	30.1.17		Battalion at Machine Gun Farm. Companies acted as yesterday, combining training with improvement of Defences. Battalion Headquarters (or about 75% thereof) were turned out for some very useful drill, including musketry, physical training, semaphore, manual, and squad drill. Parades 9 am to 12 noon 2 pm to ~~3~~ 3.30 pm.	[illegible initials]

Instructions regarding War Diaries and Intelligence Summaries are contained in F. S. Regs., Part II. and the Staff Manual respectively. Title pages will be prepared in manuscript.

WAR DIARY
or
INTELLIGENCE SUMMARY.
(Erase heading not required.)

Army Form C. 2118.

Place	Date	Hour	Summary of Events and Information	Remarks and references to Appendices
MACHINE GUN FARM SHW F5 C 88)	31.1.17		Battalion at Machine Gun Farm. Training and work carried out as yesterday, 45% of Headquarter Staff performing a similar programme of Training.	[illegible]

Lieutenant Colonel,
Commanding 10th. Bn., S. W. Borderers (1st. Gwent.)

T2134. Wt. W708—776. 500000. 4/15. Sir J. C. & S.

Instructions regarding War Diaries and Intelligence Summaries are contained in F. S. Regs., Part II. and the Staff Manual respectively. Title pages will be prepared in manuscript.

WAR DIARY
or
INTELLIGENCE SUMMARY.
(Erase heading not required.)

Army Form C. 2118.

10 SWB

Vol 14

Place	Date	Hour	Summary of Events and Information	Remarks and references to Appendices
MACHINE GUN F.M. 28NW H2B88	1.2.17		Battalion at Machine Gun Farm. Normal Training combined with work on Elverdinghe Defences, & Line carried out during the day. H.Qr. Company carried out squad drill, semaphore, and map reading	G.Y.O.
"	2.2.17		Battalion at Machine Gun Farm. Normal training combined with work on defenses carried out as yesterday. Commanding Officer inspected the Battalion Transport Lines and Stores. H.Qr. Company carried on as yesterday.	G.Y.O.
"	3.2.17		Battalion at Machine Gun Farm. Normal Training and work on Defences carried out as yesterday. Practice 'Stand To' was done about 6.30pm until 7.30pm.	G.Y.O.

T2134. Wt. W708 500000. 4/15. Sir J. C. & S.

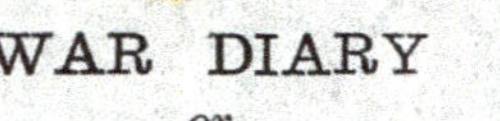

Instructions regarding War Diaries and Intelligence Summaries are contained in F. S. Regs., Part II. and the Staff Manual respectively. Title pages will be prepared in manuscript.

WAR DIARY
or
INTELLIGENCE SUMMARY.
(Erase heading not required.)

Army Form C. 2118.

Place	Date	Hour	Summary of Events and Information	Remarks and references to Appendices
MACHINE GUN FARM (28 NW) H.5.c.8.8	4.2.17		Battalion at Machine Gun Farm. Church Parades arranged, but afterwards were cancelled owing to indisposition of Chaplain. Work on Defences continued as before	J.G.O.
"	5.2.17		Battalion at Machine Gun Farm. Work on defences and Normal Company training carried out under Company Commanders	J.G.O.
"	6.2.17		Battalion at Machine Gun Farm. Work on defences and normal Company Training carried out as yesterday under Officers Commanding Companies. Baths @ Elverdinghe.	J.G.O.
	7.2.17		Battalion at Machine Gun Farm. Work on Elverdinghe Defences and "L" line an Company	J.G.O.

T2134. Wt. W708—776. 500000. 4/15. Sir J. C. & S.

Instructions regarding War Diaries and Intelligence Summaries are contained in F. S. Regs., Part II. and the Staff Manual respectively. Title pages will be prepared in manuscript.

WAR DIARY
or
INTELLIGENCE SUMMARY.
(Erase heading not required.)

Army Form C. 2118.

Place	Date	Hour	Summary of Events and Information	Remarks and references to Appendices
			Training carried on under Company arrangements.	G.L.O.
MACHINE GUN FARM H 5 c. 6.8	8/2/17		Battalion at Machine Gun Farm. Work on Defences, and Company Training carried out under Company arrangements.	G.L.O.
"	9-2/17		Battalion at Machine Gun Farm. Work on Defences and Company Training carried out as before	G.L.O.
"	10-2/17		Battalion at Machine Gun Farm Work on Defences and Company Training carried out under Company arrangements.	G.L.O.

T2134. Wt. W708—776. 500000. 4/15. Sir J. C. & S.

Instructions regarding War Diaries and Intelligence Summaries are contained in F. S. Regs., Part II. and the Staff Manual respectively. Title pages will be prepared in manuscript.

WAR DIARY
or
INTELLIGENCE SUMMARY.
(Erase heading not required.)

Army Form C. 2118.

Place	Date	Hour	Summary of Events and Information	Remarks and references to Appendices
MACHINE GUN FARM I.5.c.8.8	11.2.17		Battalion at Machine Gun Farm. Work on Defences and Company Training carried out under Company arrangements.	G.L.O.
"	12.2.17		Battalion at Machine Gun Farm. Preliminary inter Company Bayonet Fighting & Bombing Competitions held. Work on Defences and Company Training carried out under Company arrangements.	G.L.O.
"	13.2.17		Battalion at Machine Gun Farm. Inter Company Musketry Competition fired on range near Elverdinghe Chateau. "A" Company proved the victors. Work on defences and usual Company Training carried out as usual.	G.L.O.

T2134. Wt. W708–776. 500000. 4/15. Sir J. C. & S.

Instructions regarding War Diaries and Intelligence Summaries are contained in F. S. Regs., Part II. and the Staff Manual respectively. Title pages will be prepared in manuscript.

WAR DIARY
or
INTELLIGENCE SUMMARY.
(Erase heading not required.)

Army Form C. 2118.

Place	Date	Hour	Summary of Events and Information	Remarks and references to Appendices
[M]ACHINE [G]UN FARM 45 c 88	14/2/17		Battalion at Machine Gun Farm. Musketry (firing) practiced, with Box Respirators on. Battalion relieved by 16th Bn. Welch Regiment (Cardiff City) at dark and marched, by very small parties with suitable intervals between parties, to BLUET FARM, relieving the 17th Bn. Royal Welsh Fusiliers in Support Line. Relief completed about 9 p.m. Casualties nil. C Coy & A Coy in the line C on right A left.	S.G.O. D Coy in reserve at Bluet Farm. B Coy at [illegible] Farm
BLUET FARM. B.10.c 2.3	15/2/17		Battalion at Bluet Farm in Support to 17th Bn. R.W.F. in the Front Line Left Sector. Box respirator drill. Inspection of helmets, rifles, bayonets, ammunition and feet. Bathing in afternoon. Working parties of 6 off and 120 Men. Similar dispositions.	S.G.O.

T2134. Wt. W708—776. 500000. 4/15. Sir J. C. & S.

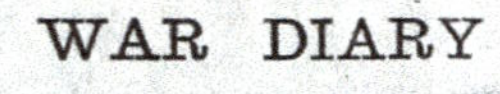

Instructions regarding War Diaries and Intelligence Summaries are contained in F. S. Regs., Part II. and the Staff Manual respectively. Title pages will be prepared in manuscript.

WAR DIARY
or
INTELLIGENCE SUMMARY.
(Erase heading not required.)

Army Form C. 2118.

Place	Date	Hour	Summary of Events and Information	Remarks and references to Appendices
Bre.C.2.3	16 2/7		Battalion in support to 17th Batt. R.W.F. Inspection of rifles equipment, feet, identity discs. Box respirator drill. Testing Box respirators in gas cloud. Bathing. Battalion course of rangefinding. Working parties of 6 Off. and 120 O.R. Casualties Nil. Similar dispositions	E.L.O.
"	17 2/7		Battalion in support to 17th Batt R.W.F. Inspection of rifles bayonets, equipment and oil tins. Usual box respirator drill. Testing same in gas cloud. Battalion course of rangefinding. Working parties of 6 Off and 120 O.R. Casualties Nil. Similar dispositions	E.L.O.
"	18 2/7		Battalion in support to 17th Batt. R.W.F. Church parade at Battalion Headquarters. Officers Commanding Companies & Coy. Sergeant Majors visited the front line. Battalion relieved 17th Batt R.W.F. in front line. Relief started	E.L.O.

T2134. Wt. W708—776. 500000. 4/15. Sir J. C. & S.

WAR DIARY
or
INTELLIGENCE SUMMARY.
(Erase heading not required.)

Army Form C. 2118.

Instructions regarding War Diaries and Intelligence Summaries are contained in F. S. Regs., Part II. and the Staff Manual respectively. Title pages will be prepared in manuscript.

Place	Date	Hour	Summary of Events and Information	Remarks and references to Appendices
[illegible] C.10.c.2.3.	8/2/17 (cont.)		at 2.15 p.m. and completed at 7.30 p.m. Battalion on left Premier regiment des Grenadiers Belges. Battalion on right 15th Batt. R.W.F. Work :– Work in trenches. Throwing off top of parapet to give field of fire. Building up-cover on dug-outs in Village Street. Wiring :– 7 Concertinas put out in Front line. 5 coils put out in X line. Hostile machine-guns somewhat active. During the night our artillery fired short bursts at intervals. Casualties Nil. Disposition A + B Coys in Front line A on right. C Coy in village line D. Coy in Boesinghe Redoubt.	[illegible]
Boesinghe Chateau Sn C.5.5.	9/2/17		Battalion in Front line. Battalion on left :– Premier regiment des Grenadiers Belges. Battalion on right :– 16th Batt. R.W.F. Our artillery fired bursts at intervals during the day. Our machine guns active during early part of the night. Enemy used rifle grenades at stand to in the evening. His artillery retaliated about 9.30 p.m. with H.E. + shrapnel on Chateau Grounds and X line. His machine-guns somewhat	[illegible]

T2134. Wt. W708—776. 500000. 4/15. Sir J. C. & S.

Instructions regarding War Diaries and Intelligence Summaries are contained in F. S. Regs., Part II. and the Staff Manual respectively. Title pages will be prepared in manuscript.

WAR DIARY
or
INTELLIGENCE SUMMARY.
(Erase heading not required.)

Army Form C. 2118.

Place	Date	Hour	Summary of Events and Information	Remarks and references to Appendices
[illegible] [illegible]	19/2/17	cont.	active during night. Work:- Working parties on Front line under R.E. supervision. Clearing falls in communication trenches. Draining; repairing and re-laying trench-boards; making brick pathways around Battalion Headquarters. Clearing village street. Salvaging. Re-establishing Dumps. Shaving off lip of parapet to give field of fire. Camouflaging. 16 concertinas put out on front line. Strengthening wire on S. line. Casualties 3 O. Ranks wd., one remained at duty. Disposition similar.	E.Z.O.
[illegible] [illegible] [illegible]	20/2/17		Battalion in front line:- Battalion on left:- Premier Regiment des Grenadiers belges. Battalion on right:- 15th R.W.F. Hostile artillery fired a few rounds on Boesinghe during the morning. Enemy fired Rifle Grenades near the end of Railway Street, but did no damage. We retaliated with Grenades immediately and he ceased. Work:- Working parties under R.E. supervision.	E.Z.O.

T.2134. Wt. W708—776. 500000. 4/15. Sir J. C. & S.

Army Form C. 2118.

Instructions regarding War Diaries and Intelligence Summaries are contained in F. S. Regs., Part II. and the Staff Manual respectively. Title pages will be prepared in manuscript.

WAR DIARY
or
INTELLIGENCE SUMMARY.
(Erase heading not required.)

Place	Date	Hour	Summary of Events and Information	Remarks and references to Appendices
	1/2/17 (Cont.)		Clearing falls in Bridge St. Building new sick changing dug-out for HQr Coy. Camouflaging. Wiring. Mine concertinas put out in front line. Shelter bolts on S. Line. Casualty :- One other rank w/d. Dispositions similar.	R.L.O.
[illegible] Sector Sub [illegible]	2/2/17		Battalion in Spur line. Battalion on left :- 1st Regiment des Grenadiers Belges. Battalion on right :- 15th R.W.F. [illegible] fired some light Trench Mortars on our front. At 12 noon he fired about 20 Trench Mortars on front & S. Line. His artillery shelled village street and Chateau about 3pm. Our artillery retaliated heavily on each occasion. We also retaliated with grenades. Work :- Working parties under R.E. supervision. Clearing and opening up drains. Repairing and relaying trench boards. Clearing falls in Bridge Street. Rebuilding damaged part. Casualties One O.R. k. Two O.R. w/d one at duty. Disposition C & D in Front line. C on right. A Coy in village line B Coy in Bosnythe Redoubt	R.L.O.

T2134. Wt. W708—776. 500000. 4/15. Sir J. C. & S.

Army Form C. 2118.

Instructions regarding War Diaries and Intelligence Summaries are contained in F. S. Regs., Part II. and the Staff Manual respectively. Title pages will be prepared in manuscript.

WAR DIARY
or
INTELLIGENCE SUMMARY.
(Erase heading not required.)

Place	Date	Hour	Summary of Events and Information	Remarks and references to Appendices
[illegible]	[illegible] 22/1/17		Battalion in Front line. Enemy artillery quiet during day and night. Fired a few rifle grenades on to our front line during the morning but did no damage. Enemy snipers somewhat active on extreme left. Our artillery shelled the enemy's front and support lines during the morning. Rifle Grenades on to enemy's front line. Battalion on left – [illegible] regiment de [illegible]. Battalion on right – 15th Batt. R.W.F. Work – Work on front line under R.E. supervision. Clearing widening & levelling Bridge St in Chateau Wood. Improving & changing dug-outs. Pumping water from cellars at Battalion Headquarters. Wiring. Battalion was relieved by 11th Batt. S.W.B. Relief complete at 10.5 p.m. Battalion marched to X Camp A 16 central, in place of 17th Batt. R.W.F. Casualty. One O.R. w/a. at duty.	Disposition Similar [illegible]

T2134. Wt. W708—776. 500000. 4/15. Sir J. C. & S.

Instructions regarding War Diaries and Intelligence Summaries are contained in F. S. Regs., Part II. and the Staff Manual respectively. Title pages will be prepared in manuscript.

WAR DIARY
or
INTELLIGENCE SUMMARY.
(Erase heading not required.)

Army Form C. 2118.

Place	Date	Hour	Summary of Events and Information	Remarks and references to Appendices
X. Camp A16 Central	23/2/17		Battalion at Camp X. Working parties of 6 officers and 276 O. Ranks. Paraded at 7.45 a.m. Returned at 4 p.m. General Clean up. Band and Drum practice.	[illegible]
"	24/2/17		Battalion at Camp X. Working parties of 6 officers and 276 O. Ranks. Battalion Concert at Cornish Hall proved most successful. Inspection of huts by the C.O.	[illegible]
"	25/2/17		Battalion at Camp X. Church Parade C.E. in Cornish hut at 10.30 a.m. N.C. 9.30 a.m. R.C. 8.45 a.m. Inspection of kit by the C.O. 9.45 a.m – 10.25 a.m. Medical Inspection by Medical Officer.	[illegible]
"	26/2/17		Battalion at Camp X. Working parties of 6 officers and 276 O.R. Band & Drums paraded 9.30 and marched to H. Camp whence they played a party of reinforcements to X. camp. Drill	[illegible]

Instructions regarding War Diaries and Intelligence Summaries are contained in F. S. Regs., Part II. and the Staff Manual respectively. Title pages will be prepared in manuscript.

WAR DIARY
or
INTELLIGENCE SUMMARY.
(Erase heading not required.)

Army Form C. 2118.

Place	Date	Hour	Summary of Events and Information	Remarks and references to Appendices
X Camp A.6 central	26/2/17	(Cont)	platoon & company carried out from 10.30 a.m. to 12 noon. Then were played back to the camp. Packing up preparatory to moving into support. Battalion left X Camp at 4 p.m. Working parties proceeded direct to Roussel Farm where they had tea. Then marched to Bluet Farm, relieving 17th Batt. R.W.F. Casualties Nil. C. Coy in reserve at (Bluet) Paradou Farm A Coy at Emile Farm B and D Coys in X line. B on left.	J.L.D.
Bluet Farm B.10 c.2.3.	27/2/17		Battalion in support to 17th Batt. R.W.F. Working parties of 4 officers & 99 O.R. One N.C.O. & 4 men reported at Batt. Hqrs for instruction in the upkeep of trenches. Casualties Nil. Disposition Similar	J.L.D.
"	28/2/17		Battalion in support to 17th Batt. R.W.F. Working parties of 1 off & 41 O.R. from 9 a.m. – 12.30 p.m. Clearing of support trenches. Inspection of Rifles & equipment. Lecture on the "water cart" at Batt. Hqrs. Casualties Nil. Disposition Similar	J.L.D.

G. Rees Major
Commanding 10th S.W.B. (1st Gwent)

T2134. Wt. W708–776. 500000. 4/15. Sir J. C. & S.

Instructions regarding War Diaries and Intelligence Summaries are contained in F. S. Regs., Part II. and the Staff Manual respectively. Title pages will be prepared in manuscript.

WAR DIARY or INTELLIGENCE SUMMARY.

(Erase heading not required.)

Army Form C. 2118.

10 S W B

Vol 15

Place	Date	Hour	Summary of Events and Information	Remarks and references to Appendices
Bluet Farm B10 c.2.3.	1/3/17		Battalion at Bluet Farm in support to 17th Batt. R.W.F. Working parties of 4 Off and 150 O.R. Lecture on "The Watercart" at Battn. Headquarters at 10.45 a.m. Testing of new box respirators in gas cloud at 2 p.m. Details of B Coy for baths 7-7.30 a.m. One Officer and 8 N.C.O. proceeded to H Camp at 12 noon and conducted 136 reinforcements to Bluet Farm. Casualties nil	[illegible]
"	2/3/17		Battalion in support to 17th Batt. R.W.F. Working parties of 4 Off and 150 O.R. Lecture on "The Watercart" at 10.30 a.m. Reinforcements paraded at Battn. Hqrs. at 9 a.m. for lecture. Battalion relieved 17th Batt. R.W.F. in Front line. Relief started at 5 p.m. and completed about 11.30 p.m. Battalion on left ~~Division~~ 4th Regiment des Carbiniers. Battalion on right:- Dispositions. Front line. A Coy on right. "C" Coy on left. "B" Company in Village line. "D" Company in the Redoubt. Work:- Work on front line under R.E. Supervision. Clearing + Relaying	[illegible]

T2134. Wt. W708–776. 500000. 4/15. Sir J. C. & S.

Instructions regarding War Diaries and Intelligence Summaries are contained in F. S. Regs., Part II. and the Staff Manual respectively. Title pages will be prepared in manuscript.

WAR DIARY
or
INTELLIGENCE SUMMARY.
(Erase heading not required.)

Army Form C. 2118.

Place	Date	Hour	Summary of Events and Information	Remarks and references to Appendices
Front line	7/3/17	(contd)	trench-boards. Wiring Cardiff St, Apron wire - 3 coils used. South of Railway St., 6 French Concertinas & 9 coils barbed wire. Front line. 29 concertinas put out. 8 French concertinas & 3 coils of barbed wire. Owing to high visibility, our wiring party was seen and heavily fired on. The N.C.O. in charge 10/20955 Cpl P. Grant Killed &. 10/22093 Pte J Cosgrove W/a.	[illegible]
Boesinghe Sector B.11. c. 8.5.	8/3/17		Battalion in Front Line. Battalion on left 4th Regiment de Carbiniers Battalion on right - 14th R.W.I. Dispositions:- as ~~yesterday~~ on 2nd inst. Hostile artillery fired a few shells on Boesinghe Village. Our artillery retaliated promptly. Work:- Revetting front line. Erecting dugout. Clearing & opening drains in front line. Wiring:- 150 yds apron fence put out S. of Railway St. Wiring of posts continued 22 coils used. Casualties Nil.	[illegible]

T2134. Wt. W708-776. 500000. 4/15. Sir J. C. & S.

Instructions regarding War Diaries and Intelligence Summaries are contained in F. S. Regs., Part II. and the Staff Manual respectively. Title pages will be prepared in manuscript.

WAR DIARY
or
INTELLIGENCE SUMMARY.
(Erase heading not required.)

Army Form C. 2118.

Place	Date	Hour	Summary of Events and Information	Remarks and references to Appendices
Boesinghe Chateau B.16.b.8.5.	4/3/17		Battalion in Front Line. Battalion on left:- 9th Regiment des Carbiniers. Battalion on right - 14th R.W.F. Hostile aircraft activity during afternoon. Artillery inactive. We fired a few grenades on to enemy front line at 2 a.m. Work:- Working parties under R.E. supervision. Completing dug-outs. Wiring:- S. of Railway St. 24 coils used on apron wire. Front line 50 gooseberries put out. Dispositions similar. Casualty one O.R. 7/20492 Cpl James T. w/a.	J.P.W.
"	5/3/17		Battalion in Front Line. Battalion on left:- 4th Regiment des Carbiniers relieved in afternoon by 2nd Regiment de Carbiniers. Battalion on right:- 14th R.W.F. Dispositions similar. Hostile artillery [illegible] active. Our artillery [illegible] [illegible]. Work:- Work on new dug-outs. Cleaning [illegible] [illegible] [illegible]. Wiring:- South of Railway St. 23 coils used. [illegible] [illegible] existing wire. 167 Gooseberries put out in front line. Casualties nil.	J.P.W.

T2134. Wt. W708–776. 500000. 4/15. Sir J. C. & S.

Instructions regarding War Diaries and Intelligence Summaries are contained in F. S. Regs., Part II. and the Staff Manual respectively. Title pages will be prepared in manuscript.

WAR DIARY
or
INTELLIGENCE SUMMARY.
(Erase heading not required.)

Army Form C. 2118.

Place	Date	Hour	Summary of Events and Information	Remarks and references to Appendices
Boesinghe Chateau B.11.b.2.5			Battalion in front line. Battalion on left :- 2nd Regiment de [illegible]. Battalion on right 14th R.W.F. Operations: Enemy [illegible] inactive. Quiet day. Work completing dug outs in front line. Clearing & draining [illegible]. General maintenance of trenches. Wiring :- South of Railway apron fence continued. The Battalion was relieved by 16th Welsh Regt. (Cardiff City). Relief started at 2.30 p.m. & completed about 10 p.m. Battalion marched to Camp X. A.16. central. Casualties Nil.	
X Camp A.16 central			Battalion at X Camp. Working parties of 6 off. and 200 O.R. for construction under R.E. supervision. Details left in camp paraded at 11 a.m. for training bayonet fighting and box respirator drill. Retreat sounded by Band and drums at 5 p.m.	

T2134. Wt. W708—776. 500000. 4/15. Sir J. C. & S.

Instructions regarding War Diaries and Intelligence Summaries are contained in F. S. Regs., Part II. and the Staff Manual respectively. Title pages will be prepared in manuscript.

WAR DIARY
or
INTELLIGENCE SUMMARY.
(*Erase heading not required.*)

Army Form C. 2118.

Place	Date	Hour	Summary of Events and Information	Remarks and references to Appendices
X Camp. A.6 central	2/7		Battalion at X Camp. Working parties of 6 Officers & 300 O.R. on railway construction under R.E. supervision. Paraded at 7.30 a.m. Details left in camp showed kit to the Commanding Officer at 11 a.m. Retreat sounded by Band & Drums at 6 p.m.	
"	3/7		Battalion at X Camp. Working parties of 6 Officers & 300 O.R. on railway construction under R.E. supervision. Details in camp paraded in Drill order at 10 a.m. All available Officers & Company Sergeant Majors attended parade. Two men per Company attended an elementary Lewis Gun class under Lewis Gun Officer. A concert was held at the Comrades Hut at 6 p.m. proving most successful. A draft of 49 O. Ranks joined the Battalion.	
"	4/7		Battalion at X Camp. Working parties of 6 Officers & 300 O.R. on railway construction under R.E. supervision. Details in camp paraded at 10 a.m. in drill order for company drill, bayonet	

T2134. Wt. W708–776. 500000. 4/15. Sir J. C. & S.

Instructions regarding War Diaries and Intelligence Summaries are contained in F. S. Regs., Part II. and the Staff Manual respectively. Title pages will be prepared in manuscript.

WAR DIARY
or
INTELLIGENCE SUMMARY.
(*Erase heading not required.*)

Army Form C. 2118.

Place	Date	Hour	Summary of Events and Information	Remarks and references to Appendices
	10/3/17	(contd)	fighting and bombing. Packing up preparatory to moving into support area. Working party proceeded direct to Roussel Farm for tea. Battalion left Camp X at 4.30 p.m. and marched to Bluet Farm in support to 17th Batt. R.W.F. Disposition: Battalion Headquarters – Bluet Farm; C Coy. X line left Coy. A Coy X line right Coy; B Coy – Farm Paradis; D Coy – Ferme Emile.	870
Bluet Farm B10 c.2.3.	11/3/17	(contd)	Battalion at Bluet Farm in support to 17th Batt R.W.F. Working parties of 4 Off and 146 O.R. Clean up 7.0 a.m. to 8.0 a.m. Inspection 8 a.m. 9.30 – 12.30 a.m. Bombing, bayonet-fighting, box respirator drill, instruction in use of rifle grenades. Elementary Lewis Gun class under Lewis Gun Officer. Casualties Nil. Dispositions similar	870
"	12/3/17	(contd)	Battalion at Bluet Farm, in support to 17th Batt R.W.F. Working parties of 4 Off and 146 O.R. Bathing at Elverdinghe Chateau for 176 O.R. Clean up 7.0 a.m. to 8.0 a.m.	870

T2134. Wt. W708–776. 500000. 4/15. Sir J. C. & S.

Instructions regarding War Diaries and Intelligence Summaries are contained in F. S. Regs., Part II. and the Staff Manual respectively. Title pages will be prepared in manuscript.

WAR DIARY
or
INTELLIGENCE SUMMARY.
(Erase heading not required.)

Army Form C. 2118.

Place	Date	Hour	Summary of Events and Information	Remarks and references to Appendices
Bluet Farm Sh. C.2.3	12/3/17	(cont.)	9.30 - 12.30. Bombing, bayonet fighting and box respirator drill. Elementary Lewis Gun course at Battalion Headquarters under Lewis Gun Officer. Dispositions similar. Casualties Nil.	[illegible]
"	13/3/17		Battalion at Bluet Farm in support to 17th Batt. R.W.F. Working parties of 4 Off. + 146 O.R. Clean up 7 to 8.0 a.m. Inspection 9.0 a.m. 9.30 - 12 noon Bombing, Bayonet fighting, gas helmet drill + musketry. Bathing from 7.0 a.m. - 5.0 p.m. Dispositions similar. Casualties Nil.	[illegible]
"	14/3/17		Battalion at Bluet Farm in support to 17th Batt. R.W.F. Working parties of 4 Off + 146 O.R. Clean up 7.0 to 8.0 a.m. Inspection 9.0 a.m. 9.30 - 12 noon. Bombing, Bayonet fighting, gas helmet drill + musketry. Battalion relieved 17th Batt. R.W.F. in front line. Relief started 5.30 p.m. and completed about 9.30 p.m. Dispositions:- Front line - "B" Coy on the right. "D" Coy on the left. "A" Coy. Village Line. "C" Coy in Redoubt. Batt. on left:- 3rd Battalion. 2nd Carabiniers. Armée Belge. On Right:- 16th R.W.F. Casualties Nil.	[illegible]

Instructions regarding War Diaries and Intelligence Summaries are contained in F. S. Regs., Part II. and the Staff Manual respectively. Title pages will be prepared in manuscript.

WAR DIARY
or
INTELLIGENCE SUMMARY.
(Erase heading not required.)

Army Form C. 2118.

Place	Date	Hour	Summary of Events and Information	Remarks and references to Appendices
Boesinghe Chateau B.6.8.5	15/3/17		Battalion in Front Line. Battalion on left:- 3rd Battalion, 2nd Carabiniers Armée Belge. Battalion on right:- 16th R.W.F. Dispositions similar. Hostile artillery quiet. A few stick bombs fired on to our front line at 7.0 a.m. We retaliated with 15 grenades. Our "heavies" registered on enemy front with good effect. Work:- Working parties under R.E. supervision. Clearing and draining front line and repairing trench boards. Work on new dug outs in the front line. Wiring:- Front line, 17 concertinas put out. 'S' line 50 yds Apron fence. Casualties Nil.	[illegible]
"	16/3/17		Battalion in Front Line. Battalion on left - 3rd Battalion, 2nd Carabiniers Armée Belge. Battalion on right:- 16th R.W.F. Dispositions similar. Hostile artillery shelled Chateau Wood S. line 8.30-9.0 a.m. Our artillery somewhat active. We fired some grenades on to enemy front line during the morning. Clearing and draining front line. Revetting Bridge Street. Work on new dug outs. Wiring. Front line:- 17 Concertinas put out. 'S' line 210 yds Apron wiring. Casualties Nil.	[illegible]

T2134. Wt. W708–776. 500000. 4/15. Sir J. C. & S.

Instructions regarding War Diaries and Intelligence Summaries are contained in F. S. Regs., Part II. and the Staff Manual respectively. Title pages will be prepared in manuscript.

WAR DIARY
or
INTELLIGENCE SUMMARY.
(Erase heading not required.)

Army Form C. 2118.

Place	Date	Hour	Summary of Events and Information	Remarks and references to Appendices
Boesinghe Chateau Su. 6.8.5.	1/3/17		Battalion in the Front Line. Hostile Artillery somewhat active. Shelled Railway Street & Station. Enemy fired a number of stick-bombs on to our front-line, causing three casualties. We retaliated with No 20 Rifle Grenades. Retaliation for enemy's shellings was prompt and effective. – Dispositions similar. Battalion on left :– 3ème Battalion, 2ème Carabiniers, Armée Belge. Battalion on right :– 14th R.W.F. Work :– Clearing and draining in front & S^t lines. Work on new dug-outs. Repairing & revetting Bridge Sts. Shaving top of parapet. Wiring – Front Line – 18 concertinas. St Line. 44 coils wire. Cardiff St. Apron fence. 35 coils. Casualties 1 OR K/a. 2 OR W/a.	
	2/3/17		Battalion in the Front Line. Dispositions similar. Battalion on the left. 2ème Carabiniers. Armée Belge. Battalion on the right 14th Batt R.W.F. Hostile artillery inactive. Shelled Boesinghe Village Chateau, Wood and Park St. Our artillery registered on	

T2134. Wt. W708—776. 500000. 4/15. Sir J. C. & S.

Instructions regarding War Diaries and Intelligence Summaries are contained in F. S. Regs., Part II. and the Staff Manual respectively. Title pages will be prepared in manuscript.

WAR DIARY
or
INTELLIGENCE SUMMARY.
(Erase heading not required.)

Army Form C. 2118.

Place	Date	Hour	Summary of Events and Information	Remarks and references to Appendices
[illegible] Plateau [illegible] b.8.5	18/3/17	Cont.	various points behind the enemy's line. Work:- Clearing & draining front line. Building up parados. Work on new dug-outs. The Battalion was relieved by 16th Batt. Welsh Regt. Relief started at 5.30 p.m. and completed about 9.0 p.m. Battalion marched to X Camp. A.16. central. Casualties Nil.	B.T.O.
X Camp A.16.central	19/3/17		Battalion at X camp. Working parties of 4 Off. & 250. O.R. Details left in Camp paraded at 10. a.m. for drill. Elementary Classes in Lewis Gun and Range-finder assembled at 9.30 a.m. Cleaning Lewis Guns & S.A.A.	B.T.O.
	20/3/17		Battalion at X Camp. Working parties of 4 Off & 250 O.R. Details in Camp paraded at 10.0 a.m. for musketry. R.S.M. Leckie. G. awarded The Italian Bronze Medal for Military Valour. Elementary Classes in Lewis Gun & Range-finder. Practice by Band & Drums.	B.T.O.

Instructions regarding War Diaries and Intelligence Summaries are contained in F. S. Regs., Part II. and the Staff Manual respectively. Title pages will be prepared in manuscript.

WAR DIARY
or
INTELLIGENCE SUMMARY.
(Erase heading not required.)

Army Form C. 2118.

Place	Date	Hour	Summary of Events and Information	Remarks and references to Appendices
~~X Camp.~~ A.6.central	21/3/17		Battalion at Camp. X. Working parties of 4 Off. and 250 O.R. Details in Camp paraded 9.15 a.m. for Musketry. Lewis Gun and Range-finding classes under Lewis Gun Officer. Battalion left Camp X at 6 p.m. and was joined by working parties on the line of march. Marched to support position of Centre Area. A draft of 61 Other Ranks joined Batt. from Reinforcement Camp.	[illegible]
Canal Bank B24 b.9.4 Sheet 28 N.W. 2.	22/3/17		Battalion in support to 17th Batt. R.W.F. Inspection of rifles. Musketry. Box respirator drill. Working parties of 3 Off and 185 O.R. Two men per Coy. detailed for upkeep of trenches. Dispositions A.B.C & D Coys from Bridge 6 to Bridge 6 W. Right Coy. A; Right Centre B; Left Centre C; Left Coy. D: Casualties Nil	[illegible]
"	23/3/17		Battalion in support to 17th Batt. R.W.F. Inspection of rifles. Musketry. Box respirator drill. Working parties as on 22nd inst. Clearing refuse from [illegible]. Dispositions similar. Casualties Nil.	[illegible]

T2134. Wt. W708—776. 500000. 4/15. Sir J. C. & S.

Instructions regarding War Diaries and Intelligence Summaries are contained in F. S. Regs., Part II. and the Staff Manual respectively. Title pages will be prepared in manuscript.

WAR DIARY
or
INTELLIGENCE SUMMARY.
(Erase heading not required.)

Army Form C. 2118.

Place	Date	Hour	Summary of Events and Information	Remarks and references to Appendices
Canal Bank B.24 b.9.4 Sheet 28 N.W. 2.	24/3/17		Battalion in support to 17th Batt R.W.F. Inspections of rifles and equipment. Musketry. Rapid loading. Box respirator drill. Working parties of 3 off and 200 O.R. General upkeep of trenches. Clearing refuse from sperlees. Dispositions similar Casualties Nil	870
"	25/3/17		Battalion in support to 17th Batt R.W.F. Inspection of Rifles. Working parties of 3 Off. and 200 O.R. Work as on 24th inst. Dispositions similar. Casualties Nil.	870
"	26/3/17		Battalion in support to 17th Batt. R.W.F. Physical training. Musketry. Bayonet Fighting. Passing messages. Box respirator drill. Work:– General upkeep of trenches. Battalion relieved 17th Batt. R.W.F. in Front line. Dispositions:– A Coy – Right Front; C Coy – Left Front. B Coy – Right Support; D Coy – Left Support;. Battalion on right – 13 Welch Regt; Battalion on left – 16th Batt Welch Casualties Nil.	870

Instructions regarding War Diaries and Intelligence Summaries are contained in F. S. Regs., Part II. and the Staff Manual respectively. Title pages will be prepared in manuscript.

WAR DIARY
or
INTELLIGENCE SUMMARY.
(Erase heading not required.)

Army Form C. 2118.

Place	Date	Hour	Summary of Events and Information	Remarks and references to Appendices
Canal Bank B24 b.9.4. Sheet 28 N.W. 2	27/2/17		Battalion in front line. Dispositions:- similar. Battalion on right:- 16th Welsh Regt. Battalion on left 13th Batt Welsh Regt. Our artillery active throughout the day. One of our Lewis Guns dispersed an enemy working party at 9.0 a.m. Our aeroplanes active during the afternoon. Enemy artillery somewhat active during the day. Work:- Repairing and draining front line. Excavating for new fire-bays. Making Lewis Gun emplacement in Butt 17. Excavating for new dug-outs in Fargate, Butt 22, West Bank of Canal and front line. Casualties Nil.	870
"	28/2/17		Battalion in front line. Dispositions:- similar. Battalions on flanks:- similar. Hostile artillery active on back areas. Our artillery shelled enemy's front & support lines during the day. Work as on 27th inst. Cleaning bombs. Work on new Mess Kitchen at Battn Hqrs. Wiring:- Thickening existing wire. 13 Concertinas & 18 Coils were used. Casualties Nil	870

T2134. Wt. W708—776. 500000. 4/15. Sir J. C. & S.

Instructions regarding War Diaries and Intelligence Summaries are contained in F. S. Regs., Part II. and the Staff Manual respectively. Title Pages will be prepared in manuscript.

WAR DIARY
or
INTELLIGENCE SUMMARY
(Erase heading not required.)

Army Form C. 2118

Place	Date	Hour	Summary of Events and Information	Remarks and references to Appendices
Canal Bank B.4 b 9.4 Sheet 28NW2	28/8/17		Battalion in Front Line. Battalion on left 11th [illegible]. On right 10th Welch. Dispositions similar. Our heavy Trench Mortars fired during the afternoon. Enemy retaliated with minenwerfers on our front line. We fired about a dozen No 20 Rifle Grenades during the morning. Work – Draining & Repairing front line. Work on dug-outs. Rebuilding cook house in Bell 17. Work on New Mess kitchen at Batt. Hqrs. Clearing Yperlee. General trench maintenance.	870
	29/8/17 3 a.m.		During the night our artillery shelled Caesar's Nose and enemy retaliated heavily on Right Battalion front causing S.O.S. to be sent up. Within two minutes of signal our artillery opened fire putting up a barrage on No Man's Land. Our Light & Heavy Trench Mortars in retaliation for enemy "pineapples". Our artillery & T.M. fire was continuous from 3.55 a.m. to 5.15 a.m. Casualties. 3 Other Ranks killed i/a. 9 O.R. w/a. 5. O.R. w/a at Duty. Our patrols reconnoitred No Man's Land after bombardment.	

1875 Wt. W593/826 1,000,000 4/15 J.B.C. & A. A.D.S.S./Forms/C. 2118.

Instructions regarding War Diaries and Intelligence Summaries are contained in F. S. Regs., Part II. and the Staff Manual respectively. Title Pages will be prepared in manuscript.

WAR DIARY
or
INTELLIGENCE SUMMARY
(Erase heading not required.)

Army Form C. 2118

Place	Date	Hour	Summary of Events and Information	Remarks and references to Appendices
Canal Bank B24 b.9.4 sheet 28 N.W. 2.	30/3/17		Battalion in front line. Dispositions similar. Battalions on flanks as on 29th inst. During morning our artillery shelled enemy line intermittently damaging his parapet. No retaliation. Work as on 29th inst. Repairing damaged firebays. Wiring:- Repairing gaps in wire and thickening same. Our patrols reconnoitred No Mans Land without opposition. Casualties Nil.	
	31/3/17		Battalion in front line. Dispositions similar. Battalion on left. On right 10th Batt Welsh Regt. Our artillery active during the morning. Enemy's retaliation weak. Work:- as on 30th inst. Battalion was relieved in front line by 17th Batt. R.W.F. Relief started 6 p.m. Completed about 8.30 p.m. Casualties Nil	

C.G. Rees Major
for Lieut. Colonel.
Commanding 10th S. Batt. S.W.B.

1875 Wt. W593/826 1,000,000 4/15 J.B.C. & A. A.D.S.S./Forms/C. 2118.

Instructions regarding War Diaries and Intelligence Summaries are contained in F. S. Regs., Part II. and the Staff Manual respectively. Title Pages will be prepared in manuscript.

WAR DIARY
or
INTELLIGENCE SUMMARY
(Erase heading not required.)

Army Form C. 2118

10th Lwb Vol 16

Place	Date	Hour	Summary of Events and Information	Remarks and references to Appendices
Canal Bank B24. b. 9. 4. Sheet 8 N.W. 2.	1/4/17		Battalion in Support to 17th Batt. R.W.F. Dispositions from Bridge 6 to Bridge 6W A. B. C. & D Coys respectively. Working parties of 3 off and 300 O.R. Inspections of rifles, bayonets & equipment. Inspection of Dug outs. 9.45 – 10.30 am Physical Training. 11.0 am to 11.45 a.m. Musketry. 11.45 – 12.15 Box respirator & P.H. Helmet drill. General Trench maintenance. Clearing [illegible] from [illegible]. Casualties nil.	E.L.O.
	2/4/17		Battalion in Support to 17th Batt. R.W.F. Dispositions similar. Training as on 1st inst. Intercompany bombing competition between 'D' & 'B' Companies at L. line. D Coy proving victors. Working parties of 3 Off & 300 O.R. Work as on 1st inst. Casualties Nil.	E.L.O.
	3/4/17		Battalion in Support to 17th Batt. R.W.F. Dispositions similar. Training as on 1st inst. Lewis Gunners [illegible] for [illegible] practice. Bombing and Bayonet fighting [illegible] practised in L. line. Working parties of 3 Off and 300 O.R. Work as on 1st inst. Casualty 14/20449 Sgt Bull W.J.	E.L.O.

1875 Wt. W593/826 1,000,000 4/15 J.B.C. & A. A.D.S.S./Forms/C. 2118.

Army Form C. 2118

WAR DIARY
or
INTELLIGENCE SUMMARY
(Erase heading not required.)

10th SWB

Instructions regarding War Diaries and Intelligence Summaries are contained in F. S. Regs., Part II. and the Staff Manual respectively. Title Pages will be prepared in manuscript.

Place	Date	Hour	Summary of Events and Information	Remarks and references to Appendices
Canal Bank C.24.b.9.4. Sheet 28 N.W. 2	4/4/17		Battalion in support to 17th Batt. R.W.F. Dispositions similar. Work as on 1st inst. Musketry. Box respirators & P.H. helmet drill. General trench maintenance. Clearing [illegible]. Working parties of 4 Off & 350 O.R. Casualties Nil.	E.L.O.
"	5/4/17		Battalion in support to 17th Batt. R.W.F. Dispositions similar. Bathing for B. Coy. Musketry. Box respirator drill. Inspection of rifles & equipment. Battalion relieved 17th Batt. R.W.F. in the front line. Relief started at 6 p.m. and completed at 8.30 p.m. Dispositions D - left Coy. front; B - right Coy front; A - left support Coy; C - right support Coy: Casualties O.R. w/ya. 1 O.R. w/ya at duty.	E.L.O.
"	6/4/17		Battalion in front line. Dispositions similar. Battalion on left 11th S.W.B. on right 16th R.W.F. Permanent working & carrying parties of 6 Off & 250 O.R. Building new dug-outs in Butts 20 & 22. Making Lewis Gun emplacements in [illegible]gate. Work on dugouts in Harkness Ave. Enemy artillery inactive. His machine guns active on support lines & Canal Bank. Casualties nil. Patrol left our line at 11.15 p.m. and withdrew at 12.5 a.m. Discovered party of enemy apparently acting as covering party. Identifications nil. Casualties Nil.	E.L.O.

1875 Wt. W593/826 1,000,000 4/15 J.B.C. & A. A.D.S.S./Forms/C. 2118.

Army Form C. 2118

Instructions regarding War Diaries and Intelligence Summaries are contained in F. S. Regs., Part II. and the Staff Manual respectively. Title Pages will be prepared in manuscript.

WAR DIARY
or
INTELLIGENCE SUMMARY
(Erase heading not required.)

10th SWB

Place	Date	Hour	Summary of Events and Information	Remarks and references to Appendices
Canal Bank B24.b.9.4 Sheet 28 N.W.2.	7/4/17		Battalion in Front Line. Dispositions similar. Enemy seemed somewhat ~~active~~ nervous during the night and bombed his own wire several times during the night. His machine guns also active. Our 'Heavies' shelled CAESARS. NOSE. about 11.10 p.m. Enemy artillery inactive. Test Gas Alarm at 10. a. m.: German Deserter gave himself up at No 31 Post. Work. Draining & clearing front line. Work on new dug-outs. Rebuilding firebays. General trench maintenance. Wiring: 70 feet of Apron Wire & 1½ coils used. Casualties Nil. 17/23200 L.Cpl J. Allen awarded Military Medal for meritorious act performed on night 29-30th March.	S.Y.O.
"	8/4/17		Battalion in Front Line. Dispositions similar. At 'Stand-to' Enemy machine guns were active. His artillery inactive during day. Our artillery shelled rear lines of enemy during the day. A Reconnoitring Party left our lines at 11.30 p.m. and returned at 1.15 a.m. Work:- Thickening of parapets. Work on firebays. Work on dug-outs. Laying down Trench-boards. General trench maintenance. Aerial activity on both sides. Casualties Nil.	S.Y.O.
"	9/4/17		Battalion in Front Line. Dispositions similar. Enemy machine guns active during the night. His artillery shelled Canal Bank with about 40 L.H.V. Our Lewis Guns fired from points in front of our line. We fired some Rifle Grenades on to Caesars Nose during the afternoon. A Reconnoitring Patrol left our line at 11.30 p.m. and returned at 1.15 a.m. Casualties Nil.	S.Y.O.

1875 Wt. W593/826 1,000,000 4/15 J.B.C. & A. A.D.S.S./Forms/C. 2118.

Army Form C. 2118

WAR DIARY
or
INTELLIGENCE SUMMARY
(Erase heading not required.)

Instructions regarding War Diaries and Intelligence Summaries are contained in F. S. Regs., Part II. and the Staff Manual respectively. Title Pages will be prepared in manuscript.

10th LWB

Place	Date	Hour	Summary of Events and Information	Remarks and references to Appendices
Canal Bank. B 24. b. 9. 4. Sheet. 28 N.W. 2	10/4/17		Battalion in Front line. Dispositions similar. Artillery inactive on both sides. Considerable machine Gun fire on part of the enemy. A Test Gas Alarm was carried out at 9.30 p.m. Work:- Thickening Parapets, work on new Firebays and Cookhouses and dug-outs. Draining Barn Trench. Casualties Nil. Battalion was relieved by 14th Batt. R.W.F. Relief started at 5 p.m. & completed by 8 p.m. Battalion moved into Support on Canal Bank and were relieved by 15th Batt. R.W.F. at 12 m.n. Battalion marched to Camp X. A 16 central	[illegible]
"	11/4/17		Battalion in Camp X. General Clean up. Inspection of kits by O.C. Companies. Inspection of rifles. Casualties Nil. Lecture by C.O. on "Training" to all Officers & N.C.O.s	[illegible]
"	12/4/17		Battalion in Camp A. Working parties of 1 Off and 86 Other Ranks for Road Construction. Battalion formed up in Mass at 9.0 a.m.	[illegible]
		9.30/10.30	Close order Drill by Sections. Saluting	
		10.30/11.0	Platoon musketry. Rapid loading and firing	
		11.15/12.45	Bombing, Bayonet fighting, Physical Training, Lewis Gun instruction, Scouting and semaphore signalling.	
		2.30/3.30	~~Cross Country Run~~. Football Match.	
		7'	Casualties Nil.	

1875 Wt. W593/826 1,000,000 4/15 J.B.C. & A. A.D.S.S./Forms/C. 2118.

Instructions regarding War Diaries and Intelligence Summaries are contained in F. S. Regs., Part II. and the Staff Manual respectively. Title Pages will be prepared in manuscript.

WAR DIARY
or
INTELLIGENCE SUMMARY
(Erase heading not required.)

Army Form C. 2118

10th SWB

Place	Date	Hour	Summary of Events and Information	Remarks and references to Appendices
X Camp A 16 central	13/4/17		Battalion in Camp X. Working parties of 1 Off and 86 Other Ranks. Training as on 12th inst. 2.30 - 3.30 p.m. Cross Country Run.	
		7 p.m.	Concert at Cornish Hut proved most successful.	
		5.15 pm	Lecture by Platoon commanders on next day's work. Casualties Nil	[illegible]
"	14/4/17		Battalion in Camp X. Working parties as on 12th inst.	
		9/11 a.m.	Kit inspection by Commanding Officer 11.15 a.m. Battalion formed up in Mass.	[illegible]
		11.20 to 1.0 pm	Close Order drill. Handling of arms by platoons. Practice trench to trench attack. Open and artillery formation.	
		2 p.m.	Inter-company football competition. Casualties Nil.	
"	15/4/17		Battalion in Camp X. Working parties as on 12th inst. Divine service Baths. Hut inspection. Revolver practice for officers. Lecture by C.O. to officers. Football Match. Casualties Nil.	[illegible]
	16/4/17		Battalion in Camp X. Working parties as on 12th inst. Also 1 N.C.O. & 6 men for loading lorry at Mont Rouge. Disinfection parade at Corps Disinfection Station. Bathing. Usual training programme. Inter-company football match. Casualties Nil.	[illegible]

1875 Wt. W593/826 1,000,000 4/15 J.B.C. & A. A.D.S.S./Forms/C. 2118.

Instructions regarding War Diaries and Intelligence Summaries are contained in F. S. Regs., Part II. and the Staff Manual respectively. Title Pages will be prepared in manuscript.

WAR DIARY
or
INTELLIGENCE SUMMARY
(Erase heading not required.)

Army Form C. 2118

10th SWB

Place	Date	Hour	Summary of Events and Information	Remarks and references to Appendices
X Camp A.16 central.	17/4/17		Battalion in Camp X. Usual training programme. Instruction in firing Rifle Grenades and in Lewis Guns. Fumigation as on 16th inst. Cross country run in the afternoon. Casualties Nil. Inter-company Cooker Competition	[illegible]
"	18/4/17		Battalion in Camp X. Usual training programme. Instruction in Rifle Grenades & Lewis Guns as on 17th inst. Fumigation. Concert at Cornish Hut at 1.30 p.m. was most successful. Casualties Nil.	[illegible]
"	19/4/17		Battalion in Camp X. Usual training programme. Packing up preparatory to moving into the line. The Battalion left Camp X at 7.30 p.m. and marched into front line. Boesinghe Sector. Completed Relief 1.30 a.m. 20th. Cross-country team of C. Company proceeded to Brigade Headquarters for training. Disposition of Coys in line. C Coy - left front; A Coy - right front; B Coy - Boesinghe Redoubt; D Coy - Village St.; Battalion on right - 13th R.W.F. Battalion on left - 2nd Grenadiers. Casualties Nil.	[illegible]

1875 Wt. W593/826 1,000,000 4/15 J.B.C. & A. A.D.S.S./Forms/C. 2118.

Instructions regarding War Diaries and Intelligence Summaries are contained in F. S. Regs., Part II. and the Staff Manual respectively. Title Pages will be prepared in manuscript.

WAR DIARY
or
INTELLIGENCE SUMMARY
(Erase heading not required.)

Army Form C. 2118

10th Innis

Place	Date	Hour	Summary of Events and Information	Remarks and references to Appendices
Front line. Birmingham Redoubt Bn. [illegible]	[illegible]/4/17		Battalion in front line. Dispositions as above. Battalion on left – [illegible] Grenadiers [illegible] Bge. Battalion on left right – 14th R. W. F. Enemy artillery inactive. Our artillery fired on enemy's support lines. [illegible] We fired some Rifle Grenades on to enemy front line. Work – Drawing [illegible] [illegible] General trench maintenance. [illegible] the Redoubt. [illegible] Strengthening wire in front of posts. 246 [illegible] put out. Casualties Nil.	[initials]
	2[illegible]/4/17.		Battalion in front line. Dispositions similar. Battalions on flanks similar. Enemy artillery active against [illegible] Wood, [illegible] Line & Village St. Our heavies shelled enemy's rear lines in retaliation. We fired Rifle Grenades on to his front line, provoking no retaliation. Work. Drawing front line. Excavating for dug-outs. Camouflaging. Strengthening wire in front of posts. Casualties Nil.	[initials]
	[illegible]/4/17		Battalion in front line. Dispositions similar. Battalions on flanks similar. Enemy artillery [illegible] inactive. Our heavies shelled his support lines. Work as on 21st inst. Improving front line. Strengthening wire in front of posts. 240 [illegible] put out. Casualties Nil. Inter-Company relief. B (Left) & D (Right) to front line. A. to Birmingham Redoubt. C. to Village St.	[initials]

1875 Wt. W593/826 1,000,000 4/15 J.B.C. & A. A.D.S.S./Forms/C. 2118.

Instructions regarding War Diaries and Intelligence Summaries are contained in F. S. Regs., Part II. and the Staff Manual respectively. Title pages will be prepared in manuscript.

WAR DIARY
or
INTELLIGENCE SUMMARY.
(Erase heading not required.)

Army Form C. 2118.

10th S.W.B.

Place	Date	Hour	Summary of Events and Information	Remarks and references to Appendices
Front Line Boesinghe Chateau B.11.D.8.5	23/4/17 Monday		Battalion in Front Line. Dispositions similar. Enemy lightly shelled Village St. and Railway St. Our artillery active. Our aircraft active throughout the latter part of the day. Work:– General trench maintenance; improving Front Line. 250 Gooseberries put out. Between 12.30 & 12.45 pm 15 rounds from our Heavies fell short between Front Line & Village causing Casualties {1 O.R. Killed, 3 O.R. Wounded	G.J.D
"	24/4/17 Tuesday		Battalion in Front Line. Dispositions similar. Enemy fired about a dozen shells on Chateau Wood, doing no damage. Our guns fired in retaliation and our heavies fired consistently throughout the day. Rifle grenades fired at Stand-to and at 10 am. provoking some retaliation. Our aircraft very active. Work:– General trench maintenance. 80 Gooseberries put out. Batt. Stood-to during heavy shelling on Right at about 10 pm. Casualties:– 2 O.R. wounded	G.J.D
"	25/4/17 Wed.		Battalion in Front Line. Dispositions similar. A few enemy shells dropped in the Village lines causing slight damage. Our artillery shelled Canal Avenue, Cable Support & Babbon Support. In reply to our rifle grenade fire, the enemy sent over a few 'Pineapples' which did no damage. Battalion moved into support. Hqrs. at Bleuet Farm. Relief complete at 11.15 pm. Casualties nil. (Batt. relieved by 17th R.W.F.)	G.J.D.

T2134. Wt. W708–776. 500000. 4/15. Sir J. C. & S.

Instructions regarding War Diaries and Intelligence Summaries are contained in F. S. Regs., Part II. and the Staff Manual respectively. Title pages will be prepared in manuscript.

WAR DIARY
or
INTELLIGENCE SUMMARY.
(Erase heading not required.)

Army Form C. 2118.

10th Innis

Place	Date	Hour	Summary of Events and Information	Remarks and references to Appendices
Bleuet Farm B.10.C.33	26/4/17 Thur.		Battalion in Support. Hqrs at Bleuet Farm. A (right) + C (left) Companies in "X" Lines. B. Coy. at Barn Farm. D. Coy. at Roger Farm. Our planes active during the day. Batt. supplying Working Parties to work under R.E. supervision. Also undergoing instruction in Bombing, Musketry + map-reading + Box respirator drill. Physical drill. Casualties. Nil.	JHD (5 officers 150. O.R.)
do.	27/4/17 Fri.		Battalion in Support. Dispositions similar. Working parties as on 26th. Training continued as on 26th. Casualties. Nil.	JHD
do.	28/4/17 Sat.		Battalion in Support. Dispositions similar. Working parties and training as on 26th. Inter-company relief complete at 7.30pm. B. Coy. relieved A. Coy. D. Coy. relieved C. Coy. Casualties. Nil.	JHD
do.	29/4/17 Sun.		Battalion in Support. B (right) + D (left) Companies in "X" lines. A. Coy. at Barn Farm. C. Coy. at Roger Farm. Working parties and training as on 26th. Bathing at Elverdinghe. Casualties. Nil.	JHD

T2134. Wt. W708—776. 600000. 4/15. Sir J. C. & S.

Instructions regarding War Diaries and Intelligence Summaries are contained in F. S. Regs., Part II. and the Staff Manual respectively. Title pages will be prepared in manuscript.

WAR DIARY
or
INTELLIGENCE SUMMARY.
(Erase heading not required.)

Army Form C. 2118.

10th S.W.B.

Place	Date	Hour	Summary of Events and Information	Remarks and references to Appendices
Blcuet Farm. B.10. c.2.3	30/1/17 Mon.		Battalion in support. Dispositions similar. Working parties as on 26th. Training continued. Major Bowen, 2nd. in Command, instructed half of C. Coy. in sandbagging. Bathing at Elverdinghe continued this morning. Leather jerkins and blankets (one per man) called in yesterday were examined by a Board of Survey. President Lieut. J. P. C. Hornby. Advance party under Lt. A. J. Evans, proceeded to Rollezeele to arrange for billetting &c. Casualties nil.	J.S.O.

W. Hawe. Lt. Colonel.
Commanding 10th (Service) Battalion
South Wales Borderers.

Instructions regarding War Diaries and Intelligence Summaries are contained in F. S. Regs., Part II. and the Staff Manual respectively. Title pages will be prepared in manuscript.

WAR DIARY
or
INTELLIGENCE SUMMARY.
(Erase heading not required.)

10TH. SERVICE BATT'N. ORDERLY ROOM - - MAY 1917 No. .... SOUTH WALES BORDERERS (1ST. GWENT)

Army Form C. 2118.

Vol 17

Place	Date	Hour	Summary of Events and Information	Remarks and references to Appendices
Bleuet Farm B.10.c.2.3 "	1/5/17 Tues.		Battalion at Bleuet Farm in support to 17th R.W.F. A. & C. Coys. and Hqrs. had Physical Training before breakfast. Training comprised extended order drill, passing of messages, outpost duty, practising new formation in attack by platoons, & musketry. Battalion were relieved (between 9 p.m. & 10 p.m.) by 10th Welsh. Batt. marched to Poperinghe en route for Bollezeele. Rested at the Hop Factory. Casualties. nil.	B.G.O.
Bollezeele Sheet 27 A.24.C.5.3	2/5/17 Wed.		Battalion entrained at 7.30 a.m. Arrived at Esquelbec at 10.45 a.m. and marched thence to Bollezeele. Companies accomodated in various barns. Rest during remainder of day. Casualties:- nil	B.G.O.
do.	3/5/17 Thur.		Battalion at Bollezeele. Physical training (20 mins) before breakfast. Inspection of Battalion by C.O. Training on Batt. parade ground included Platoon drill, handling of arms, instruction in saluting and sentry-go, extended order drill & musketry. Inter-platoon football matches, A. Coy., 6.0 p.m. to 7.30 p.m. Casualties:- nil.	B.G.O.

T2134. Wt. W708—776. 500000. 4/15. Sir J. C. & S.

Instructions regarding War Diaries and Intelligence Summaries are contained in F. S. Regs., Part II. and the Staff Manual respectively. Title pages will be prepared in manuscript.

WAR DIARY
or
INTELLIGENCE SUMMARY.
(Erase heading not required.)

Army Form C. 2118.

Place	Date	Hour	Summary of Events and Information	Remarks and references to Appendices
Bollezeele Sheet 27 A.24.C.5.3	4/5/17 Fri.		Battalion at Bollezeele. Physical training before breakfast. Route march to Brigade Training Ground* at 9.15 a.m. Platoon drill and handling of arms followed by instruction (by sections) in the use of arms, Lewis guns, rifle grenades, bombs; also bayonet fighting and scouting. Dinner on the field followed by practising new formations by platoons with Tactical Schemes. Route march back to Bollezeele 3 - 3.45 pm. Inter-platoon football matches, B. Coy. 6.0 pm to 7.30 pm. D. Coy. succeeded in winning the Divisional Bayonet-Fighting Competition. Casualties :- Nil.	*: G.3.c. & d. E.L.O.
do.	5/5/17		Battalion at Bollezeele. Similar training to yesterday's. Also rapid wiring and entrenching tool drill. Inter-company football matches during evening. D. & C. Companies defeated A. & B. Companies respectively. Casualties :- Nil.	E.L.O.

Instructions regarding War Diaries and Intelligence Summaries are contained in F. S. Regs., Part II. and the Staff Manual respectively. Title pages will be prepared in manuscript.

WAR DIARY
or
INTELLIGENCE SUMMARY.
(Erase heading not required.)

Army Form C. 2118.

Place	Date	Hour	Summary of Events and Information	Remarks and references to Appendices
Bollezeele. Sheet 27. A 24. C. 5. 3.	6/5/17 Sunday		Battalion at Bollezeele. Divine Services attended this morning. The C. of E. party marched to the Training Ground & joined with the remainder of the Brigade in a Drum-head Service. During the afternoon the Batt. was inspected by the Medical Officer. C. & D. Coys. defeated A. & B. Coys. at Rugby Football. Casualties:- nil.	E.F.O.
do.	7/5/17 Mon.		Battalion at Bollezeele. A route march through Rubrock occupied from 7.30 a.m. to 11 a.m. Inspection of feet followed. Lectures on "Outposts". Afternoon devoted to Musketry. Inspection of Box Respirators & P.H. Helmets followed by drill with same. Casualties:- nil.	E.F.O.
do.	8/5/17 Tue.		Battalion at Bollezeele. March to Training Area for further training. A successful Sports Gathering was held on the Batt. Parade Ground from 4 p.m. to 8 p.m. Casualties:- nil.	E.F.O.
do.	9/5/17 Wed.		Battalion at Bollezeele. Companies carried on with training independently, practising Advance Guards, Outpost duty, Scouting, Attacking in open order, and a Concentration March to the Training Ground. Casualties:- nil. Firing on Miniature Range.	E.F.O.

Instructions regarding War Diaries and Intelligence Summaries are contained in F. S. Regs., Part II. and the Staff Manual respectively. Title Pages will be prepared in manuscript.

WAR DIARY
or
INTELLIGENCE SUMMARY
(Erase heading not required.)

Army Form C. 2118.

Place	Date	Hour	Summary of Events and Information	Remarks and references to Appendices
Bollezeele. Sheet 27. 24.C.5.3	10/5/17 Thur.		Battalion at Bollezeele. Training similar to yesterdays — Companies carrying on independently. Casualties :— Nil.	
do.	11/5/17 Fri.		Battalion at Bollezeele. Training continued as on 9th. inst. Casualties :- Nil.	
do.	12/5/17 Sat.		Battalion at Bollezeele.	
		7.15-7.35 a.m.	Physical training by Companies in vicinity of billets.	
		9.15-10.15	Battalion parade & drill on Batt. Parade Ground.	
		11.40 a.m.	Battalion formed up in column of route and marched to the Training Ground. Practised advancing in "Waves" under cover of "Artillery Barrage," represented by Signallers moving forward with flags. General Sir Herbert Plumer, G.C.M.G., K.C.B., A.D.C., Commanding Second Army, was present and expressed great satisfaction at the smartness with which the operations were carried out. Casualties :- Nil.	

2449 Wt. W14957/M90 750,000 1/16 J.B.C. & A. Forms/C.2118/12.

Army Form C. 2118.

Instructions regarding War Diaries and Intelligence Summaries are contained in F. S. Regs., Part II. and the Staff Manual respectively. Title Pages will be prepared in manuscript.

WAR DIARY
or
INTELLIGENCE SUMMARY

(Erase heading not required.)

Place	Date	Hour	Summary of Events and Information	Remarks and references to Appendices
Bollezeele Sheet 27. A.24.C.5.3.	May 13th. Sunday		Battalion at Bollezeele. Parades for Divine Services were held during the morning. Baths were allotted to the Battalion from 8.0 am. to 5 p.m. The 115th. Brigade Sports were held on the Training Ground during the afternoon and evening. This Battalion proved very successful, winning nearly every event; flat racing, and also exhibitions of mules, field kitchens & Lewis gun limbers. Casualties:- nil.	
	May 14th. Monday	7.45 am 9am - 11.30am 12 noon - 2 pm	Battalion at Bollezeele. Route march to Training Area. Practising an advance from trenches as on 12th. inst. Advancing over open country; Scouts being sent forward to report "all clear" or otherwise, followed by an advance party in open order, & the main body in Artillery formation. Afternoon free, as the Batt. had been employed on Saturday afternoon.	

2449 Wt. W14957/M90 750,000 1/16 J.B.C. & A. Forms/C.2118/12.

Instructions regarding War Diaries and Intelligence Summaries are contained in F. S. Regs., Part II. and the Staff Manual respectively. Title Pages will be prepared in manuscript.

WAR DIARY
or
INTELLIGENCE SUMMARY

(Erase heading not required.)

Army Form C. 2118.

Place	Date	Hour	Summary of Events and Information	Remarks and references to Appendices
Bollezeele. Sheet 27 A.24.c.5.7.	15th. May. 1917 Tues.	8.45am 9.15 to 12.30pm. 1pm.	Battalion at Bollezeele. Route march to Training Ground. Practising advance from trenches as on 14th. The 11th. S.W.B. supporting us on our left & the Machine Gun Company bringing up the rear. The Signal Sections had good practise in communicating with an aeroplane that was present during the operations, flying at a low altitude. March back to billets. Packing up preparatory to a move away to-morrow morning. Casualties:- Nil.	E.F.O
Bollezeele Sheet 27. A.24.c.5.3. Houtkerque Sheet 27 E.14.d.	16th. May 1917 Wed.	7.15 am 12 noon	Battalion marched away from Bollezeele. Proceeded via Zeggers Cappel, Esquelbecq, Wormhoudt, Herzeele to Houtkerque, arriving in new area at 12 noon. The Companies accommodated in various barns on the West side of the village. Cleaning up during afternoon. Casualties:- Nil.	E.F.O

2449 Wt. W14957/M90 750,000 1/16 J.B.C. & A. Forms/C.2118/12.

Instructions regarding War Diaries and Intelligence Summaries are contained in F. S. Regs., Part II. and the Staff Manual respectively. Title Pages will be prepared in manuscript.

WAR DIARY
or
INTELLIGENCE SUMMARY
(Erase heading not required.)

Army Form C. 2118.

Place	Date	Hour	Summary of Events and Information	Remarks and references to Appendices
Houtkerque Sheet 27 E.14.d.	17 May 1917.	11am	Battalion at Houtkerque. Kit inspection by Officers Commanding Companies at 11 a.m.	
Camp Z F.25.d.8.1	Thurs.	5pm.	Battalion moved off again at 5 pm. and marched via	
		6.30pm	Watou to Camp "Z", arriving at 6.30 p.m. Casualties:– Nil.	8.7.0
Camp Z Sheet 27 F.25.d.8.1.	18 May 1917. Fri.		Battalion at Camp "Z". Physical drill by companies, followed by Lectures by Officers Commanding Companies.	8.7.0
		3pm.	Battalion marched to Roussel Farm, via the Switch Road, Poperinghe. Headquarters, B. & C. Companies proceeded to billets at Roussel Farm; A. and D. Companies to	
Roussel Farm. Sheet 28. B.13.a.2.6		5.30pm	Chateau Grounds, Elverdinghe. We relieved 15th. Welsh Regt. Casualties:– Nil.	
~~Camp~~ Roussel Farm. Sheet 28 B.13.a.2.6	19 May 1917 Sat.		Battalion Hqrs., B. & C. Coys. at Roussel Farm. A. and D. Companies manning part of Elverdinghe Defences. Coy. Hqrs. at B.14.c.1.4 (A) and B.14.a.8½.7.(B). Major Bowen (2nd. in Command) and two officers per Company attended a demonstration of camouflaging	8.7.0
		10.30 am	screens at Elverdinghe Chateau at 10.30 am. Those not on	

2449 Wt. W14957/M90 750,000 1/16 J.B.C. & A. Forms/C.2118/12.

Instructions regarding War Diaries and Intelligence Summaries are contained in F. S. Regs., Part II. and the Staff Manual respectively. Title Pages will be prepared in manuscript.

WAR DIARY
or
INTELLIGENCE SUMMARY
(Erase heading not required.)

Army Form C. 2118.

Place	Date	Hour	Summary of Events and Information	Remarks and references to Appendices
Roussel Farm Sheet 28. B.13.a.2.6.	19 May (contd)		fatigue were paraded for Physical drill and musketry. Working parties of 3 officers and 120 Other Ranks found for fatigues in Front Line, Elverdinghe, Roussel Farm and Turque Farm; and for carrying material from Belmont dump & the Chateau, Elverdinghe, to Village St. and "X" Lines; also for Sanitation work at Roussel Farm. Casualties:- Nil.	E.F.O.
do.	20 May (Sunday)	11 a.m. to 12.15 pm.	Battalion at Roussel Farm. Dispositions of Companies similar. Divine Services held during the morning. "B" and "C" Companies paraded for Gas Helmet inspection and drill, followed by handling of arms and bombing. Working parties as yesterdays. During the afternoon, the Chateau Grounds were heavily shelled, A. and D. Companies suffering the following casualties:- 1 O.R. Killed; 2 O.R. Wounded, one remaining at duty.	E.F.O.
do.	21 May (Mon)	9.15 a.m. to 12 noon	Battalion at Roussel Farm. Dispositions similar. Training during the morning consisted of musketry, Open and Close Order Drill & bombing. Signallers instructed by the Commanding Officer and Signalling Sergeant. Usual working parties provided. The Chateau Grounds at Elverdinghe were again shelled during the morning. Casualties:- 4 O.R. Wounded. (2 at duty)	E.F.O.

2449 Wt. W14957/M90 750,000 1/16 J.B.C. & A. Forms/C.2118/12.

WAR DIARY
or
INTELLIGENCE SUMMARY

(Erase heading not required.)

Instructions regarding War Diaries and Intelligence Summaries are contained in F. S. Regs., Part II. and the Staff Manual respectively. Title Pages will be prepared in manuscript.

Army Form C. 2118.

Place	Date	Hour	Summary of Events and Information	Remarks and references to Appendices
Roussel Farm. Sheet 28. B.13.a.2.6.	22 May 1917 (Tue.)		Battalion at Roussel Farm. Dispositions similar. Training continued during the morning. Usual Working Parties found. Also 2 N.C.O.s and 20 Other Ranks for work on new Transport lines near camp "G". Casualties:– Nil. Bathing at Elverdinghe 8 a.m. to 10 a.m.	
do.	23 May 1917. (Wed.)	9.15 am – 12.15	Battalion at Roussel Farm. Dispositions similar. Baths at Elverdinghe were allotted to the Battalion from 8 a.m. – 10 a.m. This morning's parades comprised Physical Training, extended order drill, handling of arms, musketry and bombing. Elverdinghe was again shelled during the morning but we suffered no casualties. Usual Working Parties.	
do.	24 May 1917 (Thur.)	8.30 pm.	Battalion at Roussel Farm. Dispositions similar. The usual working parties were found. Morning parades the same as yesterday's. A successful concert was held in the Church Army Hut adjoining Roussel Farm. Casualties: Nil.	
do.	25 May 1917 (Fri.)		Battalion at Roussel Farm. Dispositions similar. Parades and working parties as usual. Casualties:– Nil.	

2449 Wt. W14957/M90 750,000 1/16 J.B.C. & A. Forms/C.2118/12.

Army Form C. 2118.

WAR DIARY
or
INTELLIGENCE SUMMARY

(Erase heading not required.)

Instructions regarding War Diaries and Intelligence Summaries are contained in F. S. Regs., Part II. and the Staff Manual respectively. Title Pages will be prepared in manuscript.

Place	Date	Hour	Summary of Events and Information	Remarks and references to Appendices
Roussel Farm Sheet 28 B.13.a.2.6.	26 May 1917 Sat.		Battalion at Roussel Farm. Dispositions similar. Morning parades were arranged by Officers Commanding Companies. The usual Working Parties were found by the Battalion. Casualties: Nil.	[illegible]
do.	27 May 1917 Sun.		Battalion at Roussel Farm. Dispositions similar. Divine Services were held during the morning, B. & C. Companies attending at the Church Army Hut, Roussel Farm; and A. and D. Companies proceeding to Mouton Farm Hospital Hut. Blankets were withdrawn to-day. Casualties - Nil. Usual Working parties furnished.	[illegible]
do.	28 May 1917 Mon.		Battalion at Roussel Farm. Dispositions similar. Training under Company arrangements during the morning. Some night working parties cancelled, in order that men going on trench digging fatigue to morrow night be rested. Casualties: Nil.	[illegible]
	29 May 1917 Tue.		Battalion at Roussel Farm. Dispositions similar. Morning spent in practising silent trench digging and resting for the nights fatigue. Working parties:- 1 Company [illegible] new Front Line. 20 Officers and 300 Other Ranks were employed with the 10th and 14th Welsh Regts. in digging a new front line trench in 'No man's land' - near [illegible] Nose. We sustained one casualty - One Other Rank wounded.	[illegible]

2449 Wt. W14957/M90 750,000 1/16 J.B.C. & A. Forms/C.2118/12.

Army Form C. 2118.

Instructions regarding War Diaries and Intelligence Summaries are contained in F. S. Regs., Part II. and the Staff Manual respectively. Title Pages will be prepared in manuscript.

WAR DIARY
or
INTELLIGENCE SUMMARY
(Erase heading not required.)

Place	Date	Hour	Summary of Events and Information	Remarks and references to Appendices
Roussel Farm Sheet 28. B.a.26	30 May 1917 (Wed)	10 am	Battalion at Roussel Farm. Dispositions similar. Rest and a general clean up after yesterdays fatigue. The usual night working parties were provided. A Board of survey - Presdt. Lieut J. R. L. Hornsby was held to examine and report on the condition of the blankets recently withdrawn. Casualties - nil.	
do.	31 May 1917 (Thur)		Battalion at Roussel Farm. Dispositions similar. Baths at Elverdinghe were allotted to the Battalion from 7.0 a.m. to 11.0 a.m. All available men paraded at Headquarters at 9 a.m for the usual morning training. Working parties of 3 officers and 120 Other Ranks provided. Casualties :- nil.	

[signature]
Capt. & Adjt.
for Cl. 10th S.W.B.
31 May 1917.

OPERATION ORDERS NO. 42. by LIEUT COL. C. D. HARVEY
COMMANDING D. L. R.

Secret.

Copy No 2

28.5.1917.

Ref. Map. 28 N.W. BELGIUM. 5.a.
" " St. JULIEN. 28. N.W.

1. NATURE OF TASKS.

On the night of 29th-30th May, a trench will be dug from C.13.3. to C.7.c.0.6. The Trench will be dug to the following dimensions:- 2 ft. deep, 3 ft. broad and each man will take 6 ft. task. All earth will be thrown forward in the direction of the enemy, leaving a berm of 2 ft. Officers will carry template. No party will be allowed to stop work until it has been passed by an officer.
The task will be divided into three sectors:-

"A" Sector - 10TH WELCH REGT.
"B" " - 10TH S. W. B.
"C" " - 14TH WELCH REGT.

10th Welch Regt will dig and wire Front Trench from C.13.3. to C.7.d.4.1. 10th S. W. B. will dig and wire front trench from C.7.d.4.1. to C.7.c.7¾. 3¾. 14th Welch Regt will dig and wire front trench from C.7.c.7¾.3¾. to C.7.c.0.6. The 124. Coy. R.Es will dig three Communication Trenches as under:-

"A" From C.13.a.07.83. to C. 7.d.10.30.
"B" " C.7.c.30.25. to C. 7.d.50.45.
"C" " C.7.c.60.15. to C. 7.c .85.40.

2. WIRING.

The Wire Dumps will be established at POSTS 32 and 35. These Posts will be pointed out to the Battalions on the night of the Operation by a Guide of the 14th Welch Regt. The wire to be erected will be a single apron fence along the whole of our front.

3. PERSONNEL.

COVERING PARTIES.

The Covering Party under Lieut. Cottam consisting of 2. Lewis Guns, Strength, 3. Lewis Gunners and 4. Rifle men detailed from "D" Company under the senior N. C. O., and one Riflemens Post of one N.C.O., and 6. Other Ranks under Sgt. Jackson will take position as follows:-

One Lewis Gun at C.7.2. to be in Liaison with Lewis Gun of 14th Welch Regt., firing towards KIEL COTTAGE.
One Lewis Gun at C.7. d.4.1. bringing cross fire on to the same point which will be in Liaison with the 10th Welch Regt..
Riflemens Post at C.7.d.2.4.

These Parties will go out at 10.30.p.m. with the Tape Laying Parties, remaining out about 40. or 50. yards in front of the tape. At.2.25.a.m., these parties will withdraw. All the Covering Parties will have their faces blackened prior to going out.

WIRING PARTIES.

Four parties consisting of One N. C. O., and 11. O. Rs each to be found by "A" Company under 2nd Lieut. C. A. Sundy will go out at 11.p.m. or when it has been reported that the necessary tapes have been laid, carrying as much wire and stakes as possible. One N. C. O., and 11. Men of "A" Company will be detailed as Carrying Party to carry wire from the dumps forward..

No.1.Party will be under	10/20256.Sgt.D.H.Thomas.	of A. Coy.
" 2. " " " "	10/20540.Cpl.P.Power.	"
" 3. " " " "	10/21447.Sgt.A.King.	"
" 4. " " " "	10/20335.L.Sgt.Edward. W.J.	"

Each party will wire 100. yards of single apron fence and the wiring will commence from the right of each task, parties being numbered from right to left. Each Man will carry one pr. of wire cutters and one pair of Hedging Gloves which will be

obtained from the other Companies.
One Gap will be cut in the centre of each task, otherwise, the wire must be continuous. Wire will be put out 20. YARDS IN FRONT of the trench. Rifles will be carried with the Bayonet fixed, slung over the left shoulder. Wire Parties will withdraw at 2.15 a.m., but if their work has been completed before that time they will withdraw to the trench and assist in digging.

DIGGING PA RTIES.

Digging Parties will be divided into eight parties of 25. O.Rs each of the same platoon under a sergeant, One Officer will command two parties. Pa rties will have their task allotted to them on the ground working from right to left, each man pla-cing his rifle, bayonet fixed, in rea r of the left of his task with the point of the bayonet towards the enemy.
The Parties will be found as under:-
No. 1. Party will be found by "B" Coy under 20408. Sgt.J.H.Williams.
No. 2. " " " " " "B" " " 20464.L.Sgt.Pratten.
No. 3. " " " " " "B" " " 204 30.L.Sgt.Rogers.
No. 4. " " " " " "C" " " 21216. Sgt. Rose. F.
No. 5. " " " " " "C" " " 20932.L.Sgt.Blake.A.C.
No. 6. " " " " " "D" " " 40353. Sgt. Dutton. T.
No. 7 " " " " " "D" " " 21346.L.Sgt.Hughes. J.
No. 8. " " " " " "D" " " 20727.LSgt.Parsons.G.

Officers will be in charge of parties as under:-
Nos. 1. and 2. Parties 2nd Lieut. H. E. Brighton.
Nos. 3. and 4. do. Lieut. D. B. Hitchings.
Nos. 5. and 6. do. Capt. F.R.E.Henward.
Nos. 7. and 8. do. 2nd Lieut. D. P. Clayton.

Nos. 1. to 4.parties inclusive will be under Capt. W.O.Jones.
Nos. 5. to 8. do. do. will be under Capt. J. A. Jones.

These parties will leave their assembly positions at 11.15 .p.m., and will commence working on their tasks immediately, on arrival.

All the parties will withdra w at 2.15.a.m.

4. ASSEMBLY POSITIONS.

Parties of "D" and "C" Companies will assemble in ALMA TRENCH.
do. of "A" and "B" do. will assemble in YORKSHIRE TRENCH.
All Parties will be formed up in their assembly positions at 11.p.m. Wireswill be run back from the Front Line tape to the right of each working party. 2. men per party will go out with the R. E. Officer to lay the tape.

5. T ALKING.

Absolute silence will be maintained during work.. Men must not talk until it is absolutely necessary to do so and then, not above a whisper. No Smoking will be allowed. Great care must be taken that no noise is made when carrying the tools. This must be practised All men will lay flat on the ground when a Very Light is sent up and will remain so until a bout five seconds after it is extinguished.

6. TOOLS.
Ea ch man of the Digging Parties will carry a shovel and in addition, four picks per party will be carried.

7. DRESS.
Steel Helmets, Bandolier around waist, rifle with magazine charged and Bayonet fixed, Bos Respirator at the ALERT position and First Field Dressing. Scabbards will be tied to the tape of the Ba nd-olier and fastened in the centre of the ba ck. All Bayonets will be dulled. Boots will be muffled, each man taking two sandbags for this purpose. These will be put on when they reach the Canal Bank.

8. BOMBS.
NO BOM BS WILL BE CARRIED .

9. ALARM.

9. ALARM.

In the event of any unforeseen tactical emergency, the Battalion will be prepared to move to suita-ble positions in shell-holes near the place to which they are working, and their right thrown back so as to gain touch with Post 31.

INX ON THE DISCHARGE OF A VARIEGATED ROCKET from POST S.2. the Battalion will move to places as above. The VARIEGATED SIGNAL ROCKET will not be used if it is possible to communicate by other means.

In the event of our Covering party seeing two or three boches in NO MANS LAND, NO BOMBS will be thrown but the boches will be allowed to approach our covering party when they will be dealt with by the Bayonet. The DEFENSIVE WILL BE ASSUMED during these operations and no firing will take place unless it is absolutely necessary so as not to delay ~~for~~ the carrying on of the work.

10. MEDICAL ARRANGEMENTS.

All Casualties will be sent down to the Regtl. Aid Post of the 13th WELCH REGT., on the Canal Bank, using the Medical Trolley on the WINDSOR-CASTLE LINE. Four Stretcher bearers will go with each Company under the charge of Sgt. J. Campbell

11. SYNCHRONIZATION OF WATCHES.

All Watches will be synchronised at 8 .30.p.m., o n the evening of the 29th inst.

12. BATTALION HEADQUARTERS.

Battalion Headquarters will be established at POST S.2, (Junction of Barnsley Road and White Trench) where all reports are to be sent.

One runner per Company will remain at Battalion Headquarters.

Negative Reports or Otherwise will be sent to Bn. Hqrs every half hour.

13. RECONNOISANCE.

All Officers and Non-commissioned Officers in charge of Parties will reconnoitre the route from ELVERDINGHE TO THE CANAL BANK to be taken, also the SITES OF THE TASKS AND ASSEMBLY POSITIONS on the evening of the 28th inst and will assemble at 114th Inf. Brigade Headquarters on Canal Bank (Map.Ref.C.19.c.1.4.). at 10.45.p.m.

C.W. Hawes
LIEUTENANT COLONEL.
COMMANDING 10TH BN. SOUTH WALES BORDERERS. (1st GWENT.)

28.5.1917.

Copy No. 1. to 114th. Inf. Brigade.
" " 2. to 115th do.
" " 3. to 13th Welch Regt.
" " 4. to Commanding Officer.
" " 5 .to O.C."A" COY.
" " 6. to O.C."B" "
" " 7. to O.C."C" "
" " 8. to O.C."D". "

MARCH ORDERS FOR OPERATION ORDERS NO. 42. by
LT.COL. C.D.HARVEY COMMANDING
10TH BN. S. W. B.
-:-:-:-:-:-:-:-:-:-:-:-

REF. MAP. 28.N.W. BELGIUM. 5.a.
" " ST.JULIEN. 28. N.W.

28.5.1917.

Onthe evening of 29th May and morning of 30th May next, the following Orders will be observed.

As laid down in O.Orders No. 42, of today's date, the Battalion will march from ELVERDINGHE AND ROUSS ELL FARM to BRIDGE 6.D. on the CANAL BANK.

"A" Company will leave ELVERDINGHE at 5.30.p.m. route - ELVER DINGHE - DAWSON'S CORNER - B.22.c. "D" Company will follow them and both companies will assemble in their respective parties in the WOOD in B.2 3.a. and d.

"B" Company will leave ROUSSELL FAR M AT 6.15 .p.m. route - Via ELVERDINGHE - DAWSON'S CORNER to the Wood. "C" Company will follow "B".

Not more than FIVE MEN will march together. An interval of ~~xxxxxxxxxx~~ 100 yards will be kept between each group of five men.

At 9.15.p.m., Companies will leave the Wood via the tract across country already reconnoitred to BRIDGE 6.D in the Order:-

"D" COY.
"A" "
"B" "
~~xx~~ "C" COY.

Companies will move by platoons at 200 yards intervals.

Two Pack Mules will be detailed to carry up 2. Lewis Guns and Ammunition. They will move in rear of the Battalion.

At 10.p.m., the parties as already detailed in Operation Orders will ~~xxxxx~~ in the following order:-

"A" Carrying Party Company.
"B" do.
"C" do.
"D" do.

Across BRIDGE 6.D, and will proceed by HARKNESS AVENUE, ALMA TRENCH to their positions of ass embly and be formed up in their positions at 11.p.m.

On withdrawal at set time at 2.25.a.m., Companies will file out of trenches in the same route as they entered them crossing BRIDGE 6.D. Marching Back in small parties to the Wood before daylight breaks and will then march back to the Billets in the same order as they left on the previous evening.

C.D. Harvey Lieut. Colonel.

28.5.1917. Commanding 10th Bn. S. W. B.

Copy No. 1. to 114th Inf. Brigade.
" " 2. to 115th Inf. do.
" " 3. to 13th Welch Regt.

P.T.O.

Instructions regarding War Diaries and Intelligence Summaries are contained in F. S. Regs., Part II. and the Staff Manual respectively. Title Pages will be prepared in manuscript.

WAR DIARY
or
INTELLIGENCE SUMMARY
(Erase heading not required.)

Army Form C. 2118.

10 SWB
Vol 18

Place	Date	Hour	Summary of Events and Information	Remarks and references to Appendices
Roussel Farm Sheet 28 B.13.a.2.6.	June 1st. 1917 Friday	9.0am 12.30pm 2-2.30pm	Battalion Hqrs. at Roussel Farm. B & C. Companies at Roussel Farm. A. and D. Companies at Elverdinghe. Training under Company arrangements from 9.0 a.m. to 12.30 p.m. Company Signallers and Scouts paraded at Headquarters for instruction. "C" Company and details bathing at Elverdinghe from 8.0.am. to 9.0.am. Available men paraded from 2pm. to 2.30 pm. for Box respirator and P.H. Helmet drill. Working parties as follows:- One Company digging Cable Trench. 22 Other Ranks at new Transport Lines. Remainder of Batt. available digging continuation of "X" Lines from rear of Boesinghe to Canal Bank. Casualties:- Nil.	HWK
	June 2nd. 1917 Sat.		Battalion at Roussel Farm. Dispositions similar. General clean up of huts and equipment, followed by Inspection of feet. Working parties of 3 Officers and 120 Other Ranks provided by the Battalion. The Commanding Officer (Lt. Col. Harvey) proceeded to U.K. on leave. Casualties :- Nil.	HWK
	June 3rd. 1917 Sun.		Battalion at Roussel Farm. Dispositions similar. Divine Service was held in the Church Army Hut at 10.30 a.m. During the afternoon the Elverdinghe Defences were heavily shelled but we sustained only one casualty – One Other Rank wounded. Usual Working parties.	HWK

2449 Wt. W14957/M90 750,000 1/16 J.B.C. & A. Forms/C.2118/12.

Army Form C. 2118.

Instructions regarding War Diaries and Intelligence Summaries are contained in F. S. Regs., Part II. and the Staff Manual respectively. Title Pages will be prepared in manuscript.

WAR DIARY
or
INTELLIGENCE SUMMARY

(Erase heading not required.)

Place	Date	Hour	Summary of Events and Information	Remarks and references to Appendices
Roussel Farm. Sheet 28. B.13.a.2.6.	June 4th. 1917. Mon.		Battalion at Roussel Farm. Dispositions similar. Morning training included bombing signalling and scouting for the various sections. The usual day-time fatigues were carried on with, but night parties were cancelled. Casualties :- Nil.	JWRK
	June 5th. 1917 Tue.		Battalion at Roussel Farm. A fatigue party of 18 officers and 300 Other Ranks left at 3.30 a.m. for Peselhoek to load and unload ammunition. During the morning Elverdinghe was heavily shelled. Roussel Farm also received some attention from the German Artillery. Our casualties were :- 1 O.R. killed and 1 O.R. wounded.	JWRK
	June 6th. 1917 Wed.		Battalion at Roussel Farm. The fatigue party from Peselhoek returned at 2 a.m. this morning. At 10 a.m. Roussel Farm and its immediate neighbourhood were shelled. No damage was done, but the camp was evacuated & the trenches at the rear occupied. The chateau grounds at Elverdinghe were also lightly shelled. Working parties of 1 officer & 40 other Ranks provided. Casualty :- One Other Rank wounded. Included in the Birthday Honours list is Capt. & Adjt. E.F. Orford who has been awarded the Military Cross. The following officers of this Battalion have been mentioned in Despatches :- Capt. W.F. Havard; Capt. J.A. Jones; Capt. G.F.H. Charlton.	JWRK

2449 Wt. W14957/M90 750,000 1/16 J.B.C. & A. Forms/C.2118/12.

Instructions regarding War Diaries and Intelligence Summaries are contained in F. S. Regs., Part II. and the Staff Manual respectively. Title Pages will be prepared in manuscript.

WAR DIARY
or
INTELLIGENCE SUMMARY

(Erase heading not required.)

Army Form C. 2118.

Place	Date	Hour	Summary of Events and Information	Remarks and references to Appendices
Roussel Farm. Sheet 28 B.13.a.2.6.	June 7th. 1917 Thur		Battalion at Roussel Farm. Dispositions similar. As there was no renewal of the shelling the trenches were vacated and the huts occupied again. Parades during morning and afternoon included Arm drill, extended Order drill, musketry, Lewis Gun instruction and kit inspection. Working parties of 15 officers and 130 Other Ranks provided. The Elverdinghe Defences were again lightly shelled but we suffered no Casualties.	JWK
	June 8th 1917 Fri.		Battalion at Roussel Farm. Dispositions similar. Morning parade similar to yesterdays. During the day there was intermittent shelling of the Elverdinghe Defences – heavy shells coming over for the most part. Seven Other Ranks were wounded but four of these remained at duty. Working parties as usual.	JWK
	June 9th 1917. Sat.		Battalion at Roussel Farm. Dispositions similar. The usual morning and afternoon parades were held. Working parties of 12 officers and 100 Other Ranks provided. Very slight shelling of Elverdinghe but no casualties.	JWK
	June 10th 1917 Sun		Battalion at Roussel Farm. Dispositions similar. Divine services were held during the morning. Working parties as yesterday. Casualties:- Nil.	JWK

2449 Wt. W14957/M90 750,000 1/16 J.B.C. & A. Forms/C.2118/12.

Instructions regarding War Diaries and Intelligence Summaries are contained in F. S. Regs., Part II. and the Staff Manual respectively. Title Pages will be prepared in manuscript.

WAR DIARY
or
INTELLIGENCE SUMMARY
(Erase heading not required.)

Army Form C. 2118.

Place	Date 1917	Hour	Summary of Events and Information	Remarks and references to Appendices
Roussel Farm. Sheet 28 B.13.a.2.6.	June 11th. Mon.		Battalion at Roussel Farm. Dispositions similar. In the early hours of the morning the billets occupied by "A" Coy. at Elverdinghe were again heavily shelled by a 15 cm. How. Battery. The usual training parades were held this morning. Working parties as yesterdays. Capt. J. J. Williams in charge of a cable laying party was wounded. One Other Rank wounded this morning.	JRK
do.	June 12 Tue.		Battalion at Roussel Farm. Dispositions similar. Morning parades as yesterdays. At dusk the Battalion was relieved by a Battalion of the 16th. Welsh Regt. We moved to the Boesinghe sector of the Front Line, relieving the 11th. S.W.B. Relief was complete shortly after midnight. Casualty – One O.R. wounded (at duty)	JRK
Front Line (Boesinghe Chateau) B.11.c.8.5	June 13 Wed		Batt. in Front Line. Dispositions as follows:– A. Coy. Front Line (Right); D Coy. Front Line (Left) B. Coy. in S. Line & Redoubt. C Coy in Boesinghe Redoubt. Batt. on Right:– 15th. R.W.F. Batt. on Left:– 1st Company 10th. Regt. of the Belgian Army. Shortly after relief was completed the sector was shelled – mostly in "F" Line region and near Batt. Hqrs. Headquarters were shelled by "whizz-bangs" and 10·5 cms. intermittently throughout the day. Capt. & Adjt. E. F. Orford, M.C. was wounded in the right arm by shell splinters whilst subduing a burning camouflage that had been set alight by a previous shell. Work – usual trench	JRK

2449 Wt. W14957/M90 750,000 1/16 J.B.C. & A. Forms/C.2118/12.

Instructions regarding War Diaries and Intelligence Summaries are contained in F. S. Regs., Part II. and the Staff Manual respectively. Title Pages will be prepared in manuscript.

WAR DIARY
or
INTELLIGENCE SUMMARY

(Erase heading not required.)

Army Form C. 2118.

Place	Date	Hour	Summary of Events and Information	Remarks and references to Appendices
Front Line. Boesinghe Chateau. B. 11. b. 8.5	June 13 (contd.)		maintenance. The front line was further strengthened by the addition of 16 "gooseberries" to the parapet. Casualties:- Capt. Orford, wounded. One other rank killed. Three other ranks wounded - two remaining at duty. Batt. now attached to XIV Corps. Fifth Army.	HRbK
do.	June 14 Thur.		Battalion in Front Line. Dispositions similar. During the day Batt. Headquarters were again heavily shelled, but very little damage was done. Our artillery retaliation appeared to silence the enemy. Trench mortars were fired at intervals on the enemy's front line. Work:- general trench maintenance. Casualties:- nil.	HRbK
do.	June 15 Fri.		Battalion in Front Line. Dispositions similar. Our artillery was fairly active throughout the day, shelling principally the enemy's support lines. The enemy's artillery was fairly quiet, being confined almost exclusively to Elverdinghe neighbourhood. The 1st. Batt., Coldstream Guards, relieved us, relief being complete just before midnight. The Batt. marched to a wood at A. 8. d. 2.3, near Coppernollehoek; accommodation provided included a few tents for the officers & waterproof 'bivouac' shelters for the ranks. Lt. Col. Harvey returned from leave. Casualty:- 1 Other Rank wounded.	HRbK
Coppernollehoek A. 8. d. 2.3	June 16 Sat.		Battalion bivouacked at A. 8. d. 2. 3. Rested until midday and then	HRbK

2449 Wt. W14957/M90 750,000 1/16 J.B.C. & A. Forms/C.2118/12.

WAR DIARY
or
INTELLIGENCE SUMMARY.
(*Erase heading not required.*)

Army Form C. 2118.

Instructions regarding War Diaries and Intelligence Summaries are contained in F. S. Regs., Part II. and the Staff Manual respectively. Title pages will be prepared in manuscript.

Place	Date 1917	Hour	Summary of Events and Information	Remarks and references to Appendices
Coppernollehoek A.8.d.2.3.	Sat. June 16. (contd)		had a general clean up. Casualties :- nil. 33658. Pte. D. Hancock received the Military Medal for services in the Field.	JPWK
do.	June 17 (Sun.)		Battalion at Coppernollehoek Woods. Divine Services were held at 10 a.m. the Band assisting at the Church of England service. The Battalion moved off again at 11 a.m. and marched to a wood South of De Wippe Cabaret at A.10.b.6.4, arriving at 1 pm. The new bivouac is situate just within the Belgian Area. The remainder of the day was devoted to a general clean up and arrangement of the bivouac. Casualties :- nil.	JPWK
De Wippe Cabaret. A.10.b.6.4	June 18 (Mon)		Battalion in bivouac near De Wippe Cabaret. During the day Working parties of 4 officers and 200 Other Ranks were provided for camouflaging and preparing gun pits &c. for heavy artillery. Casualties :- nil.	JPWK
do.	June 19 (Tue.)		Battalion in bivouac near De Wippe Cabaret. Companies paraded under orders of Officers Commanding Companies, "A" proceeding to "H" Camp for training on the Assault Course. Stretcher bearers received instruction on First Aid from the Medical Officer. Signallers and	JPWK

Army Form C. 2118.

Instructions regarding War Diaries and Intelligence Summaries are contained in F. S. Regs., Part II. and the Staff Manual respectively. Title pages will be prepared in manuscript.

WAR DIARY
or
INTELLIGENCE SUMMARY.
(*Erase heading not required.*)

Place	Date	Hour	Summary of Events and Information	Remarks and references to Appendices
De Wippe Cabaret A.10.b.6.4.	June 19 (contd)		Scouts & runners paraded for general instruction. Working parties of 6 officers and 300 were provided. Casualties :- Nil.	JRBK
	June 20 (Wed)		Battalion in bivouac. Working parties of 9 officers and 449 Other ranks provided for making gun-emplacements, unloading ammunition & making camouflages. Scouts received special training. Casualties:- Nil.	JRBK
		9am 1pm	All available officers paraded for Tactical Exercise - Attacking a village.	
	June 21 (Thurs)		Battalion in bivouac. Working parties of 10 officers and 397 Other ranks provided. Signallers employed on training during the morning, & later worked on camouflage. "D" Company moved 'en bloc' to Woesten - S.30.a.1.9 - in order to obviate the necessity of a long march each day. Casualties :- Nil.	JRBK
	June 22 (Fri)		Battalion in bivouac. Working parties of 12 officers and 402 Other ranks provided. None available for training. Casualties :- Nil.	JRBK
	June 23 (Sat)		Battalion in bivouac. Working parties of 10 officers and 450 Other ranks provided. Nobody available for training. Casualties :- Nil.	JRBK
	June 24 (Sun)		Battalion in bivouac. Similar working parties. During the morning "D" Coy were subjected to light shell fire and suffered the following Casualties :-	JRBK

A6945 Wt. W11422/M1160 350,000 12/16 D. D. & L. Forms/C./2118/14.

Instructions regarding War Diaries and Intelligence Summaries are contained in F. S. Regs., Part II. and the Staff Manual respectively. Title pages will be prepared in manuscript.

WAR DIARY
or
INTELLIGENCE SUMMARY.
(*Erase heading not required.*)

Army Form C. 2118.

Place	Date	Hour	Summary of Events and Information	Remarks and references to Appendices
nr. De Wippe Cabaret A.10.b.6.4	June 24 (contd.)		2/Lt. Benfield, W.T. and one O.R. wounded, the latter remaining at duty. One O.R. (attached to 151 Coy. R.E's) was also wounded to-day. "D" Company returned to Headquarters this afternoon.	JPBK
do.	June 25 (Mon)		Battalion in bivouac. Working parties the same as on 23rd. inst. Casualties:- Nil.	JPBK
do.	June 26 (Tue)		Battalion in bivouac. Working parties similar to yesterdays. A Draft of 43 O.R.s joined the Battalion to-day. Casualties:- Nil. A hostile aeroplane appeared over the neighbourhood of the camp at 8.45 pm flying very low. It was subjected to heavy M.G. and A.A fire but appeared to escape.	JPBK
do. Caestre Sheet 27. W.3.a.4.5.	June 27 (Wed)		The Battalion moved to-day. Marched from bivouac to Proven, where busses were in waiting to convey the Battalion to Caestre. Arrived in new area at 1 p.m. The afternoon was devoted to a rest and general clean-up. Casualties:- Nil.	JPBK
do. Lavies.	June 28 (Thur)		The Battalion moved again to-day. Embussed on the Caestre-St. Sylvestre Road at 8.30 a.m. and were conveyed to Lavies. Map refce:- Sheet Hazebrouck 5a. 6.D. The route followed was via. Hazebrouck, Morbecque, Steenbecque, Aire, Lambres,	JPBK

A6945 Wt. W11422/M1160 350,000 12/16 D. D. & L. Forms/C./2118/14.

Instructions regarding War Diaries and Intelligence Summaries are contained in F. S. Regs., Part II. and the Staff Manual respectively. Title pages will be prepared in manuscript.

WAR DIARY
or
INTELLIGENCE SUMMARY.
(Erase heading not required.)

Army Form C. 2118.

Place	Date	Hour	Summary of Events and Information	Remarks and references to Appendices
Laires 6.D. (Hazebrouck 5A.)	June 28 (contd)		St. Hilaire, Lieres, Auchy and Westrehem. Arrived in new Area at 2 p.m. and proceeded to billets. Remainder of day devoted to cleaning up and rest. The transport section arrived at 10 p.m. Casualties:- Nil.	A draft of 59 O.R. joined at Laires.
	June 29 (Fri)		Battalion at Laires. The day was devoted to training under Company arrangements – platoon drill, handling of arms, musketry, physical drill & bayonet fighting practise. Casualties:- Nil. A draft of 10 O.R. arrived at 10 p.m.	
	June 30 (Sat.)		Battalion at Laires. To-days training included handling of arms, physical training; bayonet and bullet practice; and platoon drill. Signallers, band and drummers received special instruction from their respective leaders. "Draft" men paraded under the R.S.M. at 2.0 p.m. for gas helmet inspection and drill. Casualties:- Nil.	

J R C Kennard
Capt. & Adjt.
1 July 1917. for O.C. 10th. (Service) Bn. South Wales Borderers.

A6945 Wt. W11422/M1160 350,000 12/16 D. D. & L. Forms/C./2118/14

Instructions regarding War Diaries and Intelligence Summaries are contained in F. S. Regs., Part II. and the Staff Manual respectively. Title pages will be prepared in manuscript.

WAR DIARY
or
INTELLIGENCE SUMMARY.
(Erase heading not required.)

Army Form C. 2118.

10th S.W.B.

Vol 19

Place	Date	Hour	Summary of Events and Information	Remarks and references to Appendices
Laires Sheet Hazebrouck 5A C.D.	July 1 1917 (Sun)		Battalion at Laires. Divine services were held during the morning, a drum head service (C.E.) being held in one of the Training fields, Roman Catholics proceeding to Laires Church. Kits were inspected by O.s C. Companies between 11 a.m. and 12 noon. The afternoon was devoted to washing of clothes and equipment. Casualties - Nil.	
	July 2 (Mon)		Battalion at Laires. Training as follows:- 7.0 a.m. to 7.45 a.m. Handling of Arms. 9.0 a.m. to 12.30 p.m. Close order drill, physical training, musketry, extended order drill and mobility of sections. 2.0 p.m. to 4.10 p.m. "Bullet & bayonet" practice, platoon drill in battle formation and Company drill. At 9.0 am the Commanding Officer inspected the whole Battalion (including employed men), dressed in Fighting Order. Signallers were engaged on a 'scheme' between 9 a.m. and 5 p.m. Hqr. runners received instruction in map reading and message carrying from 2 p.m. to 4.30 p.m. A draft of 50 Other Ranks joined to-day. Major C. V. Reece rejoined & took over duties of 2nd. in Command. Casualties - Nil	

Instructions regarding War Diaries and Intelligence Summaries are contained in F. S. Regs., Part II, and the Staff Manual respectively. Title pages will be prepared in manuscript.

WAR DIARY
or
INTELLIGENCE SUMMARY.
(Erase heading not required.)

Army Form C. 2118.

Place	Date	Hour	Summary of Events and Information	Remarks and references to Appendices
Laires Sheet Hazebrouck 5A 6. D.	July 3 Tues.		Battalion at Laires. Paraded in column of route at 4.0 am. and marched to the Divisional Training Area at P. of Therouanne to dig trenches &c. and prepare the ground for later practice. Arrived back at about 7 pm. The draft that arrived yesterday paraded at 9 a.m. in full marching order for inspection by the R.S.M. and for gas helmet drill. Casualties :- Nil.	
	July 4 Wed.		Battalion at Laires. Paraded at 10 a.m. with Lewis Gun limbers, Cookers and Pack Animals loaded with tools, ammunition and water, and proceeded to the Training Area. Each Company practised independently schemes previously arranged by O.C. Companies. Battalion returned to billets at 8 p.m. Casualties :- Nil.	
	July 5 Thurs.		Battalion at Laires. Companies carried on training independently. Nos. 1 and 2 of all Lewis Gun teams remained off parade to clean guns and ammunition. Casualties :- Nil.	
	July 6 Fri.		Battalion at Laires. Marched to Training Area, with Transport. Further training was arranged by Brigade. Batt. out from 8 am. to 4 pm. Casualties :- Nil.	

Instructions regarding War Diaries and Intelligence Summaries are contained in F. S. Regs., Part II. and the Staff Manual respectively. Title pages will be prepared in manuscript.

WAR DIARY
or
INTELLIGENCE SUMMARY.
(Erase heading not required.)

Army Form C. 2118.

Place	Date	Hour	Summary of Events and Information	Remarks and references to Appendices
Laires Sheet Hazebrouck 5A. 6.D.	July 7 Sat.		Battalion at Laires. Marched to the Training Area at 6 a.m. Transport and Field Kitchens accompanying the Battalion. A rehearsal of proposed forthcoming attack was carried out, in conjunction with the remainder of the Division. Arrived back at Laires at 4 pm, marching via Bomy. Casualties Nil.	
	July 8 Sun.		Battalion at Laires. Divine Services were held this morning, Roman Catholics attending at the local church and other denominations parading for drumhead service. During the day the whole of the Battalion bathed (in an improvised bath fitted up at Hqrs.) & the men were afterwards inspected by the M.O. The Commanding Officer visited billets after church Parade. Casualties Nil.	
	July 9 Mon.		Battalion at Laires. Gas Helmet drill and Inspection was carried out between 7 a.m. and 7.30 a.m. Companies paraded at 9 a.m. and carried on independently with training – musketry, bullet-bayonet practise &c. All stretcher bearers (including 16 extra men drawn	

A6945 Wt. W11422/M1160 350,000 12/16 D. D. & L. Forms/C./2118/14.

Instructions regarding War Diaries and Intelligence Summaries are contained in F. S. Regs., Part II. and the Staff Manual respectively. Title pages will be prepared in manuscript.

WAR DIARY
or
INTELLIGENCE SUMMARY.
(Erase heading not required.)

Army Form C. 2118.

Place	Date	Hour	Summary of Events and Information	Remarks and references to Appendices
Laires Sheet - Hazebrouck 5A 6D	1917 July 9 (Contd)		from the Band) received instruction from the M.O. during the day. A miniature range is made use of when the Batt. remains at Laires. Casualties - Nil. Capt. Dunnington - Yukon Pack specialist - demonstrated their uses.	
	July 10 (Tue)		Battalion at Laires. Divisional training was again carried out on the Training Area, the Batt. leaving Laires at 7 a.m. and arriving back at 5 pm. Battalion Observers remained behind for special instruction. Casualties - Nil.	
	July 11 (Wed)		Battalion at Laires. Companies carried on independently with musketry, Bullet - bayonet - bullet practice, wiring, handling of arms &c. Battalion observers again received special instruction. Casualties - Nil.	
	July 12 (Thu)		Battalion at Laires. Marched to Training Area at 6.30. Rehearsal of forthcoming operations was carried on with until 4 pm. when Batt. moved to bivouac & rested till midnight. Casualties Nil	
	July 13 (Fri)		Further operations were practised just before & after dawn. Another bivouac was formed & breakfast partaken of at 6.30am. Before moving off to Billets the G.O.C. addressed the 115th Brigade	

A6945 Wt. W11422/M1160 350,000 12/16 D. D. & L. Forms/C./2118/14.

Instructions regarding War Diaries and Intelligence Summaries are contained in F. S. Regs., Part II. and the Staff Manual respectively. Title pages will be prepared in manuscript.

WAR DIARY
or
INTELLIGENCE SUMMARY.
(*Erase heading not required.*)

Army Form C. 2118.

Place	Date	Hour	Summary of Events and Information	Remarks and references to Appendices
Laires Sheet Hazebrouck 5A 6 D.	July 13 (contd)		& expressed his pleasure at the keenness displayed by all ranks during the training. Batt returned to Laires at 10.30 am. and rested for the remainder of the day. Casualties - Nil.	
do	July 14 Sat.		Battalion at Laires. Training under Company arrangements included Field Firing, rapid wiring, bayonet fighting and gas helmet drill. Casualties - Nil.	
do	July 15 (Sun)		Battalion at Laires. No parades were ordered for the day. A good number voluntarily attended a C E Service this morning. Casualties - Nil	
do	July 16 (Mon)		Battalion at Laires left at 5.30 a.m. and marched to Molinghem via Febvin-Palfart, Westrehem, St Hilaire and Norrent Fontes arriving at destination at 11.30 am. Remainder of the day devoted to rest. Casualties: Nil.	
Molinghem Sheet Hazebrouck 5A 5 F.	July 17 (Tue)		Battalion at Molinghem marched off at 2.30 am. and proceeded to Caestre via Steenbecque and Hazebrouck, arriving at destination at 11 am. Remainder of the day was devoted to rest. Casualties:- Nil.	

A6945 Wt. W11422/M1160 350,000 12/16 D. D. & L. Forms/C./2118/14.

Instructions regarding War Diaries and Intelligence Summaries are contained in F. S. Regs., Part II. and the Staff Manual respectively. Title pages will be prepared in manuscript.

WAR DIARY
or
INTELLIGENCE SUMMARY.
(*Erase heading not required.*)

Army Form C. 2118.

Place	Date	Hour	Summary of Events and Information	Remarks and references to Appendices
Caestre Sheet Hazebrouck 5A. 3H.	July 18 (Wed)		Battalion at Caestre moved again at 8.30 am. and proceeded to Eecke. Box respirators and P.H. Helmets were inspected during the afternoon. Casualties - Nil	
Eecke Sheet Hazebrouck 5A. 3H. Watou Sheet 27 E.10.&9.5.	July 19 (Thur)		Battalion at Eecke left at 5.30 a.m. and marched to a camp North of Watou, arriving at 12 noon. Remainder of day devoted to a general clean up and rest. Casualties - Nil	
do.	July 20 (Fri)		Battalion N of Watou. The Commanding Officer inspected the Battalion at 9a.m. Between 10 am. and 12 noon Company Commanders carried on with drill and training. A gas helmet inspection was held during the afternoon. A Working party of 4 Officers and 200 O.R. was sent to [illegible] lines on a cable burying fatigue. Casualties - Nil	
do. Stoke Farm Sheet 27 F.5.c.	July 21 (Sat)		Battalion N of Watou moved again this morning and marched to Stoke Farm bivouac at F.5.c. - N of Poperinghe. Arrived in new area at 11 am. Remainder of day devoted to a clean up and rest. Casualty - One Other Rank accidentally wounded.	
do.	July 22 (Sun)		Battalion at Stoke Farm. Divine Services were held during the morning. Inspection of feet, boots, field dressings, iodine tubes, identity discs	

A6945 Wt. W11422/M1160 350,000 12/16 D. D. & L. Forms/C./2118/14.

Instructions regarding War Diaries and Intelligence Summaries are contained in F. S. Regs., Part II. and the Staff Manual respectively. Title pages will be prepared in manuscript.

WAR DIARY
or
INTELLIGENCE SUMMARY.
(Erase heading not required.)

Army Form C. 2118.

Place	Date	Hour	Summary of Events and Information	Remarks and references to Appendices
Stoke Fm (Ubest 7) F. 5 c.	July 22 (contd)		Cardigans & braces followed. 2/Lt Cobb W.T and two O.R. proceeded to the Yser Canal to investigate the depth of water north of Bridge 6. Casualties - Nil. A party of 2 officers & 500 O.R. left for Cardoen Fm for fatigue.	
do	July 23 (Mon)		Battalion at Stoke Farm. The C.O. inspected the Batt at 9 a.m. Battalion drill followed by training - chiefly extended order drill - occupied the remainder of the morning. A fatigue party of 4 officers and 200 O.R. proceeded to Canal Bank to bury cable. The party was subjected to considerable gas shelling and the following casualties were incurred: - 16 O.R. gassed and 7 O.R. wounded - one remaining at duty.	
do	July 24 (Tue)		Battalion at Stoke Farm. Battalion drill and training were carried out. The G.O.C. inspected the Battalion at 11 a.m. & visited the Transport Lines during the afternoon, afterwards expressing approval with all he had seen. Casualties - Nil.	
do	July 25 (Wed)		Battalion at Stoke Farm. Companies paraded under Major Rus for general instruction and were later inspected by the	

A6945 Wt. W11422/M1160 350,000 12/16 D. D. & L. Forms/C./2118/14.

Army Form C. 2118.

WAR DIARY
or
INTELLIGENCE SUMMARY.

(Erase heading not required.)

Instructions regarding War Diaries and Intelligence Summaries are contained in F. S. Regs., Part II. and the Staff Manual respectively. Title pages will be prepared in manuscript.

Place	Date	Hour	Summary of Events and Information	Remarks and references to Appendices
do	July ([illegible])		Commanding Officer – two Companies at a time. A demonstration of the new S.O.S. signal was given at 6 pm. The G.O.C. was present, and he afterwards presented a silver bugle to No 15 Platoon, the victors of the 38th Divisional Bayonet Fighting Competition. Casualty – Nil	
do	July [illegible] ([illegible])		Battalion at Stoke Farm. Both the Commanding Officer and Major Rees closely inspected the Battalion & ensured that everybody was properly equipped. Casualties – 5 O.R. who were on fatigue & slightly gassed on night 23/24th were sent to Hospital to-day.	
do	July ([illegible])		Final preparations and inspections – preparing for forthcoming operations – were made and the Battalion was warned to be in readiness to move at an hour's notice. All men not previously put through gas were sent to Coy H.Q. where they went into a gas chamber. Casualties – Nil	

A6945 Wt. W11422/M1160 350,000 12/16 D. D. & L. Forms/C./2118/14.

Instructions regarding War Diaries and Intelligence Summaries are contained in F. S. Regs., Part II. and the Staff Manual respectively. Title pages will be prepared in manuscript.

WAR DIARY
or
INTELLIGENCE SUMMARY.
(*Erase heading not required.*)

Army Form C. 2118.

Place	Date	Hour	Summary of Events and Information	Remarks and references to Appendices
Stoke Fm. Sheet 27 F.5.c.	July 28 (Sat)		Battalion at Stoke Farm. Further "preparedness" inspections and a little bombing practice occupied the morning. A fatigue party of 2 officers and 50 OR proceeded to the new Transport lines at A10 d 4 9 and made their Hqrs while working on Fatigue at Ondank Dump. Casualties	Nil.
Stoke Fm. Sheet 27 F.5.c.	July 29 (Sun)		Battalion at Stoke Farm. Divine Services had been arranged for this morning but were abandoned owing to the inclement weather. The Divisional Baths at St Sixte were in use between 8am and 3pm. The Batt. moved to "G" Camp at 8.30pm. Casualties - Nil	
Camp G A.16.a.	July 30 (Mon)		Battalion at Camp "G". Final preparations for to-morrow's attack were made. 18 officers and 509 other Ranks left at 8.30 pm and proceeded to their assembly position at B22 a marching via Infantry Track No. 9. Major E T Rees MC was in command. Batt Hqrs including QM. Stores and Transport moved to woods at A 10 d 4 9. (28 NW) Forward Transport (pack mules for carrying rations, ammunition etc) was situated on the West of the Yser Canal at B 24 d (28 NW). One Company which had been detailed to lay trench boards across the Canal were to form the Carrying party [illegible]	

A6945 Wt. W11422/M1160 350,000 12/16 D. D. & L. Forms/C./2118/14.

WAR DIARY
or
INTELLIGENCE SUMMARY.
(*Erase heading not required.*)

Army Form C. 2118.

Instructions regarding War Diaries and Intelligence Summaries are contained in F. S. Regs., Part II. and the Staff Manual respectively. Title pages will be prepared in manuscript.

Place	Date	Hour	Summary of Events and Information	Remarks and references to Appendices
	1917 July 30 (contd)		remainder of the Battalion. Battalion reserves included the following – (1) 3 officers & 65 O.R. who joined the 38th Divn Reinforcement Batt at Hagrade – having been detached from the Batt. on the 28th inst (2) A party of 1 officer and 50 O.R. who had been detached to keep Infantry track 9 in repair and also to act as guides for troops using the track (3) 10 officers and 72 O.R. remaining at Transport lines. (4) A Draft of 30 O.R. who joined the Battalion to-day. (5) Men away on leave – about 35 O.R.	
	1917 July 31 (Tue)		18 Officers and 509 OR go into action – for details see next month's Summary.	

[illegible] Lt-Col
Comdg 10th S.W.B.

A6945 Wt. W11422/M1160 350,000 12/16 D. D. & L. Forms/C./2118/14.

Instructions regarding War Diaries and Intelligence Summaries are contained in F. S. Regs., Part II. and the Staff Manual respectively. Title pages will be prepared in manuscript.

WAR DIARY
or
INTELLIGENCE SUMMARY.
(Erase heading not required.)

10 SWB

Army Form C. 2118.

115/38

10th (Service) Bn South Wales Borderers

Vol 20

Place	Date	Hour	Summary of Events and Information	Remarks and references to Appendices
[illegible] (28)	30/7/1917	9pm	The Battalion less one Company which had been detailed to carry [illegible] Bridges across the Canal d'Yser, left [illegible] Camp by march route at 9pm 30/7/1917 and following Route 9	
		11.15pm	arrived at Assembly Trenches at B22a at 11.15 pm.	
Assembly Trenches [illegible] B22.a[illegible]	31/7/17	3am	At 3am July 31st the Battalion left Assembly Trenches for KIEL COT proceeding via Route 10 crossing the canal by Bridge 6D. There was little hostile shelling at the time. 2nd Lt [illegible] Evans was wounded at this juncture.	
KIEL COTT		6.50am	Kiel Cottage was reached at 6.50 am (Zero + 3 hours) the scheduled time of arrival. By this time, the 113th and 114th Brigades had made their attack in accordance with pre-arranged plans, and were fighting for final occupation of the famous Pilckem Ridge which for so long had dominated the Ypres Salient. The Guards Division on our left, with their usual dash, had taken the high ground opposite BOESINGHE, and the Welsh Divisions' Objective was the village of PILCKHEM. The Battalion took up position immediately North of Caddy Lane, until a few hours previously one of the Hun's strongholds. Arrangements were made for a quick move to be effected if necessary, and touch was at once gained with the 16th Welch Regt. From here a party was sent to reconnoitre the way to IRON CROSS.	
		3pm	At 3pm the Bn was ordered to move forward to the Western Slopes of the IRON CROSS Ridge, which was now in British hands having been taken by the other Brigades of the Division. The march was commenced, moving in Artillery Formation in half platoons, but on reaching PILCKHEM, such a fierce hostile fire was opened on the men that orders were given for columns to split into Sectional Columns, which was quickly done, at a cost of only about a dozen casualties. The behaviour of the men while passing through the exceedingly heavy barrage	

A6945 Wt. W11422/M1160 350,000 12/16 D. D. & L. Forms/C./2118/14.

August 1917

Instructions regarding War Diaries and Intelligence Summaries are contained in F. S. Regs., Part II. and the Staff Manual respectively. Title pages will be prepared in manuscript.

WAR DIARY
or
INTELLIGENCE SUMMARY.

10th Bn (*Erase heading not required.*) S.W. Borderers

Army Form C. 2118.

Place	Date	Hour	Summary of Events and Information	Remarks and references to Appendices
PILCKHEM + IRON CROSS RIDGES N of YPRES	August 1, 2, 3, /1917		which was put down by the enemy Artillery at this point deserves the highest commendation, especially when it is remembered that about 150 of them were recent drafts of reinforcements, and were for the first time under serious fire.	
			The rendezvous was reached by 4.10 pm, and work was commenced digging a series of strong points along a line 300 yards in advance and parallel to the road running SE from IRON CROSS. This line was, incidentally, in continuation of the line along which the 5th Gordon Highlanders, on our right, were consolidating. Battalion Headquarters were at C.3. b.4.3	
			At this time, orders were received for a company to reinforce the front line, and accordingly "D" Company under Lieutenant H Cottam were despatched. The line was reached by this company by 8.00pm and communication was established with units on flanks	
			Rain was now falling heavily, and men were experiencing great difficulty in keeping their rifles, and especially their Lewis Guns, in good working order. The Lewis Gun difficulty was overcome when Battalion Headquarters moved next day to RUDOLPHE FARM where there were four strong machine gun emplacements. Here the 4 Headquarter Lewis Gun teams gave their guns a thorough overhauling and cleaning, and exchanged with 4 teams in the line, which were again cleaned by HQ teams. In this way a continual supply of clean guns was maintained throughout the operations.	
			Facilities were afforded at RUDOLPHE FARM for making hot tea, and the constant supply was greatly appreciated by the men.	
			During the night of July 31/Aug 1 a great deal of promiscuous	

August 1917

Instructions regarding War Diaries and Intelligence Summaries are contained in F. S. Regs., Part II, and the Staff Manual respectively. Title pages will be prepared in manuscript.

WAR DIARY
or
~~INTELLIGENCE SUMMARY.~~

10th (S) Bn (Erase heading not required.) S W Borderers

Army Form C. 2118.

Place	Date	Hour	Summary of Events and Information	Remarks and references to Appendices
			shelling took place. AID POST at RUDOLPHE FARM received no little attention and Lt G.L. Gall, the medical officer in charge was wounded, as also was the Medical Officer of the 11th S W Borderers.	
			August 1st was comparatively quiet until about 5 pm, when the enemy put down an exceedingly heavy barrage along:-	
			(a) Front Line	
			(b) A line 200x in rear of Front Line	
			(c) Line known as "Green Line"	
			(d) Roads { IRON CROSS to STEENBEEK YARNA FARM to STEENBEEK	
			(e) RUDOLPHE FARM and houses at IRON CROSS	
			SOS Signals were observed, and messages were received from Lieut Cottam, i/c D Company who were in the Front Line to the effect that he feared counter attack by the Bosche, and that his ranks were much depleted by casualties. At 4.57 pm B Company were ordered to the front under 2/Lieutenant Cobb, and at 5.30 pm A Company, under Captain Galsworthy advanced to form a line immediately forward of THE INGS and parallel to the Front line. Here they consolidated and eventually made a strong support line, use being made of existing Hun wire and gun positions.	
			SAA beginning to get short, a party was organised from C Company, and sent to IRON CROSS DUMP, for SAA and bombs, and a dump was made at Battalion Headquarters from which Companies could draw their requirements.	
			By this time, casualties had become heavy, and two Company	

A6945 Wt. W11422/M1160 350,000 12/16 D. D. & L. Forms/C./2118/14.

August 1917

Instructions regarding War Diaries and Intelligence Summaries are contained in F. S. Regs., Part II. and the Staff Manual respectively. Title pages will be prepared in manuscript.

WAR DIARY

or

~~INTELLIGENCE SUMMARY.~~

10th Bn (*Erase heading not required.*) S.W. Borderers

Army Form C. 2118.

Place	Date	Hour	Summary of Events and Information	Remarks and references to Appendices
PILCKEM RIDGE and IRON CROSS RIDGE	1/8/17		Commanders were amongst them. 2/Lieutenant W T Cobb therefore took over command of the front line and reorganised the garrison, making three strong points, each containing 20 men, under an officer. About 60x in front of main line were three Battle Outposts, well sited, from each of which good enfilade fire could be brought to bear on both flanks. Each battle outpost had its own small protective party 20x in front.	
			A patrol was sent to discover position &c of troops on our left, and returned with the news that remnants of A Company of 11th S.W. Borderers, a LG Post of 14th Welsh Regt, and a post of one officer and 50 O.Ranks of 17th RWF were there. The Scots were still in touch on our right.	
			Another patrol under an officer was sent about 11 pm along Western Banks of the STEENBEEK. None of the enemy were seen, but a Machine Gun which had been barraging the roads was located at PEITRES FARM. This was afterwards dealt with effectively by the Artillery. About midnight, shelling became ~~very~~ less intense, ~~but~~ it never ceased altogether. During this trying period runners and stretcherbearers performed extraordinarily good work.	
	2/8/17		On August 2nd there was much shelling, which became intense on both sides when the SOS signal went up at 8.30pm and 10.30pm. The garrison was now well entrenched. Use having been made of coils of wire left by the enemy.	
			During the night of August 2/3 constant patrolling was done. The chief points of interest being The STEENBEEK, both flanks, between	

August 1917.

Instructions regarding War Diaries and Intelligence Summaries are contained in F. S. Regs., Part II, and the Staff Manual respectively. Title pages will be prepared in manuscript.

WAR DIARY
or
~~INTELLIGENCE SUMMARY.~~

10th Bn S.W. Borderers

(*Erase heading not required.*)

Army Form C. 2118.

Place	Date	Hour	Summary of Events and Information	Remarks and references to Appendices
PILCKHEM RIDGE			battle outposts, and between Posts in the main line.	
	3/8/17	5am	5am brought welcome relief, the relieving unit being the 15th Royal Welsh Fusiliers, and by 7am relief was complete, and the Battalion was more or less comfortably ensconced in CANDLE TRENCH	
	4/5/8/17	-	and CANCER TRENCH, where they remained until August 5th. At 2.30pm on 5th August, the battalion was relieved by the 7th Bn of the Somerset Light Infantry, and proceeded to ELVERDINGHE CHATEAU, which was reached	
Elverdinghe Chateau	5/8/17		at 5.15pm. An excellent and much needed hot dinner was immediately served, and was very much appreciated by the men, as also were the hot baths which some were fortunate to get. Particular and necessary attention was paid to the mens feet. At 9pm, the Battalion entrained at the Chateau, and detrained at INTERNATIONAL CORNER whence a short march brought them to	
Stoke Farm Camp 27.15.c.			STOKE FARM CAMP, where another hot meal was ready, after which all settled down to hardearned and welcome sleep.	
	6/8/17		The day was spent by cleaning as much as possible, preparing indents, and a muster roll call was had, to decide the exact casualties, which were 22 Killed, 139 wounded, 2 missing 3 died of wounds. Officer casualties were, Capt Galsworthy,	

A6945 Wt. W11422/M1160 350,000 12/16 D. D. & L. Forms/C./2118/14.

August 1917

Instructions regarding War Diaries and Intelligence Summaries are contained in F. S. Regs., Part II, and the Staff Manual respectively. Title pages will be prepared in manuscript.

WAR DIARY
or
~~INTELLIGENCE SUMMARY.~~

10th Bn (Erase heading not required.) S W Borderers

Army Form C. 2118.

Place	Date	Hour	Summary of Events and Information	Remarks and references to Appendices
Stoke Farm 27/P.5.c	6/8/17		2/Lieutenant L Gower Williams, 2/Lieutenant W H Evans, Lieutenant H Cottam, 2/Lieutenant H O Jones and Lieutenant H H Davenport (attached 115 Brigade) all wounded. Lieutenant G L Gall, RAMC attached as Medical Officer in charge, was also wounded. Capt C H Morgan was wounded but remained at duty. A draft of 81 men was received today.	
-do-	7/8/17		More roll calls and inspections of kit &c. which were finished during the morning, and the men had the afternoon and evening to themselves.	
-do-	8/8/17		During the morning, kit &c was finally cleaned and inspected by Company Commanders at noon. Owing to shortage of men, Companies were reorganised on a two-platoon basis. Runners, Lewis Gunners &c were paraded under various officers. A medical inspection was held during the day.	

A6945 Wt. W11422/M1160 350,000 12/16 D. D. & L. Forms/C./2118/14.

August. 1917.

Instructions regarding War Diaries and Intelligence Summaries are contained in F. S. Regs., Part II. and the Staff Manual respectively. Title Pages will be prepared in manuscript.

WAR DIARY

or

~~INTELLIGENCE SUMMARY~~

(Erase heading not required.)

10th Bn South Wales Borderers

Army Form C. 2118.

Place	Date	Hour	Summary of Events and Information	Remarks and references to Appendices
Stoke Farm Camp 27, &5.c	9/8/17		Intermixed with Baths, companies were at disposal of Company Commanders, who for the most part utilized the opportunity to make necessary inspections of Paybooks and identity discs. Specialists were under their respective officers	
-do-	10/8/17		The Battalion was inspected by the Brigadier General Commanding the Brigade during the morning, and was drawn up in Battle formation Battalion Mass, at 8.30 am., the Band being in attendance. Dress was Battle order with steel helmets. After the preliminary inspection, the GOC inspected Companies sections &c at work, which was carried out as detailed, and included Gas helmet drill, musketry, Rapid wiring, a demonstration of a platoon attacking a Strong point. Specialists were under their respective officers	
-do-	11/8/17		The usual training was carried out, including musketry and Bombing. Rifle Grenades were also fired as practice. The Attack on a Strong Point was practised in the morning.	
-do-	12/8/17 (Sun)		Divine Services. CE at 10.30 am, NC 11 am RC 10 am. Rifles and bayonets were inspected at 11.45 am. A reinforcement of 4 men arrived, and were posted to Companies	

2449 Wt. W14957/M90 750,000 1/16 J.B.C. & A. Forms/C.2118/12.

·August 1917·

Instructions regarding War Diaries and Intelligence Summaries are contained in F. S. Regs., Part II. and the Staff Manual respectively. Title Pages will be prepared in manuscript.

WAR DIARY
or
~~INTELLIGENCE SUMMARY~~
(Erase heading not required.)

Army Form C. 2118.

10th Bn South Wales Borderers.

Place	Date	Hour	Summary of Events and Information	Remarks and references to Appendices
Stoke Farm 27/[illegible]5c.	13/8/17		Training in accordance with Brigade suggestions was carried out, which included Battalion drill, Company drill, Gas helmet drill, Musketry, fire orders, rapid reorganising and consolidating, bombing, rapid wiring, use of cover, tactical scheme for officers. Specialists were under respective officers. A lecture on fire control was delivered by Company Commanders at 5·30 pm	
-do	14/8/17		Similar training to that carried out yesterday was gone through. Companies were formed on a two-platoon basis and a demonstration was arranged and carried out of 'The Normal Formation for a Company in the Attack'.	
-do	15/8/17		A similar programme of training was again adopted for today's training. Officers & ½ NCOs were engaged on a tactical scheme from 2pm to 2·45 pm.	
-do-	16/8/17		Training as before. Intimation received of the following Honours and awards granted by Corps Commander:- 20405 Sgt J H Williams, 20236 Sgt L G Bull, 20641 Pte J Bevan, 44468 Dr Hales, 20847 L/Sgt Hulbert, 20414 Pte I Watkins, 23148 Pte T Hiscock, 39687 Pte Baker R, 21202 Cpl D J Morgan, 20982 Cpl J James, 21430 Pte Tooke E, 20305 A/Cpl Reece (attd TMB), all awarded MILITARY MEDALS.	
			Notification was received on 20th inst that the Commander-in-Chief had awarded the Military Cross to the following Officers:- Capt & A/Adjt H R E Kenward, 2/Lt D T George, 2/Lt L G Williams, Lt H Coltam.	

2449 Wt. W14957/M90 750,000 1/16 J.B.C. & A. Forms/C.2118/12.

August 1917

Instructions regarding War Diaries and Intelligence Summaries are contained in F. S. Regs., Part II. and the Staff Manual respectively. Title Pages will be prepared in manuscript.

WAR DIARY
or
~~INTELLIGENCE SUMMARY~~
(Erase heading not required.)

10th Bn South Wales Borderers

Army Form C. 2118.

Place	Date	Hour	Summary of Events and Information	Remarks and references to Appendices
Stoke Farm Camp 27/B.5.c	7/8/17		The usual programme of training was carried out during the day, use being made between 2 and 4pm of the Brigade Training Ground west of Saville Row. Aeroplanes of the enemy were busy during the night, and dropped several bombs on Transport lines, inflicting the following casualties – 3 Killed 17 wounded.	
Stoke Farm Camp 27/F.5.c..	8/8/17		After the usual preparations, the Bn left STOKE CAMP at 8am, and marched to INTERNATIONAL CORNER, where, at 9 am they entrained on the Light Railway. Detraining place was ELVERDINGHE, which was reached at 10 am. The Bn then marched to CANAL BANK at B24 b (28 NW) via DAWSONS CORNER, arriving at 12.30 pm. ~~[illegible]~~ Artillery formation was necessarily adopted 200x W of MARENGO HOUSE, on the W side of YPRES - BOESINGHE Road. The Commanding Officer and Company Commanders immediately reconnoitred the old British Front Line Trenches and decided on positions companies should occupy. On their return at 2.30 pm an order was received from Brigade Headquarters that the Battalion was to proceed to CANDLE TRENCH. Dinner was served at 5pm. 2/Lieut Sundy returned at 5.50pm, and reported that CANDLE TRENCH was in a very bad state, and possessed only one good dugout. The Battalion moved away at 7pm and proceeded in Artillery formation to CANDLE TRENCH via Bridge 6$\frac{x}{3}$ and the newly	

2449 Wt. W14957/M90 750,000 1/16 J.B.C. & A. Forms/C.2118/12.

August 1917

Instructions regarding War Diaries and Intelligence Summaries are contained in F. S. Regs., Part II. and the Staff Manual respectively. Title Pages will be prepared in manuscript.

WAR DIARY
or
INTELLIGENCE SUMMARY
10th (S) Bn S. Wales Borderers
(Erase heading not required.)

Army Form C. 2118.

Place	Date	Hour	Summary of Events and Information	Remarks and references to Appendices
Candle Trench			~~made wooden roadway, arriving at 8 pm. However did not take over~~ from the 10th Welsh until they moved forward at 9 pm. Dispositions were as follows:- Bn Hqrs. C8. c.8.6.(28NW) "B" Coy on Right, "C" Coy Centre Coy and "D" Coy on Left. "A" Coy (Carrying Coy) and Headquarters Coy were situated in rear of CANDLE TRENCH. Bombs were drawn from a dump on the side of the road soon after arrival. The vicinity in rear was fairly heavily shelled between 10 pm & midnight. "A" Coy suffered the following casualties:- 1 O.R. Killed 13 O.R. Wounded.	
	19/8/17		Rations etc brought up on pack mules arrived at 2 am. All water and a few rations had been destroyed by shell fire, but another party brought up the deficiencies at 10 am. Work:- Trenches were drained, strengthened & deepened & fire steps were placed in position. The ground had now dried well enough to allow of these improvements being made without difficulty. The G.O.C. visited the C.O. and positions held by the Battn at 1 pm. Battery positions about a mile in rear of the Battn were heavily shelled between 4 pm and 6-30 pm, several ammunition dumps being destroyed,	

2449 Wt. W14957/M90 750,000 1/16 J.B.C. & A. Forms/C.2118/12.

August 1917

Instructions regarding War Diaries and Intelligence Summaries are contained in F. S. Regs., Part II. and the Staff Manual respectively. Title Pages will be prepared in manuscript.

WAR DIARY
or
~~INTELLIGENCE SUMMARY~~
(Erase heading not required.)

10th Batt South Wales Borderers

Army Form C. 2118.

Place	Date	Hour	Summary of Events and Information	Remarks and references to Appendices
Candle Trench	19/8/17		but the remainder of the evening was fairly quiet. Improvements to trenches impossible to carry out in daylight owing to enemy observation, were made at nightfall. Battn Hqrs were screened by a sandbagged wall and trenches were dug leading to Bn Hqrs. Aircraft of both sides were very active throughout the day. B. C & D. Coys were ordered to send one platoon each 150 yds in front of CANDLE TRENCH and dig themselves in by joining up shell holes. This was completed during the night. Dispositions of the Battn were now as follows:- 1 platoon each of B.C & D Coys respectively from Right to Left occupying the line C.2 d.9.1 to C.2.d.1.3. One platoon each of B. C & D Coys from C.8 b.9.8. to C.2.d.½.½. Two platoons of A Coy from C.8 b 77 to C.8.b.47. Hqr Coy - C.8 b.4.7 to C.8.b.1.6. Battn Hqrs at C.8.b 8.8. Four platoons (1 from each Coy) each under an officer were detailed for a working party on the tramway at STRAY FARM - from 8-30 pm to 1 am. Casualty:- 1 O.R. Wounded	

2449 Wt. W14957/M90 750,000 1/16 J.B.C. & A. Forms/C.2118/12.

August 1917

Instructions regarding War Diaries and Intelligence Summaries are contained in F. S. Regs., Part II. and the Staff Manual respectively. Title Pages will be prepared in manuscript.

WAR DIARY
or
~~INTELLIGENCE SUMMARY~~

10th Battn South Wales Borderers (Erase heading not required.)

Army Form C. 2118.

Place	Date	Hour	Summary of Events and Information	Remarks and references to Appendices
	20/8/17		Good weather continued. The artillery of both sides were fairly quiet throughout the morning; but at 3 pm our artillery bombarded the enemy's Front Lines and Communications. The enemy retaliated slightly, directing his fire on the STEENBEEK and on our gun positions behind PILKEM. During the morning the C.O. with the four Coy Commanders and the I.O. reconnoitred the IRON CROSS RIDGE and afterwards proceeded across the STEENBEEK to AU BON GITE (u 28. d. 3. 9). Platoon Commanders and all available 2 - Cos reconnoitred the same positions during the afternoon. Liaison with the 14th Welch Rgt was obtained at AU BON GITE. Aircraft of both sides were active during the morning. Casualty 1 O.R. Wounded	
	21/8/17		Fine weather continues & the ground is drying rapidly. At 3-30 am S.O.S. Signals from our Front Line were observed. Brigade & Artillery Hqrs were immediately warned and the Battn stood to for ½ an hour. There was slight intermittent shelling by both sides throughout the day. One Pack Mule with rations came under shell fire on the way to the Battn. Two mules being killed & one injured. Two stretcher bearers were killed while attending one of the wounded.	

Lambe Lieut

2449 Wt. W14957/M90 750,000 1/16 J.B.C. & A. Forms/C.2118/12.

August 1917

Instructions regarding War Diaries and Intelligence Summaries are contained in F. S. Regs., Part II. and the Staff Manual respectively. Title Pages will be prepared in manuscript.

WAR DIARY

or

~~INTELLIGENCE SUMMARY~~

10th Battn South Wales Borderers (Erase heading not required.)

Army Form C. 2118.

Place	Date	Hour	Summary of Events and Information	Remarks and references to Appendices
Candle Trench	21/8/17		Improvements to dispositions were continued and instruction given on the Lewis Gun. The C.O. attended a Conference at CANAL BANK (E.D.1) at 4-30 pm. Casualties 2 Killed 3 Wounded	
Au Bon Gite	22/8/17		At 4.50 am the division on our right, attacked on a four Battn front, gaining all their objectives. A very heavy barrage was put up by our artillery. The enemy's artillery was very active during the morning. At 9.15 the C.O. & C. Coms with one runner per Coy went to AU BON GITE to reconnoitre positions to be taken over from the 15th Welsh Regiment tonight. Captain W. C. Jones and 2/Lt. Silby proceeded by bus to St Omer to attend a demonstration on "How to attack a hostile machine gun emplacement". At 9pm the Battn to new position in support of the Front Line Battalions, relieving the 15th Welsh. Headquarters were at AU BON GITE a large concrete shelter, that had suffered very little damage from shell fire. Arrived at new positions at 10pm, Relief was complete at 11 pm. Aircraft were particularly active during the day, the weather being very fine. Casualties. Nil	
	23/8/17		~~The Commanding Officer visited all Companies during the morning.~~ Hostile shelling during the day was intermittent, at times very heavy, especially at dawn & dusk. Our artillery carried out a Bombardment during the day, with guns of various calibres, on the enemy's front line, chiefly EAGLE TRENCH, this trench being the most important target. During the day D Coy suffered the following Casualties:- 6 O.R. Killed 12 O.R. Wounded. Total Casualties 7 O.R. Killed 15 O.R. Wounded.	
	24/8/17		Hostile shelling was again intermittent, & mostly directed against the positions of D Coy & Battalion Headquarters, during the morning. The afternoon was comparatively quiet.	

2449 Wt. W14957/M90 750,000 1/16 J.B.C. & A. Forms/C.2118/12.

August 1917

Instructions regarding War Diaries and Intelligence Summaries are contained in F. S. Regs., Part II. and the Staff Manual respectively. Title pages will be prepared in manuscript.

WAR DIARY
or
~~INTELLIGENCE SUMMARY.~~
(Erase heading not required.)

10th South Wales Borderers

Army Form C. 2118.

Place	Date	Hour	Summary of Events and Information	Remarks and references to Appendices
	24/8/17		Our artillery maintained a fairly heavy shelling of EAGLE TRENCH & its rear, throughout the day. All Coys were visited by the C.O. during the morning. Capt Evans and 2/Lt Selby were each in charge of Carrying Parties to transport barbed-wire, screw stakes & bombs, to the front line. Both parties were subjected to heavy shell fire, but suffered few casualties. Rations were brought up along the new Trolley line, and drawn by carrying parties from west of the STEENBEEK. The ration parties also came under heavy shell fire. The enemy appeared to be concentrating his fire on the tracks as marked by tape line. Total Casualties Capt [illegible] (remained at duty) 5 O.R. Wounded.	
	25/8/17		The G.O.C. visited Headquarters at 7am. Hostile shelling was again intermittent throughout the day D Coy receiving most attention. Our artillery was also active. Several of our shells however fell short between the FRONTLINE and the STEENBEEK at different times of the day. At about 12noon C Coy H'qrs were shelled, C.S.M. [illegible] and a [illegible] of the [illegible] being killed. Enemy Aircraft appeared over our lines, flying at a height of about 600ft. They were engaged by our Anti-Aircraft-Mounted Lewis Guns. One of our planes which was however brought down by the enemy, the pilot escaping slightly injured.	
			At 5.30pm concentrated fire was brought to bear on Battn H'qrs - AU BON GITE, two	

A6945 Wt. W11422/M1160 350,000 12/16 D. D. & L. Forms/C./2118/14.

August 1917

Instructions regarding War Diaries and Intelligence Summaries are contained in F. S. Regs., Part II. and the Staff Manual respectively. Title pages will be prepared in manuscript.

WAR DIARY

or

~~INTELLIGENCE SUMMARY.~~

(Erase heading not required.)

10th Batt South Wales Borderers

Army Form C. 2118.

Place	Date	Hour	Summary of Events and Information	Remarks and references to Appendices
Au Bon Gite	25/8/17		direct hit, at least, being obtained by 4.2s, but the Hun concrete withstood the bombardment. Just before & after midnight B Coy HQrs were shelled with gas shells and suffered considerably, Capt H. O. Jones being killed, 2/Lt J. F. Taylor being wounded, 2 O.R. killed 3 O.R. wounded & 4 O.R gassed. The C.O. visited all Coys during the day. R.S.M. Lockie left the Battalion sick. 2/Lt Lewton assumed command of B Coy. The M.O. investigated the wells existing in LANGEMARCK and found that no water could be obtained. A Track was run out by tape from the Aid Post on the STEENBEEK to approximately 100xs of REITRES FARM, and also from the latter place along the mule track to the STEENBEEK. Casualties 5 Killed 12 Wounded. The Commanding Officer visited all Companies, as usual, during the day.	
	26/8/17		Enemy aircraft appeared over our lines at intervals, throughout the morning, usually flying in formations consisting of from 5 to 7 machines. One machine was brought down in our lines. Enemy artillery was fairly quiet throughout the day, but a heavy barrage was dropped to the right of C Coys position U 29.a.25, late in the afternoon. Our artillery shelled EAGLE TRENCH and neighbourhood, and a practice barrage was put on the German front line. Rain began to fall at 8 pm and continued intermittently throughout the night. The ground at once became	

D. D. & L., London, E.C.
(A7883) Wt. W803/M1672 350,000 4/17 Sch. 52a Forms/C/2118/14

August 1917

1

Instructions regarding War Diaries and Intelligence Summaries are contained in F. S. Regs., Part II. and the Staff Manual respectively. Title pages will be prepared in manuscript.

WAR DIARY
or
~~INTELLIGENCE SUMMARY.~~

10th Batt. Border (Erase heading not required.)

Army Form C. 2118.

Place	Date	Hour	Summary of Events and Information	Remarks and references to Appendices
Nr Pilckem Ridge	26/8/17		very muddy. At midnight B & C Coys moved forward to Assembly Position in support of 16th Welsh Regt, who had been detailed to capture part of EAGLE TRENCH & Cemetery (Squares U23 - 24). These Coys came under the orders of the O.C. 16th Welsh and were lined up in their support positions by 1.30 am on 27th inst. Runners Pte [illegible] & W. Knight (to 16th S.W.B.) & Cpls. Kitchen (to 17 R.W.F.) went out with messages under heavy barrage fire. A fatigue party consisting of 1 NCO & 15 men was sent out to dig a Machine Gun Emplacement. A carrying party consisting of 1 Officer & 25 OR carried stores, ammunition, bombs etc. Casualties Capt. W. G. Jones killed Lt Taylor wdd 2 OR killed 4 OR wounded 4 OR gassed.	
	27/8/17		The C.O. visited H'qrs at 8 am. The artillery of both sides were fairly active during the morning. Our artillery commenced its barrage of the enemy's line at 1.53 pm. The 16th Welsh attacked EAGLE TRENCH their first objective but failed to take it. The enemy replied with heavy barrages on our Front and LANGEMARCK - POEL CAPELLE ROAD (C.9) line of STEENBEEK (from C2 & d) PILKEM RIDGE. This barrage was maintained until 5.30 pm, quietened until 7 pm then recommenced with its former intensity, stopping at 8 pm. One Coy of HELEN (15 RWF's) was attached under the orders of the C.O.	

D. D. & L., London, E.C.
(A7883) Wt. W209/M1672 350,000 4/17 Sch. 52a Forms/C/2118/14

August 1917

Instructions regarding War Diaries and Intelligence Summaries are contained in F. S. Regs., Part II. and the Staff Manual respectively. Title pages will be prepared in manuscript.

WAR DIARY
or
~~INTELLIGENCE SUMMARY.~~
(Erase heading not required.)

10th Batt^n South Wales Borderers

Army Form C. 2118.

Place	Date	Hour	Summary of Events and Information	Remarks and references to Appendices
Au Bon Gite	27/8/17		at 1 p.m. A message from Brigade was received at 6-30 pm to be prepared to reinforce the right support Coy of the 11th S.W.B who had suffered heavy casualties from shelling. A Coy was warned to be in readiness. A message was despatched at 7-10 pm to 11th S.W.B asking if they required reinforcements. Two runners (Ptes I. & C. Williams) took this message & returned with the answer through a very heavy barrage at 8-40 pm. The O.C. 11th S.W.B. requested the O.C. to send up two platoons & 2 Officers to support him as soon as possible. This request was complied with & a message sent to Brigade that "A" Coy had been sent to reinforce 11th S.W.B at 8-55 pm under 2/Lt Selby. B & C Coys remained in their original positions & were not utilised during the attack by the 11th Welsh. The enemy obtained 5 direct hits on Batt^n H.Qrs - AU BON GITE, between 3-4 pm & 5pm with 5.9s. Drizzly rain commenced to fall at 1-30 pm & continued throughout the day. The ground developed into a quagmire. Capt Cobb joined from the transport lines & assumed command of "B" Coy. Casualties 3 O.R. killed 7 O.R. wounded.	
	28/8/17		Rain ceased at 4 am & strong wind developed. "C" Coy reported 1 killed 1 wounded & 3 missing during operations in connection with (16th Welsh) HUGE. The enemy artillery were very	

(A7883) Wt. W803/M1672 350,000 4/17 Sch. 52a Forms/C/2118/14
D. D. & L., London, E.C.

August 1917

10th Battn South Wales Borderers

28/8/17 quiet throughout the day excepting between 4·30pm & 5·30pm, when he somewhat heavily shelled the neighbourhood of ALOUETTE FARM (U 29 a 5.2. to U 27. a. 9. 2.) Our artillery was quieter than usual, but maintained a systematic shelling of the enemy's rear lines & strong points. Rations were drawn from terminus of TROLLEY LINE by 25 O.R. from 'D' Coy taken to Battn Hqrs whence they were collected by parties of 1 N.C.O. & 12 men sent from each Coy. Capt Cobb 'B' Coy reported he had lost ~~[illegible]~~ 2 killed & 5 wounded since being attached to 15th Welch HUGE. His Coy headquarters being at U 23. d. 2.5. C. Coy headquarters were situated with C. Coy of 17th R.W.F.s at U 23. C. 60. 75. C. Coy have suffered no casualties since the 25th inst. Both the C.O. & Adjt paid visits to the Companies. At 9pm 'B' & 'C' Coys were placed again under the orders of the C.O. & remained in their same positions, 'B' at U 23. d 30.50 'C' at U 23. C. 60.75. The 15th Welch moved out of the line at 9pm the 17th R.W.F. & 11th S.W.Bs holding the front line. 'A' Coy remained under orders of O.C. 11th S.W.Bs Capt Evans proceeded to establish a forward COMMAND POST at 8·30pm but reported that Capt Cobb was in direct communication with Battn Hqrs from his Coy Hqrs and his remaining at the COMMAND POST, was cancelled.

An 1Bn Cite

August 1917

War Diary

10th Batt South Wales Borderers

Place	Date	Hour	Summary of events & information	Remarks & references
Au Bon Gite	28/8/17		Evening very fine; with bright moon shining. A working party was furnished by 'D' Coy for carrying Ammunition & digging Machine Gun Emplacements. Casualties 1 OR Wnd 1 OR D of W	
	29/8/17		The G.O.C. visited Battn Hqrs and AID POST at 10 am. The enemys artillery operations during the morning were practically NIL. Our artillery maintained a systematic shelling of the enemys lines. The Hun opened up a weak barrage of the line LANGEMARCK-ALOUETTE FARM n.29.a u.20.b.2.6 & AU BON GITE from 12 noon to 1 pm. One runner was wounded severely. Pte Ross (Total casualties to Runners 2 killed 3 wounded) Our artillery opened sleeping, sending thick barrages between 1.55 pm and 5.30 pm on enemys lines near position. Officers of the 13th RWF came to take over our dispositions before relieving us tonight. The Commanding Officer again visited Companies this morning. At 11 pm the enemy began to shell AU BON GITE and the LANGEMARCK-PILKEM road in the vicinity. Shelling ceased at 11-30 pm. The Battalion was relieved by the 13th RWF the latter taking up old positions occupied by 'A' & 'B' Coys & not the forward ~~station~~ positions occupied by them. Relief completed at 2 am on the 30th inst. Casualties 3 OR Wnd.	
Canal Bank C.13.c.15.8 (28.N.W)	30/8/17		The Battn proceeded by Coys to dugouts N of BARD CAUSWAY on CANAL BANK, which were reached between 4.30 am & 5 am. The Battn rested in the dugouts until 1 pm when hot dinners were provided by the Field Kitchens. Orders to leave this position were received & the Battn moved to L2 lines E of DAWSONS CORNER (Hqrs moving at 4.30 pm). All Coys proceeded to ELVERDINGHE	

August 1917.

War Diary

10th. Battn. South Wales Borderers.

Place	Date	Hour	Summary of events & information	Remarks & References
L.2. Lines B.22.d.7.7 (28 N.W.)	30/8/17		to obtain a bath and clean change of clothing. One Company only managed to obtain clean clothing but nobody was bathed. Coys. rejoined at L.2. Lines. The Roll of each Company was called and the strength of the Battn. ascertained to be 10 Offrs. and 202 O.R. Another hot meal was provided at 7 pm.	
	31/8/17		There was no reveille. Breakfast was ready at 9 a.m. Companies called the Roll again, from the Acquittance Rolls. Inspections of Rifles, Lewis Guns & Battle Order Kit during the morning. No Parades were held during the afternoon. Casualties — nil. Total Casualties suffered during operations now known to have been as follows:– Officers. Capt. W.O. Jones. Killed. Capt. J.P.S. Hornsby. Wounded. Capt. S.A. Fearly Wounded (Rem. at Duty) Lt. T.J. Taylor, M.C. Wounded. Other Ranks 21 Killed, 81 Wounded, 4 wounded (Rem. at Duty) 4 died of wounds, 4 gassed. Total 114. In addition, about 50 O.R. went to Hospital "sick" or suffering from apparent "Shell-Shock" during the Operations.	

Decorations. The Corps Commander awarded the Military Medal to the following: 20936 L/Sgt. S.W. Patrick, 20138 Pte. T. Pask. 20846 Pte. T.C. Williams

W. Hoover. Lt. Col. Commdg. 10th S.W.B.

Army Form C. 2118.

10 SWB

Vol 21

Instructions regarding War Diaries and Intelligence Summaries are contained in F. S. Regs., Part II. and the Staff Manual respectively. Title pages will be prepared in manuscript.

WAR DIARY
or
~~INTELLIGENCE~~ SUMMARY.
(*Erase heading not required.*)

Place	Date	Hour	Summary of Events and Information	Remarks and references to Appendices
L.2. B.22.d.7.7 (Sh.28)	1/9/17		At L.2. Bivouac. A German Aeroplane was brought down by Lewis and Machine Gun fire at 11am about ½ mile E. of the bivouac. The pilot was made prisoner but the observer escaped. During the morning Company Commanders supervised their men cleaning up their clothing, kit, equipment and arms, and afterwards inspected them. Arrangements for the use of the Brigade Rifle Range during the afternoon had been made, and "D" Company were sent off to fire. Orders were received at 1.30 pm that all available men were to participate in a "drive" to capture the escaped Hun observer. The Bn. in extended order, stretching from the DAWSON'S CORNER – CHEAPSIDE ROAD on its left, in conjunction with the Guards on the left and the 17th R.W.F. on the right, searched all ground from the ELVERDINGHE – BRIELEN ROAD to CANAL BANK. Then information was received that the German had been captured at BANK FARM – C 24 c. A fatigue party of 1 Off. and 40 O.R. was provided for pushing trucks of R.E. material from BROAD ST. DUMP. Casualties – Nil.	[illegible]
do.	2/9/17		Divine Services were held during the morning. Afterwards there were inspections of all Box Respirators and P.H. Helmets. An enemy long range gun fired on positions	

D. D. & L., London, E.C. (A7893) Wt. W593/M1672 350,000 4/17 Sch. 52a. Forms/C/2118/14

Instructions regarding War Diaries and Intelligence Summaries are contained in F. S. Regs., Part II. and the Staff Manual respectively. Title pages will be prepared in manuscript.

WAR DIARY

~~or~~

~~INTELLIGENCE SUMMARY.~~

(*Erase heading not required.*)

Army Form C. 2118.

Place	Date	Hour	Summary of Events and Information	Remarks and references to Appendices
L.2. B.22 d.7.7 (Sh. 28)	2/9/17 (contd)		near the bivouac intermittently throughout the day. Baths at B.7.3.9.3 were allotted to the Battalion from 2.30 pm to 5.30 pm all men of the Battn bathing. Same fatigues as yesterday. Also a party from D Coy repairing Range at B.23.b.8½.8. There was intermittent bombing by Hun planes during the night. Casualties Nil.	[illegible]
do	3/9/17		Training as follows:- 10 men per Company instructed in Lewis Gun. 4 men per Coy received Signalling Instruction. 3 men per Coy were trained as Runners. Remainder of Battn carried on as follows:- 9am – 10am Physical Training; 10am – 11am Bayonet fighting; 11am to 12.15 pm Musketry; 2pm – 3pm Platoon Drill and Saluting; 3pm to 4pm Rapid Loading [illegible]. The G.O.C. decorated recent	
		6pm	recipients of the M.C. and M.M. in the presence of the remainder of the Battn formed up in a square. The following fatigue parties were provided. 1 offr and 130 O.Ranks carrying ammunition and grenades from MACKENSEN DUMP to the STEENBEEK. Also 1 offr and 40 OR as yesterday. Hun planes were active bombing throughout the night. Casualties:- One OR. killed.	[illegible]
do.	4/9/17		Companies fired in turn on range at B.23.b.8½.8. When not so occupied carried out Training as follows:- 9am – 10am Platoon Drill and Saluting; 10am to 11am	

D. D. & L., London, E.C.
(A7883) Wt. W593/M1672 350,000 4/17 Sch. 52a Forms/C/2118/14

Instructions regarding War Diaries and Intelligence Summaries are contained in F. S. Regs., Part II, and the Staff Manual respectively. Title pages will be prepared in manuscript.

WAR DIARY ~~or INTELLIGENCE~~ SUMMARY.

(*Erase heading not required.*)

Army Form C. 2118.

Place	Date	Hour	Summary of Events and Information	Remarks and references to Appendices
			Ref Sheet 28	
L.2. B.22.d.7.7	4/9/17 (Contd)		Physical Training. 11.15am to 12.15am Musketry, rapid loading and aiming. 2pm to 3pm Rapid Solution Schemes. 3pm to 4pm Guard mounting drill. Lewis gun, Signalling & runners classes were continued. All ammunition was cleaned during the day, and inspected by Company Commanders. The CO visited Transport Lines and Battn Details at A Camp this morning. The Battn relieved the 10th Welsh on Canal Bank. Relief was complete at 8pm. The fatigue party of 1 off. and 40 OR was provided by D Coy. Casualties Nil.	[illegible]
CANAL BANK C.13.c.1½.8.	5/9/17		Battn at Canal Bank in Reserve to Front & Support lines. Dispositions as follows:- Bn Hqrs on W Side at C.13.c.1½.8. A Coy C.13.c.4.9. B C.13.c.4.4. C C.13.a.4.2. D C.13.a.4.1. A fatigue party of ½ Battn furnished by A & B Companies was furnished for work on duckboard track from MALAKOFF to HUDDLESTONE ROAD. The party of 1 off & 40 OR was found by D Coy. A miniature range from E to W Bank of the Canal was in use during the afternoon and evening. Casualties – 2 OR Wounded	[illegible]
do.	6/9/17		Both sides of the CANAL were heavily shelled between 1am and 1.30am. All available NCOs and men received instruction on the Lewis Gun.	

D. D. & L., London, E.C. (A7833) Wt. W803/M1672 350,000 1/17 Sch. 52a Forms/C/2118/14

Instructions regarding War Diaries and Intelligence Summaries are contained in F. S. Regs., Part II. and the Staff Manual respectively. Title pages will be prepared in manuscript.

WAR DIARY
or
~~INTELLIGENCE SUMMARY.~~
(Erase heading not required.)

Army Form C. 2118.

Place	Date	Hour	Summary of Events and Information	Remarks and references to Appendices
			Ref Map Sh 28.	
CANAL BANK C.13.c.15.8	6/9/17 (Sd)		Good use was made of the Rifle Range. The ½ Battn fatigue party was furnished by A and C Coys. 'B' Coy provided men for the Tunneller party. Casualties – 1 O.R. Killed. 7 O.R. Wounded (1 remaining at duty)	[illegible]
do	7/9/17		In a cricket match arranged between Hqrs and 'D' Coy, the latter proved the victors. Firing continued on the Range until orders were received from Brigade at 11 am to cease, as the range was considered to be unsafe for use. Salvage parties were sent out to collect stores, kit and equipment and all the area occupied by the Battn was thoroughly cleared of rubbish. Large fatigue party furnished by C & D Coys. Small party by A Coy. The G.O.C. visited the Battn at 7 pm. Information was received that 215716 Pte S. [illegible] Wright, 20975 Pte Hall J. and [illegible] had been awarded the MILITARY MEDAL. Casualties – nil	[illegible]
do	8/9/17		Instruction on the Lewis Gun was continued, special attention being paid to loading and unloading. Inspections of P.H. Helmets and Box Respirators were held during the afternoon. Orders were received that the Battn was to proceed to the PROVEN Area to-morrow and preparations were accordingly made. Situation quiet throughout the day. Casualties – nil.	

D. D. & L., London, E.C. (A7893) Wt. W503/M1672 350,000 4/17 Sch. 52a Forms/C/2118/14

Instructions regarding War Diaries and Intelligence Summaries are contained in F. S. Regs., Part II, and the Staff Manual respectively. Title pages will be prepared in manuscript.

WAR DIARY or INTELLIGENCE SUMMARY.

(Erase heading not required.)

Army Form C. 2118.

Place	Date	Hour	Summary of Events and Information	Remarks and references to Appendices
			Ref Map Sh 28 & Sh 27	
CANAL BANK C.13.c 1.8 (Sh. 28)	9/9/17		The Battalion left the CANAL BANK at 8.30 am and marched to ELVERDINGHE, entraining there at 11am. Detrained at PROVEN at 11.45 am and marched to PERSIA CAMP at E.16 d 9.5 arriving at 1.30pm. No parades were held but a general clean up was ordered. Casualties nil.	[illegible]
PERSIA CAMP (Sh. 27) E.16.d.9.5	10/9/17		Battn at Persia Camp. Company Stores, equipment and kit were inspected. Baths at COUTHOVE were allotted to the Battn from 10am to 2pm. A draft of 1 officer and 82 O.Ranks joined the Battn today, with the Battn Reserve of 1 officer and 36 O.Ranks from Herzeele. Inter Company cricket matches were arranged for the afternoon. Casualties nil.	[illegible]
do	11/9/17		At 10 am the G.O.C. distributed Military Medals to recent recipients of the honour, the Battn being formed up in mass. Kit inspections followed. Further inter-Company cricket matches were played during the afternoon.	
		4.30pm to 5.30pm	A lantern lecture on "The reading of aeroplane photos" at the Richmond and Kew Church Army Hut, PROVEN, was attended by the C.O. and as many available officers & O.Ranks as possible. Casualties nil.	[illegible]

Instructions regarding War Diaries and Intelligence Summaries are contained in F. S. Regs., Part II. and the Staff Manual respectively. Title pages will be prepared in manuscript.

WAR DIARY

~~or~~

~~INTELLIGENCE SUMMARY.~~

(Erase heading not required.)

Army Form C. 2118.

Place	Date	Hour	Summary of Events and Information	Remarks and references to Appendices
PERSIA CAMP. (Sh. 27) E16 d 9.5	12/9/17		The Battalion left Persia Camp at 8.15 a.m. and proceeded via WATOU to STEENVOORDE (in the EECKE Billetting Area). Billets in farmhouses about ½ mile South of the town were provided.	
STEENVOORDE			Remainder of the day was devoted to a clean up and rest. Casualties nil.	[illegible]
STEENVOORDE	13/9/17		The Battalion left STEENVOORDE at 9.30 a.m. and marched to MORBECQUE via EECKE, St SYLVESTRE and HAZEBROUCK arriving at 1.30 p.m. Billets	
MORBECQUE			in farmhouses ½ mile West of the town were provided. Rifle & feet inspections were held on arrival in new area. Casualties – nil	HWR
MORBECQUE	14/9/17		A party under Major [illegible] M.C. proceeded to the LEPINETTE Sub-sector of the Line to reconnoitre position to be taken over by the Battn. on 16th inst. The remainder of the Battalion left MORBECQUE at 8.30 a.m. and marched via STEENBECQUE Station and	
LA GORGUE			MERVILLE to LA GORGUE, arriving at 4 p.m. Inspections of Rifles and feet were held. On the march the C.O. acted for the 2 i/c who had gone forward with the advance party. Casualty 1 O.R. [illegible]	HWR

D. D. & L., London, E.C. (A7883) Wt. W803/M1672 350,000 4/17 Sch. 52a Forms/C/2118/14

Instructions regarding War Diaries and Intelligence Summaries are contained in F. S. Regs., Part II. and the Staff Manual respectively. Title pages will be prepared in manuscript.

WAR DIARY
or
INTELLIGENCE SUMMARY.
(*Erase heading not required.*)

Army Form C. 2118.

Place	Date	Hour	Summary of Events and Information	Remarks and references to Appendices
			Map Ref Sh. 36.	
LA GORGUE	17/9/17		The Battalion, less Lewis Gunners, left LA GORGUE at 10.30 a.m	
			and marched via ESTAIRES and CROIX du BAC to WATERLANDS SOUTH	
WATERLANDS SOUTH B.20.d.8.7			West of ARMENTIERES, arriving in new area at 4 pm.	
			Inspections of feet and rifles were held. All Lewis Gun	
			teams remained behind, and proceeded to the Front	
			and Subsidiary Lines later, leaving LA GORGUE at 4.15 pm.	
			The C.O. acted for the G.O.C. again. [signature] Lt Col	[initials]

D. D. & L., London, E.C. (A7883) Wt. W80/M1672 350,000 4/17 Sch. 52a. Forms C/2118/14

Instructions regarding War Diaries and Intelligence Summaries are contained in F. S. Regs., Part II. and the Staff Manual respectively. Title pages will be prepared in manuscript.

WAR DIARY
~~or~~
~~INTELLIGENCE SUMMARY.~~
(*Erase heading not required.*)

Army Form C. 2118.

Place	Date	Hour	Summary of Events and Information	Remarks and references to Appendices
WATERLANDS SOUTH B.20.d.8.9 (Sh. 36)	16/9/17		Between 10.30 am and Noon, Companies were at the disposal of their Commanders for the issue of Company Equipment and for the telling off of Posts. An Advance Party left at 3pm. to take over L'EPINETTE Sub-Sector of the Front Line. Remainder of the Battn left at 7.30 pm. for the Line, and relieved the 7th Loyal North Lancs. Relief was completed at 1.15 a.m. Two Companies of the 11th Bn. S.W.B. were stationed in the Subsidiary Line, and came under the orders of the C.O. 10th S.W.B. Casualties nil	
FRONT LINE L'EPINETTE Sub Sector I.3.d.35.70	17/9/17		Battalion in Front Line. L'EPINETTE Sub-Sector. Battn on Right - 7th South Lancs Rgt. On left - 16th Welsh Rgt. Dispositions as follows. H.qrs at I.3.d.35.70. "A" Coy: I.4.b.95.55. B Coy. I.4.b.60.90. C Coy. I.10.c.95.70. D Coy. I.10.c.75.95. Two Companies of 11th S.W.B. in Subsidiary Line. A Fighting Patrol (under Lt. Lindsay) of 10 O.R. left our lines at 3.10 am and returned at 5.10 pm. Discovered that the ground was in good condition, excellent cover being provided by long grass and ditches. No enemy Patrols were seen or heard. Throughout the day operations of both sides were extremely quiet. Work - Maintenance and general cleaning of trenches. Widening Support Line at entrance to PLANK AVENUE. 2 Concertinas and one plain coil were put out in disused trench N. of No. 5 Post & N.E. of No. 6 Post.	

D. D. & L., London, E.C. (A7883) Wt. W809/M1672 350,000 4/17 Sch. 52a Forms/C2118/14

Instructions regarding War Diaries and Intelligence Summaries are contained in F. S. Regs., Part II, and the Staff Manual respectively. Title pages will be prepared in manuscript.

WAR DIARY

~~or~~

~~INTELLIGENCE SUMMARY.~~

(Erase heading not required.)

Army Form C. 2118.

Place	Date	Hour	Summary of Events and Information	Remarks and references to Appendices
			Ref. map. 36.	
L'EPINETTE Sub-sector I.3.d.35.70.	17/9/17 (contd)		40 yards of Apron Fencing were put out in front of Support & Front Lines. 174 yds. put out in front of Supporting Line. A fighting Patrol of 1 Officer & 12 O.Ranks, under 2/Lt Silby, reconnoitred NO MANS LAND between 9.15 pm and 11.15 pm. Enemy neither seen nor heard. Casualties Nil.	[illegible initials]
do	18/9/17		Enemy Artillery was fairly active, about 80 L.H.V. and 20, 4.2 cm. How. Shells falling between our Front & Support Lines. The DISTILLERY at I.4.a.5.9 was shelled by 4.2 cm. Hows. during the morning. A few minnies were fired on HEADQUARTER WALK and SUPPORT LINE. Aircraft inactive. A Patrol of 1 Officer & 11 O.R. under 2/Lt W.J. Williams reconnoitred craters at I.11.c.31.30. Craters found to be unoccupied (10.15 pm to 12.15 am.) A Patrol of 1 officer & 10 O.Ranks under 2/Lt Lundy patrolled NO MANS LAND between I.5.a.55.70 and a point 300 yards left. No enemy were encountered. Casualties - Patrols - Nil. Others 1 O.R. Wounded. Work:- General trench maintenance. 200 yards of wire were put out.	[illegible] [illegible initials]
do	19/9/17		Between 9 am. and 2.30 pm. 4.2 cm How shells were dropped around Battn. H.qrs. at the rate of about 1 every 8 minutes. Very little damage was done. Enemy aircraft fairly active. At 7.30 pm the enemy opened a heavy bombardment on Right	

D. D. & L., London, E.C. (A7883) Wt. W593/M1672 350,000 4/17 Sch. 52a Forms C/2118/14

Army Form C. 2118.

Instructions regarding War Diaries and Intelligence Summaries are contained in F. S. Regs., Part II. and the Staff Manual respectively. Title pages will be prepared in manuscript.

WAR DIARY *or* INTELLIGENCE SUMMARY.

(Erase heading not required.)

Place	Date	Hour	Summary of Events and Information	Remarks and references to Appendices
L'EPINETTE Sub Sector I.3.d.35.70.	19/9/17 (Contd)		Company Front, directing fire particularly on No 1 Post. The bombardment was most intense at 7.55 pm when our S.O.S. was sent up. Shortly afterwards a large party of the enemy estimated at 40 strong attempted to raid this Post. They were beaten off, however by Lewis Guns and rifle fire, and bombs. They did not succeed in entering the Post at any point and secured no identification. The bombardment slackened at 8.20pm and ceased at 8.35pm. One of the enemy was made prisoner, and one dead German was found. Wiring gaps in front of Posts in front & support lines. Improvements to & general maintenance of trenches. Casualties - 1 O.R. Killed 7 O.R. wounded (3 remaining at duty)	[illegible]
do.	20/9/17		There was fairly heavy shelling of Battn. Hqrs. during the morning which ceased when our artillery retaliated. Enemy planes flew over our lines at 3.30 pm, 5 pm and 7 pm. Our aircraft were active throughout the day. 500 yards of wire were put out in front of Forward Posts & Support Line. 76 [illegible] were	

D. D. & L., London, E.C. (A7883) Wt. W593/M1672 350,000 4/17 Sch. 52a. Forms/C/2118/14

Instructions regarding War Diaries and Intelligence Summaries are contained in F. S. Regs., Part II, and the Staff Manual respectively. Title pages will be prepared in manuscript.

WAR DIARY

~~or~~

~~INTELLIGENCE SUMMARY.~~

(*Erase heading not required.*)

Army Form C. 2118.

Place	Date	Hour	Summary of Events and Information	Remarks and references to Appendices
L'EPINETTE Sub-Sector I.3.d.35.70	20/9/17 (Contd)		put out on flanks of Nos 4 & 5 Posts. Other work – General maint. & repair of trenches, strengthening dug-outs and repairing L.G. emplacements. A party 1 offr & 12 Ranks, which had acted as a covering party to a wiring squad, afterwards went out as a Fighting Patrol. Nothing exceptional was encountered in No mans land. Casualties – Nil	[illegible]
do.	21/9/17		Enemy artillery was fairly active during the morning, some 4.2 Hows dropping on the Subsidiary Line at I 4 a 45.50. A cookhouse was destroyed. Three enemy planes flying over enemy front line were engaged by three of our planes. Two of the enemy's were brought down. A fighting patrol of 1 officer and 10 O.Ranks was in No mans land between 10.30 pm. & 12.15 am (22nd inst.) but none of the enemy was encountered and nothing unusual observed. Work – 350 yards of 'double apron' were put out, & 270 yds of single apron. The task of strengthening the line by the provision of better trenches was continued. Casualties 1 O.R. D of W.	[illegible]
do.	22/9/17		Enemy artillery shelled Left Coy. Front and rear areas intermittently, mostly with L.H.V. but fired little on the remainder of the sector.	

D. D. & L., London, E.C. (A7883) Wt. W5o7/M1672 350,000 4/17 Sch. 52a Forms C/2118/14

WAR DIARY
or
INTELLIGENCE SUMMARY.
(Erase heading not required.)

Army Form C. 2118.

Instructions regarding War Diaries and Intelligence Summaries are contained in F. S. Regs., Part II. and the Staff Manual respectively. Title pages will be prepared in manuscript.

Place	Date	Hour	Summary of Events and Information	Remarks and references to Appendices
L'EPINETTE Sub-sector I.3.d.35.70	22/9/17 (contd)		A few "minnies" were fired on the Support line (Centre Coy) but did no damage to the trench. Our artillery fired on suspected enemy T.M. emplacements between 8.40 am and 10.30 am and remained fairly quiet for the remainder of the day. The constant presence of our air patrols accounts for the days enemy aerial inactivity. Work – 350 yards of double apron fencing were put out in front of Subsidiary Line. 50 yards of wire & 20 gooseberries were put out on the flanks of Nos. 4 & 5 posts; and 20 gooseberries were put out on the left of No. 6 Post. Also general maintenance & repair of trenches. Clearing & repairing LOTHIAN AVENUE and JAPAN AVENUE. A Fighting Patrol of 1 officer and 10 O.Ranks went out reconnoitring No Man's Land from 10 pm to midnight. Heavy machine gun bursts were fired on the Patrol but no casualties were incurred. Casualties for the day – Nil.	[illegible]
do.	23/9/17		Excepting for two periods – from 2 pm to 2.30 pm, and from 3 pm to 4.30 pm when CHAPELLE-D'ARMENTIERES was shelled with 4.2 cms, the enemy's artillery was very quiet. At frequent intervals throughout	

D. D. & L., London, E.C. (A7883) Wt. W803/M1672 350,000 4/17 Sch. 52a Forms/C/2118/14

Instructions regarding War Diaries and Intelligence Summaries are contained in F. S. Regs., Part II. and the Staff Manual respectively. Title pages will be prepared in manuscript.

WAR DIARY ~~or~~ ~~INTELLIGENCE~~ SUMMARY.

(*Erase heading not required.*)

Army Form C. 2118.

Place	Date	Hour	Summary of Events and Information	Remarks and references to Appendices
L'EPINETTE Sub Sector I.3.d.35.70	23/9/17 (contd)		the day our Heavies fired on PREMESQUES. Enemy aircraft were active especially at about 7pm when 20 machines appeared over our lines flying at a great altitude. A fighting patrol consisting of 1 officer and 12 other ranks reconnoitred in No Man's Land between 10pm and midnight. Nothing unusual occurred. Work - General maintenance of trenches. The task of levelling LOTHIAN AVENUE and linking up with No.1 Post was completed. Casualties:- Nil.	[illegible]
do.	24/9/17		There was slight intermittent shelling, mostly with 4.2's on our Front & Support Lines between 9am and 4pm. Our artillery registered during the afternoon in direction C.29.d.00.25. Aircraft of both sides were fairly active throughout the day. The Battalion was relieved by the 11th. Bn. A.&S.H. who took over the Front and Support Lines. "C" & "D" Companies of the Battalion moved into the Subsidiary Line and came under the orders of O.C. 11th A&SH. Battn. H.Qrs. and A and B. Compan	

D. D. & L., London, E.C. (A7883) Wt. W803/M1672 350,000 4/17 Sch. 52a Forms/C/2118/14

Instructions regarding War Diaries and Intelligence Summaries are contained in F. S. Regs., Part II. and the Staff Manual respectively. Title pages will be prepared in manuscript.

Army Form C. 2118.

WAR DIARY ~~or~~ ~~INTELLIGENCE~~ ~~SUMMARY.~~

(*Erase heading not required.*)

Place	Date	Hour	Summary of Events and Information Ref. map Sheet 36.	Remarks and references to Appendices
	24/9/17		moved to THE LAUNDRIES ERQUINGHEM. Relief completed at 9 pm Casualties - Nil.	H.R.K.
THE LAUNDRIES ERQUINGHEM H.5.a.4.7	25/9/17		Battn Hqrs, A & B Companies at ERQUINGHEM. The Commanding Officer inspected all available NCOs and men at [illegible]. A platoon from A Company was detailed to be in readiness to move away at 5 minutes notice for the protection of ARMENTIERES. A fatigue party of 1 off. and 40 OR. was provided for cable burying in ARMENTIERES. Casualties Nil	H.R.K.
do.	26/9/17		Baths near Battn Headquarters were in use by the Battn. between 8 am. and 5 pm. "C" and "D" Companies were relieved by platoons from A & B Companies for the purpose of letting available N.C.O.s and men received instruction under Company arrangements. Fatigue party as yesterday was provided. Official intimation was received that the Corps Commander had awarded the MILITARY MEDAL to 21240 L/c. T. Edmunds; 40341 L/c. J Taylor and 42449 Pte. G. E. Dover for conspicuous	

D. D. & L., London, E.C.
(A7883) Wt. W803/M1672 350,000 4/17 Sch. 52a. Forms/C/2118/14

Army Form C. 2118.

Instructions regarding War Diaries and Intelligence Summaries are contained in F. S. Regs., Part II, and the Staff Manual respectively. Title pages will be prepared in manuscript.

WAR DIARY ~~or~~ ~~INTELLIGENCE SUMMARY.~~

(*Erase heading not required.*)

Place	Date	Hour	Summary of Events and Information	Remarks and references to Appendices
			Ref Map 36.	
LAUNDRIES ERQUINGHEM			gallantry during the enemy raid on the 19th inst. Casualties: nil	JWBH
do. H.5 a.4.7	27/9/17		Training under Battalion arrangements was carried on to-day on the Brigade Training Ground. The same fatigue party of 1 off. and 40 O.R. was provided. Casualties: nil	JWBH
do	28/9/17		All Headquarter Details, Lewis Gunners and the worst shots of "A" and "B" Companies fired on the Range, on Brigade Training Ground. Those not using the Range carried on with training under Battalion arrangements. A successful concert was held at Hqrs. this evening. The cable-burying fatigue party was not sent out. The C.O. visited the two Companies in Subsidiary Line. Casualties: nil	JWBH
do.	29/9/17		All available N.C.Os. and men paraded at 7.30 a.m. and proceeded to the Range at H.8 b.20.32. which was made use of until 12 noon. A platoon from "B" Company relieved a platoon from the Subsidiary Line – the latter Platoon having been selected to attend the First Course at the newly formed Brigade School	

D. D. & L., London, E.C. (A7883) Wt. W593/M1672 350,000 4/17 Sch. 52a Forms/C/2118/14

Army Form C. 2118.

Instructions regarding War Diaries and Intelligence Summaries are contained in F. S. Regs., Part II. and the Staff Manual respectively. Title pages will be prepared in manuscript.

WAR DIARY ~~or~~ ~~INTELLIGENCE SUMMARY.~~

(*Erase heading not required.*)

Place	Date	Hour	Summary of Events and Information Ref Map 36.	Remarks and references to Appendices
LAUNDRIES ERQUINGHEM H.5.a.4.7	29/9/17 (contd)		A fatigue party of 1 officer and 80 O.Ranks was required to-night for cable burying. Casualties nil.	JWBH
do.	30/9/17		An empty hostile Observation Balloon was found intact at H.11.b.90.90 this morning having probably broken loose and come ~~down~~ down during the night. A guard was placed on it until it was deflated and taken away at 10 a.m. Available N.C.Os & men continued with training according to Battalion programme. The usual fatigue party was provided. Casualties nil.	JWBH
			1/10/17 [signature] Major Commanding 10th Battn South Wales Borderers	

D. D. & L., London, E.C. (A7883) Wt. W593/M1672 350,000 4/17 Sch. 52a Forms C/2118/14

Instructions regarding War Diaries and Intelligence Summaries are contained in F. S. Regs., Part II. and the Staff Manual respectively. Title pages will be prepared in manuscript.

WAR DIARY or ~~INTELLIGENCE SUMMARY.~~

(Erase heading not required.)

Army Form C. 2118.

10 S.W.B.

Vol 22

Place	Date 1917.	Hour	Summary of Events and Information	Remarks and references to Appendices
			Reft up. Sheet 36.	
ERQUINGHEM THE LAUNDRIES. 4.5.a.0.7	1/10/17		Training was carried out in accordance with Battalion Programme, "A" Company and Headquarters firing on the Range. In addition to the fatigue party of Sappers and [illegible] required for Cable-burying, all available men were sent to ARMENTIERES to patrol the streets in search of supposed enemy Huns. Casualties - Nil	[illegible]
do	2/10/17		No parades were ordered, but Companies cleaned up generally and made all necessary arrangements for move to the Front Line to-night, detailing Posts &c. The Battalion left THE LAUNDRIES at 6.15 pm. and proceeded to take over as follows:- "D" Coy. Left Coy. Hqrs. at I.4.b.95.95. "B" Coy. Centre Coy. Hqrs. at I.10.b.60.90. "A" Coy. Right Coy. Hqrs. at I.10.c.95.55. "C" Coy. in Support. Hqrs. at I.10.c.75.95. Battn. Headquarters at I.3.d.35.70. Relief was complete at 8.5 pm. Work:- Strengthening parapets at Posts Nos. 1, 2, 3, 9, 11 and 12. Clearing debris in PLANK AVENUE. 6 Coils of wire fence was put out. Casualties - Nil	[illegible]

(A7883) Wt. W593/M1672 350,000 4/17 Sch. 52a Forms/C/2118/14
D. D. & L., London, E.C.

Army Form C. 2118.

WAR DIARY
or
~~INTELLIGENCE SUMMARY.~~
(Erase heading not required.)

Instructions regarding War Diaries and Intelligence Summaries are contained in F. S. Regs., Part II. and the Staff Manual respectively. Title pages will be prepared in manuscript.

Place	Date	Hour	Summary of Events and Information	Remarks and references to Appendices
			Ref. Map. Sh. 36.	
Front Line L'EPINETTE SUB-SECTOR I.3.d.35.70	3/10/17		Both our own and the enemy's artillery were very quiet throughout the day. We retaliated when the enemy shelled CHAPELLE D'ARMENTIERES. Aircraft inactive owing to poor visibility. Work – Repairing and improving Posts. General maintenance of trenches. 95 coils of wire and 40 Gooseberries were put out in front of Posts. A Patrol, consisting of 1 off. and 9 OR left I.5.c.6.6. at 9.5 pm & worked in a N.E. direction. The Patrol returned at midnight having encountered none of the enemy. Casualties – nil	[illegible]
do.	4/10/17		The enemy fired a few 5.9s and L.H.V.s on CHAPELLE D'ARMENTIERES at 10.30 am, and 10 rounds of 4.2s on Cross roads at I.9.c.35.55. Our artillery fired occasional bursts of 20 rounds on various targets. Aircraft activity practically nil. Work:– General improvement of all posts i.e. repairing parapets, fixing new fire steps &c. A new Company Hqrs. is being constructed in HEADQUARTER WALK, and a new officers' cook-house in PORTUGAL AVENUE. A Reconnoitring Patrol was out from 9 pm to 11.30 pm. examining the ground in the area of L'EPINETTE SALIENT. Casualties nil	[illegible]

D. D. & L., London, E.C. (A7883) Wt. W809/M1672 350,000 4/17 Sch. 52a Forms C/2118/14

Instructions regarding War Diaries and Intelligence Summaries are contained in F. S. Regs., Part II. and the Staff Manual respectively. Title pages will be prepared in manuscript.

WAR DIARY ~~or INTELLIGENCE SUMMARY.~~

(*Erase heading not required.*)

Army Form C. 2118.

Place	Date	Hour	Summary of Events and Information	Remarks and references to Appendices
Front Line L'EPINETTE SUB-SECTOR I.3.d.35.70			B Company of the 4th Batt. 5th Provisional Bde C.E.F. were attached to the 10th S.W.B. for instruction in the line. One platoon each was attached to "A" "B" and "D" Companies. A Coy of the C.E.F. were attached the the 16th Welch Regt. — on our Right.	MWS
do.	5/10/17		Enemy fired on JARRY AVENUE and Support line from PORT EGAL AVE to VAUXHALL AVE with L.H.V. The fire of our artillery was active all day. Three hostile planes which attempted to cross our lines between 8am & 11am were driven back by our A.A. guns. Our aircraft were very active. Machine gun and Trench Mortar fire was normal. Work — general trench maintenance. Reclamation of AUCKLAND — VAUXHALL C.T. was commenced under R.E. supervision. 134 Coils of wire were put out. A patrol of one officer and 9 O.Ranks left at I.5.a.50.65 at 10.15pm to reconnoitre NO MAN'S LAND. A party of the enemy was encountered & there was quick exchange of rifle and revolver fire. The enemy soon retreated to his lines, & search was made for	

D. D. & L., London, E.C. (A7883) Wt. W803/M1672 350,000 4/17 Sch. 52a Forms/C/2118/14

Instructions regarding War Diaries and Intelligence Summaries are contained in F. S. Regs., Part II. and the Staff Manual respectively. Title pages will be prepared in manuscript.

WAR DIARY
~~or~~
~~INTELLIGENCE SUMMARY.~~
(Erase heading not required.)

Army Form C. 2118.

Place	Date	Hour	Summary of Events and Information Ref map Sh 36.	Remarks and references to Appendices
Front Line L'EPINETTE I.3.d.35.70			any enemy dead or identification that may have been left. But none was found. Enemy party was estimated to be between 30 and 40 strong. Our party returned at 1.55 pm. Casualties – nil.	[illegible]
do.	6/10/17		Enemy fired at intervals a few 5.9s into our Front & Support Line, & shelled back areas later in the day. Two enemy planes flew over our lines at low altitude between 8 am and 10 am. They were fired on by L.Gs & M.G. Our aircraft were inactive. There was very little T.M. and ordinary M.G. fire. Work:- General maintenance of trenches. Work on LOTHIAN AVE, VAUXHALL - AUCKLAND C.T. and JAPAN AVENUE was continued with. 150 Coils of wire and 50 gooseberries were put out. A patrol of 1 Offr and 9 O.Rs reconnoitred No Man's Land. Nothing exceptional occurred. Casualties nil	[illegible]

D. D. & L., London, E.C. (A7883) Wt. W803/M1672 350,000 4/17 Sch. 52a. Forms C/2118/14

Army Form C. 2118.

WAR DIARY
or
~~INTELLIGENCE SUMMARY.~~
(Erase heading not required.)

Instructions regarding War Diaries and Intelligence Summaries are contained in F. S. Regs., Part II, and the Staff Manual respectively. Title pages will be prepared in manuscript.

Place	Date	Hour	Summary of Events and Information	Remarks and references to Appendices
Front line L'EPINETTE SUB-SECTOR I.3.d.35.70	7/10/17		Between 9-0 am and 12 noon the DISTILLERY was shelled intermittently. Our artillery fired all the morning in the direction of WEZ MACQUART. Aircraft of both sides quiet excepting between 9 am & 10 am. T.Ms, R.Gs and M.Gs were quiet. Between 2 am and 2.30 am flashes from a clear white lamp were observed coming from an ENE direction. Work – General trench maintenance. 120 coils of wire were put out in front of Posts and 20 gooseberries were also put out in front of No 21 Post. A Patrol of 1 officer and 9 O.Ranks reconnoitred in NO MANS LAND. None of the enemy was seen. The attached Portuguese Troops were relieved in the line this evening, "C" & "D" Coys. relieving "A" and "B" Coys. Battalion Hqrs. of the C.E.P. became attached to Battn Hqrs. 10th S.W.B. Casualties – Nil.	[illegible]

D. D. & L., London, E.C.
(A7883) Wt. W803/M1672 350,000 4/17 Sch. 52a Forms/C/2118/14

Army Form C. 2118.

WAR DIARY
or
INTELLIGENCE SUMMARY.
(*Erase heading not required.*)

* Instructions regarding War Diaries and Intelligence Summaries are contained in F. S. Regs., Part II. and the Staff Manual respectively. Title pages will be prepared in manuscript.

Place	Date	Hour	Summary of Events and Information	Remarks and references to Appendices
			Ref map. Sheet 36.	
Front Line. LEPINETTE SUB-SECTOR I.3.d.35.70	8/10/17		Batt. in Front Line. Visibility was very poor and both artillery and aircraft were inactive. A heavy rain began to fall at 6 pm. The Battalion was relieved in the front line by the 11th. S.W.B. this evening. "A" and "B" Companies and one Platoon of "C" Company became attached to the 11th. S.W.B. and were quartered in the Subsidiary Line. The remainder of the Battn. proceeded to the LAUNDRIES, ERQUINGHEM. Relief was complete at 8 pm. [illegible]	Lt Col Harvey took over command of the 11th Bde School on returning from leave. [illegible]
THE LAUNDRIES ERQUINGHEM H.5.a.4.7.	9/10/17		A general clean up was ordered until 11.30 am. The C.O. inspected all available N.C.O.s and men in Battle Order at 12 noon. Fatigue parties of 3 officers and 100 O.Ranks were provided. [illegible]	[illegible]
do	10/10/17		Batt. Hqrs, "A" Coy. and part of "C" Coy. at ERQUINGHEM. "A" & "B" Coys. and one Platoon of "C" Coy. attached to 11th. S.W.B. in the Line. All from last nights fatigue were resting during the day. Fatigue parties of 2 officers and 80 O.Ranks	

D. D. & L., London, E.C.
(A7883) Wt. W593/M1672 350,000 4/17 Sch. 52a Forms/C/2118/14

Army Form C. 2118.

WAR DIARY
or
INTELLIGENCE SUMMARY.
(*Erase heading not required.*)

Instructions regarding War Diaries and Intelligence Summaries are contained in F. S. Regs., Part II. and the Staff Manual respectively. Title pages will be prepared in manuscript.

Place	Date	Hour	Summary of Events and Information Ref Map H.36.	Remarks and references to Appendices
THE LAUNDRIES ERQUINGHEM			were provided for Cable burying. Casualties nil	HRK
H 5 a 4 7	11/10/17		Dispositions similar. Available men from Headquarters were engaged upon trench digging, the trench being required for practice purposes at the Brigade School. Fatigue parties as yesterday were provided. Casualties nil	HRK
do.	12/10/17		Dispositions similar. The trench digging was continued and the usual night fatigue parties furnished. Casualties nil	HRK
do.	13/10/17		Dispositions similar. Details paraded for inspection by the C.O. at 11 a.m. The usual fatigue parties were provided. Intimation was received that the Commander-in-Chief had awarded the MILITARY CROSS to 2/Lt. F. S. Silby for gallantry during the recent attempted raid on one of our front line posts. Casualties nil	HRK
do.	14/10/17		Dispositions similar. Divine services were held for C, D and Headquarter Companies. Afterwards kits were inspected by the Commanding Officer. "A" and C Companies moved to the	

D. D. & L., London, E.C. (A7883) Wt. W603/M1672 350,000 4/17 Sch. 52a Forms/C/2118/14

Army Form C. 2118.

WAR DIARY ~~or~~ ~~INTELLIGENCE SUMMARY.~~

(*Erase heading not required.*)

Instructions regarding War Diaries and Intelligence Summaries are contained in F. S. Regs., Part II, and the Staff Manual respectively. Title pages will be prepared in manuscript.

Place	Date	Hour	Summary of Events and Information	Remarks and references to Appendices
THE LAUNDRIES ERQUINGHEM H.5.a.4.7	14/10/17 (Contd.)		Front line and came under the orders of O.C. 11th S.W.B. "B" Company (from the Subsidiary Line) and "D" Company were attached for training to the 115th. Brigade School at the LAUNDRIES, ERQUINGHEM. Battn. Hqrs. remained at the LAUNDRIES. Casualties:- 2 O.R. wounded.	J.R.H.
do.	15/10/17		Dispositions as follows:- Batt. Hqrs. at "The Laundries". "A" and "C" Companies in Front Line. "C" and "D" Companies at Brigade School. Baths at "the Laundries" were made use of by Batt. Hqrs., "B" & "D" Companies from 8 a.m. to 12 noon. Spare men from Hqrs. continued digging practice trenches, whilst "B" & "D" Companies commenced training under the direction of Lt. Col. Harvey, during the afternoon. Casualties:- Nil.	J.R.H.
do.	16/10/17		Dispositions similar. Trench digging by Hqrs. and training of "B" and "D" Companies were continued with. Casualties 1 O.R. wounded.	J.R.H.
do.	17/10/17		Dispositions similar. The working party, composed of Band, Signallers, Drums paraded at 6 a.m. to dig a bombing pit for the	

D. D. & L., London, E.C. (A7883) Wt. W803/M1672 350,000 4/17 Sch. 52a Forms/C/2118/14

Instructions regarding War Diaries and Intelligence Summaries are contained in F. S. Regs., Part II. and the Staff Manual respectively. Title pages will be prepared in manuscript.

WAR DIARY
or
~~INTELLIGENCE SUMMARY.~~
(*Erase heading not required.*)

Army Form C. 2118.

Place	Date	Hour	Summary of Events and Information	Remarks and references to Appendices
			Ref Map Sh. 36	
THE LAUNDRIES ERQUINGHEM	17/10/17 (contd)		Brigade School. B and D Companies carried on with special training. Casualties – nil.	[illegible]
do	18/10/17		Dispositions similar. Between 11 am and 12 noon Headquarters relieved Headquarters of 11th S.W.B. in the line. The four Companies of 11th S.W.B. and A and C Companies of 10th S.W.B. came under the orders of Major Rees. Dispositions as follows – "C" Coy. (10th) Left Front I.4 b 95 75. A Coy (10th) Centre Front I.10 b [illegible] "D" Coy (11th) Right Front I.10 c 95 95. "A" Coy (11th) Support Coy I.10 c 75 95	
FRONT LINE L'EPINETTE SUB-SECTOR I.3 d 35 70		x	"B" & "C" Coys of 11th S.W.B. in the Subsidiary Line. Between 12 noon and 4.30 pm our artillery fired 150 rounds on various targets. Armentieres was fairly heavily shelled during the afternoon. Aircraft of both sides active. A Patrol went out to examine enemy wire at I.11.a Casualties – nil.	[illegible]
do.	19/10/17		Dispositions similar. Our Artillery fired on FRELINGHEM, CENTRAL SUPPORT and CENTRAL SWITCH, TRAMWAY DRIVE and SWITCH, and CENSORS NOSE. The enemy lightly shelled ARMENTIERES and HOUPLINES. Aircraft were active. Our T.Ms	[illegible]

D. D. & L., London, E.C.
(A7883) Wt. W593/M1672 350,000 1/17 Sch. 52a Forms/C/2118/14

WAR DIARY ~~or INTELLIGENCE SUMMARY.~~

Army Form C. 2118.

Instructions regarding War Diaries and Intelligence Summaries are contained in F. S. Regs., Part II. and the Staff Manual respectively. Title pages will be prepared in manuscript.

(*Erase heading not required.*)

Place	Date	Hour	Summary of Events and Information	Remarks and references to Appendices
			Ref Map No 36.	
FRONT LINE L'EPINETTE SUB-SECTOR I.32 [illegible]	19/10/17		fired on enemy wire and new work. Work – general maintenance and repair of trenches. Improving drainage. A party was furnished for cable burying under supervision of Brigade Signalling Officer. 130 coils of wire were put out. A patrol left our lines at I.[illegible] to examine NO MANS LAND. "D" Company 1st Battalion C.E.F. were attached to the front line Companies for training, from to-night to the 25th inst. Casualties nil.	JRH
do.	20/10/17		Dispositions similar. Our Artillery were chiefly engaged in providing covering fire for T.M.s who were destroying enemy's wire and firing on new work. The enemy fired about 200 rounds on various targets chiefly [illegible] and [illegible]. Our planes were active. 10 enemy planes crossed our lines between 7.30 am & 4 pm. Work:- General maintenance & repair of trenches. The Subsidiary line is being strengthened by the addition of a revetted parados. A patrol left our lines to examine enemy wire. Two prisoners, one an acting officer, were taken at I.16.b. at 5.45 am. They were two of a patrol of 3 seen outside our wire. The 3rd escaped. Casualties:- nil	JRH

D. D. & L., London, E.C. (A7883) Wt. W503/M1672 350,000 1/17 Sch. 52a. Forms/C/2118/14

Instructions regarding War Diaries and Intelligence Summaries are contained in F. S. Regs., Part II. and the Staff Manual respectively. Title pages will be prepared in manuscript.

Army Form C. 2118.

WAR DIARY or ~~INTELLIGENCE~~ SUMMARY.

(Erase heading not required.)

Place	Date	Hour	Summary of Events and Information	Remarks and references to Appendices
			Ref. map. Sheet 36.	
FRONT LINE L'EPINETTE SUB-SECTOR T 5 d 35 70	21/10/17		Dispositions similar. Artillery fairly active on both sides. Enemy planes continually patrolled over our front during the afternoon. They were engaged by A.A. and M.G. fire. Our aircraft were active throughout the morning. A direct hit by a "minnie" was obtained by the Hun [illegible] to [illegible] Post at 9.30 a.m. Our T.M. battery fired on enemy's wire, causing considerable damage thereto. Work: general maintenance of trenches. 120 coils of barbed wire and 30 gooseberries were put out. A fighting patrol of 1 officer and 10 Ranks left our lines at 8 pm. Nothing of importance was seen or heard. B and D Coys of 10th R.I.R. relieved A and D Coys of 11th R.I.R. during the evening. Casualties nil.	[illegible]
do	22/10/17		Dispositions similar except that "B" and "D" Companies occupy Centre and Right Front Sections respectively. Our artillery were chiefly engaged in retaliation, and firing on enemy T.M. The enemy paid most attention to C.22.b, firing 130 rounds (4.2 and 77 mm)	

D. D. & L., London, E.C. (A7893) Wt. W593/M1672 350,000 4/17 Sch. 52a. Forms/C/2118/14

Instructions regarding War Diaries and Intelligence Summaries are contained in F. S. Regs., Part II. and the Staff Manual respectively. Title pages will be prepared in manuscript.

WAR DIARY ~~or~~ ~~INTELLIGENCE SUMMARY.~~

(*Erase heading not required.*)

Army Form C. 2118.

Place	Date	Hour	Summary of Events and Information — Map Ref. No 36	Remarks and references to Appendices
FRONT LINE LEPINETTE SUB-SECTOR I.3.d.35.70	27/10/17 (contd)		Between 3pm and 4.30 pm. Our T.Ms were much more active than the enemy's. Our aircraft were active, but only two enemy planes were seen throughout the day. A fighting patrol left our lines at C.3.a.15.20, but no enemy were encountered. The days work consisted of the usual trench maintenance, and wiring round Posts. Casualties – Nil	[illegible]
do.	28/10/17		Dispositions similar. Our Artillery was fairly active firing on various targets including LA PROVOTE Cross Roads CENSOR FARM. The enemy fired intermittently throughout the day mostly on our forward positions. Aircraft of both sides was quiet. T.M. and M.G. fire was normal. A reconnoitring patrol left our lines at I.11.a.0.5. Nothing exceptional was seen or heard. Work – Improvements to drainage, and general upkeep of trenches. 125 Coils of wire were put out. Casualties – Nil	[illegible]

D. D. & L., London, E.C. (A7883) Wt. W803/M1672 350,000 4/17 Sch. 52a Forms/C/2118/14

Instructions regarding War Diaries and Intelligence Summaries are contained in F. S. Regs., Part II, and the Staff Manual respectively. Title pages will be prepared in manuscript.

WAR DIARY ~~or~~ ~~INTELLIGENCE SUMMARY.~~

(*Erase heading not required.*)

Army Form C. 2118.

Place	Date	Hour	Summary of Events and Information — Ref Map Sh 36.	Remarks and references to Appendices
FRONT LINE. L'EPINETTE SUB-SECTOR I 11 d 35 70	24/10/17		Dispositions similar. Our artillery fired on various targets throughout the day. The enemy shelled ARMENTIERES heavily in the neighbourhood C 26 c + d and C 27 b firing 400 rounds of 10.5 cms between 9 am and 12 noon. Aircraft activity was above normal. An indecisive combat took place between two of our planes and five enemy. Our L.T.M. fired 100 rounds on a strong point at I 5 d 6 5. 40 minnie dropped in the neighbourhood of PLANK AVENUE. General maintenance and improvements to trenches were continued. A reconnoitring patrol left our lines at I 11 a 0 4. Nothing unusual occurred. Casualties as follows were caused by a direct hit by a 'minnie' on one of our F.L. Posts. 1 O.R. killed 3 O.R. wounded.	[illegible initials]
	25/10/17		Dispositions similar. FRELINGHIEN received a large amount of attention between 2.30 and 3.30 pm and our artillery fired on numerous other targets. Harassing fire was kept up during the night on enemy wire at I 11 a + b. The enemy fired 50 gas shells on CAMBRIDGE AVENUE at about 10.30 a.m. but no casualties were	

D. D. & L., London, E.C. (A7883) Wt. W593/M1672 350,000 1/17 Sch. 52a Forms/C/2118/14

Army Form C. 2118.

Instructions regarding War Diaries and Intelligence Summaries are contained in F. S. Regs., Part II, and the Staff Manual respectively. Title pages will be prepared in manuscript.

WAR DIARY or INTELLIGENCE SUMMARY.

(*Erase heading not required.*)

Place	Date	Hour	Summary of Events and Information	Remarks and references to Appendices
			Ref Map Sh. 36.	
FRONT LINE L'EPINETTE SUB-SECTOR (contd) I.11.d.35.70	25/10/17		moved. Aircraft were inactive. Work – maintenance and repair of trenches. Wiring around the front line posts was continued with. Casualties – nil	[illegible]
do	26/10/17		Dispositions similar with the exception that "C" Company are now left Company in the subsidiary line, having been relieved yesterday by "C" Company of 11th S.W.B. Harassing fire was directed by our artillery on various targets (including enemy wire) throughout the day. The enemy fired intermittently, chiefly on our forward area. Aircraft of both sides were inactive. A Patrol left our lines [illegible] to ascertain damage done to enemy wire by our artillery and T.M. fire. No enemy were encountered. Casualties – nil.	[illegible]
do	27/10/17		Dispositions similar. Headquarters were relieved by Hqrs 11th S.W.B. during the morning, relief being completed by noon, when O.C. 11th S.W.B. took over command of L'EPINETTE SUB-SECTOR. Hqrs. moved to the LAUNDRIES, ERQUINGHEM. Casualties – nil	[illegible]

D. D. & L., London, E.C. (A7893) Wt. W803/M1672 350,000 4/17 Sch. 52a Forms/C/2118/14

Army Form C. 2118.

WAR DIARY
or
INTELLIGENCE SUMMARY.
(*Erase heading not required.*)

Instructions regarding War Diaries and Intelligence Summaries are contained in F. S. Regs., Part II. and the Staff Manual respectively. Title pages will be prepared in manuscript.

Place	Date	Hour	Summary of Events and Information	Remarks and references to Appendices
			Ref Map Sheet 36	
LAUNDRIES ERQUINGHEM H.5.a.4.7	28/10/17		Dispositions as follows:- Batt. Hqrs at Laundries, ERQUINGHEM. "A" and "C" Companies in Support and Subsidiary Lines (L'EPINETTE) respectively. "B" and "D" Companies, Centre and Right Front Companies, respectively. Divine Services were held this morning at the Laundries. "B" Coy. suffered two casualties to-day - 1 O.R. Killed and 1 O.R. wounded.	JBR
do.	29/10/17		Dispositions similar. All available men of Headquarters were engaged on trench digging under orders of Brigade School. "A" and "C" Companies were relieved to-night by two Companies of 11th. S.W.B. and moved from the Line to the Laundries, where they came under orders of 115th. Brigade School. Casualties nil.	JBR
do	30/10/17		Dispositions as follows. Batt. Hqrs., "A" and "C" Companies at the LAUNDRIES. "B" and "D" Companies in the Line under orders of 11th. S.W.B. All available men of "Hqrs" were again employed on trench digging, whilst "A" and "C" Companies were given the morning in which to clean up, and were inspected by the Commandant during afternoon. The Brigade Gas Officer afterwards	

D. D. & L., London, E.C. (A7883) Wt. W593/M1672 350,000 1/17 Sch. 52a. Forms/C/2118/14

Army Form C. 2118.

Instructions regarding War Diaries and Intelligence Summaries are contained in F. S. Regs., Part II. and the Staff Manual respectively. Title pages will be prepared in manuscript.

WAR DIARY or INTELLIGENCE SUMMARY.

(Erase heading not required.)

Place	Date	Hour	Summary of Events and Information	Remarks and references to Appendices
			Ref. map. Sh 36.	
LAUNDRIES ERQUINGHEM			inspected their box respirators. Casualties - nil.	JWBH
H.5. a 4 7	31/10/17		Dispositions similar. The two 'school' companies and available men of Hqrs. were engaged on trench digging this morning and afternoon. Casualties: nil	JWBH
			[signature] Major Commanding 10th S.W.B.	

D. D. & L., London, E.C. (A7834) Wt. W209/M1672 350,000 4/17 Sch. 52a Forms/C/2118/14

Operation Orders No. 10A. by Major. A.T.Rees. [illegible]
Commanding HANGAR.

13.10.1917.

1. A. and C. Companies less L. Guns will relieve B. and C. Companies of HASTEN in the Front Line L'EPINETTE SUBSECTOR on the night 14/15th October and will be under the direct orders of O. C. HASTEN for this tour of duty in the Trenches.

2. Dispositions:-

Centre Company.	A. Company.
Left Company	C. do.

3. A. Company will move forward from SUBSIDIARY LINE at 7.30.p.m.

4. O.C. C. Company will take precautions that his Company does not pass East of a Line drawn North and South through H.6.b.0.9. before 7.pm.

5. Os. C. A. and C. Companies will tell their men off by Posts before proceeding to the front line. Intervals of 100 yards between parties of 16 men will be maintained.

6. D. Company will remain in their present billets.

7. On Completion of relief with Company of Hasten B. Company will march off by parties of 30 with intervals of 100 yards and take over Brigade School Billets at the Laundry.

8. All Trench Stores, Permanent Working Parties, Defence Schemes and all information relating to the Line will be taken over and receipts passed. Receipts will also be obtained for cleanliness of Dugouts etc, All receipt s will be rendered to Battalion Headquarters by 10.a.m. 15th inst.

9. Lewis Guns. The Lewis Gun Teams of A. and C. Companies will relieve the Lewis Gun teams of B. and C. Companies Hasten under arrangement s to be made between the L. G. Officer Hasten and Sgt. Beavan. Relief to be complete by 12.noon 14th Octr with the exception of One L.G. team of Hasten and one L. G. Team of C. Company Hangar who will report at Bn. Hqrs Hasten at 3.30.p.m. marching off from Brigade School at 2.p.m.

10. Transport. A. Companies Officers Valises. B. Company's Officers Valises, Mess kit or L. G. Ammunition will be at SQUARE FARM AT 5.p.m. ready for removal by the Transport Officer.

11. Rations. A. Company's Rations and Lt. Mercer's Platoon Rations of C. Company will go up in the usual way, remainder of C. Coys Rations will be delivered at present billets by 4.p.m. 14th inst and will be carried up by the men to the front line. Headquarters & B. and D. Companies rations will be delivered at Support Bn. Headqrs.

12. Taking Over. One Officer and 2. N.C.Os each of A. and C. Coys will proceed to the front line to take over on the afternoon of the 14th in[illegible]

13. Completion of relief will be reported to Battalion Hqrs. in Code.

14. ACKNOWLEDGE.

(Signed.)
F. A. [illegible] Heyward.
Capt. and Adjutant.

Issued at 6.p.m.

Copies:-
1. File.
2. O.C. Hasten.
3. O.C. A. Coy. Hangar.
4. O.C. B. " "
5. O.C. C. " "
6. O.C. D. " "
7. Lt. D.P.Mercer.
8. Hearty.
9. T.O. and Qmr.
10. RSM.
11. Officer i/c Hqrs.

Operation Orders No.12a by Major E.T.Rees M.C.,
Commanding Hangar and Hasten.

Copy No. 8

S E C R E T. October 18th.1917.

1. "D" Company, 1st Battalion, C.E.P. will be attached to these Units from the 19th.October for six days in the Line.

2. Officers Commanding "A" "B" and "C" Companies of Hasten will detail one Officer and One N.C.O from their respective companies to report at The Factory at B.30.a.7.0. (Sheet 36) at 5.30.p.m. 19th.instant, to conduct platoons of "D" Company, 1st.Bn.C.E.P. up to their positions in the Subsidiary and Support Lines.

3. Dispositions will be as follows:-

No.1 Platoon, "D" Co. 1st.Bn.C.E.P. attached "A" Co.Hasten.
No.2 Platoon, "D" Co. 1st.Bn.C.E.P. attached "B" Co.Hasten.
No.3 Platoon, "D" Co. 1st.Bn.C.E.P. attached "C" Co.Hasten.

4. Company Commanders will ensure that guides are ready at Company Headquarters to conduct C.E.P. to their respective positions, so as to avoid any crowding at Company Headquarters.

5. All Officers' kit, Camp kettles, baggage etc. of "D" Co. 1st.Bn. C.E.P. will be carried up to the Line from the Factory by men of that company detailed by the Company Commander.

6. O.C."B" Company Hasten will have attached to him the Company Commander of "D" Co. 1st.Bn.C.E.P., as well as the Platoon Officer. Os.C."A" and "C" Companies, Hasten, will accommodate Platoon Officers of Nos.1 and 3 platoons of "D" Co.1st.Bn.C.E.P. respectively.

7. These platoons will be rationed up to ~~and including~~ the night of the 20th.instant, after which they will be rationed by Hangar.

8. Officers Commanding companies concerned will ensure that Ration Parties are detailed to draw the attached platoons' rations from the Dump each evening.

9. The code word "COMPLETE" will be sent by wire when the C.E.P. are in position.

10. ACKNOWLEDGE.

(Signed) F.R.E.Kenward.
Captain and Adjutant.
HANGAR.

Copy No.1. Commanding Officer.
2. O.C."A" Co.Hasten.
3. O.C."B" Co.Hasten.
4. O.C."C" Co.Hasten.
5. O.C."D" Co.Hasten.
6. O.C."A" Co.Hangar.
7. O.C."C" Co.~~Hasten~~. Hangar
8. 115 Brigade.
9. R.S.M. Hangar.
10. T.O & Q.M. Hangar.
11. File.

10th SWB

Army Form C. 2118.

Instructions regarding War Diaries and Intelligence Summaries are contained in F. S. Regs., Part II, and the Staff Manual respectively. Title pages will be prepared in manuscript.

WAR DIARY
~~or~~
~~INTELLIGENCE SUMMARY.~~
(*Erase heading not required.*)

Vol 23

Place	Date	Hour	Summary of Events and Information (Ref Map. Sh 36.)	Remarks and references to Appendices
LAUNDRIES ERQUINGHEM H.5.a.4.7	1/11/17		Dispositions as follows:- Batt. Hqrs, "A" "B" & "C" Companies at the Laundries ERQUINGHEM. D Company in the Subsidiary Line L'EPINETTE under orders of 11th SWB. A B & C Companies were training for the proposed forthcoming raid; whilst available men of Headquarters were employed on digging and improving the model of the Hun trenches that were to be raided. An inter-platoon football match was played during the afternoon. Casualties - Nil.	
do	2/11/17		Dispositions similar. Training similar to yesterday's was continued with. Patrols from training companies were sent out to reconnoitre No Man's Land and gaps in enemy's wire. Casualties: Nil. A rehearsal of the attack was made to-night on the prepared training ground.	
do	3/11/17		Dispositions similar. Training was continued. Three Patrols were sent to reconnoitre No Man's Land. One of these was fired on by M.Gs and we suffered the following casualty:- One OR wounded.	

D. D. & L., London, E.C. (A7883) Wt. W593/M1672 350,000 4/17 Sch. 52a Forms C/2118/14

WAR DIARY

Ref map Sh 36.

Place	Date	
LAUNDRIES ERQUINGHEM H.5.a.4.7 FRONT LINE L'EPINETTE I.3.d.80.85	4/11/17	Dispositions similar. Battalion Hqrs. relieved Hqrs. of 11th SWB., the command of ~~the~~ L'EPINETTE SUB-SECTOR passing to OC. 10th SWB at 3 p.m. Dispositions now as follows:- Batt Hqrs. at I 3 d 80.85.; A, B & C. Companies at Brigade School ERQUINGHEM; C 11th Left Front Hqrs. I 4 b 95.95; B 11th Centre Front Hqrs. I 4 b 60.90; D 11th, Right Front Hqrs. I 10 c 95.95; A 11th Reserve Coy. Hqrs. I 4 c 75.95; D 10th in Subsidiary Line. A and B Coys. 17th Battn [illegible] were attached for training. Between 10.30 pm and 11 pm. and again from 11.30 pm. to 11.45 pm. there was a gas bombardment over practically the whole of the Battalion front, the neighbourhood of BUTTERNE FARM, the DISTILLERY, Left Subsidiary Line and Battalion Headquarters being heavily and continuously shelled. About 100 gas T.Ms. were also sent over. Our artillery fired in retaliation. Three Patrols were sent out to reconnoitre NO MANS LAND and examine gaps in enemy wire. One was unsuccessful owing to M.G. fire and bombing by the enemy. Work:- general trench maintenance. Excavating for dug-out under R.Es. at BUTTERNE FARM. Casualties:- 4 O.R. gassed.
do.	5/11/17	Dispositions similar. Enemy ~~activity~~ was rather quiet. Our artillery fired throughout the day on INCANDESCENT TRENCH and on wire in I 11 a. Only one plane seen throughout the day. M.Gs. and T.Ms were quiet. Four patrols went out at different times during the night to examine enemy wire, especially in neighbourhood of INCANDESCENT TRENCH. None of the enemy

Ref. map. Sh. 36. WAR DIARY

Place	Date	Summary	Remarks
FRONT LINE. – L'EPINETTE – 1.3.d.80.85.	5/11/17 (contd)	were encountered, excepting a dead body. Identifications were obtained from it. Work:- General trench maintenance - chiefly clearing and improving drains. 50 men were provided for burying cable in BUTTERNE LANE. Parties were also provided for carrying R.E. material and T.M. ammunition. Casualties:- two O.R. wounded one accidentally. An officer from the American Expeditionary Force was attached to this Battn. for instruction.	J.R.W.
do.	6/11/17	Dispositions similar. The enemy's artillery was active throughout the day. Our batteries in front of ARMENTIERES were shelled. Our activity was greatest between 11 a.m. and 3.30 p.m. when we fired on enemy's line and wire. Aircraft of both sides inactive. Our T.M's shot at enemy wire, and M.Gs. kept up harassing fire on gaps throughout the night. 3 Patrols were sent out to examine enemy wire and to reconnoitre NO MANS LAND. No enemy were encountered. Work:- Draining and improving trenches and posts. Night work was interfered with by inter-Company reliefs. "D" Coy. 10th. S.W.B. relieved "B" Coy. ~~11th~~ 11th. S.W.B. "A" and "C" Companies of 11th. S.W.B. exchanged positions. Casualties:- Nil.	J.R.W.
do.	7/11/17	ARMENTIERES was shelled between 2 p.m. and 3.20 p.m. The enemy's wire and trenches in I.11.a. were shelled throughout the day. One of our planes appeared at 7.15 a.m., and one enemy plane flew low over our lines at 2.15 p.m. No other appearance. Our 6" T.M.s. fired on enemy front line and wire between 12 noon and 3 p.m.	

WAR DIARY

Place	Date	Entry	
FRONT LINE – L'EPINETTE – 13.d.8.5	7/11/17 (contd.)	Patrols were sent out at once after dusk to see if enemy wire in I.11.a had been completely destroyed. Work. – General maintenance of trenches and drainage system. Carrying R.E. material and T.M. ammunition. Casualties – nil.	[illegible]
do.	8/11/17	Dispositions similar. We made a successful raid on the enemy's front and support lines during the early hours of the morning. "A", "B" & "C" Companies who had completed their training at the Brigade School, assembled in our front line, in accordance with the pre-arranged scheme, at midnight. At 1.30 a.m. aided by our artillery which put a heavy barrage on enemy front line, our men gallantly led by Capt. W.T. Cobb began the attack. As soon as our barrage lifted to enemy's support trenches, our troops dashed forward and easily passing over enemy's wire (which had been systematically destroyed by our artillery and T.Ms during the past few days) they entered the enemy trenches and killed or captured any huns who had withstood our artillery fire. Soon our T.Ms, M.Gs and artillery put a box barrage around our objective. The enemy's trenches and dug-outs were thoroughly searched. The latter were afterwards destroyed by the R.Es. who successfully exploded ~~Bangalore torpedoes~~ mobile charges in the concrete shelters. We captured 14 prisoners and killed at least 50 huns. Seven of our gallant lads were killed and	

WAR DIARY.

Ref map. Sh. 36.

Place	Date	Summary of Events	
FRONT LINE EPINETTE I. 3. d. 80. 85.	8/11/17 (contd).	48 wounded. 5 officers (including Capt Cobb, who remained at duty) were also wounded. The operation successfully accomplished, the three Companies returned to the Brigade School. Throughout the remainder of the day the situation was unusually quiet. Two patrols were sent out to reconnoitre NO MANS LAND, one at 7.30 pm. and the other at 10.30 pm. Nothing exceptional occurred. Work:- General maintenance of trenches, building parados in SUBSIDIARY LINE and carrying R.E. material.	JRSM
do	9/11/17	Dispositions similar. Enemy artillery was active, his special targets being PLANK AVENUE, the DISTILLERY, ARMENTIERES and SQUARE FARM. Our guns were engaged in counter-battery work, and fired twice during the afternoon in retaliation for enemy T.M. fire. An enemy wiring party was successfully dispersed at 7.30 pm. Our aircraft were active during the afternoon. T.Ms. were quiet, and M.G. fire was chiefly directed against enemy aircraft. Three patrols left our lines at I. 11. a. 00. 60., I. 5. c. 30. 30 and I. 10. b. 94. 30 respectively. "D" & "B" Companies, 11th. S.W.B., changed positions immediately after "Stand down" this evening. Work:- Repairing damage at No. 2 Post and in CENTRAL AVENUE, General maintenance of trenches, repairing duck-boards &c, carrying R.E. material. One OR. wounded. Casualty	JRSM

W.A.R. DIARY

Place	Date	Summary of Events	Remarks
FRONT LINE. – L'EPINETTE – I.3.d.80.85	10/11/17	Dispositions similar except that "B" Coy. 11th S.W.B. are now Right Front Company and "D" Company are in Subsidiary Line. Enemy artillery was very quiet. Our field artillery fired on INCANDESCENT TRENCH during afternoon. Salvoes were fired between 5 pm. and 5.30 pm. and again at 6.30 pm. in retaliation for enemy T.M. shooting, which was directed on front line, FORT EGAL FARM and Centre Company Headquarters. Our M.Gs. and T.Ms. also retaliated. Work:- General maintenance of trenches. A fighting patrol of 1 officer and 9 other Ranks went out at 3.30 am. The two Companies of Portuguese troops, who had been in the line for training, moved out immediately after "Stand-down." Later, A B C Companies, 10th S.W.B., relieved "A", "B" and "C" Companies 11th S.W.B. Casualties – Nil.	JWBH
do.	11/11/17	Dispositions as follows:- "C" Coy, Left Front; "D" Coy, Centre Front; "A" Coy, Right Front. "B" Coy, Support Coy; two Companies of 16th Welsh Regt. in Subsidiary Line under orders of O.C. 10th S.W.B. Enemy ~~activity~~ artillery showed more than usual activity throughout the day. From 10 a.m. to 11.30 a.m. the road in I. 9. a. and b., the DISTILLERY and the sector on the left were heavily shelled with 4.2s and heavy shrapnel. The CHAPELLE D'ARMENTIERES Road, PLANK AVENUE and FOCKABER DUMP received considerable attention during the afternoon. Our artillery was much less active. Howitzers fired	

WAR DIARY

Place	Date	Summary of Events and Information	Remarks
FRONT LINE. – L'EPINETTE – I.3.d.80.85.	11/11/17 (contd.)	during the afternoon. Enemy aircraft were much more active than our own, one unusually large plane dropping six bombs on the road in I.15.a. M.G. and T.M. fire was normal. Work:- General trench maintenance, carrying R.E. material and burying cable. Three Patrols were sent to reconnoitre NO MANS LAND. An enemy patrol was sighted and dispersed by rifle fire. Casualties:- Nil.	JRBR
do	12/11/17	Dispositions similar. Between 7.45 a.m. and 8.40 a.m. the enemy put a barrage of 4.2's and 77mm on the left front support and subsidiary lines. No infantry action of any sort followed & little damage was done. Enemy artillery was also active throughout the day, the chief targets being WILLOW WALK, ARMENTIERES and CHAPPELLE D'ARMENTIERES. Our guns fired on various targets, dispersing a working party at 11.30am. M.G. and T.M. fire was normal. Our planes were active morning and afternoon but enemy machines were only seen during the morning. Work – General repair & maintenance of trenches. Building parados for Subsidiary line is still being continued. The usual R.E. carrying parties & cable burying party were provided. A patrol went out from our lines at I.5.1. No enemy were encountered. Casualties – Nil.	JRBR

Instructions regarding War Diaries and Intelligence Summaries are contained in F. S. Regs., Part II. and the Staff Manual respectively. Title pages will be prepared in manuscript.

WAR DIARY

or

~~INTELLIGENCE SUMMARY.~~

(Erase heading not required.)

Army Form C. 2118.

Place	Date	Hour	Summary of Events and Information	Remarks and references to Appendices
			Ref Map Sh 36	
FRONT LINE – L'EPINETTE I.3.d & 8.5 –	13/11/17		Dispositions similar. Enemy artillery activity was below normal but at 10pm, 11.15pm and after midnight the SUBSIDIARY LINE, SUPPORT LINE and CHAPPELLE D'ARMENTIERES were heavily shelled with Gas and 77mm. The gas shelling was intense but only lasted a short time. Helmets had to be worn for two hours. Our guns fired at intervals on enemy front and support lines. There was no unusual M.G. or T.M. fire. A thick mist rendered patrolling difficult. Parties left our lines at I.10.a and C.29.1 Nothing exceptional was seen or heard. Work:- General maintenance and repair of trenches. Improving "wire" around front line Posts. The two Companies of 11th Bn continued building parados in SUBSIDIARY LINE and furnished Cable burying party. Casualties - 2 O.R. w/a	Major E.J. Rees M.C. proceeded to UK on Leave. Major A.L. Bowen took over Command of the Battn. [initials]
do.	14/11/17		Dispositions similar. The Centre Company was shelled with 77mm and 5.9s during afternoon. ARMENTIERES and HOUPLINES also received some attention. Our artillery activity was below normal, chief targets being INCANDESCENT TRENCH and FRELINGHEM. M.G. and T.M. fire was normal. A thick mist rendered aircraft observation useless. A patrol which went out to reconnoitre the Railway Embankment was heavily bombed but suffered no loss. Work: General trench maintenance. Draining trenches. Building parados in SUBSIDIARY LINE. Casualties - nil.	[initials]

A7092). Wt. W12839/M1293 750,000. 1/17. D. D & L. Ltd. Forms/C2118/14.

Instructions regarding War Diaries and Intelligence Summaries are contained in F. S. Regs., Part II. and the Staff Manual respectively. Title pages will be prepared in manuscript.

WAR DIARY

or

~~INTELLIGENCE SUMMARY.~~

(*Erase heading not required.*)

Army Form C. 2118.

Place	Date	Hour	Summary of Events and Information (Ref map Sh. 36.)	Remarks and references to Appendices
FRONT LINE. – L'EPINETTE – I.3.d.80.85	15/11/17		Dispositions similar. Between 3.0 a.m. and 4.0 a.m. there was a general gas shelling of the line, necessitating the donning of respirators in several parts. Enemy artillery showed greater activity than usual throughout the day. Enemy planes flew persistently, observing the effect of the Huns fire. Our guns fired on CENSOR and CHASTOL FARMS, hostile T.M.s and on FRELINGHEM by night. Our M.G.s were actively engaged with enemy planes throughout the day. 7 of our planes crossed enemy lines during the day, but no aerial fights took place. Enemy T.M.s fired on our Centre Company and on PORT EGAL FARM. Our patrols reconnoitred in front of INCANDESCENT TRENCH and the TWIN CRATERS. None of the enemy were encountered. Work:– Usual trench maintenance, building parados in SUBSIDIARY LINE and carrying R.E. material and T.M. ammunition. Casualties Nil	JRM
do	16/11/17		Dispositions similar. Artillery was quiet throughout the morning, but the enemy shelled WESSEX AVENUE PLANK AVENUE and trenches in C.22.a., C.22 and C.17. Three of our planes flew low over the enemy's lines at intervals. The Battalion, less Lewis guns, was relieved in the Front Line by the 11th. S.W.B. Batt. Hqrs. moved to H.5.b.8.7 – West of ARMENTIERES. The four Companies moved to the SUBSIDIARY LINE. 'A' and 'D' occupying Right and Left positions	

A7092). Wt. W12839/M1293 750,000. 1/17. D. D & L. Ltd. Forms/C2118/14.

Instructions regarding War Diaries and Intelligence Summaries are contained in F. S. Regs., Part II. and the Staff Manual respectively. Title pages will be prepared in manuscript.

WAR DIARY
or
INTELLIGENCE SUMMARY.
(Erase heading not required.)

Army Form C. 2118.

Place	Date	Hour	Summary of Events and Information	Remarks and references to Appendices
			Ref Sheet 36	
ARMENTIERES H.5.b.8.7	16/11/17 (contd)		respectively in L'EPINETTE sub. sector and coming under the orders of O.C. 11th S.W.B.; whilst 'B' and 'C' Companies took up Left and Right positions respectively in the HOUPLINES sub. sector, and came under the command of O.C. 16th Welsh Regt. Relief was completed by 8pm. Casualties:- Nil.	[illegible]
ARMENTIERES. H.5.b.8.7	17/11/17		Dispositions as follows:- Batt. Hqrs. at H.5.b.8.7. 'A' and 'D' Companies in SUBSIDIARY LINE, L'EPINETTE. 'B' and 'C' Companies in SUBSIDIARY LINE - HOUPLINES. The Commanding Officer (Major Bowen) inspected Hqr. Company's equipment at 11am. after the men had cleaned up. Lewis Gun teams were relieved & joined their Companies. Casualties:- Nil.	[illegible]
do.	18/11/17		Dispositions similar. Divine services were attended by all available NCOs and men of Hqrs, the Church of England service being held at the LAUNDRIES. Casualty: One other rank gassed.	[illegible]
do.	19/11/17		Dispositions similar. The Co. attended as president of a F.G.C.M. There was an inspection of small kit by the Adjutant this morning. Signallers received special instruction. Casualties:- Nil.	[illegible]

A7092). Wt. W12839/M1293 750,000. 1/17. D. D & I. Ltd. Forms/C2118/14.

Instructions regarding War Diaries and Intelligence Summaries are contained in F. S. Regs., Part II. and the Staff Manual respectively. Title pages will be prepared in manuscript.

WAR DIARY
or
~~INTELLIGENCE SUMMARY.~~

(Erase heading not required.)

Army Form C. 2118.

Place	Date	Hour	Summary of Events and Information Ref Map Sh 36.	Remarks and references to Appendices
ARMENTIERES H.5.b.8.7	20/11/17		Dispositions similar. The Commanding Officer inspected Headquarter Coy in Battle Order at 10.30 am. Signallers again received special instruction in view of forthcoming classification tests. During shelling of the left sector Subsidiary Line, we suffered the following casualties:- 2 O.Ranks killed and 1 O.R. wounded.	JRBH
do	21/11/17		Dispositions similar. Our artillery retaliated effectively on hostile T.M.s and fired on various targets, chiefly CENSUS TRENCH and Reserve. Our Companies in the SUBSIDIARY LINE received attention from enemy guns both morning and afternoon, but no casualties were incurred. Headquarter Company cleaned up and prepared for move to the line tomorrow. Casualties:- Nil.	JRBH
do	22/11/17		Dispositions similar. At 12 noon "A" and "B" Companies commenced relief of the Right and Centre Front Companies of 11th S.W.B. On completion of this relief, "C" & "D" Coys. moved, by half companies to the Left and Support Coys. respectively, relieving the other two Coys. of 11th S.W.B. Batt. Hqrs moved from billets at 3 p.m. and relieved Hqrs. of 11th S.W.B. Relief was complete at 6 p.m. There was little artillery activity after dark. At 11.30 p.m.	

A7092). Wt. W12839/M1293 750,000. 1/17. D. D & L. Ltd. Forms/C2118/14.

Instructions regarding War Diaries and Intelligence Summaries are contained in F. S. Regs., Part II. and the Staff Manual respectively. Title pages will be prepared in manuscript.

WAR DIARY
or
INTELLIGENCE SUMMARY.
(Erase heading not required.)

Army Form C. 2118.

Place	Date	Hour	Summary of Events and Information	Remarks and references to Appendices
			Ref map. Sh 36.	
FRONT LINE. L'EPINETTE 13.d.80.85	22/11/17 (contd)		an enemy patrol was seen approaching our Right Post near PEAR TREE FARM. Accurate L.G. fire was directed and shrieks were heard. Later a patrol of ours went out and the body of a dead German officer was brought in. No further trace of the enemy could be found. Casualties:- Nil	JRSH
do.	23/11/17		Dispositions as follows:- Batt. Hqrs. 13.d.80.85. 'A' Coy. Right Front. I.10.c.95.55. 'B' Coy. Centre Front. I.10.b.60.90. 'C' Coy. Left Front. I.10.b.75.95. 'D' Coy. Support Coy. I.10.c.75.95. This morning our 6" Hows. carried out a shoot on FRELINGHEM. Our guns also fired on hostile T.Ms and shelled in retaliation when called for. Enemy artillery was active all day, shelling our communication trenches, and also firing on HOUPLINES, DISTILLERY and ARMENTIERES. T.M. and M.G. fire was normal. Our aircraft were active all day. Seven planes crossed the enemy's lines at 10.30 am. A patrol which went into No Mans Land at dusk, recovered the body of a German who had been seen close to our wire and shot at daybreak this morning. Casualties:- 2 O.Ranks wounded.	JRSH
do.			Dispositions similar. Shortly before 5 a.m. the enemy bombarded our front and support lines in I.5.a and C.29.c with guns of	

A7092. Wt. W12839/M1293 750,000. 1/17. D. D & L. Ltd. Forms/C2118/14.

Instructions regarding War Diaries and Intelligence Summaries are contained in F. S. Regs., Part II. and the Staff Manual respectively. Title pages will be prepared in manuscript.

WAR DIARY

~~or~~

~~INTELLIGENCE SUMMARY.~~

(*Erase heading not required.*)

Army Form C. 2118.

Place	Date	Hour	Summary of Events and Information	Remarks and references to Appendices
			Ref. map. Sh 36.	
FRONT LINE. L'EPINETTE 1.3.d. 80.85	24/11/17		all calibres, M.Gs and TMs co-operating. Our old unoccupied Front Line in I 5 a seemed to be the principal enemy target. A small party was believed seen approaching the old Front Line. Upon S.O.S. being sent up, our guns opened promptly. Enemy bombardment slackened at 6.0 am. and ceased at 6.30 am. No infantry action accompanied the shelling, and a patrol which went out found no trace of the enemy afterwards. We suffered the following Casualties:- Lt. A. Lowe and 1 O.Rank killed. 6 other ranks wounded, and 3 other ranks wounded, remaining at duty. Artillery of both sides was quiet for the remainder of the day. Aircraft inactivity probably due to the misty atmosphere, which rendered observation almost impossible. A patrol went out at dusk and scoured the area of the enemy's intended raid. A German stretcher, five small white flags, a large number of stick bombs and 3 mobile charges were found. There was no hostile activity in No Man's Land.	JRBR
do.	25/11/17		Dispositions similar. Our artillery carried out a destructive shoot on INANE DRIVE and fired on CENSOR and CELL trenches.	

A7092). Wt. W12839/M1293 750,000. 1/17. D. D & L. Ltd. Forms/C2118/14.

Instructions regarding War Diaries and Intelligence Summaries are contained in F. S. Regs., Part II. and the Staff Manual respectively. Title pages will be prepared in manuscript.

WAR DIARY
or
~~INTELLIGENCE SUMMARY.~~

(Erase heading not required.)

Army Form C. 2118.

Place	Date	Hour	Summary of Events and Information	Remarks and references to Appendices
			Ref. map Sh. 36	
FRONT LINE L'EPINETTE 13.d.80.85	25/11/17 (contd)		The enemy displayed only slight artillery activity. One of our planes was seen early this morning, and one of the enemy's appeared at 3 pm.; but there was no further activity. MGs. directed harassing fire on INANE DRIVE and CIRCUS LANE. T.M. fire was normal. Work – General maintenance and cleaning of drains and trenches. Strengthening the SUBSIDIARY LINE by adding a strong parados, carrying R.E. material etc. and improving wire of front line Posts. Casualties. Nil	JRSM
do	26/11/17		Dispositions similar. Our artillery shelled enemy trenches at intervals during the day, and directed harassing fire on INANE DRIVE by night. The enemy actively shelled our trenches in I.9.a.&b., the DISTILLERY and ARMENTIERES. Three enemy planes which flew over our lines particularly low were actively engaged by our M.Gs and L.Gs. Our planes were active all the afternoon, one dropping bombs on hostile trenches. Two patrols went out to reconnoitre No man's Land. There was no hostile activity. Work – Maintenance and repair of trenches, cleaning drains, improving SUBSIDIARY LINE. Wiring front line Posts. Casualties:– 1 OR ~~k~~ wd.	JRSM

A7092). Wt. W12839/M1293 750,000. 1/17. D. D & L Ltd. Forms/C2118/14.

Instructions regarding War Diaries and Intelligence Summaries are contained in F. S. Regs., Part II. and the Staff Manual respectively. Title pages will be prepared in manuscript.

WAR DIARY
or
INTELLIGENCE SUMMARY.

(*Erase heading not required.*)

Army Form C. 2118.

Place	Date	Hour	Summary of Events and Information	Remarks and references to Appendices
			Ref. Map. Sh. 36.	
FRONT LINE L'EPINETTE – 13 d 80 85 –	27/11/17		Dispositions similar. Enemy artillery activity was below normal. The SUBSIDIARY LINE was shelled during the day and a few gas shells were fired into CHAPELLE D'ARMENTIERES. Our guns shelled INANE, CENTURY and CENSUS DRIVES, and retaliated for enemy T.M. fire. Three of our planes were flying throughout the day, but only one enemy machine was seen. Our M.Gs. fired intermittently on enemy trenches. A great deal of movement was observed in the neighbourhood of PREMESQUES. Work – maintenance of trenches & improvements to drainage. Carrying R.E. material and T.M. ammunition. Improving wire around our Posts. A patrol was sent out to reconnoitre No Mans Land. No enemy activity was observed. Casualties:– Nil.	[illegible]
do.	28/11/17		Dispositions similar. There was no unusual activity during the morning. At 10 am. the relief of the Battalion from the Front Line commenced. Two companies at a time were relieved by the 11th SWB., the relieved companies moving to positions in the SUBSIDIARY LINE formerly occupied by 16th Welsh Regt. The 17th RWF. then relieved our companies in the SUBSIDIARY LINE & the Battalion moved to the LAUNDRIES, ERQUINGHEM. Relief was	

A7092). Wt. W12839/M1293. 750,000. 1/17. D. D. & L. Ltd. Forms/C2118/14.

Instructions regarding War Diaries and Intelligence Summaries are contained in F. S. Regs., Part II. and the Staff Manual respectively. Title pages will be prepared in manuscript.

WAR DIARY
~~or~~
~~INTELLIGENCE SUMMARY.~~
(*Erase heading not required.*)

Army Form C. 2118.

Place	Date	Hour	Summary of Events and Information	Remarks and references to Appendices
			Ref map Sh 36.	
LAUNDRIES			Completed at about 10 pm. Casualties – nil	
ERQUINGHEM H.5.a.4.7	29/11/17		Battalion at the LAUNDRIES, ERQUINGHEM. 'A' and 'D' Companies became attached to the Brigade School for training. The day was spent in cleaning kit and equipment, and bathing. The Baths were at the disposal from 8.30 am. until 5 pm. Casualties. nil	
do	30/11/17		Battalion at ERQUINGHEM. 'A' and 'D' Coys commenced training at Brigade School. 'B' & 'C' Companies and available men of Headquarters paraded for inspection (in drill order) and for physical training. There was a kit inspection afterwards. Fatigue parties of 2 offrs. and 80 O.Ranks were provided for Cable-burying; making dug-outs in the SUBSIDIARY LINE, near CAMBRIDGE AVENUE; and for conducting parties of Portuguese troops from the JUTE FACTORY to the SUBSIDIARY LINE for continuing with the parados building. Lt. Col. C.B. Harvey relinquished command of the Brigade School and proceeded on leave to PARIS. Casualties. nil	

C. Bower Major
Commanding 10th S.W.B.

A7092. Wt. W12839/M1293 750,000. 1/17. D. D & L. Ltd. Forms/C2118/14.

10th S.W.B.

Instructions regarding War Diaries and Intelligence Summaries are contained in F. S. Regs., Part II. and the Staff Manual respectively. Title pages will be prepared in manuscript.

WAR DIARY
or
~~INTELLIGENCE SUMMARY.~~
(Erase heading not required.)

Army Form C. 2118.

10 SWB
Vol 24

Place	Date	Hour	Summary of Events and Information — Ref. map. Sh. 36.	Remarks and references to Appendices
LAUNDRIES ERQUINGHEM – H.5.a.4.7 –	1/12/17		Battalion at the LAUNDRIES, ERQUINGHEM; "A" and "D" Companies being attached to the Brigade School for training. The Commanding Officer inspected available men of Headquarters and "B" & "C" Coys in "battle" order, this morning. Physical training followed. A football match between "B" & "C" Coys. and Batt. Hqrs. was played this afternoon. Working parties of 2 officers and 80 other ranks were provided for cable-burying, making dug-outs in the SUBSIDIARY LINE near CAMBRIDGE AVENUE, and for conducting parties of Portuguese troops from the JUTE FACTORY to the SUBSIDIARY LINE for work on the new parados. Casualties – nil.	[initials]
do.	2/12/17		Battalion at ERQUINGHEM. Divine Services were held at the LAUNDRIES this morning, the Brigadier General attending the C.E. Parade Service. All employed men of Batt. Hqrs. and the four Companies were inspected by the Commanding Officer at 3 p.m. Dress worn – "battle" order. Fatigues as yesterday. Casualties – nil.	
do.	3/12/17		Battalion at ERQUINGHEM. Inspections of B, C and Headquarter Coys. in "drill" order were held this morning. "Arms" drill and physical training followed. The usual working parties were provided. Casualties – nil.	

A7092) Wt. W12839/M1293 750,000. 1/17. D. D & L. Ltd. Forms/C2118/14.

Instructions regarding War Diaries and Intelligence Summaries are contained in F. S. Regs., Part II. and the Staff Manual respectively. Title pages will be prepared in manuscript.

WAR DIARY
or
~~INTELLIGENCE SUMMARY.~~
(Erase heading not required.)

10th S.W.B.

Army Form C. 2118.

Place	Date	Hour	Summary of Events and Information — Ref. map. Sh. 36.	Remarks and references to Appendices
LAUNDRIES ERQUINGHEM H.5.a.4.7	4/12/17		Battalion at ERQUINGHEM. Preparations for to-days relief were made during the morning. The Battalion paraded at 4 pm. and moved off in small parties, Headquarters leading. The 11th. Battn. S.W.B. were relieved in the Front Line, relief being completed by 7pm. Dispositions now as follows:- Batt. Hqrs. behind the SUBSIDIARY LINE (I.3.d.80.85). "A" Coy., Right Front (I.10.c.95.55). "B" Coy., Centre Front (I.10.b.60.90). "D" Coy., Left Front (I.4.b.95.95) "C" Coy. Reserve Coy. (I.10.c.75.95). Two Companies of the 16th Bn. Welsh Rgt. garrisoned the SUBSIDIARY LINE in L'EPINETTE sub-sector, and came under orders of O.C. 10th. S.W.B. There was very little artillery fire during the evening. L.G.s and M.Gs. kept up harassing fire on enemy trenches, wire and tramways. Casualties:- Nil.	AL
FRONT LINE. L'EPINETTE I.3.d.80.85				
do.	5/12/17.		Battalion in Front Line. Enemy artillery was active throughout the day. HEADQUARTER WALK was shelled with 4.2s and 5.9s. the shelling being especially heavy at 10.30 am. and 3.15 pm. The Right Coy. Front, neighbourhood of Gde PORTE EGAL FARM, and the Support line of Centre Coy. Front also received considerable attention. Battery positions in ARMENTIERES were heavily engaged throughout the day. Our guns were fairly quiet and only put over	

(A7092). Wt. W12839/M1293 750,000 1/17 D. D & L. Ltd. Forms/C2118/14.

10th L.N.B.

Army Form C. 2118.

WAR DIARY
or
INTELLIGENCE SUMMARY.

(Erase heading not required.)

Instructions regarding War Diaries and Intelligence Summaries are contained in F. S. Regs., Part II. and the Staff Manual respectively. Title pages will be prepared in manuscript.

Place	Date	Hour	Ref map. Sh. 36. Summary of Events and Information	Remarks and references to Appendices
~~ERQUINGHEM~~ – FRONT LINE – L'EPINETTE – I.3d.80.85 –	5/12/17 (contd)		a weak retaliation in reply to the enemy's fire. Aircraft activity was normal. Three enemy balloons were up opposite our front between "stand down" and 3 p.m. MGs were most active at "stand-to" and "stand-down". Trench mortars were quiet. Two fighting patrols reconnoitred NML, but no enemy were encountered. Work – General maintenance of trenches; widening No. 26 Post; clearing trenches where blown in; working on new dug-outs; building parados in SUBSIDIARY LINE. Carrying water for Left, Centre and Support Coys. Casualties:- Nil.	AR
do.	6/12/17		Battalion in Front Line. The enemy again shelled HEADQUARTER WALK, both morning and afternoon. Between 3.30 p.m. & 4.30 p.m. the shelling was intense, and appeared to be directed against camouflage behind Coy. Hqrs. Some damage was done to HEADQUARTER WALK, but no casualties were suffered by "A" Coy. Battery positions in ARMENTIERES received considerable attention this morning. Our guns were fairly active; but our artillery retaliation for hostile shelling of HEADQUARTER	

A7092. Wt. W12839/M1293 750,000. 1/17. D. D & I. Ltd. Forms/C2118/14.

10th SWB

Army Form C. 2118.

WAR DIARY
or
INTELLIGENCE SUMMARY.
(*Erase heading not required.*)

Instructions regarding War Diaries and Intelligence Summaries are contained in F. S. Regs., Part II. and the Staff Manual respectively. Title pages will be prepared in manuscript.

Place	Date	Hour	Summary of Events and Information	Remarks and references to Appendices
			Ref Map. Sh. 36.	
FRONT LINE – L'EPINETTE – I.3.d.80.85	6/12/17 (contd)		WALK was slow and inadequate. A hostile plane, flying low, directed the afternoon shoot. Four of our planes were up this morning, whilst two flew over HOUPLINES during the afternoon. Enemy H.T.M's fired on JAPAN AVE. and SPY. causing considerable damage. Our M.G's fired on enemy planes, and also on targets in rear of enemy line. Work:– Usual trench maintenance; building parados in SUBSIDIARY LINE etc. Two patrols (each of 1 officer and 9 O.R.) reconnoitred No man's Land. Nothing exceptional occurred. Casualties: Nil	H.L.
do.	7/12/17		Battalion in Front Line. At about 3.40 a.m. an enemy patrol approached No. 5 Post, from the direction of No. 6 Post. Our sentries opened fire and an unwounded Hun was captured. Later, another prisoner from the same patrol was caught. A third Hun was found dead on our wire at I.5.c.62.75. Valuable identifications were secured from these prisoners, who belonged to a Division recently transferred from the Russian Front. Enemy artillery was much quieter to-day, only a few L.H.V's being fired into our Communication trenches. Our guns were more active. They	

A7092. Wt. W12839/M1293 750,000. 1/17. D. D & L. Ltd. Forms/C2118/14.

10th LWB

Army Form C. 2118.

Instructions regarding War Diaries and Intelligence Summaries are contained in F. S. Regs., Part II. and the Staff Manual respectively. Title pages will be prepared in manuscript.

WAR DIARY or ~~INTELLIGENCE SUMMARY.~~

(Erase heading not required.)

Place	Date	Hour	Summary of Events and Information (Ref Map Sh 36)	Remarks and references to Appendices
FRONT LINE – L'EPINETTE – I.3.d.80.85 –	7/12/17		provided covering fire for a shoot by our M.T.M.s this afternoon. A hostile formation of 5 planes, flying very high, crossed our lines at 12.45 pm. Several times this morning 5 of our planes crossed the enemy line, persisting in their reconnaissance in spite of heavy hostile A.A. & M.G. fire. Two of our machines drove off an enemy plane at 4 pm. Patrols left our line at I.5.a.50.60 and I.11.c.10.50 to reconnoitre No Man's Land. Nothing exceptional occurred. Casualties:- Nil.	A/2
-do-	8/12/17		Battalion in Front Line Dispositions similar. Enemy Machine Guns normally active throughout the night, fire being directed chiefly on Front and Support Lines and Communication Trenches. The Hun appears to take a very lively interest in the roads in the Battalion Front of lake. A larger number of signals than usual were put up during the night, probably on account of a thick ground mist. Our artillery fired a heavy burst on enemy trench-tramway in rear of INCANDESCENT TRENCH at about 9.30pm. ~~Some~~ A patrol of one officer and 9 other ranks and another of one officer and 9 other ranks were sent	

A7092). Wt. W12839/M1293 750,000. 1/17. D. D & L. Ltd. Forms/C2118/14.

Instructions regarding War Diaries and Intelligence Summaries are contained in F. S. Regs., Part II. and the Staff Manual respectively. Title pages will be prepared in manuscript.

WAR DIARY
or
INTELLIGENCE SUMMARY.
(Erase heading not required.)

10th LN(?)B

Army Form C. 2118.

Place	Date	Hour	Summary of Events and Information	Remarks and references to Appendices
FRONT LINE L'EPINETTE I.3.d.80.85	8/12/17		out during last night to reconnoitre No Mans Land and Enemy wire No casualties Enemy Artillery fired on THE DISTILLERY and Left Batt's front with H.V at 11.30am, and again at 12.45pm At 1.45pm hostile fire, in retaliation for our Artillery fire, was directed on HAYSTACK FARM, where he was searching for our 9.4 TM emplacement. During the shelling some damage was done to HEADQUARTER WALK. Five hostile planes flew over our lines during the afternoon. Enemy working party was spotted and fired on at Stand To this morning. Our Artillery were vigorously active during the day	[illegible]
-do-	9/12/17		Battalion in Front Line. dispositions similar. Enemy artillery was far less active than usual during the day. though ours heavily shelled CENTRAL TRENCH and INANE TRENCH. Owing to inclemency of the weather aerial activity was nil. Machine Guns, on both sides, were uncomfortably active. New wire was observed in C29c central. Casualties NIL	

A7092). Wt. W12839/M1293 750,000. 1/17. D. D & L. Ltd. Forms/C2118/14.

10th S.W.B.

Army Form C. 2118.

Instructions regarding War Diaries and Intelligence Summaries are contained in F. S. Regs., Part II. and the Staff Manual respectively. Title pages will be prepared in manuscript.

WAR DIARY
or
INTELLIGENCE SUMMARY.
(Erase heading not required.)

Place	Date	Hour	Summary of Events and Information	Remarks and references to Appendices
~~FRONT LINE~~ L'EPINETTE Subsector 13 d 80 88	10/12/17		Battalion in the Front Line Dispositions similar. Our Artillery has been fairly active during the night firing on selected targets. Enemy Artillery was normally lively, firing a fair number of rounds on sundry targets. Patrols were sent out for reconnaissance purposes but encountered difficulty through intense darkness. No enemy patrols were encountered. Battalion was relieved at dusk by 11th S.W. Borderers, and relieved 17th Bn R.W.F. in the Subsidiary Line. Dispositions now as follows:- A Company I 9 b 50 35, B Company I 4 a 60 90, C Coy - C 22 b 00 10, D Company C 28 a 80 70. Bn Headquarters H 5 b 8 7. A + B Coys on relief came under orders of OC L'Epinette Subsector, and C + D Coys under orders of OC Houplines Sub sector. Relief was satisfactorily carried out, without casualties, and was completed by 11 pm.	W/R

Instructions regarding War Diaries and Intelligence Summaries are contained in F. S. Regs., Part II. and the Staff Manual respectively. Title pages will be prepared in manuscript.

WAR DIARY
or
INTELLIGENCE SUMMARY.
(Erase heading not required.)

10th SWB

Army Form C. 2118.

Place	Date	Hour	Summary of Events and Information	Remarks and references to Appendices
In Subsidiary Lines. 19.b.50.80 to 28.a.80.70 H.Q. at H.5.b.8.7	11/12/17		Ref Map 36. Dispositions unchanged. Battalion Headquarters paraded for inspection by the Commanding Officer at 3pm. having occupied the morning by cleaning up kit and equipment. Companies operated under orders of their respective Commanders on work on Subsidiary Line Defences. Casualties nil	AB
Do.	12/12/17		Dispositions similar. Bn Headquarters were inspected by the Commanding Officer at 10.am. in battle order. Signallers carried out flag drill under senior N.C.O. Companies as yesterday. Casualties nil. Gas helmets and box respirators of all Headquarters were inspected 3pm	
Do	13/12/17		Dispositions similar. Headquarters utilized baths ~~all day~~ between 9.30am and 11.0 am. Signallers under N.C.O.'s carried out Station Practice with flags and lamp. Companies under respective Commanding Officers. Casualties nil.	
Do	14/12/17		Dispositions similar. Headquarters, Commanding Officers' inspection 9.40am. Signallers carried out training under senior N.C.O. in flash lamp work. Companies in Subsidiary Lines under respective Sub sector Commanders. Casualties nil.	

A7092). Wt. W12839/M1293 750,000. 1/17. D. D & L. Ltd. Forms/C2118/14.

Instructions regarding War Diaries and Intelligence Summaries are contained in F. S. Regs., Part II. and the Staff Manual respectively. Title pages will be prepared in manuscript.

WAR DIARY
or
INTELLIGENCE SUMMARY.
(Erase heading not required.)

10th LWB

Army Form C. 2118.

Place	Date	Hour	Summary of Events and Information (Ref Map 36.)	Remarks and references to Appendices
Coys in Subsidiary Lines from I.9.b.50.35 to C.28.a.80.30	15/12/1917		Dispositions similar. Bn Headquarters carried out usual training and bathing. Coys under their respective Subsection Commanders. Casualties nil	A.F.C.
H.Quarters H.5.b.8.7. Front Line L'Epinette I.3.d.80.85	16/12/1917		Dispositions similar. Bn Headquarters relieved Bn HQrs of 11th LWB in the front line at 7pm. Coys. simultaneously relieved companies of the 11th [illegible]. Dispositions now Headquarters I.3.d.80.85. "A" Coy Reserve Coy, "B" Company Centre front Coy, "C" Coy Left front and "D" Company Right front Coy. Relief satisfactorily completed without casualties. Enemy activity well below normal during the night.	

A7092). Wt. W12839/M1293 750,000. 1/17. D. D & L. Ltd. Forms/C2118/14.

Instructions regarding War Diaries and Intelligence Summaries are contained in F. S. Regs., Part II. and the Staff Manual respectively. Title pages will be prepared in manuscript.

WAR DIARY
or
INTELLIGENCE SUMMARY.
(Erase heading not required.)

10th LIB

Army Form C. 2118.

Place	Date	Hour	Summary of Events and Information	Remarks and references to Appendices
Frontline L'Epinette T.3.d.80.85	17/12/1917		Dispositions as yesterday. Enemy activity chiefly confined to desultory shelling of back areas. Casualties nil. Patrols sent out during the evening encountered no enemy opposition. Artillery almost inactive all day. ~~Cas~~	AG
-do-	18/12/1917		Dispositions unchanged. Advance parties of Australian Brigade arrived, which indicates an early relief of this Brigade. Artillery almost inactive with the exception of a couple of bursts in the forenoon in retaliation for some T.M's on front line post. Casualties nil. Enemy aircraft rather unusually active. One plane appeared to become out of control in the midst of brisk expostulation from our AA and planed down, apparently behind J Houp lines. Our casualties nil.	

A7092). Wt. W12839/M1293 750,000. 1/17. D. D & L. Ltd. Forms/C2118/14.

Instructions regarding War Diaries and Intelligence Summaries are contained in F. S. Regs., Part II. and the Staff Manual respectively. Title pages will be prepared in manuscript.

WAR DIARY
or
INTELLIGENCE SUMMARY.
(Erase heading not required.)

10th Lw B

Army Form C. 2118.

Place	Date	Hour	Summary of Events and Information	Remarks and references to Appendices
Frontline. L'Epinette. I 3 d 85 80	19/12/1917		Dispositions similar. Battalion relieved during the evening by 33rd Australian Battalion, and marched companies moving indepentantly, to billets at ESTAIRES. Relief was compleete about 2am 20/12/1917. Casualties nil.	[illegible]
Estaires. 36a/L 30 a 5.2	20/12/1917		Battalion in Rest billets at Estaires. Company Commanders inspected Companies indepently and then dismissed.	
-do	21/12/1917		Dispositions similar. Battalion paraded for inspection by the Commanding Officer at 9 am, and were then turned over to Company Commanders for kit inspection etc	

A7092. Wt. W12839/M1293 750,000. 1/17. D. D & L. Ltd. Forms/C2118/14.

Instructions regarding War Diaries and Intelligence Summaries are contained in F. S. Regs., Part II. and the Staff Manual respectively. Title pages will be prepared in manuscript.

WAR DIARY
or
INTELLIGENCE SUMMARY.
(Erase heading not required.)

10th Inf B

Army Form C. 2118.

Place	Date	Hour	Summary of Events and Information	Remarks and references to Appendices
ESTAIRES. L30.a.5.2	22/12/1917		Dispositions similar. Battalion paraded at 9am and, after inspection by the Commanding Officer proceeded on a Route March in accordance with prearranged programme, passing through Merville en route. Officers were given instruction in guard mounting during the afternoon. Inter Company football matches were arranged. A+B Companies proceeded to Baths at SAILLY during the afternoon.	[illegible]
do	23/12/1917		Dispositions similar. Divine Service was held after which a short gas helmet practice was carried out. Commanding Officer inspected billets.	
do	24/12/1917		Battalion drill, bayonet fighting, Physical Training and Musketry were the main features of morning parade. Extended order drill, handling of arms and gas helmet drill, and a tactical scheme for officers were carried out during the afternoon	

A7092. Wt. W12839/M1293 750,000. 1/17. D. D & L. Ltd. Forms/C2118/14.

Army Form C. 2118.

10th LWB

WAR DIARY
or
INTELLIGENCE SUMMARY.
(Erase heading not required.)

Instructions regarding War Diaries and Intelligence Summaries are contained in F. S. Regs., Part II. and the Staff Manual respectively. Title pages will be prepared in manuscript.

Place	Date	Hour	Summary of Events and Information	Remarks and references to Appendices
ESTAIRES L.30.a.5.2	25/12/1917		Xmas Day. After Church Parade, Companies marched to places selected for dinner. A B D + HQ Coys dined all together in the School Room and C Coy and Transport were in the Sergeants Mess. No training was carried out. Sergeants Mess dinner was held at 6pm, at which speeches were made by the Commanding Officer and Adjutant.	NE
-do-	26/12/17		Battalion Route March with Transport via Lestrem L'Epinette &c. Feet and rifles were inspected during the afternoon	
-do-	27/12/17		Recreational Training and Bayonet Fighting, and Musketry were the main items during the morning. Staff Officers and NCOs had a tactical scheme. Cross country run and football during the afternoon	

A7092). Wt. W12839/M1293 750,000. 1/17. D. D & L. Ltd. Forms/C2118/14.

Instructions regarding War Diaries and Intelligence Summaries are contained in F. S. Regs., Part II. and the Staff Manual respectively. Title pages will be prepared in manuscript.

WAR DIARY
or
INTELLIGENCE SUMMARY.
(Erase heading not required.)

10th LWB

Army Form C. 2118.

Place	Date	Hour	Summary of Events and Information	Remarks and references to Appendices
ESTAIRES L30.a.5.2	28/12/1917		Battalion drill, recreational training and wiring practice were carried out during the morning. During the afternoon tactical training was indulged in, practice being carried out of Battalion taking up a defensive line of posts &c	AZ
-do-	29/12/1917		Battalion drill was carried out after an inspection by the Commanding Officer, of the Battalion turned out in full marching order. A Battalion scheme, fighting a rear guard action across country was also performed. Sports had been arranged for the afternoon but severity of the weather prevented these and football matches were organized and played instead.	
do-	30/12/1917		Sunday Divine Services attended ~~and~~ Small kits were inspected by the Commanding Officer after Church Parade.	

A7092). Wt. W12839/M1293 750,000. 1/17. D. D & L. Ltd. Forms/C2118/14.

Instructions regarding War Diaries and Intelligence Summaries are contained in F. S. Regs., Part II. and the Staff Manual respectively. Title pages will be prepared in manuscript.

WAR DIARY
or
INTELLIGENCE SUMMARY.
(Erase heading not required.)

10th SWB

Army Form C. 2118.

Place	Date	Hour	Summary of Events and Information	Remarks and references to Appendices
ESTAIRES L30a.52	31/12/1917		Dispositions unchanged Battalion Route march with advanced and rear guards, through Merville, occupied the morning's training, and during the afternoon feet and rifles were inspected	WJ

C. W. Hawes
Lieutenant Colonel
Commanding 10th Bn S. W. Borderers

A7092. Wt. W12839/M1293 750,000. 1/17. D. D & L. Ltd. Forms/C2118/14.

1918

Instructions regarding War Diaries and Intelligence Summaries are contained in F. S. Regs., Part II. and the Staff Manual respectively. Title pages will be prepared in manuscript.

WAR DIARY
or
INTELLIGENCE SUMMARY.
(Erase heading not required.)

10th Bn S.W.Borderers

Army Form C. 2118.

Vol 25

Place	Date	Hour	Summary of Events and Information	Remarks and references to Appendices
			Reference Map 36a	
ESTAIRES L 30 a 5 2	1/1/1918		Recreational training, Company drill revetting Construction of Strong Points Rapid wiring and Musketry were the items of todays training. Baths were available at Sailly and were fully utilized each company being allotted one hour	AH
-do-	2/1/1918		C Company paraded for Musketry on Range at 9am. Grouping Application and rapid practices were carried out. Remainder of Battalion did Battalion drill and Physical Training and Bayonet Fighting. Signallers ~~Band~~ Lewis Gunners paraded for special training under Signalling NCOs ~~Bandmaster~~ and Lewis Gun Officer respectively The Band	AH

A7092. Wt. W12839/M1293 750,000. 1/17. D. D & L. Ltd. Forms/C2118/14.

10th LWRB

January 1918 Army Form C. 2118.

WAR DIARY
or
INTELLIGENCE SUMMARY.

(Erase heading not required.)

Instructions regarding War Diaries and Intelligence Summaries are contained in F. S. Regs., Part II. and the Staff Manual respectively. Title pages will be prepared in manuscript.

Place	Date	Hour	Summary of Events and Information (Refce. Map 36A)	Remarks and references to Appendices
			paraded for Arm drill under CSM Burgess. Drummers received instruction, as stretcher bearers under the Medical Officer. NCOs as available, received instruction in wiring under Sergeant Price ~~and~~ Rose and Hughes. A number of men were inoculated by the Medical Officer at 9 am. Three men per Company paraded under 2Lt Rayner and Sgt Campbell for instruction in boxing	AK
ESTAIRES L.30.a.5.2	3/1/1918		Companies were paraded for inspection by Company Commanders at 8.45 am, and afterwards carried out a varied programme including Company & Battalion Drill, musketry. Physical training, & Bayonet	AK

A7092. Wt. W12839/M1293 750,000. 1/17. D. D & I. Ltd. Forms/C2118/14.

Instructions regarding War Diaries and Intelligence Summaries are contained in F. S. Regs., Part II. and the Staff Manual respectively. Title pages will be prepared in manuscript.

WAR DIARY
or
INTELLIGENCE SUMMARY.
(Erase heading not required.)

Army Form C. 2118.

Place	Date	Hour	Summary of Events and Information	Remarks and references to Appendices
[illegible]	3/1/18		fighting Lewis Gun Class under Lt Clayton, proceeded to the Range for practice. Signallers, Band and Drums were under instruction under their respective NCOs. Platoon Roll Books, Company Conduct Sheets & Company Books were inspected by the Commanding Officer at 4 pm. The inspection, being longer than was expected, was adjourned until tomorrow. Boxing was carried out under 2/Lt Rayner during the afternoon.	[illegible]

A7092). Wt. W12839/M1293 750,000. 1/17. D. D & L. Ltd. Forms/C2118/14.

10th IWB

Instructions regarding War Diaries and Intelligence Summaries are contained in F. S. Regs., Part II. and the Staff Manual respectively. Title pages will be prepared in manuscript.

WAR DIARY
or
INTELLIGENCE SUMMARY.
(Erase heading not required.)

January 1918

Army Form C. 2118.

Place	Date	Hour	Summary of Events and Information	Remarks and references to Appendices
			Ref Map 36a	
Estaires	4/1/1918		Companies paraded as usual at 8.45 am for inspection by Company Commanders. Physical Training and Bayonet fighting was carried out between 9 am and 10 am, Extended Order drill between 10 am and 11 am, Rifle bombing practice, bombing + arm drill from 11.15 am to 12.30 pm, during which period Lewis Gunners practised application of fire to ground During the afternoon, musketry instruction and Company Drill were carried out. NCO. were paraded for wiring instruction under Sergeants Price and Rose C Company were allotted the Range, and carried out Grouping, Application, and Rapid practice.	HE

A7092). Wt. W12839/M1293 750,000. 1/17. D. D & L. Ltd. Forms/C2118/14.

10 LWB

Instructions regarding War Diaries and Intelligence Summaries are contained in F. S. Regs., Part II. and the Staff Manual respectively. Title pages will be prepared in manuscript.

WAR DIARY
or
~~INTELLIGENCE SUMMARY.~~

(Erase heading not required.)

Army Form C. 2118.

Place	Date	Hour	Summary of Events and Information	Remarks and references to Appendices
			Signallers and Lewis Gunners under instruction carried out special instructions under their respective instructors between 10 am and 12.30 pm. Drums paraded as stretcher bearers at 9 am and were then given instruction under the Medical Officer. Band paraded for Musketry, drill and Physical training under Sergeant Harrison from 9 am to 11 am, and were then at the disposal of the Bandmaster for practice for the remainder of the day. 10 men per Company were inoculated. Notification received that the Commanding Officer, Lt Colonel C D Harvey has been awarded Distinguished Service Order and Capt W T Havard C4 attached as	A/E

A7092. Wt. W12839/M1293 750,000. 1/17. D. D & I. Ltd. Forms/C2118/14.

10th LWB

Instructions regarding War Diaries and Intelligence Summaries are contained in F. S. Regs., Part II. and the Staff Manual respectively. Title pages will be prepared in manuscript.

WAR DIARY or INTELLIGENCE SUMMARY.

(Erase heading not required.)

January 1918

Army Form C. 2118.

Place	Date	Hour	Summary of Events and Information	Remarks and references to Appendices
			Chaplain, the Military Cross.	AC
Estaires L30a.52	5/1/18		The following were Mentioned in Despatches for Distinguished Service in the Field - Lieut Col C D Harvey DSO, Major T G T Rees MC, Capt A Ackworthy, 20220 Sgt. D H Thomas. Battalion paraded at 8 am, and proceeded by Companies to Fleurbaix, where some excellent wiring was carried out in conjunction with 151st Field Coy Royal Engineers.	
-do-	6/1/18		Companies paraded at 9.30 am, and proceeded in the order Band, Headquarters, A Co, B Co, Drums, C Co, D Co, Transport, to new Billeting area RUE BATTAILLE, J 13 d. Intervals of 300x were maintained between Companies. New area was reached by 11 am, and the	

A7092). Wt. W12839/M1293 750,000. 1/17. D. D & L. Ltd. Forms/C2118/14.

10th LWB.

Instructions regarding War Diaries and Intelligence Summaries are contained in F. S. Regs., Part II. and the Staff Manual respectively. Title pages will be prepared in manuscript.

WAR DIARY
or
~~INTELLIGENCE SUMMARY.~~

(*Erase heading not required.*)

January 1918

Army Form C. 2118.

Place	Date	Hour	Sheet. 36 — Summary of Events and Information	Remarks and references to Appendices
			men quickly settled down. Headquarters were installed at H 13 b 5.5, and two Coys were billeted in the immediate vicinity, the remaining Companies proceeded to G 24 c 8 8, Transport to L 4 c 9 9 (Sheet 36a) ~~Major Bowen returned from leave in UK~~	R.G.O.
H 13 b 5 5	7/1/1918		Two Companies at G 24 c 8 8 were moved in the afternoon to billet near Battalion Headquarters. D Company proceeded to the Range, and carried out necessary repairs and improvements before firing rapid and application practices. A Company carried out Physical Training and Bayonet Fighting from 9am to 10am, and then proceeded to clean and repair various hutments near Headquarters so as to make them habitable for Coys from G 24 c 8 8	R.G.O.

A7092). Wt. W12839/M1293 750,000. 1/17. D, D & L. Ltd. Forms/C2118/14.

10th SWB

Instructions regarding War Diaries and Intelligence Summaries are contained in F. S. Regs., Part II. and the Staff Manual respectively. Title pages will be prepared in manuscript.

WAR DIARY
or
INTELLIGENCE SUMMARY.
(Erase heading not required.)

January 1918 Army Form C. 2118.

Place	Date	Hour	Summary of Events and Information	Remarks and references to Appendices
36/Nf A 13 b 5 5	7/1/1918		Sheet 36 B + C Companies carried out Physical Training and Running between 9 am and 10 am, Extended order drill from 10 am to 11 am and Company Drill. Practice with Rifle Grenades + bombing and Musketry between 11 am and 12.30 pm. Lewis Gunners instructed, under LG Officer + NCOs, in Application of fire to Ground. Coy + Battalion Signallers paraded under Signalling NCO's for instruction. Band, Physical Training, Musketry and drill were carried out. Drummers were given instruction in Stretcher work under Medical Officer. After 11 am Band and Drums practised under Bandmaster and Sergeant Drummer respectivily. 10 men per Coy were inoculated by MO.	J.Y.D.

A7092). Wt. W12839/M1293 750,000. 1/17. D. D & L. Ltd. Forms/C2118/14.

10th SWB

Instructions regarding War Diaries and Intelligence Summaries are contained in F. S. Regs., Part II. and the Staff Manual respectively. Title pages will be prepared in manuscript.

WAR DIARY
or
INTELLIGENCE SUMMARY.

(*Erase heading not required.*)

January 1918 Army Form C. 2118.

Place	Date	Hour	Summary of Events and Information	Remarks and references to Appendices
			Sheet 36	
			Major A.H. Bowen rejoined from leave, as also did Capt A.W. Newton	
	8/1/1918		C Company proceeded to the Range for Range practices at 9 am. Remaining Companies carried out Physical Training 9am to 10am, Extended Order drill 10am to 11am, Bayonet Fighting and Musketry 11.30 am to 12.30 pm. Lewis Gunners carried out drill and Application of fire to ground under Instructors. Junior NCOs were taken in Communication Drill under the R.S.M., and 50% of the remaining NCOs were given instruction in Map reading under Major Bowen and Lieut Clayton. Officers carried out a tactical scheme arranged by the Adjt	

A7092. Wt. W12839/M1293 750,000. 1/17. D. D & L Ltd. Forms/C2118/14.

10th SWB

Instructions regarding War Diaries and Intelligence Summaries are contained in F. S. Regs., Part II. and the Staff Manual respectively. Title pages will be prepared in manuscript.

WAR DIARY
or
INTELLIGENCE SUMMARY.
(Erase heading not required.)

January 1918.

Army Form C. 2118.

Place	Date	Hour	Sheet 36 Summary of Events and Information	Remarks and references to Appendices
	8/1/18		between 2pm and 3pm Signallers trained and untrained were under instruction 10am to 12.30pm and 2pm – 3.30pm, in signalling and did ½ hour box respirator drill afterwards Band and Drums, after an hours physical training under Sgt Blake and afterwards practised RSM Stocker awarded Distinguished Conduct Medal. Notification received through Divisional Orders. 2/Lt Hughes returned from a course of Musketry. Lieut W D Lt Mercer proceeded on leave to UK	To [illegible]

136 5.5.

A7092I. Wt. W12839/M1293 750,000. 1/17. D. D & L. Ltd. Forms/C2118/14.

10th S W Borderers

WAR DIARY
or
~~INTELLIGENCE~~ SUMMARY.
(Erase heading not required.)

January 1918

Army Form C. 2118.

Instructions regarding War Diaries and Intelligence Summaries are contained in F. S. Regs., Part II. and the Staff Manual respectively. Title pages will be prepared in manuscript.

Sheet 36

Place	Date	Hour	Summary of Events and Information	Remarks and references to Appendices
H 13 b 5 5	9/1/1918		Baths at Sailly being allotted to the Battalion were utilized as follows:- A Coy 8-9 am, B Coy 9-10 am, C Coy 10-11 am, D Coy 2-3 pm, H Qrs 3-4 pm, details 4-5 pm. Training was carried out as far as practicable as follows:- 9-10 am Physical Training, 10-11 am Extended order drill, 11-20 - 12-30 pm Bayonet fighting and musketry, 2-3 pm Bombing + Rifle Grenade practice and handling of arms, 3-3.30 pm Box Respirator drill. Specialists, as they became available after bathing, carried out instruction under Instructors. Band and Transport carried out firing on the Range. Lt W D P Mercer and 3 O R proceeded on leave.	9 J.O

A7092). Wt. W12839/M1293 750,000. 1/17. D. D & L. Ltd. Forms/C2118/14.

10th LWB

Instructions regarding War Diaries and Intelligence Summaries are contained in F. S. Regs., Part II. and the Staff Manual respectively. Title pages will be prepared in manuscript.

WAR DIARY
or
INTELLIGENCE SUMMARY.
(Erase heading not required.)

January 1918

Army Form C. 2118.

Place	Date	Hour	Summary of Events and Information	Remarks and references to Appendices
			Sheet 36	
H.D.c. 5.5	10/1/1918		Battalion marched to Fleurbaix for wiring; marching off in the order D, C, B, A, at 8.45, 8.50, 8.55 and 9.0 am respectively. Wire was strengthened, filled in, and otherwise improved. Available Headquarters signallers & personnel proceeded with their Companies. Lewis Gunners under instruction continued as usual under Lt Clayton. Band and drums carried out practice under Bandmaster and Sergeant Drummer respectively.	
	11/1/1918		B Company proceeded to the Range for firing practice. Lewis Guns of the Company were also fired. C Company Lewis Guns were fired whilst B Coy were having dinner. The remainder of the Battalion carried out Physical Training & recreational training 9-10 am, Company drill and Bayonet fighting from 10 to 11 am, Musketry and Box Respirator drill 11.30 to 12.30 pm. Bombing and rifle bombing 2-3 pm and Company drill 3 to 3.30 pm. Lewis Gunners of	

A7092. Wt. W12839/M1293. 750,000. 1/17. D. D. & L. Ltd. Forms/C2118/14.

10th SWB

Instructions regarding War Diaries and Intelligence Summaries are contained in F. S. Regs., Part II. and the Staff Manual respectively. Title pages will be prepared in manuscript.

WAR DIARY
or
INTELLIGENCE SUMMARY.
(Erase heading not required.)

January 1918

Army Form C. 2118.

Sheet 36

Place	Date	Hour	Summary of Events and Information	Remarks and references to Appendices
H17c55	11/1/18		A + D Coys ~~will~~ carry out Gun drill and application of fire to ground. Signallers under instruction carried out training under Cpls Saunt and White. Junior NCO's were taken in Communication Drill by the RSM. Guard Mounting, Squad drill + fire orders were also practised. Half of the remaining NCOs were taken in Map reading by ~~Major Bowen~~ Capt Hornsby. The farmhouse at H13a 45 40 was burnt to the ground during the early hours of this morning. The battalion was turned out but owing to a very strong wind, nothing could be done to save the farm. A considerable amount of Medical and Signalling equipment and mens clothing &c were destroyed. A Board of Enquiry was assembled by order of the Commanding Officer to investigate the cause of the fire. Board was adjourned until tomorrow after a considerable number of witnesses had been interrogated.	

A7092). Wt. W12839/M1293 750,000. 1/17. D. D & L. Ltd. Forms/C2118/14.

10th LWB

Instructions regarding War Diaries and Intelligence Summaries are contained in F. S. Regs., Part II. and the Staff Manual respectively. Title pages will be prepared in manuscript.

WAR DIARY
or
INTELLIGENCE SUMMARY.
(Erase heading not required.)

January/1918

Army Form C. 2118.

Place	Date	Hour	Summary of Events and Information	Remarks and references to Appendices
			Sheet 36	
H.13.b.5.5	13/1/1918		Board of Enquiry on the fire re assembled at 9.15 am under Major Bowen, and continued the taking of evidence. Battalion marched to Fleurbaix for wiring moving off in the order C, B, A, D, at 8.45, 8.50, 8.55, 9 am respectively. Some very satisfactory progress was made with the work, and men returned to billets about 2.30 pm. Lewis Gunners + Signallers were allotted the range, and carried out practice under Lt Clayton and 2Lt Hughes. Band + Drums practised under the Bandmaster + Sergeant Drummer respectively. Some junior NCOs attended a Gymnastic Class under Brigade Staff Instructor. A large number of NCOs promotions were approved by the Commanding Officer.	J.F.O.

A7092). Wt. W12839/M1293 750,000. 1/17. D. D & L. Ltd. Forms/C2118/14.

10th SWB

Instructions regarding War Diaries and Intelligence Summaries are contained in F. S. Regs., Part II. and the Staff Manual respectively. Title pages will be prepared in manuscript.

WAR DIARY or ~~INTELLIGENCE SUMMARY.~~

(Erase heading not required.)

January 1918

Army Form C. 2118.

Place	Date	Hour	Summary of Events and Information	Remarks and references to Appendices
H13d 55	13/1/1918		Church parades were arranged for the morning, which, owing to lack of accommodation, had to take place twice – right and left half battalion having seperate services Battalion paraded at 12.30pm, full marching order, and proceeded to billets at ESTAIRES Sheet 36a, L 30 ~~a~~ 5 2 (as before occupied) Intervals of 500x were maintained between companies en route in accordance with Brigade Orders. Dinners were served on arrival in hutments.	G.F.O.
Estaires L30a52	14/1/1918		Battalion paraded at 9.0am, and after inspection by the Commanding Officer, carried out training as follows 9.30am to 10.30am. Physical Training and recreational games. 10.45am to 11.30am Company drill, 11.30am to 12.30pm Musketry and Bayonet fighting. Afternoon training:– 2pm to 2.30pm, box respirator drill, 2.30pm to 3.0pm, Throwing bombs, & firing rifle bombs.	G.F.O.

A7092). Wt. W12839/M1293 750,000. 1/17. D. D & I. Ltd. Forms/C2118/14.

10th SWB

Instructions regarding War Diaries and Intelligence Summaries are contained in F. S. Regs., Part II. and the Staff Manual respectively. Title pages will be prepared in manuscript.

WAR DIARY
or
~~INTELLIGENCE~~ SUMMARY.

(Erase heading not required.)

January 1918

Army Form C. 2118.

Place	Date	Hour	Summary of Events and Information	Remarks and references to Appendices
ESTAIRES 2o a 5 2	14/1/18		A Company was detailed for Range practice, but owing to inclemency of the weather, this was abandoned, & Company carried Training on similar lines to the remainder of the Battalion. Lieut Colonel C. D. Harvey DSO proceeded on leave to UK for one month (special) and command of the Battalion devolves on Major A. L. Bowen	
	15/1/18		Commanding Officer inspected the Battalion as usual at 9 am, after which a Route March was commenced Dress fighting order. Band headed the Battalion, followed seriatum by Headquarters, D Coy, A Coy Drums, B Coy C Coy Route:- Estaires, Neuf Berquin, Merville, Northern Road to Estaires. Battalion returned about 1 pm. Weather was very bad during the march. After dinner, feet and rifles were inspected.	

A7092. Wt. W12839/M1293 750,000. 1/17. D. D & L. Ltd. Forms/C2118/14.

10th LivB

Instructions regarding War Diaries and Intelligence Summaries are contained in F. S. Regs., Part II. and the Staff Manual respectively. Title pages will be prepared in manuscript.

WAR DIARY
or
~~INTELLIGENCE SUMMARY.~~

(Erase heading not required.)

January 1918

Army Form C. 2118.

Place	Date	Hour	Sheet 36a & 36 — Summary of Events and Information	Remarks and references to Appendices
E STAIRES	16/1/1918		Physical drill, recreational games company drill, Musketry were carried out during the morning. Instruction in Guard Mounting duties and Box respirator drill occupied time during the afternoon. 2/Lt Hughes took a Musketry Class of 8 men per Coy, assisted by Sgt Harrison & Hughes. Lewis Gun Class and Signalling Class carried out instruction as usual. 50% of Officers and NCO's proceeded to reconnoitre to be taken up by this unit in the event of hostile attack	J. F. O.
	17/1/1918		Morning training was as follows - 9.15 to 10, Bayonet fighting, 10 to 10.45, Arms drill, 11 to 12.30 Musketry. During the afternoon Musketry and Box Respirator drill were carried out. Lewis Gun, Signalling and Musketry Classes carried on as usual under their respective instructors. Band and Drums carried out Physical training from 9.15 to 10, after which Musketry and Stretcher drill respectively were performed. The remaining 50% of officers and NCOs reconnoitred position of defence 2/Lt J J Powell proceeded to XV Corps School of Instruction. 2/Lieut J Ellis, H P Carefull, and C Bissell joined for duty. No 25423 Pte H Wiltshire proceeded to UK for Commission Capt FRR Kenward MC rejoined from leave	J. F. O.

A7092). Wt. W12839/M1293 750,000. 1/17. D. D & L. Ltd. Forms/C2118/14.

10th LWB

Instructions regarding War Diaries and Intelligence Summaries are contained in F. S. Regs., Part II. and the Staff Manual respectively. Title pages will be prepared in manuscript.

WAR DIARY
or
INTELLIGENCE SUMMARY.
(Erase heading not required.)

January 1918

Army Form C. 2118.

Place	Date	Hour	Summary of Events and Information (Reference Map 36A)	Remarks and references to Appendices
ESTAIRES	18/1/1918		Training during the morning was devoted chiefly to Musketry. Fire positions. Aiming positions. Care of Arms. Trigger pressing. Judging distance were all embodied. Platoon and Physical drill were also carried out. Signallers and Lewis Gunners Class carried out training under their Instructors. All available runners commenced a Class of Map Reading under 2/Lt P B King. Stretcher Bearers received instruction in their work under the M.O. Capt and Adjt E F Orford MC DCM rejoined from Base 20244 Sgt J Jones proceeded to UK for Commission Capt A J Evans proceeded on leave to UK	E.F.O.
	19/1/1918		Morning Training was as follows:- 9.15 - 10 Platoon Drill, 10 to 10.30 Bayonet fighting, 10.45 - 12.30 Musketry, including Aiming Instruction, Visual training, Aiming instruction. A Battalion Cross Country Run was organized and carried out in the afternoon, the first home being Pte Jeffreys, the Commanding Officer's servant. Signallers, runners, Lewis Gunners, Stretcher bearers Band and drums carried out instruction under their various instruction under their Instructors. 2/Lt Lewis and platoon (of B Coy) proceeded to Brigade School.	E.F.O.

A7092. Wt. W12839/M1293 750,000. 1/17. D. D & L. Ltd. Forms/C2118/14.

10th LWB

Instructions regarding War Diaries and Intelligence Summaries are contained in F. S. Regs., Part II. and the Staff Manual respectively. Title pages will be prepared in manuscript.

WAR DIARY
or
INTELLIGENCE SUMMARY.

(Erase heading not required.)

January 1918

Army Form C. 2118.

Place	Date	Hour	Summary of Events and Information — Reference Map 36A	Remarks and references to Appendices
ESTAIRES	20/1/1918		After Divine Service, kit inspections were held. Two Working parties numbering 110 each were found for digging Corps Defences. Hours of work 9 am to 3.30	
	21/1/1918		Working parties were again provided, as yesterday. Lewis Gun Class, Runners Class Stretcher bearers, ~~Signallers~~ carried on as usual. Lewis Gun and Musketry Classes carried out Range practices. All Signallers, under 2/Lt RM Morgan, proceeding to Divisional Signal School, were inspected at 2pm. Brigade Gas Expert attended during the afternoon and imparted instruction. Company Equipment was inspected by the Adjutant at 12 noon. Junior Officers carried out reconnaissance under Capt FRR Kenward MC	
	22/1/1918		Working parties provided as before. Signallers under 2/Lt Morgan proceeded to Div. Signal School. Specialists, as available, paraded under their respective instructors. Junior Officers reconnoitred Strong Posts in Corps Defences under Capt FRR Kenward MC. Boxing took place at 5pm, the band being in attendance.	

A7092. Wt. W12839/M1293 750,000. 1/17. D. D & L. Ltd. Forms/C2118/14.

10th SWB — War Diary — January 1918

Place	Time	Date	Ref Map 36A. Summary of Events	Remarks
ESTAIRES		25/1/1918	Working Parties furnished as before Lewis Gunners, Runners, Map reading Class Musketry Class &c carried on under Instructors. A new Lewis Gun Class was assembled comprising six men per Company Battalion Concert was given at 130th Field Ambulance, and proved very successful Inter-Battalion Boxing Contest took place in the evening This unit did not win the event, but some very excellent boxing was observed. ~~Brigade Retreat was sounded by Massed Bands of this unit & 17th RWF~~	G.Y.O.
		26/1/1918	Working parties unaltered Specialists carried on as usual A Company showed kit for Commanding Officer at 11 am. Brigade Retreat sounded by Massed Bands of 17th RWF and this unit 4pm	G.Y.O.
		27/1/1918	Working parties as usual. Divine Services were attended by those remaining in Camp. B Coy Band and Drums laid down their kits for inspection by the Commanding Officer	G.Y.O.

10th LWB

January 1918

ESTAIRES

Reference Map 36A

23/1/1918 Working parties proceeded as before.
Details of C Company carried out general instruction under Company Commander. Runners Lewis Gunners Drummers carried on under instructors.
Charge Reports and Company Records were checked by the Commanding Officer at 2pm. (B+D Coys only)
Lieut D.P. Clayton proceeded on leave.
Junior Officers carried out Map Reading under Capt A.R.R. Kennard M.C. Bde Cross Country run 2pm.
G.F.O.

24/1/1918 Working Parties as usual.
Musketry Class, Lewis Gun Class, runners, + Map reading Class paraded as usual under their respective instructors.
Reports + Company Records of B+D Coys were checked by the Commanding Officer at 2pm.
Brigade Cross Country Race which took place yesterday was won by 'C' Coy team.
G.F.O.

10th S.W. Borderers

WAR DIARY
or
INTELLIGENCE SUMMARY.
(Erase heading not required.)

Army Form C. 2118.

Instructions regarding War Diaries and Intelligence Summaries are contained in F. S. Regs., Part II. and the Staff Manual respectively. Title pages will be prepared in manuscript.

February 1918.

Vol 26

Place	Date	Hour	Summary of Events and Information	Remarks and references to Appendices
			Reference Map 36A	
Estaires	1/2/18		Battalion in Billets at Estaires 280 men provided for working parties on Corps Defences Four runners per Company paraded for instruction under 2/Lt P B King between 3 and 4 pm. Elementary Stretcher bearers class, under Sgt Campbell, paraded 3 to 4 pm. Inter Company Wiring competition took place on Battalion Parade Ground winners being D Company whose team were very much congratulated by the Commanding Officer for their excellent performance Platoon Drill Competition was completed, resulting in a win for 'C' Company team. Lt & QM M Whitworth joined Battn for duty	OH
	2/2/18		Working Parties furnished as usual. Inter company runners contest took place, winner A Coy runners Medals ribbon were presented in the Square by Major General C J Blackader CB DSO, ADC after which Retreat was sounded by massed bands of 17th RWF + 10th SWB. Inter battalion transport competition took place during the morning.	OH

A5834 Wt. W4973/M687 750,000 8/16 D. D. & L. Ltd. Forms/C.2118/13.

10th SWB

WAR DIARY
or
INTELLIGENCE SUMMARY.
(Erase heading not required.)

Army Form C. 2118.

February 1918

Instructions regarding War Diaries and Intelligence Summaries are contained in F. S. Regs., Part II. and the Staff Manual respectively. Title pages will be prepared in manuscript.

Place	Date	Hour	Summary of Events and Information	Remarks and references to Appendices
			Reference Map 36A	
	3/2/18		Working parties detailed as hitherto. Lewis Gun Competition (inter-company) was held, resulting in a win for an "A" Company team. Pioneers, Sanitary men, Shoemakers and Tailors showed kits to the CO at 10 am Battalion cross country run was held in the afternoon, commencing 2.15 pm. Box Respirators and P.H. Helmets were inspected	O.H.
Zotaires	4/2/18		Usual working parties were furnished. Transport Section showed kits to the Commanding Officer at 2 pm. A platoon of D Company under 2/Lt Rayner proceeded to Bde School relieving platoon of B Company under 2/Lt J.A. Lewis which rejoined about dinnertime. Inter Company rifle bombing competition was held & was won by D Company. Elementary Stretcher bearers and Lewis Gunners carried under their respective instructors 2.30 pm to 3.30 pm. 4 NCOs per Coy map reading under Capt F.R. Kenward MC Capt A.J. Evans rejoined from leave 2/Lt F.J. Williams rejoined from Course	9.H.

A5834 Wt. W4973/M687 750,000 8/16 D. D. & L. Ltd. Forms/C.2118/13.

10th SWB

Instructions regarding War Diaries and Intelligence Summaries are contained in F. S. Regs., Part II. and the Staff Manual respectively. Title pages will be prepared in manuscript.

WAR DIARY
or
INTELLIGENCE SUMMARY.
(Erase heading not required.)

February 1918

Army Form C. 2118.

Place	Date	Hour	Reference Map 36A — Summary of Events and Information	Remarks and references to Appendices
Rb Faines	5/2/1918		Working parties furnished as usual.	
			Captain A. J. Evans and 2 NCOs per company paraded at Battalion Headquarters at 9 am and proceeded on a reconnaissance.	OK
			Drummers paraded for practice under the sergeant drummer.	
			Officers Musketry class assembled under 2/Lieut W. J. Hughes.	
			Battalion and Company Gas NCOs attended lecture by Brigade Gas Officer.	
			Junior NCOs had communication drill in the afternoon and all elementary classes assembled for instruction.	
			Officers & NCOs Musketry class assembled 2.30 - 3.30pm	
			Capt Harris and Lieut W L Williams rejoined from course	

A5834 Wt. W4973 M687 750,000 8/16 D. D. & L. Ltd. Forms/C.2118/13.

10th S.W.B.

WAR DIARY
or
INTELLIGENCE SUMMARY.
(Erase heading not required.)

February 1918

Army Form C. 2118.

Instructions regarding War Diaries and Intelligence Summaries are contained in F. S. Regs., Part II. and the Staff Manual respectively. Title pages will be prepared in manuscript.

Place	Date	Hour	Summary of Events and Information	Remarks and references to Appendices
			Reference Map 36A	
	6/2/18		Working parties as usual Range being allotted to Battalion was re-allotted to Lewis Gunners of "A" Coy 7.45 - 9.30 am, "B" Coy 10.15 - 12 noon "C" Coy 1.30 pm to 3 pm BGs 3 - 4 pm Transport 4 pm - 4.30 pm Baths at Estaires were allotted, 2 - 2.30 pm 25 men each of "A" & "B" Coys 2.30 - 3 pm 25 each of "A" & "D" Coys. 3 pm - 3.30 pm "C" Coy 50 men 3.30 - 4 pm Details of "A" Coy. 2/Lt J B King proceeded on a Course Time of Retreat was altered to 5 pm. 51 Reinforcements joined from 11th Bn SWB	OJ+
Estaires	7/2/18		Working parties as usual. Officers Class assembled as usual under Capt A J Evans After digging was finished Companies were placed at the disposal of Company Commanders Capt A B Harrower proceeded on leave. 2/Lt J A Lewis proceeded to UK for transfer to RFC	OJ+
	8/2/18		Working parties provided as usual. Officers Class assembled under Capt A J Evans. Elementary Lewis Gunners paraded 9 - 12 am S.A.A. was inspected during the afternoon Brigade Retreat was sounded by Bands & Drums of 2nd, 17th R.W.F. and 10th SWB at 5 pm [illegible] Sgt T C Jones were awarded Belgian Croix de Guerre 2/Lt B P Clayton returned from leave.	

A5834 Wt. W4973/M687 750,000 8/16 D. D. & L. Ltd. Forms/C.2118/13.

10th SWB

Instructions regarding War Diaries and Intelligence Summaries are contained in F. S. Regs., Part II. and the Staff Manual respectively. Title pages will be prepared in manuscript.

WAR DIARY
or
~~INTELLIGENCE SUMMARY.~~
(Erase heading not required.)

February 1918

Army Form C. 2118.

Place	Date	Hour	Summary of Events and Information Ref Map 36A	Remarks and references to Appendices
Bostaines	8/2/18		Working parties provided as usual. Officers Class under Capt A. J Evans paraded as usual. Band and drums under Bandmaster and Sergeant drummer. All elementary classes paraded for instruction during the afternoon. Musketry practice was arranged for all available NCOs & men. Lewis Guns and Spare parts were thoroughly overhauled under Company arrangements. Lieut Clayton rejoined from leave	[initials]
	9/2/18		Working parties as usual. Officers Class assembled under Capt Evans. Elementary Lewis Gun Class paraded for instruction between 9am and 12 noon. SAA was inspected during the afternoon. Brigade Retreat was sounded by Massed Band and drums of 2nd & 17th RWF and this Battalion at 5pm. Sergeant Pembrey and 30272 Cpl TC Jones (Transport Section) awarded Belgian Croix du Guerre. Lieut DP Clayton proceeded on a Course at XV Corps School	[initials]

A5834 Wt. W4973/M687 750,000 8/16 D. D. & L. Ltd. Forms/C.2118/13.

10th S.W.B.

Instructions regarding War Diaries and Intelligence Summaries are contained in F. S. Regs., Part II. and the Staff Manual respectively. Title pages will be prepared in manuscript.

WAR DIARY
or
~~INTELLIGENCE SUMMARY.~~
(Erase heading not required.)

February 1918 Army Form C. 2118.

Place	Date	Hour	Summary of Events and Information — Reference Map 36A	Remarks and references to Appendices
Zolaous [?]	10/2/1918		No working parties. Divine Services were attended. Baths being available were allotted HQ 25, A Coy 50, B Coy 50, C Coy 50, D Coy 30. Reinforcement received recently were inspected by the Commanding Officer at 12.15 pm. 2/Lieut S J Powell rejoined from 15th Corps School.	O.H.
	11/2/1918		Working parties furnished as before. Officers Class assembled under Capt A J Evans at 9 am. Elementary Classes paraded under their respective Instructors at 9 am. Identity discs were inspected at pay which took place during the afternoon under Company arrangements. ~~Class~~ Capt J R S Hornsby rejoined from leave.	O.H.
	12/2/1918		Working parties furnished as usual. All Elementary Classes carried out usual training under their respective instructors. Retreat was sounded by band and drums between the huts at 5.30 pm.	O.H.

A5834 Wt. W4973/M687 750,000 8/16 D. D. & L. Ltd. Forms/C.2118/13.

10th LWB

February 1918

Army Form C. 2118.

WAR DIARY
or
INTELLIGENCE SUMMARY.

(*Erase heading not required.*)

Instructions regarding War Diaries and Intelligence Summaries are contained in F. S. Regs., Part II. and the Staff Manual respectively. Title pages will be prepared in manuscript.

Place	Date	Hour	Summary of Events and Information	Remarks and references to Appendices
			Reference Map 36 + 36A	
Estaires + H4d88	13/2 1918		Battalion left Billets at Estaires and proceeded to the Line relieving 7th LIVL Regt Wez Macquart Sector. Headquarters B Coy and D Coy left Estaires at 10.30 am and marched to Erquinghem and A + C Coys left at 2.30 pm by bus, which brought them to Erquinghem from where A Coy proceeded to reserve position at Subsidiary Line with Headquarters at I 20 a 60 68, and C Coy to front line Headquarters at I 20 b 90.50. Advanced Headquarters were established at I 20 a 60 70, and Rear-Administrative Headquarters at Erquinghem, H4d88. B + D Coys proceeded to Atlas Camp near Erquinghem. Relief completed by 10.50 pm.	WH
H4d88	14/2 1918		Dispositions similar. Companies in reserve and Administrative Headquarters had a general clean up, and were inspected at 12 noon. Battalion on left, 17th Bn RWF on right, Royal Sussex Regt, 12th Division. No operation of any importance were enacted. Casualties nil. Enemy and our Artillery normally active.	WH
	15/2 1918		Dispositions unchanged. Machine Guns normally active during the night. A patrol left our lines at 8 pm consisting of 2/Lt W? Hughes and three other ranks. Object of patrol to	WH

A5834 Wt. W4973/M687 750,000 8/16 D. D. & L. Ltd. Forms/C.2118/13.

10th SWB

February 1918 Army Form C. 2118.

Instructions regarding War Diaries and Intelligence Summaries are contained in F. S. Regs., Part II. and the Staff Manual respectively. Title pages will be prepared in manuscript.

WAR DIARY
or
~~INTELLIGENCE~~ SUMMARY.

(*Erase heading not required.*)

Place	Date	Hour	Summary of Events and Information (Reference Map 36)	Remarks and references to Appendices
H.4d 88) 120 69.5)	15/2/1918		reconnoitre our front. The going in no man's land was bad the ground being badly cut up. A rather unsatisfactory report was rendered as to the state of our wire, which is unsystematic in places. Some good patches were reported also, however. The first support line appears to be well wired. Patrol withdrew at 11pm without casualties. The night was very quiet. During the day Artillery was fairly active and Enemy aircraft were observed over Bois Grenier. Our Artillery fired several bursts during the day on various targets. Administrative Headquarters + B + D Coys carried out sundry training including signalling, Lewis Gunnery, map reading &c. and were engaged during the afternoon in improving the Camp. Casualties nil.	W.H.

A5834 Wt. W4973/M687 750,000 8/16 D. D. & L. Ltd. Forms/C.2118/13.

10th SWB

Instructions regarding War Diaries and Intelligence Summaries are contained in F. S. Regs., Part II. and the Staff Manual respectively. Title pages will be prepared in manuscript.

WAR DIARY
or
~~INTELLIGENCE SUMMARY.~~
(Erase heading not required.)

Feby 1918

Army Form C. 2118.

Place	Date	Hour	Summary of Events and Information	Remarks and references to Appendices
			Reference Map 36	
Hud 88 / 130.195	16/2/18		Dispositions unchanged. Machine guns were active during the night. A small patrol consisting of 2/Lt P.B. King and 6 O.R. left our lines at 8 pm 15th. to ascertain position of enemy posts and M.G. positions. The results were satisfactory. Enemy and our artillery active throughout the day, and aircraft was very active. Administrative details and Reserve boys were inspected by Capt F R Kenward M.C. after which physical drill, recreational training, platoon drill and musketry were carried out. Lewis gun class, signaller class, map reading class, runners class, drummers and bandsmen, all carried on under their various instructors. Work on improvement of Camp was continued during the afternoon. Casualties - 4 O.R. wounded.	CH
-do-	17/2/18		Dispositions similar. Aircraft and M.Gs fairly active. The day was remarkably uneventful. No patrols were sent out. Church Parade and Kit inspections were the orders for Administrative Details and B+D Coys. Casualties nil.	CH

A5834 Wt. W4973/M687 750,000 8/16 D. D. & L. Ltd. Forms/C.2118/13.

10th LWB

Instructions regarding War Diaries and Intelligence Summaries are contained in F. S. Regs., Part II. and the Staff Manual respectively. Title pages will be prepared in manuscript.

WAR DIARY
or
INTELLIGENCE SUMMARY.
(Erase heading not required.)

Feby 1918.

Army Form C. 2118.

Place	Date	Hour	Summary of Events and Information (Ref Map 36)	Remarks and references to Appendices
Hud 8 8 [?o 6 9 5]	18/2/1918		B & D Coys left Atlas Camp and proceeded to Fleurie Switch. Dispositions of Coys – B Coy Fleurie Post, D Coy La Vase Post. Other dispositions unchanged. Enemy and our ~~[illegible]~~ Artillery fairly quiet all day and no events of importance occurred. Coys & Administrative details moved as above and with the exception of Signallers and Runners classes no training could be carried out. Casualties nil.	[initials]
-do-	19/2/1918		Dispositions as yesterday. Aircraft and Artillery fairly active all day. The enemy being particularly so during the evening when all communication trenches received close attention. ~~One aeroplane appeared to come down~~ Coy at Fleurie Switch carried out work under the instructions of OC Switch under whose command they came on moving into the switch. Casualties nil.	[initials]

A5834 Wt. W4973 M687 750,000 8/16 D. D. & L. Ltd. Forms/C.2118/13.

10th LWB   War Diary   January 1918

Ref Map 36A

Place	Time	date	Summary of Events	Remarks
		28/1/1918	Working party as before with the exception that location of work was slightly changed. Commanding Officer inspected Kits of C Coy at 10 am. Elementary L.G. Class assembled at 9 am and 2 pm. Sgt Bull, Cpls J R Moss and D E Thomas proceeded to UK for commissions. Capt H Cottam MC proceeded on leave	G.F.O.
Estaires		29/1/1918	Working parties furnished as before. Range was at the disposal of the battalion all day, and inter company shooting was organised. Revolver shooting was carried by Officers and NCOs in possession of revolvers. Elementary L.G. Class underwent instruction as usual.	G.F.O.
		30/1/1918	Working parties as usual. Inter-Company Field Kitchen competition was held, the winners being B Company. Band carried out practice under Bandmaster. Baths were allotted to Battn (at Sailly) and busses were provided from the Petite Place. 150 men were bathed. Work was continued after bathing	G.F.O.

10th SWB War Diary January 1918

Place	Time	Date	Summary of Events Reference Map 36a	
Rostaines		31/1/1918	Working parties continued as usual Runners Class paraded under 2/Lt P.B. King Inter platoon Competition was decided in the afternoon Winners 'C' Company Elementary Stretcher bearers paraded under Medical Officer for instruction	R.F.O.

C Bowen
Major Commanding
10th SWB

10th LWB | WAR DIARY *or* INTELLIGENCE SUMMARY. | Feby 1918 | Army Form C. 2118.

Instructions regarding War Diaries and Intelligence Summaries are contained in F. S. Regs., Part II. and the Staff Manual respectively. Title pages will be prepared in manuscript.

(*Erase heading not required.*)

Reference Map 36

Place	Date	Hour	Summary of Events and Information	Remarks and references to Appendices
H4d88 120695	20/2/1918		Enemy artillery active on our Forward Support Line. Aircraft inactive, as also was our Artillery. B+D Coys relieved A+C Coys in the Subsidiary Line and front line respectively, and Administrative Headquarters relieved Advanced Headquarters. Relief completed about 8pm. Day uneventful and very quiet. Casualties nil	OH
-do-	21/2/1918		Disposition as yesterday. Hostile Artillery active on back areas throughout the day. One enemy aeroplane was brought down by our airmen about 1215 pm. Our artillery retaliated vigorously on enemy back areas. Our Trench Mortars fired 106 rounds on enemy territory between I 21 b 10 05 and I 21 c 95 65. Casualties nil. An Officers patrol left our lines at 1030 pm to examine enemy wire, returning at 135 am	OH

A5834 Wt. W4973/M687 750,000 8/16 D. D. & L. Ltd. Forms/C.2118/13.

10th SWB

Instructions regarding War Diaries and Intelligence Summaries are contained in F. S. Regs., Part II. and the Staff Manual respectively. Title pages will be prepared in manuscript.

WAR DIARY
or
INTELLIGENCE SUMMARY.
(*Erase heading not required.*)

February 1918 — Army Form C. 2118.

Place	Date	Hour	Summary of Events and Information	Remarks and references to Appendices
			Reference Map 36	
H4 a 8.8 I20 b 9.5	22/2/1918		Dispositions unchanged with the exception that Battalion Administrative Headquarters moved to Transport Lines at H9 b 2.8 Artillery and Aircraft fairly inactive during the day. Considerable movement were observed in the enemy lines. An officers patrol was sent from our line at 5.30pm and returned at 10.40pm. No enemy encountered 2/Lieut P.B. King proceeded to UK on leave. Casualties – 1 OR wounded, remaining at duty	OH
~~H4 a 8.8~~ H9 b 2.8 I20 b 9.5	23/2/1918		Dispositions similar A very quiet day, there being little hostile activity of any description, on our front Reconnoitring Patrols were sent out during the night to report on enemy and our wire ~~Patrol under 2/Lt R.M. Morgan encountered enemy listening post and were fired on several times. One man Pte Ivatman was killed in withdrawing~~.	OH

A5834 Wt. W4973/M687 750,000 8/16 D. D. & L. Ltd. Forms/C.2118/13.

10th SWB

WAR DIARY
or
INTELLIGENCE SUMMARY.
(Erase heading not required.)

February 1918

Army Form C. 2118.

Instructions regarding War Diaries and Intelligence Summaries are contained in F. S. Regs., Part II. and the Staff Manual respectively. Title pages will be prepared in manuscript.

Place	Date	Hour	Summary of Events and Information	Remarks and references to Appendices
			Reference Map 36	
HQ [illegible] 120b 9.5	24/2/1918		Dispositions unchanged. Another quiet day. Enemy and our aircraft fairly active, but no combats were seen. Artillery fairly quiet on both sides. Patrol under 2/Lieut R.M. Morgan was seen by enemy and fired on several times. One man, Pte Swatman was killed on withdrawal from No man's Land	OH
-do-	25/2/1918		Dispositions unchanged. Enemy again quiet. A severe bombardment in the early hours of the morning was placed on the Battalion on our left, and HE shells were placed near the Subsidiary Lines near our H.Qrs. A number of Gas shells appeared to pass over somewhere also. The remainder of the day was very quiet and uneventful. 2/Lt W.P. Hughes proceeded to Brigade School with his Platoon. Casualties nil	OH

A5834 Wt. W4973/M687 750,000 8/16 D. D. & L. Ltd. Forms/C.2118/13.

10th S.W.B. | WAR DIARY *or* ~~INTELLIGENCE SUMMARY.~~ (*Erase heading not required.*) | February 1918 | Army Form C. 2118.

Instructions regarding War Diaries and Intelligence Summaries are contained in F. S. Regs., Part II. and the Staff Manual respectively. Title pages will be prepared in manuscript.

Place	Date	Hour	Summary of Events and Information — Reference Map 36	Remarks and references to Appendices
H9 b 2 8 } I 20 d 9 5 }	26/2/1918		Dispositions similar. B & D Companies were relieved by A & C Companies and Administrative and Advanced Headquarters changed over. Relief was completed by 8pm. Dispositions now - Front Line, A Company, Subsidiary Line, 'C' Company, Support Companies in Fleurie Switch, B & D Companies. Locations of Battalion and Company Headquarters remains unchanged A very quiet day as usual. A patrol was sent out after relief to reconnoitre enemy wire and returned to our lines without casualties Capt J.P.S. Hornsby proceeded to Brigade School as Adjutant Lieut Col C D Harvey DSO rejoined from leave	OK

A5834 Wt. W4973 M687 750,000 8/16 D. D. & L. Ltd. Forms/C.2118/13.

10th SWB

Instructions regarding War Diaries and Intelligence Summaries are contained in F. S. Regs., Part II. and the Staff Manual respectively. Title pages will be prepared in manuscript.

WAR DIARY
or
~~INTELLIGENCE SUMMARY.~~
(Erase heading not required.)

February 1918 Army Form C. 2118.

Place	Date	Hour	Reference Map 36. Summary of Events and Information	Remarks and references to Appendices
H.9.b.2.8 I.20.b.9.5	27/2/1918		Dispositions similar Capt W.D. Cobb proceeded to UK (exchange of Officers &c with long service overseas). Enemy quiet, as usual. 2/Lieutenant B.J. Haworth proceeded to UK on leave Reconnoitring patrol sent out to examine enemy wire and going in NO MAN'S LAND. They returned without casualties Casualties for the 24 hours Nil Administrative Details cleaned up generally	WH
-do-	28/2/1918		Disposition similar Final of Divisional Cross Country Run was run off in the afternoon. This Battalion team finishing 4th Enemy quiet as usual. Artillery activity during the night, however was above normal. Casualties nil Patrol was sent out from our lines to inspect	WH

A5834 Wt. W4973 M687 750,000 8/16 D. D. & L. Ltd. Forms/C.2118/13.

10th SWB

Instructions regarding War Diaries and Intelligence Summaries are contained in F. S. Regs., Part II. and the Staff Manual respectively. Title pages will be prepared in manuscript.

WAR DIARY
or
INTELLIGENCE SUMMARY.

(*Erase heading not required.*)

February 1918 Army Form C. 2118.

Place	Date	Hour	Reference Map 36 Summary of Events and Information	Remarks and references to Appendices
			and report on enemy wire. Patrol returned without casualties. Capt W J Cobb proceeded to UK for a tour of six months duty. This officer left the Battalion yesterday. [illegible] Lieutenant Colonel Commanding 10th Bn S W Borderers	[illegible]

A5834 Wt. W4973 M687 750,000 8/16 D. D. & L. Ltd. Forms/C.2118/13.

10th S W Borderers.

10 SWB

March 1 1918

Vol 27

WAR DIARY
or
~~INTELLIGENCE SUMMARY.~~
(Erase heading not required.)

Army Form C. 2118.

Instructions regarding War Diaries and Intelligence Summaries are contained in F. S. Regs., Part II. and the Staff Manual respectively. Title pages will be prepared in manuscript.

Place	Date	Hour	Summary of Events and Information	Remarks and references to Appendices
			Reference Map 36	
WEZ MACQUART SECTOR I 20 a. 68. 70.	1/3/18.		Dispositions. A+C Coys front line. B+D Coys Flevon [?] Switch. Advanced Headquarters Subsidiary Line I 20 a 68 70. Administrative Headquarters Erquinghem. Transport Lines Erquinghem. QM Stores Erquinghem. Enemy quiet on our front all day. Aircraft inactive. Our artillery and aircraft active throughout the day. A patrol of one NCO and 9 men was in NO MANS LAND from 7pm to 10pm. No enemy encountered and patrol returned without casualties. Capt A B Harrower struck off on being medically boarded in UK	JWRR [?]
-do-	2/3/18		~~Dispositions similar. Enemy artillery and aircraft inactive. Our artillery and aircraft were fairly active throughout the day. Battalion on our right raided Enemy trenches in the ~~evening~~ early morning during which a few enemy shells fell on our forward lines. Our Artillery assisted in the barrage put down during the raid. A fighting patrol left our lines from 8pm to 10.45 pm but no enemy were encountered. After the raid the night was quiet~~ Cancelled	JWRR [?]

A5834 Wt. W493/M657 750,000 8/16 [illegible] Ltd. Forms/C.2118/13.

10th S.W.B.

WAR DIARY
or
INTELLIGENCE SUMMARY.
(Erase heading not required.)

~~February~~ March 1918

Army Form C. 2118.

Instructions regarding War Diaries and Intelligence Summaries are contained in F. S. Regs., Part II. and the Staff Manual respectively. Title pages will be prepared in manuscript.

Place	Date	Hour	Summary of Events and Information (Reference Map 36)	Remarks and references to Appendices
WEZ MACQUART SECTOR 120 a 68.70	2/3/18		Dispositions similar. Enemy artillery and aircraft inactive but ours were fairly active throughout the day. A fighting patrol left our lines and swept NO MANS LAND between 8 pm and 10.45 pm. No enemy were encountered. Casualties Nil	[initials]
-do-	3/3/18		Dispositions similar. Battalion on our Right raided Enemy trenches at 5.40 am. During the raid a few shells were directed at our forward post. Our artillery assisted in the barrage put on enemy's trenches. Aircraft and Artillery on both sides inactive all day. Poor visibility prevented much observation during the day. Enemy artillery opened harassing fire on our sector on the signal of two blasts of a trumpet or horn, followed by series of double lights, at 12.30 am. This fire lasted for about half an hour. No further action followed and our Artillery remained quiet. 2/Lt A.A.R. Williams proceeded on leave. 2/Lt Eatham returned from leave.	[initials]

A5834 Wt. W4973/M687 750,000 8/16 D. D. & L. Ltd. Forms/C.2118/13.

10th S.W.B.

Instructions regarding War Diaries and Intelligence Summaries are contained in F. S. Regs., Part II. and the Staff Manual respectively. Title pages will be prepared in manuscript.

WAR DIARY
or
~~INTELLIGENCE SUMMARY.~~

(Erase heading not required.)

March 1918. Army Form C. 2118.

Place	Date	Hour	Reference Map 36 — Summary of Events and Information	Remarks and references to Appendices
WEZ MACQUART SECTOR 1.20 a 68 70	4/3/1918		Dispositions similar. Enemy and our artillery inactive during the day. "Betty" post received some attention between 5.45pm and 7pm, a number of whizzbangs being generously distributed. Our artillery inactive during the day. A patrol left our lines at 1.20 d. 95 70 at 1.30 am, and returned at the same point at 2.40 am. No enemy encountered. B + D Coys relieved A + C Coys and Headquarters Advanced and Administrative Details changed over. Relief completed about 9.20 pm. Casualties Nil.	J.R.H.
WEZ MACQUART SECTOR 1.20 a 68.70	5/3/1918.		Dispositions:– B + D Coys in the line. A + C Coys in Flewme Switch. Position of Headquarters, Transport and Q.M. Stores remains unchanged. Enemy artillery inactive but ours were busy on back areas with 18 pdrs and hows. Our aircraft also fairly active all day. Enemy plane crossed our line about 10 am, but did not venture far. Other planes crossed about 3 pm at a tremendous altitude	J.R.H.

A5834 Wt. W4973/M687 750,000 8/16 D. D. & L. Ltd. Forms/C.2118/13.

10th S.W.B.

Instructions regarding War Diaries and Intelligence Summaries are contained in F. S. Regs., Part II. and the Staff Manual respectively. Title pages will be prepared in manuscript.

WAR DIARY

or

~~INTELLIGENCE SUMMARY.~~

(Erase heading not required.)

~~February~~ March 1918

Army Form C. 2118.

Place	Date	Hour	Reference Map 36 — Summary of Events and Information	Remarks and references to Appendices
WEZ MACQUART SECTOR I.20.a.68.70	6/3/1918		Dispositions unchanged. Enemy artillery sent numerous gas shells on our left, but our area was unaffected. Otherwise Enemy and our Artillery inactive during the day, though our Artillery fired some rounds on back areas after midday. Aircraft fairly active during the day. At 9pm Enemy shelled our right rear with gas shells and HE. A patrol left our lines at I.20.d.55.30 at 3am and returned to same place at 5am. No enemy were encountered though a large working party was heard and was fired on by our patrol. 2/Lt D.P. Clayton proceeded to UK for six months tour of duty.	[illegible]
-do-	7/3/1918		Dispositions similar. Enemy artillery unusually active during the day, GALLOGATE, PARK ROW and SUBSIDIARY LINE receiving special attention. WELLINGTON AVENUE C.T. was hit in two places. Our Artillery was less active than usual. Desultory firing on back areas all day. A patrol left our lines at I.21.c.55.80 at 3.30am, and returned at I.21.c.70.80 at 4.30am. No enemy encountered.	[illegible]

A5834 Wt. W4973/M687 750,000 8/16 D. D. & L. Ltd. Forms/C.2118/13.

10th S.W.B.

Instructions regarding War Diaries and Intelligence Summaries are contained in F. S. Regs., Part II. and the Staff Manual respectively. Title pages will be prepared in manuscript.

WAR DIARY
or
~~INTELLIGENCE SUMMARY.~~
(Erase heading not required.)

March 1918

Army Form C. 2118.

Place	Date	Hour	Summary of Events and Information (Reference Map 36)	Remarks and references to Appendices
WEZ MACQUART SECTOR I 20 a 68 70	8/3/1918.		Dispositions similar. Enemy artillery again showed increased activity, this time the objects of his attention being BURNT FARM and WILLOW AVENUE, which was blown in in several places. Two enemy planes were bold enough to fly fairly low over our lines during the afternoon, and the poor visibility prevented them being easy targets. Other planes passed over our lines at great heights. Our Artillery retaliated vigorously for enemy TM activity, and were continuously directing harassing fire on his back areas. Our aircraft did some daring patrol work, flying particularly low over enemy lines, and directing machine gun fire on them. Two patrols left our lines. (1) 10 other ranks from I 21 a 80 20. 3am to 4.30am and (2) one officer and 9 O.R. from I 20 d 50 15. 11pm to 12.20am. No enemy encountered.	JMRK

A5834 Wt. W4973/M687 750,000 8/16 D. D. & L. Ltd. Forms/C.2118/13.

10th SWB

Instructions regarding War Diaries and Intelligence Summaries are contained in F. S. Regs., Part II. and the Staff Manual respectively. Title pages will be prepared in manuscript.

WAR DIARY
or
~~INTELLIGENCE SUMMARY~~.
(Erase heading not required.)

March 1918

Army Form C. 2118.

Place	Date	Hour	Reference Map 36 — Summary of Events and Information	Remarks and references to Appendices
WEZ MACQUART SECTOR 120 a 68 70.	9/3/1918		Dispositions unchanged. Enemy Artillery activity continued during the day. SUBSIDIARY LINE and SUPPORT LINE received a large amount of lively attention between 2 30 pm and 5 15 pm, 5.9 shells, about 200 in number, all dropped on these points. Enemy aircraft also active seven hostile planes crossed our lines at 7 45 am. Four enemy planes attacked two of ours (RE 8) about 2.45 pm, but ~~[illegible]~~ no success attended their industry. Our Artillery fired at intervals during the day, but did not appear to be retaliating for enemy's shelling. A patrol of one officer (Capt H Cottam MC) and 9 other ranks, left our lines at I.21.c.75.78 at 2.5 am to reconnoitre (1) railway line and embankment (2) going in NOMANS LAND (3) any likely obstacle on the railway, condition of enemy wire &c. The patrol was detected and bombed on two occasions but returned without casualties, entering our lines at I.21.c.68.75 at 4.20 am MW F.F.Williams proceeded on leave	MW

A5834 Wt. W4973/M687 750,000 8/16 D. D. & L. Ltd. Forms/C.2118/13.

10th S W B

Instructions regarding War Diaries and Intelligence Summaries are contained in F. S. Regs., Part II. and the Staff Manual respectively. Title pages will be prepared in manuscript.

WAR DIARY
or
~~INTELLIGENCE SUMMARY.~~
(Erase heading not required.)

March 1918

Army Form C. 2118.

Place	Date	Hour	Summary of Events and Information — Reference Map 36	Remarks and references to Appendices
WEZ MACQUART SECTOR. 1.20.a.68.70	10/3/1918		Dispositions unchanged. Enemy Artillery opened a very heavy fire on our left (about L'EPINETTE SECTOR) at 4.30 am, lasting until 5 am. After this desultory firing took place all day until 12 noon, when hostile activity became pronounced. During the afternoon DEAD COW FARM, LA VISEE POST, RATION FARM, 2nd SUPPORT, SUBSIDIARY LINE all receiving vigorous attention with 4.2s and 5.9s. Six Enemy aeroplanes crossed our lines between 9am and 9.30am and another during the afternoon. Our artillery fired 18pounders and 4.5s in retaliation for enemy shelling. At about 7pm the enemy commenced a bombardment of Battalion Headquarters with 77mm, sending over salvoes of four at a time. This continued for about 25 minutes. Officers Mess and cookhouses were hit, causing three casualties. "A+C" Coys relieved "B+D" Coys in the line. Headquarters changed over. Headquarters on relief moved from Erquinghem to Brigade School at Blanche Maison.	[initials]

A5834 Wt. W4973/M687 750,000 8/16 D. D. & L. Ltd. Forms/C.2118/13.

10th S.W. Borderers

WAR DIARY
or
~~INTELLIGENCE SUMMARY.~~
(Erase heading not required.)

March 1918

Army Form C. 2118.

Instructions regarding War Diaries and Intelligence Summaries are contained in F. S. Regs., Part II. and the Staff Manual respectively. Title pages will be prepared in manuscript.

Place	Date	Hour	Summary of Events and Information Reference Map 36	Remarks and references to Appendices
WEZ MACQUART SECTOR I 20.a 68.70	11/3/1918.		Dispositions. A & C Coys line & subsidiary, B & D Coys Ferme Switch, Advanced Headquarters I 20.a 68.70. At 4.50 am the enemy opened an intense bombardment on our left extending gradually to our extreme right. Smoke 5.9s minnies, LTMs and 77 mm all accompanied by very heavy MG fire were the "order of the strafe" which was conducted very thoroughly. SOS was observed at 5.5 am which was promptly responded to by our Artillery. Enemy barrage ceased about 6 am. During the day the enemy continued his unpleasant industry so far as Battalion Headquarters concerned two direct hits being obtained on the Mess and one on the cookhouse. No casualties. Enemy planes were unusually active during the day, but, with their usual daring, maintained a decidedly respectable height during their operations! Our Artillery was active in retaliation for enemy shelling. A patrol left our lines to examine enemy wire and NO MAN'S LAND and returned without casualties. Lt E.R. Jeffcott proceeded on Lewis Gun Course. 2/Lt. P.B. King returned from leave	RBK

A5834 Wt. W4973/M687 750,000 8/16 D. D. & L. Ltd. Forms/C.2118/13.

10th S.W.B.

Instructions regarding War Diaries and Intelligence Summaries are contained in F. S. Regs., Part II. and the Staff Manual respectively. Title pages will be prepared in manuscript.

WAR DIARY
or
~~INTELLIGENCE SUMMARY.~~
(Erase heading not required.)

March 1918

Army Form C. 2118.

Place	Date	Hour	Summary of Events and Information Reference Map 36	Remarks and references to Appendices
WEZ MACQUART SECTOR I.20 a 68.70	12/3/1918		Dispositions similar. Enemy artillery fairly quiet during the night the only activity being a few 77 mm near Battalion Headquarters at midnight and 5 ~~pm~~ am. During the day, all parts seemed to receive attention Armentieres, L'armee, Fleury, Communication Trenches, all being shelled in turn. Enemy Aircraft very active again but all flying very high. Our arms comparatively inactive excepting Machine Guns who were busy on AA work. Fighting and reconnoitring patrols were sent out during the night, without unusual results. Transport badly disorganized owing to enemy artillery activity on back areas, all roads receiving attention	
-do-	13/3/1918		Dispositions similar. Enemy artillery fairly inactive overnight so far as our sector concerned but right and left sectors were both heavily bombarded. During the day L'armee and Flewrie Switches and all rear communications were shelled. Enemy and our aircraft both active all day	

A5834 Wt. W4973/M687 750,000 8/16 D. D. & L. Ltd. Forms/C.2118/13.

10th S.W.B.

WAR DIARY
or
~~INTELLIGENCE SUMMARY.~~

(Erase heading not required.)

March 1918

Army Form C. 2118.

Instructions regarding War Diaries and Intelligence Summaries are contained in F. S. Regs., Part II. and the Staff Manual respectively. Title pages will be prepared in manuscript

Place	Date	Hour	Summary of Events and Information — Reference Map. 36	Remarks and references to Appendices
Wez Macquart Sector. I.30.a.68.70.	14/3/1918		Dispositions unchanged Enemy artillery, as usual active on all parts of the sector A red paper balloon passed over our lines at 1.20 pm and dropped a packet of papers near Battalion Headquarters These papers were sent to Brigade Intelligence Officer Our artillery was very active during the day on enemy front and rear defences. Aircraft inactive. Fighting and reconnoitring patrols were sent out during the night. No enemy encountered	JMM
do.	15/3/1918		Dispositions similar. Enemy artillery very active with 77mm ANNIE, AGNES, and ADA Posts being the most unfortunate recipients of attention. Several direct hits appeared to be secured on LA VESEE POST also. Our artillery retaliated with alacrity to their shelling during the night. During the day, Enemy artillery favoured Subsidiary Line & Cowgate Avenue	JMM

A5834 Wt. W4973/M687 750,000 8/16 D. D. & L. Forms/C.2118/13

10th SWB

Instructions regarding War Diaries and Intelligence Summaries are contained in F. S. Regs., Part II. and the Staff Manual respectively. Title pages will be prepared in manuscript.

WAR DIARY
or
~~INTELLIGENCE SUMMARY.~~
(Erase heading not required.)

March 1918

Army Form C. 2118.

Place	Date	Hour	Summary of Events and Information — Reference Map 36	Remarks and references to Appendices
	15/3/1918		with his unwelcome attentions. Enemy planes flew over our lines at an extraordinarily low altitude. Our planes were also active during the day.	[illegible initials]
WEZ MACQUART SECTOR 1.20 a 68.70	16/3/1918		Disposition similar. Enemy artillery fairly quiet through last night. Our Artillery assisted left Division in barrage put down during a raid but were otherwise quiet. Machine guns were active at intervals throughout the night. 'B' and 'D' Companies relieved 'A' and 'C' Companies in the line. Headquarter personnel did not change over. Relief satisfactorily completed without casualties	[illegible initials]

A5834 Wt. W4973/M687 750,000 8/16 D. D. & L. Ltd. Forms/C.2118/13.

16th S.W.B.

Instructions regarding War Diaries and Intelligence Summaries are contained in F. S. Regs., Part II. and the Staff Manual respectively. Title pages will be prepared in manuscript

WAR DIARY
or
~~INTELLIGENCE SUMMARY.~~
(Erase heading not required.)

March 1918

Army Form C. 2118.

Place	Date	Hour	Summary of Events and Information Reference Map 36	Remarks and references to Appendices
Wez Macquart Sector 1.30 a.68.70	17/3/1918		Dispositions 'B' & 'D' Companies Front and Subsidiary Lines A & C Companies Fleurie and L'Armee Switchs. Advanced and Administrative HQrs and transport lines dispositions unaltered. Enemy Artillery Active all day. Wellington Avenue Communication Trench, Left Company Headquarters Rue de Bois were heavily shelled between 2 pm and 11.30 pm. Three direct hits were obtained on Company Headquarters. Fleurie Switch was the unfortunate recipient of about 20 4.2s at 11 am. 30 rounds of LHV at 4.30 pm. AA guns were busy against our planes which were very active throughout the day. Enemy Trench Mortars were active against Augusta Post, Gallowgate Post and second line. Administrative Headquarters moved from Blanche Maison back to Erquinghem.	[illegible]

A5834 Wt. W4973/M687 750,000 8/16 D. D. & L. Ltd. Forms/C.2118/13.

10th S.W.B.

Instructions regarding War Diaries and Intelligence Summaries are contained in F. S. Regs., Part II. and the Staff Manual respectively. Title pages will be prepared in manuscript.

WAR DIARY
or
~~INTELLIGENCE SUMMARY.~~
(Erase heading not required.)

March 1918

Army Form C. 2118.

Place	Date	Hour	Summary of Events and Information — Reference Map 36	Remarks and references to Appendices
Map Marquart Sector 1/20 a 68 70	18/3/1918		Dispositions similar. Quartermaster's Stores were shelled out of Erquinghem in the morning and moved to the Transport Lines at B.28 a 3 8. About 12.30 pm Enemy artillery opened heavy fire on old buildings and wire at I.8 b and d, about 300 shells being sent over. Salop Avenue and Wellington Avenue also received some attention during the day. Enemy and our aircraft very busy during the day. Headquarters personnel changed over and A & C Companies relieved B & D Companies in the line. Relief completed without casualties. Reconnoitring patrols sent out throughout the night to ascertain condition of enemy wire. Lt. E.D. Rees proceeded on leave.	JRRW

A5834 Wt. W4973/M687 750,000 8/16 D. D. & L. Ltd. Forms/C.2118/13.

10th S.W.Borderers. March 1918. Army Form C. 2118.

WAR DIARY
or
~~INTELLIGENCE SUMMARY.~~
(Erase heading not required.)

Instructions regarding War Diaries and Intelligence Summaries are contained in F. S. Regs., Part II. and the Staff Manual respectively. Title pages will be prepared in manuscript.

Place	Date	Hour	Reference Map 36 — Summary of Events and Information	Remarks and references to Appendices
Mez Macquart Sector	19/3/1918		Dispositions A + C Companies Front and Subsidiary Lines B + D Companies Fleurie and L'Ormee Switches. Advanced and Administrative Headquarters as before. Transport as before. Enemy Artillery fairly active overnight chief attractions being back areas. Machine Guns fired occasional bursts throughout the night. Our Artillery inactive with the exception of slight retaliation for enemy "whizzbanging" at 12.30 pm and 4 pm. Aircraft on both sides comparatively inactive. Two reconnoitring patrols were sent out to inspect enemy wire and returned without casualties. Administrative Headquarters moved again to Blanche Maison. A & a. Y.W. a.a. Williams returned from leave.	JRM
-do-	20/3/1918		Dispositions unchanged. Enemy Artillery was active overnight shelling Subsidiary Line near Battalion Headquarters and front line posts with 4.2s and 18 pounders about midnight. M.G.s fairly quiet. ~~Ene~~ Artillery after a quiet morning resumed activity	JRM

A5834 Wt. W4973/M687 750,000 8/16 D. D. & L. Ltd. Forms/C.2118/13.

10th S W B

Instructions regarding War Diaries and Intelligence Summaries are contained in F. S. Regs., Part II. and the Staff Manual respectively. Title pages will be prepared in manuscript.

WAR DIARY
or
INTELLIGENCE SUMMARY.
(Erase heading not required.)

March 1918

Army Form C. 2118.

Place	Date	Hour	Summary of Events and Information — Reference Map 36	Remarks and references to Appendices
	20/3/1918		on Subsidiary Line and Left Company Headquarters. A few 5.9s dropped near BETTY POST during the afternoon. Our artillery retaliated slightly for enemy activity. Two reconnoitring patrols out to inspect enemy wire etc and engage any hostile parties seen. No enemy encountered and patrols returned without casualties	[initials]
Weymacquart Sector 120 a 68.70	21/3/1918		Dispositions similar. A heavy bombardment was heard on our left about 4.30 am and continued for some considerable time. No explanation is forthcoming. Gongs and bells were heard in Enemy lines during the bombardment. Enemy Artillery of all calibres was active on our front all day and our Artillery occasionally retaliated on his back areas	[initials]

A5834 Wt. W4973/M687 750,000 8/16 D. D. & L. Ltd. Forms/C.2118/13.

10th S.W.B. March 1918

Army Form C. 2118.

WAR DIARY
or
~~INTELLIGENCE SUMMARY.~~
(Erase heading not required.)

Instructions regarding War Diaries and Intelligence Summaries are contained in F. S. Regs., Part II. and the Staff Manual respectively. Title pages will be prepared in manuscript.

Place	Date	Hour	Summary of Events and Information (Reference Map 36)	Remarks and references to Appendices
Wez Macquart Sector 1 20 a 68 70	21/3/1918		Other arms quiet all day. Three reconnoitring patrols sent out during the night with the usual object i.e. inspecting enemy wire. All returned without encountering any hostile parties.	JWH
-do-	22/3/1918		Dispositions unaltered. Enemy artillery favoured Henry and L'Armee Switches with attention during the night which was otherwise quiet. Enemy artillery active on left Battalion front and also shelled the neighbourhood of Henry Switch slightly. Our Artillery commenced seriously cutting enemy wire and some excellent results were observed. Trench Mortars ~~also~~ cooperated with Artillery in the wirecutting operations. Four patrols were sent out to investigate the result of our wirecutting and returned with excellent reports. Capt A.W. Menton returned from Course	JWH

A5834 Wt. W4973/M687 750,000 8/16 D. D. & L. Ltd. Forms/C.2118/13.

10th S.I.R.

WAR DIARY
or
INTELLIGENCE SUMMARY.
(Erase heading not required.)

March 1918.

Army Form C. 2118.

Instructions regarding War Diaries and Intelligence Summaries are contained in F. S. Regs., Part II. and the Staff Manual respectively. Title pages will be prepared in manuscript.

Place	Date	Hour	Summary of Events and Information	Remarks and references to Appendices
			Reference Map 36	
Wez Macquart Sector I 20 a 68 70	23/3/1918		Dispositions unaltered A very quiet night on both sides. Intermittent shelling of back areas was the only artillery activity The day was as quiet as the night so far as hostile activity was concerned. Desultory shelling at intervals on back areas was the only activity. Our Artillery carried out wirecutting programme from 2.30pm onwards and as before, obtained excellent results. Reconnoitring patrol out (two in number) to examine result of days shooting and satisfactorily reported thereon. No enemy encountered	JRM
-do-	24/3/1918		Dispositions similar. Another very quiet night followed by an equally quiet day. Aerial activity fairly pronounced, chiefly on our side. Three planes patrolled over enemy lines during the day, and one enemy craft was observed over our lines.	JRM

A5834 Wt. W4973/M687 750,000 8/16 D. D. & L. Ltd. Forms/C.2118/13.

10th S W Borderers

March 1918

Army Form C. 2118.

WAR DIARY
or
~~INTELLIGENCE SUMMARY.~~
(Erase heading not required.)

Instructions regarding War Diaries and Intelligence Summaries are contained in F. S. Regs., Part II. and the Staff Manual respectively. Title pages will be prepared in manuscript.

Place	Date	Hour	Summary of Events and Information — Reference Map 36	Remarks and references to Appendices
Wez Macquart Sector 1.30.a.68.70	24/3/1918		Our artillery maintained their wire cutting tactics during the day and our Trench Mortars carried out some slight registration between 2pm and 2.30pm. Reconnoitring and fighting patrol, under 2/Lieut. W.P. Hughes went into NO MANS LAND to keep watch on enemy wire. A hostile party was seen and fired on by our patrol with uncertain result.	[initials]
-do-	25/3/1918		B + D Companies relieved "A" + C Companies in the Front and Subsidiary Lines at dawn. Disposition. A + C Companies Reserve and L'Armee Switches. B + D Companies Front and Subsidiary Lines. Headquarters and Transport unaltered.	[initials]

A5834 Wt. W4973/M687 750,000 8/16 D. D. & L. Ltd. Forms/C.2118/13.

10th S.W.B. — March 1918 — Army Form C. 2118.

Instructions regarding War Diaries and Intelligence Summaries are contained in F. S. Regs., Part II. and the Staff Manual respectively. Title pages will be prepared in manuscript.

WAR DIARY
or
~~INTELLIGENCE SUMMARY.~~
(Erase heading not required.)

Place	Date	Hour	Summary of Events and Information — Reference Map 31	Remarks and references to Appendices
Hey Marquart Sector I 20 a 68.70	25/3/1918		A very quiet day. Artillery and aircraft, both Enemy and ours, being practically inactive. Headquarters changed over, relief being completed by 7.30 pm. 2/Lt A.J. Canton rejoined from Hpl (& Brigade). 2/Lt S.G. Powell & 2/Lt J.W. Rayner rejoined from Course.	JMW
	26/3/1918		Disposition unaltered. Enemy Artillery shelled back areas intermittently with 4.2s and H.E. No material damage done. Our Artillery retaliated in kind. Enemy and our aircraft fairly active. Administrative Headquarters moved from Blanche Maison to Heroux Switch, establishing at Heroux Post. Move completed by 8 pm. A & C Companies relieved B & D Companies, who moved back to their positions in the Switch. 2/Lt T.J. Williams returned from leave.	JMW

A5834 Wt. W4973/M687 750,000 8/16 D. D. & L. Ltd. Forms/C.2118/13

10th SWB

WAR DIARY
or
INTELLIGENCE SUMMARY.
(Erase heading not required.)

March 1918

Army Form C. 2118.

Instructions regarding War Diaries and Intelligence Summaries are contained in F. S. Regs., Part II. and the Staff Manual respectively. Title pages will be prepared in manuscript.

Place	Date	Hour	Summary of Events and Information — Reference Map 36.	Remarks and references to Appendices
Wez Macquart Sector I 30 a 68 70	27/3/1918		Dispositions. A + C Coys front and Subsidiary Line. B + D Coys Ferme and l'Anne Switch. Advanced Headquarters Subsidiary Line. Rear Headquarters Ferme Post. Transport unchanged. A quiet day, Artillery being fairly inactive. Aircraft also inactive	JMR [illegible]
-do-	28/3/1918		Dispositions unaltered. B + D Companies raided enemy trenches opposite the Salient at 3.30 am and secured 6 prisoners. Casualties. 8 other ranks slightly wounded. About 25 of the enemy were killed. Enemy after some retaliation for barrage put down during our raid, remained quiet all day. Planes however were active. Capt. A. T. Oxford MC DCM proceeded to Hospital	JMR [illegible]

A5834 Wt. W4973/M687 750,000 8/16 D. D. & L. Ltd. Forms/C.2118/13

10th S.W.B. March 1918 Army Form C. 2118.

Instructions regarding War Diaries and Intelligence Summaries are contained in F. S. Regs., Part II. and the Staff Manual respectively. Title pages will be prepared in manuscript.

WAR DIARY
or
~~INTELLIGENCE SUMMARY.~~
(Erase heading not required.)

Place	Date	Hour	Reference Map 36 — Summary of Events and Information	Remarks and references to Appendices
Wez Macquart Sector I.20.a.18.70	29/3/1918		Dispositions similar. Enemy artillery active, shelling vicinity of BURNT FARM heavily. Some gas shells were included in the Salvoes, and ~~gas~~ box respirators had to be worn for half an hour. Our Artillery retaliated for enemy's shelling. There was slight activity of aircraft during the day. Battalion on our left carried out a ~~successful~~ minor operation during the night. Definite results not yet to hand. Battalion relieved by 25th K.O.R.L. Regt, and moved by companies to NOUVEAU MONDE.	[initials]

A5834 Wt. W4973/M687 750,000 8/16 D. D. &

10th SWB.

WAR DIARY
or
~~INTELLIGENCE SUMMARY.~~
(Erase heading not required.)

March 1918

Army Form C. 2118.

Instructions regarding War Diaries and Intelligence Summaries are contained in F. S. Regs., Part II., and the Staff Manual respectively. Title pages will be prepared in manuscript.

Place	Date	Hour	Reference Maps 36 & 36a. Summary of Events and Information	Remarks and references to Appendices
NOUVEAU MONDE	30/3/1918		Battalion left NOUVEAU MONDE at 12 noon, and after 6 hours waiting on route, embussed for HAVERSKERQUE, arriving about 8.30 pm. Lt Schofield and 19 Snipers rejoined Battalion. Reinforcements, 144 in number, arrived.	
HAVERSKERQUE J 28 a (36a)	31/3/1918		Battalion at HAVERSKERQUE. Clean up of kits &c from 9.30 am to 11.30 am. Draft paraded at 11 am for inspection by the Commanding Officer. Sergeant Hughes (D Coy) and Lcpl Lane (D Coy) presented with ribbons of MILITARY MEDALS awarded for good services during the recent raid, by GOC XV Corps. Companies paraded at 11.30 am for inspection by the Commanding Officer and 2nd in Command. Dress, fighting (battle) order. Church parades were attended during the afternoon ~~for~~ by men of all denominations. Lt E R Jefford returned from course	[illegible]

[signature] Lt Col. Commdg 10 SWB

A5834 Wt. W4973/M687 750,000 8/16

115th Inf.Bde.
38th Div.

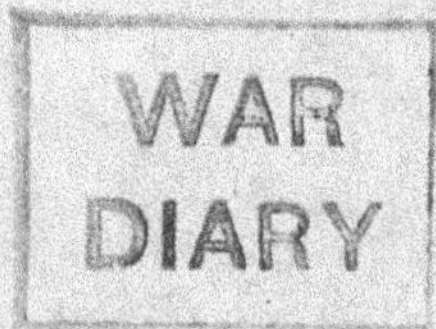

10th BATTN. THE SOUTH WALES BORDERERS.

A P R I L

1 9 1 8

10th S.W.B.

Army Form C. 2118.

WAR DIARY
or
~~INTELLIGENCE SUMMARY.~~

(Erase heading not required.)

April 1918

Vol 28

Instructions regarding War Diaries and Intelligence Summaries are contained in F. S. Regs., Part II. and the Staff Manual respectively. Title pages will be prepared in manuscript.

Place	Date	Hour	Ref. maps. Sheet 36a. & 57d. S.E. Amiens 37. Summary of Events and Information	Remarks and references to Appendices
HAVERSKERQUE J.27.d. (36a)	1/4/18 Easter Monday		Battalion at HAVERSKERQUE. "B" Coy. left at midnight and marched to CALONNE Station where they were to act as a loading party for the 38th Division. The remainder of the Battalion left at 12 noon, arriving at CALONNE at 2.15 pm. A hot dinner was served before entraining commenced. "B" Coy. remained behind when the train moved off at 3.15 pm. DOULLENS was reached at 9 pm. Here the Battalion detrained and commenced the march to VILLERS	
VILLERS BOCAGE (Amiens 37 1.D)	2/4/18 Tuesday		BOCAGE, a distance of 15 miles being covered. Our destination was not reached until 6.30 am., 2-4-18, an hours halt having been called on an open common when half the distance had been covered, and tea was served. After a short rest in billets a meal was served and the Battalion – still less 'B' Coy – moved off again at 12 noon. The Battn. marched via RUBEMPRE, HERISSART and CONTAY to HEDAUVILLE, arriving there at 9 pm. About 30 miles had then been marched since 10pm yesterday. Casualties nil	
HEDAUVILLE P.34.a. & c. (57d)	3/4/18 Wednesday		Battalion at HEDAUVILLE. 'B' Coy. rejoined, having marched direct from DOULLENS. After feet and rifle inspections the day was devoted to rest. Casualties nil	
do.	4/4/18 Thursday		Battn. at HEDAUVILLE. Inspections under Company arrangements were held this morning. 'A' & 'C' Companies were provided for a night trench-digging ~~fatigue~~ working party	

(A7092). Wt. W12839/M1293. 750,000. 1/17. D. D. & L., Ltd. Forms/C.2118/14.

Army Form C. 2118.

Instructions regarding War Diaries and Intelligence Summaries are contained in F. S. Regs., Part II. and the Staff Manual respectively. Title pages will be prepared in manuscript.

WAR DIARY
or
INTELLIGENCE SUMMARY.
(Erase heading not required.)

Place	Date	Hour	Ref. Map. Sheet 57d S.E. — Summary of Events and Information	Remarks and references to Appendices
HEDAUVILLE P.34.a & c	4/4/18 (contd.)		on a hill near ENGLEBELMER overlooking the enemy's line. The work was rendered difficult by the heavy rain which was falling, and the trench was not completed until 1am. after 5 hours work. Casualties: One OR wounded.	
do.	5/4/18 Friday		Battalion at HEDAUVILLE. Parades were held under Company arrangements. Casualties:- Nil	
do.	6/4/18 Saturday		Battalion at HEDAUVILLE. Companies were engaged on open order drill, and firing on a Range S.W. of the village. Casualties:- Nil	
do.	7/4/18 Sunday		Battalion at HEDAUVILLE. Church Parade Services, followed by open order drill, occupied the morning. 'A' & 'C' Companies packed up and marched off at 1 pm. After improving an old trench on the summit of the hill between HEDAUVILLE and VARENNES, they partook of tea and then marched to TOUTENCOURT via VARENNES and HARPONVILLE. The remainder of the Battalion moved to TOUTENCOURT during this afternoon & evening. Casualties:- Nil	
TOUTENCOURT (Lens 11)	8/4/18 Monday		Battalion at TOUTENCOURT. 'Battle Order' Inspections and musketry lectures occupied the morning. Baths were allotted for the use of the Battn. from 1 pm till 7 pm. & everybody was bathed. Casualties:- Nil	
do.	9/4/18 Tuesday		Battalion at TOUTENCOURT. The morning was devoted to training — musketry physical drill & open order drill. Rifle inspections & pay parades were held during afternoon. Casualties:- Nil	

(A7092). Wt. W12839/M1293. 750,000. 1/17. D. D. & L., Ltd. Forms/C.2118/14.

Instructions regarding War Diaries and Intelligence Summaries are contained in F. S. Regs., Part II. and the Staff Manual respectively. Title pages will be prepared in manuscript.

WAR DIARY

or

~~INTELLIGENCE SUMMARY.~~

(Erase heading not required.)

Army Form C. 2118.

Place	Date	Hour	Summary of Events and Information	Remarks and references to Appendices
			Ref. Map:- Lens 11.	
TOUTENCOURT (Lens 11) WARLOY-BAILLON (Lens 11)	10/4/18 Wednesday		Battalion at Toutencourt. Orders to move were received, and the Battalion marched to WARLOY-BAILLON, leaving present billets at 5.30 a.m. and arriving in new Area at 8 a.m. No billets were available until 12 noon. The Bttn. was therefore marshalled in neighbouring fields during the morning. A meal was served and some training was carried out, including an assault course practise, musketry + bayonet fighting. 'C' Coy. provided a fatigue party of 1 officer and 30 other ranks to carry tents and erect them in fields outside the village (3 p.m. till 6 p.m.) Casualties - Nil	
do.	11/4/18 Thursday		Battalion at WARLOY-BAILLON. Training, including musketry, physical training, bayonet fighting and assault practise was carried out this morning. Before dismissing parades, Lt.Col. Harvey D.S.O. addressed the Battalion, thanking 'B' + 'D' Coys for their splendid work in the recent raid in the WEZ MACQUART Sector, and speaking of the Battalion's prospect of being in action early in the future. Inspections of Iron Rations + Box Respirators were held this afternoon. Intimation was received that the following awards had been made for gallantry during the Raid of 28th March:- + 2/Lt. Alfred Morgan - Military Cross; 21346 Sgt. Hughes J.x and 10300 L/Cpl. Lane both awarded the Military Medal. + Capt. H. Cottam M.C. - Bar to Military Cross. Casualties:- Nil	x CH. A/C.S.M.
do.	12/4/18 Friday		Battalion at WARLOY-BAILLON. Training on similar lines to yesterday's was continued with this morning, and open order drill was practised. A fatigue party of officers and other ranks was provided for	A/D

Army Form C. 2118.

Instructions regarding War Diaries and Intelligence Summaries are contained in F. S. Regs., Part II. and the Staff Manual respectively. Title pages will be prepared in manuscript.

WAR DIARY
or
~~INTELLIGENCE SUMMARY.~~

(*Erase heading not required.*)

Place	Date	Hour	Ref Maps Lens 11. 57 D. Summary of Events and Information	Remarks and references to Appendices
WARLOY BAILLON (Lens 11)	12/4/18 (contd)		improving the Old French Line in V.18 and 24 (Sh 57 D) by sinking firesteps & levelling the parapet. Casualties - Nil	
do	13/4/18 (Saturday)		Battalion at WARLOY-BAILLON. "Stand-to" was ordered from the time of return of the fatigue party - 4.30 am - until 7.30 am. The remainder of the day was given for rest. No fatigue parties were provided this evening. Casualties - Nil	
do	14/4/18 (Sunday)		Battalion at WARLOY-BAILLON. Church Parade Services were held this morning. No fatigue parties were provided. Casualties - Nil Battn "Stood-to" from 4.45 am till 7.30 am.	
do	15/4/18 (Monday)		Battalion at WARLOY-BAILLON. "Stand-to" was ordered from 4.45 am until 7 am. A fatigue party of 1 officer and other ranks was provided for preparing shelters in V.21.c (Sh. 57 D.), working from 8 am until 5 pm. The remainder of the Battalion were provided for trench digging in V.24 and W.13 (Sh. 57 D), improving the Old French Line, the fatigue lasting from 8 pm until 4 am. (16th inst.) Casualties - Nil	G/C
do	16/4/18 (Tuesday)		Battalion at WARLOY-BAILLON: "Stand-to" from 4.45 am until 7.30 am. Morning & afternoon were devoted to resting. At 6.30 pm. B & C Coys. moved to	

(A7092). Wt. W12839/M1293. 750,000. 1/17. D. D. & L., Ltd. Forms/C.2118/14.

Army Form C. 2118.

WAR DIARY
or
INTELLIGENCE SUMMARY.

(Erase heading not required.)

Instructions regarding War Diaries and Intelligence Summaries are contained in F. S. Regs., Part II. and the Staff Manual respectively. Title pages will be prepared in manuscript.

Place	Date	Hour	Summary of Events and Information	Remarks and references to Appendices
			Ref. Map. 57 d. S.E.	
	16/4/18 (contd)		Support trenches in & bivouacs by the old French line in W.13.c. and coming under orders of 16th R.W.F. Battn. H.Q., B. & D. Coys. moved to bivouacs in V.31.c. Casualties – Nil	
V.21.c W.13.c.	17/4/18 Wed.		Battn. H.Q. A & D Coys. in W.13.c. B & C Coys. in support in V.21.c. The latter two Coys. rested during the day, and were employed improving trenches from Front Supports to Front Line during the night. A & D. Coys. were employed improving their own and Battn. H.Q. bivouacs. Casualties – One O.R. wounded	
do.	18/4/18 Thur.		Dispositions similar. B & C Coys. rested during the day and were employed in improving their bivouacs and trenches respectively at night. B. Coy. also provided a Carrying Party to carry R.E. material from Bn. H.Q. to Front Line. A & D Coys. continued improving bivouac positions during day. Casualties: – Nil. Battn. relieved 16th R.W.F. in support. [illegible] A & D Coys. moved to W.13.a & d.	
BOUZINCOURT W.13.a.37	19/4/18 Fri.		Dispositions ~~similar~~ as follows:– Bn. H.Q. at W.13.a.37. A Coy. W.13.b. B Coy. W.[illegible] C Coy. W.13.c. D Coy. [illegible] No movement was allowed during the day. At night all available men were employed under orders of [illegible] Coy R.E. improving trenches, wiring &c. Casualties – One O.R. wounded	[initials]

D. D. & L., London, E.C.
(A8001) Wt. W1771/M2031 750,000 5/17 Sch. 52 Forms/C2118/14

Army Form C. 2118.

Instructions regarding War Diaries and Intelligence Summaries are contained in F. S. Regs., Part II. and the Staff Manual respectively. Title pages will be prepared in manuscript.

WAR DIARY
or
~~INTELLIGENCE SUMMARY.~~

(Erase heading not required.)

Place	Date	Hour	Summary of Events and Information — Ref Map 57D S.E.	Remarks and references to Appendices
BOUZINCOURT W.13.a.3.7	20/4/18 (Sat)		Dispositions similar. B Coy. made further improvements to bivouac shelter in Sunken Road at W13C during the day; C Coy. keeping under cover in trench; A & D Coys. remaining also under cover from enemy observation. At nightfall A, D and part of C Coys. were engaged joining up uncompleted trench in W21a. Remr. of C Coy. unloaded barbed wire from convoy of Brigade transport at W14b. Casualties – Nil	
do. V.28.b near MILLENCOURT	21/4/18 (Sun)		Dispositions similar. Lewis musketry practice was given at stand to this morning. Working parties, similar to yesterdays, were provided. On completion of work the Battalion withdrew to bivouacs in V.28.b, the 115th Inf Bde.* being relieved by the 113th Inf Bde and becoming Reserve Brigade of the Division. Casualties – Nil	* Less 1 Battalion
do.	22/4/18 (Mon)		Dispositions. Battalion in bivouac shelters in V.28.b. The Battalion rested – under cover from enemy observation – throughout the day. From 8pm until 3 am (23rd) all available men were engaged digging new trench in V.24. On completion of their task some of the men helped to carry wounded from Aid Post at V.18.d.9.1 to Car loading point at X roads at V24 c 2 2. (Minor operation by 113th Inf. Bde.) Casualties – 15.O.R. wounded	A.P.

D. D. & L., London, E.C. (A5001) Wt. W1771/M2031 750,000 5/17 Sch. 52 Forms/C2118/14

Army Form C. 2118.

Instructions regarding War Diaries and Intelligence Summaries are contained in F. S. Regs., Part II. and the Staff Manual respectively. Title pages will be prepared in manuscript.

WAR DIARY

~~or~~

~~INTELLIGENCE SUMMARY.~~

(Erase heading not required.)

Place	Date	Hour	Ref map:- Sheet 57 D SE. Summary of Events and Information	Remarks and references to Appendices
V. 28. b near MILLENCOURT	23/4/18 (Tues)		Dispositions similar. Battalion resting, under cover by day. No fatigue parties were provided. Casualties - nil	
do.	24/4/18 (Wed.)		Same as yesterday - 23/4/18. Casualties - nil	
do. FRONT LINE W. 30. c. 7. 8 (nr. ALBERT)	25/4/18 (Thurs)		Dispositions similar. Battalion resting, under cover by day. The Battn. relieved 2nd Bn. R.W.F. in the line to-night, taking over from W. 21. b 7. 6 to W. 21. c 5. 0. Dispositions as follows:- Bn. H.Q. at W. 30. c 7. 8. 'B' Coy. Left Front Coy; 'D' Coy. Right Front Coy; 'A' Coy. in Support; 'C' Coy. in Reserve in shelters in sunken road W. 13. d 7. 4. Relief complete at midnight. Casualties - nil, Other Rank wounded	
do.	26/4/18 (Fri.)		Dispositions as taken over on last nights relief. Our Artillery directed harassing fire on enemy roads and defenses during the day and night. Our snipers were busily engaged firing at enemy who exposed themselves. The enemy directed most of his fire on our back areas. At about 7 pm. heavy fire was directed on Bn. H.Q. with 4·2s and 5·9s, a direct hit being obtained on the Orderly Room and Mess Shelters. The Battn. was relieved by 20th Australian Battn. to-night and moved in support to 17th R.W.F., Battn. H.Q. being at W. 13. a 5. 9. Casualties - 12 O.Rs W/a. & One O.R. accid. Killed	afl

D. D. & L., London, E.C. (A6001) Wt. W1771/M2031 750,000 5/17 Sch. 52 Forms C2118/14

Army Form C. 2118.

WAR DIARY

~~or~~

~~INTELLIGENCE SUMMARY.~~

(*Erase heading not required.*)

Instructions regarding War Diaries and Intelligence Summaries are contained in F. S. Regs., Part II. and the Staff Manual respectively. Title pages will be prepared in manuscript.

Place	Date	Hour	Summary of Events and Information	Remarks and references to Appendices
			Ref. map. 57 D.	
BOUZINCOURT W.13.a.5.9	27/4/18 (Sat.)		Dispositions as follows:- Battn H.Q. at W.13.a.5.9. A & B Coy in sunken road at W.13.d.7.6. 'C' Coy in Old French line in W.13.c. D Coy in sunken road at W.13.a.3.6. All available men were working under R.E. supervision during the night, carrying material, improving trenches, wiring, and generally strengthening the position. Gas shells fell thickly around Batt H.Q. between 10pm & 3am. Casualties:- 4 O.Rs. Killed and 3 Wounded in action	1 Coy & 2 platoons were placed at disposal of 17 RWF for work.
do.	28/4/18 (Sun.)		Dispositions as yesterday's. Work similar. Casualties:- One O.R. killed and 11 O.Rs. wounded in action. 2nd Lt A.A. Morgan MC wounded & D/d wds.	do.
do	29/4/18 (Mon)		Dispositions unchanged. Work similar. Casualties - 2 Killed & 6. Wounded in action	do.
do.	30/4/18		Dispositions ~~unchanged~~. 'A' Coy was placed at the disposal of 17 RWF. as Reserve Coy. for a minor operation which was carried out during night (30th/1st. May). They were not called upon, however, and suffered no Casualties. Work - consolidating the line - was carried on with as usual ~~until~~ from dusk until midnight, when it ceased owing to the minor operation. Casualties:- 4. O.Rs. Wounded in Action	do.

[illegible] Lt. Col
Comdg. 10 (S) Bn. S.W.B.

D. D. & L., London, E.C.
(A8001) Wt. W1771/M2031 750,000 5/17 Sch. 52 Forms C2118/14

Instructions regarding War Diaries and Intelligence Summaries are contained in F. S. Regs., Part II. and the Staff Manual respectively. Title pages will be prepared in manuscript.

WAR DIARY
or
~~INTELLIGENCE SUMMARY.~~
(Erase heading not required.)

10th South Wales Borderers — Army Form C. 2118.

May 1918.

Vol 29

Place	Date	Hour	Summary of Events and Information Ref. Map Sh 57D.	Remarks and references to Appendices
BOUZINCOURT W.13.a.50.85	1/5/18 (Wed)		Battalion in Support to 17th R.W.F. (holding the line from W.15.d.5.0 to W.15.a.5.5) Dispositions as follows:- Bn. HQ at W.13.a.50.85. 'D' and 'C' Coys in W.13.a. and Old French Line in W.13.c. respectively. 'A' and 'B' Coys in dugouts in Sunken Road in W.13.b. The Battalion relieved the 2/5th Staffords in the line to-night and took up the following dispositions:- Bn. HQ at W.7.c.5.1. 'D' Coy in Battn. Reserve in W.13.a.4.6. 'B' Coy in Support in Sunken Road in W.8.c; 'A' Right and 'C' Left Front Coys. at W.14.b.3.5 and W.14.b.7.1 respectively. The relief interfered with the night's work, but some improvements were made to the new accomodation taken over. One patrol went out reconnoitring N.M.L. Casualties - One O.R. W'd.	[initials]
W.7.c.5.1.				
do	2/5/18 (Thurs)		Dispositions as taken over on yesterday's relief. The enemy's artillery was active throughout the day. 50 rounds fell in vicinity of BOUZINCOURT CHURCH and Battn. H.Q. (4.2s intermixed with 5.9s) at midday. Our heavies directed harassing fire on enemy back areas throughout the day. Aircraft activity was normal. Two patrols left our lines to reconnoitre N.M.L. and engage any enemy patrol encountered, but none was met with. Work - Deepening trenches, improving dug-outs and strengthening wire in front of Posts. Casualties - 3 O.R. W'd.	[initials]

D. D. & L., London, E.C. (A8003) Wt. W1771/M2031 750,000 5/17 Sch. 52 Forms C2118/14

Instructions regarding War Diaries and Intelligence Summaries are contained in F. S. Regs., Part II. and the Staff Manual respectively. Title pages will be prepared in manuscript.

WAR DIARY

~~or~~

~~INTELLIGENCE SUMMARY.~~

(*Erase heading not required.*)

Army Form C. 2118.

Place	Date	Hour	Summary of Events and Information — Ref map Sh. 57D.	Remarks and references to Appendices
BOUZINCOURT W7 c 5.1	3/5/18 (Fri)		Battalion in front line. Dispositions similar. The enemy's artillery was more ~~the~~ active than usual throughout the day, shelling W.14, W.8 with all calibres and firing 5.9 shrapnel on BOUZINCOURT at 6pm. Our guns kept up harassing fire on the salient opposite AMIENS, to hinder enemy's transport and concentration of troops and material. Our snipers claimed several certain hits. Aircraft of both sides was very active. A fighting patrol went out from our left Company front between 12 midnight and 3am but encountered no enemy patrols. The Battn. took up the following dispositions during the night:- Bn HQ remained at W.7.c.5.1, 'C' Coy were relieved by a Coy of 16 RWF and 'side slipped' to 'A' Coys position. 'A' Coy then 'side slipped' to the Right relieving a Coy of 2nd RWF. 'B' Coy remained in support, moving slightly to the Right; whilst 'D' Coy, in Battalion Reserve, remained in the bank at W 13 a 4.6. Casualties:- 2 OR W/d (incl. 1 at duty)	[illegible]
do	4/5/18 (Sat)		Battalion in front line. Dispositions as after last nights 'side slip'. Artillery of both sides was much quieter to-day. The enemy put down several practise barrages on W 13 d and W 14 b. Aircraft was again very active especially towards dusk. Two patrols left our lines from the front line Coys. Nothing exceptional occurred. Work:-	

D. D. & L., London, E.C. (A8001) Wt. W1771/M2031 750,000 5/17 Sch. 52 Forms C2118/14

Instructions regarding War Diaries and Intelligence Summaries are contained in F. S. Regs., Part II. and the Staff Manual respectively. Title pages will be prepared in manuscript.

WAR DIARY
or
~~INTELLIGENCE SUMMARY.~~
(Erase heading not required.)

Army Form C. 2118.

Place	Date	Hour	Summary of Events and Information	Remarks and references to Appendices
			Ref. Map. Sh. 57 D.	
BOUZINCOURT W.7.c.5.1	4/5/18 (contd)		Practically nil during daytime owing to enemy observation. At night front line Coys. were engaged in wiring and deepening trenches. Support and Reserve Coys. digging new support trench in front of BOUZINCOURT. Usual carrying parties. Casualties:- Nil.	JRR
	5/5/18 (Sunday)		Dispositions similar. Our artillery continued to harass rear communications in the AMIENS salient throughout day and night; fired on Sunken Road in W9d. The enemy actively shelled our front line with 77 mm. from midday onwards, and put down two barrages - firstly at 11.30 am. on the rear of our close support line in W13.d, and secondly at 1.30 pm. on W14d. Both barrages lasted 15 mins. Our planes kept enemy's lines and communications under close observation all day. A few high flying enemy machines made an appearance. At dusk a party of 1 N.C.O. and 10 O.R. proceeded to a post known to have been occupied by the enemy. This party held the post. Two reconnoitring patrols left our lines. 2/Lt. F.F. Williams, in command of one, discovered (1) that the enemy were holding LONE TREE POST (W.15 b 00.25), (2) that 3 enemy M.G.s were located near the Post, (3) that enemy's line was not protected by wire (4) Very Lts. were being fired from points 60x + 5x N. of LONE TREE	Sgt D. H. Thomas (W 15 a 85.30) JRR

D. D. & L., London, E.C. (A8001) Wt. W1771/M2031 750,000 5/17 Sch. 52 Forms C2118/14

Army Form C. 2118.

WAR DIARY
or
~~INTELLIGENCE SUMMARY.~~
(Erase heading not required.)

Instructions regarding War Diaries and Intelligence Summaries are contained in F. S. Regs., Part II. and the Staff Manual respectively. Title pages will be prepared in manuscript.

Place	Date	Hour	Summary of Events and Information	Remarks and references to Appendices
			Ref map Sh. 57.D.	
BOUZINCOURT W.7.c.5.1	5/5/18 (contd)		and from a Post 30x South of LONE TREE. Upon withdrawal of this Patrol, L.G. fire was brought to bear on the 3 enemy posts. The second patrol, under 2/Lt. S.J. Powell, reported that Very lights had been fired from positions near W. 15 b 20.80. Work: Strengthening Posts by deepening trenches and putting out obstacle wire. Digging new support trench in front of BOUZINCOURT. Carrying parties for L.T.M.B., R.E. material & Rations. Casualties: 4 O.R. W/d 3 O.R. W/d (Rem. at duty)	J.R.B.I.
do.	6/5/18 (Mon)		Dispositions similar. Artillery of both sides was very active, our guns bombarding ALBERT continuously, and harassing any movement in enemy's back areas. BOUZINCOURT received some attention from the enemy, who also directed harassing fire over a wide area, and fired a series of crashes between 3 p.m. and 5 p.m. from W 8 d to W 14 a. Aircraft of both sides active; the enemy however rarely ventured to the low altitude favoured by our observers. L.G. fire was restricted, almost entirely, to A.A. work. Two patrols went out, one to reconnoitre N.M.L. on the Battn. front and the other to reconnoitre with a view to engaging any enemy patrols or working parties encountered. No enemy were met with. Work – Deepening &	J.R.B.

D. D. & L., London, E.C. (A8001) Wt. W1771/M2031 750,000 5/17 Sch. 52 Forms C2118/14

Instructions regarding War Diaries and Intelligence Summaries are contained in F. S. Regs., Part II. and the Staff Manual respectively. Title pages will be prepared in manuscript.

WAR DIARY

or

~~INTELLIGENCE SUMMARY.~~

(Erase heading not required.)

Army Form C. 2118.

Place	Date	Hour	Summary of Events and Information	Remarks and references to Appendices
			Ref. Map. Sh. 57.D.	
BOUZINCOURT. W.7.C.5.1	6/5/18 (contd)		improving trenches, strengthening posts, fire-stepping and continuing with the digging of new Support Trench. The usual carrying parties were provided. Casualties :- 3 O.R. W/a.	[initials]
do.	7/5/18		Dispositions similar. Artillery activity of both sides was comparatively quiet. About 20 rounds 4.2s fell on BOUZINCOURT at about 8 pm. M.G.s and T.M.s were inactive. Several planes both our own and the enemy's were seen this morning and afternoon, but heavy rain began to fall at 5 pm. and prevented flying from being of any use. Our forward trenches were soon rendered very uncomfortable. A patrol was out between 9.15 pm. and 11.30 pm. It encountered no enemy. Work:- Trench digging, wiring and improving dug-outs. The usual carrying parties were provided. News was received that the Military Medal had been awarded to 20014 Sgt. C.B. Hughes. An inter-Company relief took place to-night. Casualties :- Nil.	U.S.A. Army 7 officers, 1 First Sgt. and 1 Corpl were attached to the Battn for instruction - the first two joining the Battle Personnel at BOUZINCOURT. [initials]
do	8/5/18		Dispositions now as follows:- Battn. H.qrs. at W.7.C.5.1 (no change). 'B' Coy Left Front Coy. 'D' Coy. Right Front Coy. 'C' Coy. in Support (in 'B' Coy's old position) and 'A' Coy. in the Sunken Road at W.13.a in Reserve. Both sides opened out with heavy Artillery fire at intervals throughout the night and early morning, firing mostly on back areas. There	

D. D. & L., London, E.C. (A8001) Wt. W1771/M2031 750,000 5/17 Sch. 52 Forms C2118/14

Instructions regarding War Diaries and Intelligence Summaries are contained in F. S. Regs., Part II. and the Staff Manual respectively. Title pages will be prepared in manuscript.

WAR DIARY
or
~~INTELLIGENCE SUMMARY.~~
(Erase heading not required.)

Army Form C. 2118.

Place	Date	Hour	Ref. Map. Sheet 57.D. Summary of Events and Information	Remarks and references to Appendices
BOUZINCOURT W7C 5.1.	8/5/18 (contd)		was little activity during the day. However, an attack by the Hun was anticipated, and everybody had received orders ~~for~~ ready for immediate action. Our reconnoitring planes were busy all day. A minor operation was carried out against an enemy post at W.15.a.85.35, commencing at 10.15 p.m. 'A' and 'D' Coys. were selected for the work. Report by 'A' Coy – who captured the Post – is attached. The Section of 'D' Coy. who had gone out to hold the Post were counter-attacked by a greatly superior force, and after fighting valiantly, were forced to withdraw. Work: Improving and draining trenches, wiring around Posts, carrying R.E. material, rations and water. A Bath ~~was~~ which had been fitted up at Battn H.Q. (two cellars being used for accomodation) was first used to-day. Casualties:– 2 O.R. K/A, 4 O.R. W/A, 2 O.R. W/A rem. at duty	
do.	9/5/18 Thursday		Dispositions similar. Heavy artillery was again active on back areas, both the enemy's and our own. The enemy fired bursts of 20 rounds of 4.5 H.V. at 1½ hour intervals on valley in W13d. Our 18 pdrs. fired bursts at half hour intervals on enemy front line in W15.b. Our planes were	

D. D. & L., London, E.C. (A8001) Wt. W1771/M2031 750,000 5/17 Sch. 52 Forms C2118/14

Instructions regarding War Diaries and Intelligence Summaries are contained in F. S. Regs., Part II. and the Staff Manual respectively. Title pages will be prepared in manuscript.

WAR DIARY
or
~~INTELLIGENCE SUMMARY.~~
(Erase heading not required.)

Army Form C. 2118.

Place	Date	Hour	Ref. Map. Sheet 57 D. Summary of Events and Information	Remarks and references to Appendices
BOUZINCOURT W 7 C 5.1	9/5/18 (contd)		were active all day, but only one E.A. (which was flying very high) was seen. M.Gs and T.Ms were quiet. A reconnoitring patrol was out in N.M.L. between 11 pm. and 2 am. Nothing unusual occurred. Work:- The usual night work was continued with i.e. improving trenches by deepening, firestepping and draining. Wiring around Posts and in front of Support Lines. Casualties. - { 1 O.R. K/a, 3 O.R. missing, 19 O.R. W/a }	JRRK
do.	10/5/18 (Friday)		Dispositions similar. Our artillery was active throughout the night firing chiefly on enemy back areas and ALBERT. A heavy barrage was put down on enemy front and support lines between 9 am. and 11.30 am. Our T.Ms. co-operated. A party of Germans, apparently disturbed by the latter, left their trench at W.9.c 95.30 and ran towards Sunken Road in W9d. Our L.Gs opened fire at once on the party and claimed 6 hits. Our guns maintained harassing fire on the enemy's front line and back areas throughout the day. The enemy replied to our barrage by firing heavily on W.14.b and W8 & 9c between 9 am and 10 am. and again from 11 am. to 11.15 am. There was ~~intermittent~~ shelling of our support line in W8c between 3 pm. and 5 pm. Enemy M.Gs were active against our aircraft which were about all day. Two patrols, from the front line Companies, were reconnoitring in N.M.L. between 10 pm. and 12.30 am. and ~~1~~ between 1 am. and 3 am. respectively, but no enemy were	

D. D. & L., London, E.C. (A8001) Wt. W1771/M2031 750,000 5/17 Sch. 52 Forms C2118/14

WAR DIARY.

Place	Date	Ref Map Sh. 57.D. Summary of Events & Information	Remarks
BOUZINCOURT W7C 5.1	10/5/18 (contd)	encountered. Work:- Improvements to dug-outs and trenches. Wiring around posts and in front of Supports. Carrying R.E. material, S.A.A. & Rations. Casualties:- { 1 O.R. K/a. 8 O.R. W/a.	The 1st. party of American Corps left to rejoin Unit.
do.	11/5/18 (Sat)	Dispositions similar. The enemy was extremely quiet until midday. Before daybreak he was continually firing Very lights over N.M.L. as if expecting an infantry attack. Short bursts were fired on valley in W.20 at 1.15 pm. and at 1.45 pm.; and "crashes" fell on BOUZINCOURT at 2 pm., 4 pm. and 5 pm. from direction of AVELUY. Aircraft were quiet all day. Our guns directed harassing fire on ALBERT and AVELUY between noon and 3.30 pm. Two patrols left our lines to reconnoitre N.M.L. between dusk and dawn. No enemy were encountered. Work:- The usual night fatigues were detailed. Casualties:- { 1 O.R. K/a. 3 O.R. W/a. 1 O.R. W/a. rem. at duty	A second party of Americans (1 Offr. and 1 First Sgt.) joined for instruction.
do.	12/5/18 (Sun)	Dispositions similar. A very quiet day. The only artillery activity was early in the morning when both sides fired harassing shots on forward areas. Aircraft activity was much below normal. A reconnoitring patrol left our lines at 11.30 pm. and remained in N.M.L. until 2.30 am. (13th.) but encountered no enemy. Work:- Improving & strengthening trenches and wiring. The usual carrying parties were provided. Casualties:- { 4 O.R. W/a. 1 O.R. W/a. rem. at duty	

WAR DIARY.

Place	Date	Ref. Map. Sh. 57.D. Summary of Events & Information	Remarks.
BOUZINCOURT W 7 c 5.1	13/5/18	Dispositions similar. Our artillery continually shelled the enemy front and support lines during the night. The enemy replied with salvoes on BOUZINCOURT between 4 a.m. and 6 a.m. The remainder of the day was fairly quiet. Aircraft activity was normal, our planes as usual, being much more in evidence than the Huns'. There has been a considerable amount of night flying by our airmen during the past fortnight, and bombs have been dropped over a wide area. 2 patrols were out in N.M.L., in turn, between 9.45 pm. and 3 a.m. No enemy were encountered. Work:- Improving trenches and dugouts, wiring - especially around Posts, and carrying R.E. material &c. Casualties:- {1 O.R. W/a; 2/Lt. G.W. Rayner. W/a Rem. at duty}	JRH
do.	14/5/18	Dispositions similar. Early this morning BOUZINCOURT was shelled with 4.2s and 5.9s. 3 direct hits were obtained on H.Q. mess - a reinforced cellar, which proved strong enough to withstand the Huns' attentions. Artillery activity was less than usual after the early morning shoots. The Battalion was relieved by 2nd Battn. R.W.F. to-night, and moved into Brigade Reserve. Relief was complete by 2 a.m. A party of 30 men were attached to 178th. Tunneling Coy. for work from today onwards. Casualties:- 1 O.R. W/a	Before relief all the Battn. had bathed and had a clean change of underclothing in the improvised bath fitted up at B.H.Q. & first used on 8th inst. JRH

WAR DIARY.

Place	Date	Ref. Map. Sh. 57.D. Summary of Events & Information	Remarks.
nr. SENLIS V.22.b.4.8	15/5/18 (Wed)	Dispositions as follows:- Battn. H.Q. in Sunken Road, with 'B' and 'D' Coys. at V.22.b.4.8. 'A' and 'C' Coys. in trenches - part of the Corps line - at V 12 and 18, behind BOUZINCOURT. The day was devoted to rest, except for a rifle inspection that was held during the afternoon. No fatigue parties were provided for night work. Casualties:- Nil.	HRM
do.	16/5/18 (Thur)	Dispositions similar. Inspections of rifles and S.B. Respirators ('B' 'D' & H.Q. Coys. by Brigade Gas Officer) were held during the afternoon. All available men were employed under 124th Field Coy. R.Es. from 9pm. till 4am. on the following tasks:- 1 Company improving trenches in Divisional Line at about V.18.d.3.8; 2 Coys. Trench digging in Sunken Road at V.18.d 7.6; and the remaining Coy. wiring - in this new trench. After completion of task one platoon of 'A' Coy. moved to Old French Line at W.13.b.5.4; and one platoon of 'C' Coy. moved to W.13.c.4.4. Both these platoons were detailed to form permanent garrisons in their new positions. Casualties:- Nil.	HRM
do.	17/5/18	Dispositions similar (with the exception of the move of the 2 platoons). Inspections of rifles, equipment and S.B.Rs were held under Company arrangements, and men were employed	

WAR DIARY.

Place.	Date	Ref. Map. Sh. 57 D. Summary of Events & Information	Remarks.
nr. SENLIS V.22.b.4.8	17/5/18 (contd.)	during the day in improving their own bivouacs or shelters. Similar working parties to yesterdays were provided. Casualties – Nil.	
do.	18/5/18 (Sat.)	Dispositions similar. A range-taking class of 3 junior N.C.Os per Coy was held at Bn. H.Q. this morning. In preparation of forthcoming move an advanced party left at 10am. and proceeded to HERISSART to take over rifle ranges from 105th. Brigade. The usual working parties were provided for night work. Casualties:- Nil.	JRBr
do.	19/5/18 (Sun.)	Dispositions similar. Inspections of all S.A.A. and Battle Order equipment were held to-day, under Coy. arrangements. The Commanding Officer attended a Conference held by the Major General Commanding the Division. Reconnoitring parties from each Coy. went over the track route to be taken by the Battalion on tomorrow nights relief. At about 10.30 am. this morning a barrage was put down on our forward system, and 'A' Coy. sustained the following casualties – 1 O.R. Killed and 2 O.R. wounded. Work:- Similar to yesterdays.	JRBr
do.	20/5/18 (Mon.)	Dispositions similar. A general clean up of all trenches and positions to be handed over was ordered. The party of 30 men who had been working under 178th. Tunneling Coy. were relieved at noon, today by a party from 106th. Inf. Bde. The Battalion was relieved to-night by the 15th. Sherwood Foresters, and moved to HERISSART. 'A' Coy. were subjected to severe gas shelling	

Instructions regarding War Diaries and Intelligence Summaries are contained in F. S. Regs., Part II. and the Staff Manual respectively. Title pages will be prepared in manuscript.

WAR DIARY
or
~~INTELLIGENCE SUMMARY.~~
(Erase heading not required.)

Army Form C. 2118.

Place	Date	Hour	Summary of Events and Information	Remarks and references to Appendices
			Ref. Map. Sh. 57 D.	
HERISSART T 10. d. 2.4	20/5/18 (contd)		during the relief, and although only few of the men felt any immediate effects, several cases were sent to hospital during the ensuing 48 hours. Casualties.– { OR. K/a. 2 OR. W/a. 2nd Lt. F.H. Williams and gassed (wounded) 41 OR.	
do.	21/5/18 (Tu)		Battn in Camp at HERISSART. Surplus Battle Personnel, Rear H.Q. and Transport details had now joined the Battle Personnel, and the strength of the Battn was approx 800. All the morning was given to rest, and the afternoon occupied in cleaning up. Casualties:– Nil.	
do.	22/5/18 (Wed)		Battn at HERISSART. The CO inspected small kits, overcoats and skeleton order equipment this morning. The remainder of the day was devoted to further cleaning up and rest. Lt. Col. C.D. Harvey, DSO was admitted to hospital today. Casualties:– Nil.	Major J.H.T. Monteith assumed command of the Battn
do.	23/5/18		Battn at HERISSART. Training Commenced to-day. 'A' and 'B' Coys. were occupied all the morning in firing – the former on a two 30 yards ranges, and the latter on a 400 yds range. Whilst not actually firing, practises in saluting, judging distances, recognition of targets and musketry were carried out. These two Coys. were instructed in the fitting of Marching Order which was afterwards	

A7092. Wt. W12839/M1293 750,000. 1/17. D. D & L. Ltd. Forms/C2118/14.

Instructions regarding War Diaries and Intelligence Summaries are contained in F. S. Regs., Part II. and the Staff Manual respectively. Title pages will be prepared in manuscript.

WAR DIARY
~~or~~
~~INTELLIGENCE SUMMARY.~~
(Erase heading not required.)

Army Form C. 2118.

Place	Date	Hour	Summary of Events and Information	Remarks and references to Appendices
			Ref. Map. Sh. 57D.	
HERISSART T.10.d.2.4	23/5/18		inspected by O.s.C. Coys. during the afternoon. 'D' + 'C' Coys. had the use of the ranges this afternoon after having had 'Marching Order' inspections this morning. Lewis Gunners, Signallers and Stretcher Bearers received special instruction by their respective officers. The following Award was published to-day:- 30,624 Pte. W.J. Kemp received the Military Medal, for coolness and bravery in rescuing men of a T.M. whose gun was being shelled by the enemy. Casualties:- Nil.	WBH
do.	24/5/18		Battn. at HERISSART. Training Continued. 'A' and 'B' Coys. received Bullet-Bayonet-Bullet instruction and Physical Training exercises. 'C' + 'D' Coys. marched to a training ground N.W. of PUCHEVILLERS and carried out the following programme:- Section, platoon and extended order drill, physical training + practising rapid solutions in cases of emergency. Specialists paraded for instruction under their respective officers. The Brigade Armourer Sergeant inspected all rifles during the day. Work on the revetment of tents (as a protection against hostile bombs) commenced to-day. So far as possible all training is now being done early in the day in order to escape the midday + afternoon heat	

A7092/. Wt. W12839/M1293 750,000. 1/17. D. D & I. Ltd. Forms/C2118/14.

Instructions regarding War Diaries and Intelligence Summaries are contained in F. S. Regs., Part II. and the Staff Manual respectively. Title pages will be prepared in manuscript.

WAR DIARY

or

~~INTELLIGENCE SUMMARY.~~

(Erase heading not required.)

Army Form C. 2118.

Place	Date	Hour	Summary of Events and Information	Remarks and references to Appendices
			Ref. map. Sh. 57D.	
HERISSART T.10.d.2.4	24/5/18 (contd)		now being experienced. Casualties :- nil	JPBM
	25/5/18 (Sat.)		Battn. at HERISSART. 'A' and 'B' Coys. fired Competition practises on the Ranges to-day. Musketry instruction was given to men not actually firing. 'C' and 'D' Coys. marched to Training Area at T.2.9 a & c. and carried out Company drill, Musketry and Company Tactical Schemes. Baths at HERISSART were used by 'A', 'B' & 'C' Coys. between 8am and noon, and between 3pm & 4pm. All blankets were treated in a Foden Disinfector during the day. Casualties :- nil.	JPBM
	26/5/18 (Sun)		Battn. at HERISSART. The Range was allotted to this Battn. all day, and Competition firing was continued with. 'B' and 'C' Coys. were firing between 6am and 12.30pm.; and 'A' and 'D' Coys. between 12.30pm. and 6pm. 'A' Coy. and Transport details were allotted the Baths between 8am and 12 noon. Stretcher bearers received instruction under the M.O. this afternoon. Casualties :- nil.	Major A.J. Bowen returned from CO's Course, & assumed Command of the Battn. JPBM

A7092). Wt. W12839/M1293 750,000. 1/17. D. D & L. Ltd. Forms/C2118/14.

Instructions regarding War Diaries and Intelligence Summaries are contained in F. S. Regs., Part II. and the Staff Manual respectively. Title pages will be prepared in manuscript.

WAR DIARY

or

~~INTELLIGENCE SUMMARY.~~

(Erase heading not required.)

Army Form C. 2118.

Place	Date	Hour	Summary of Events and Information	Remarks and references to Appendices
			Ref. map. Sh 57 D.	
HERISSART T.10.d 2.4	27/5/18 (Thurs)		Battn at HERISSART. All taking part in this afternoons inspection paraded at 9am in Battle order for inspection by the C.O. The whole Brigade (including Transport) was inspected by the Corps Commander (V Corps) this afternoon. The smart turn out of all ranks was much appreciated by the Corps Commander. Casualties:- Nil	[illegible initials]
	28/5/18 (Tue)		Battn at HERISSART. The range was in use all day, all firing being done by platoons. 'A' and 'D' Coys fired this morning; and 'B' and 'C' this afternoon. The latter Companies had an hour's recreational training this morning. Specialists carried on under their respective instructors. All ranks passed through the Divisional Gas Chamber to test their respirators, between 10 a.m. and 7 p.m. Casualties - Nil	[illegible initials]
	29/5/18 (Wed)		Battn at HERISSART. 'B' and 'C' Coys. had the use of the Bullet + Bayonet Training ground at T.4.d early this morning. At 10 a.m. the Battn. marched to the Training Area at PUCHEVILLERS, and spent the remainder of the	

A7092). Wt. W12839/M1293 750,000. 1/17. D. D & I. Ltd. Forms/C2118/14.

Instructions regarding War Diaries and Intelligence Summaries are contained in F. S. Regs., Part II. and the Staff Manual respectively. Title pages will be prepared in manuscript.

WAR DIARY

or

~~INTELLIGENCE SUMMARY.~~

(Erase heading not required.)

Army Form C. 2118.

Place	Date	Hour	Summary of Events and Information	Remarks and references to Appendices
			Ref Map. Sh. 57. D.	
HERISSART T 10 d 2 4	29/5/18 (contd.)		morning in practising attacks on a strong point by platoons. An outpost scheme was carried out this afternoon. Specialists carried on as usual. Casualties - nil	[illegible]
	30/5/18 (Thurs.)		Battn. at HERISSART. The Range was in use all day, 'B' and 'C' Coys. firing between 6 am and 12 noon, and 'A' and 'D' Coys. between 1.30 pm and 8 pm. Specialists received instruction under their respective officers. Casualties nil	[illegible]
	31/5/18 (Fri.)		Battn. at HERISSART. A Brigade tactical scheme, in which 75% of officers, signallers and runners took part was practised this morning. No other parades were held, the remainder of the Battn. attending a successful Sports gathering which was held near the camp. Casualties: nil	[illegible]

C. Brown Major
Commanding
10th (S) Bn. S.W.B.

A7092. Wt. W12839/M1293 750,000. 1/17. D. D & L. Ltd. Forms/C2118/14.

W.I. [illegible]
June 1918.

Army Form C. 2118.

Instructions regarding War Diaries and Intelligence Summaries are contained in F. S. Regs., Part II. and the Staff Manual respectively. Title pages will be prepared in manuscript.

WAR DIARY

or

~~INTELLIGENCE SUMMARY.~~

(Erase heading not required.)

VR 30

Place	Date	Hour	Summary of Events and Information	Remarks and references to Appendices
			Ref. Map. Sh 57 D.	
HERISSART T.10.d.2.4	1/6/18 (Sat.)		Battalion at HERISSART. Brigade training Competitions were carried out to-day, a tactical exercise for Transport details taking place this morning and a successful Sports gathering being held during the afternoon. Competitors from this Battn. did well in all events. Casualties :- Nil	[illegible]
do.	2/6/18 (Sun)		Battalion at HERISSART. Divine Services were held this morning. A Divisional Sports gathering held this afternoon gave our men another opportunity of proving their prowess in ~~the~~ athletics. Casualties :- Nil	
do. P.14.c	3/6/18 (Mon.)		Battalion at HERISSART. Battle Surplus Personnel of 8 officers and 108 O.Ranks moved away at 9am. under the Command of Major J.W.J. Monteith, and proceeded to the Divisional Reception Camp. The remainder of the Battn. struck camp and moved away at 3.30 pm. marching via TOUTENCOURT to ACHEUX WOOD, where tents were again pitched. Casualties :- Nil	
ACHEUX WOOD P.14.c.	4/6/18 (Tue)		Battn. at ACHEUX WOOD. Battalion rested during the day & fell in at 8.30 p.m. after which they proceeded to relieve the "HOOD" BN	

A7092. Wt. W12839/M1293 750,000. 1/17. D. D & L Ltd. Forms/C2118/14.

Army Form C. 2118.

WAR DIARY
~~or~~
~~INTELLIGENCE SUMMARY.~~
(*Erase heading not required.*)

Instructions regarding War Diaries and Intelligence Summaries are contained in F. S. Regs., Part II. and the Staff Manual respectively. Title pages will be prepared in manuscript.

Place	Date	Hour	Summary of Events and Information	Remarks and references to Appendices
			of the 63rd Naval Division in SUPPORT TRENCHES of MESNIL SECTOR. Relief was complete at 12 midnight & Bn Hdqrs established at Q26a.9.2 Sht 57d.SE. Casualties Nil.	
Q26a.9.2 Sht 57d SE	5.6.18 (Wedn)		Battalion in MESNIL SECTOR - SUPPORT LINE - Very little activity by enemy artillery, consequently a somewhat calm day. A Coy carried out trench improvements under orders from OC 2nd RWF who were holding the Front Line & under whose command "A" were. Remainder of Bn improved & erected shelters & dugouts in SUPPORT SYSTEM. Casualties One OR wounded	WW
Q26a.9.2 Sht 57d.SE	6.6.18 (Thurs)		Battalion in Mesnil Sector. Support Line :- "A" Coy worked as on previous day under orders of OC Front Line Bn, "B" & "D" improved their Dugouts & during the night of 5/6th last two named Coys worked on their Defences. Brisk enemy artillery action against one of our Battery positions near Support Line. No damage done to Bty but a few shells falling short caused some casualties to this unit. The Bn "fell in" at 9/30 pm after being relieved by 14 R.W.F in above sector & proceeded to take over Front Line of RIGHT Bn of RIGHT BDE in MESNIL SECTOR from 13 WELCH REGT. Relief was completed and Bn Hdqrs established in AVELUY WOOD. Q34.a.5.2. Casualties :- 2Lt R.M. Morgan wounded 1/a 2 ORs Killed + 5 ORs wounded.	WW

A7092). Wt. W12839/M1293 750,000. 1/17. D. D & I. Ltd. Forms/C2118/14.

Instructions regarding War Diaries and Intelligence Summaries are contained in F. S. Regs., Part II. and the Staff Manual respectively. Title pages will be prepared in manuscript.

WAR DIARY
or
~~INTELLIGENCE SUMMARY.~~

(Erase heading not required.)

Army Form C. 2118.

Place	Date	Hour	Summary of Events and Information	Remarks and references to Appendices
Q34.a.5.2. Sht 57d SE	7.6.18 (Fri)		Battalion in FRONT LINE (RIGHT BN of RIGHT BDE) in MESNIL SECTOR:- Enemy fairly active with his artillery, Aircraft & T.M's all the day but in the evening, quiet up to 10.15pm when he let forth with his artillery & TMs, using all calibres, Gas & H. Explosives & made things generally uncomfortable for 30 minutes. Our retaliation was effective and the Hun was obliged to raise his Barrage off our line & MESNIL. Work was carried out on the defences but this was limited owing to shortage of material. Casualties 6 O.Rs wounded	
do.	8.6.18 (Sat)		Battalion in FRONT LINE (RIGHT BN of RIGHT Bde) in MESNIL SECTOR:- The enemy was again fairly active with his artillery, treating Squares Q34b & Q35a to occasional Bursts of H.E. & Shrapnel from 6-10pm. At about 10pm our artillery, co-operating with 17th Div on our left who were raiding the enemy's trenches, opened a heavy fire on enemy's lines to which the Hun retaliated, putting down a barrage consisting of shells of all calibres on our lines in Squares Q34b & Q35a. The enemy lifted his barrage at 10.30pm at which time our artillery had done that which was wanted of it viz:- to attract enemy's attention while neighbouring Division executed the raid. A patrol consisting of 2Lt. C.B. Excell & 4. ORs left our line at 12 midnight but beyond reconnoitring no man's land, nothing of importance occurred. Casualties:- 9. ORs wounded	

A7092. Wt. W12839/M1293 750,000. 1/17. D. D & L. Ltd. Forms/C2118/14.

Instructions regarding War Diaries and Intelligence Summaries are contained in F. S. Regs., Part II. and the Staff Manual respectively. Title pages will be prepared in manuscript.

WAR DIARY
or
~~INTELLIGENCE SUMMARY~~.
(Erase heading not required.)

Army Form C. 2118.

Place	Date	Hour	Summary of Events and Information	Remarks and references to Appendices
Q 34. a. 5. 2 Sht 57 d SE	9.6.18	(Sun)	Battalion in FRONT LINE (R. BN of RIGHT BDE) MESNIL SECTOR:- At 2pm the enemy heavy artillery shelled Battalion HQrs with 4.2s 5.9s & 8" shells, with about 200 shells. At 3am he put down a light Barrage on rides running through AVELUY WD. and concentrated his heavies on Battalion HQrs, obtaining direct hits on all dugouts which withstood the Bombardment. Bn. Reserve Water Dumps, Canteen & Limber Ambulances were all destroyed in addition to Officers Mess Kitchen which seems unfortunate in being unable to avoid the attention of enemy artillery Observers. Shelling of Bn. HQrs ceased at 4 am. Throughout the day the enemy shelled our front line system with small calibre shells, making movement and work almost impossible, nevertheless, the trenches and posts were improved as much as it was possible to do so. At 5pm the enemy attempted a daylight raid on one of our forward Posts but was beaten off losing 2 Killed and two or three wounded. Our Casualties were nil. Identification could not be secured from the dead owing to enemy's M.G. fire which he used unsparingly over his casualties, thus preventing our men from going forward and examining the bodies. Casualties - One O.R. wounded.	WG
Q 34. a. 5. 2 Sht 57 d. SE	10.6.18	(Mon)	Battalion in FRONT LINE (RIGHT BN of RIGHT BDE) MESNIL SECTOR:- comparatively quiet day all round, excepting at about 8/50 pm just before Stand To when the enemy again carried out a silent raid, against ~~one~~ No 7 Post on this occasion about 17 of	WG

Instructions regarding War Diaries and Intelligence Summaries are contained in F. S. Regs., Part II. and the Staff Manual respectively. Title pages will be prepared in manuscript.

WAR DIARY
or
~~INTELLIGENCE SUMMARY.~~

(Erase heading not required.)

Army Form C. 2118.

Place	Date	Hour	Summary of Events and Information	Remarks and references to Appendices
	10.6.18 MONDAY (continued)		the enemy attacked in light order, carrying revolvers only and succeeded in capturing one of the lost and wounding remainder of garrison (2 O.Rs.) but not without sustaining heavy casualties from our rifle fire. This is the first ~~successful~~ raid carried out by the enemy against this unit during 30 months of warfare. The Battn. was relieved in the front Line about 10 pm by 17 R.W.F. & proceeded to take over support posit[ion]. Casualties. One OR Killed, 4 wounded & One Missing	
Q 31 b 90.90 Sht 57d S.E.	11.6.18 Tuesday		Battalion in Support to Front Line Bn of Right Bde MESNIL SECTOR. Usual work org[anised] improving trenches & Dugouts, carried out. D Coy very heavily shelled in the afternoon, otherwise an unimportant day. Casualties. One OR Killed Four OR Wounded	[initials]
do.	12.6.18 Wednesday		Battalion in Support as above — usual work carried out. Battalion was relieved by 14 WELSH REGT in the evening after which we proceeded to Relieve the 14 R.W.F who were in Reserve to the Right Bde of MESNIL SECTOR. Both reliefs completed without mishap, this being a another calm day. Casualties — Nil	[initials]
Q 19 c 5.8 Sht 57d S.E.	13.6.18 Thursday		Battalion in RESERVE (N of ENGLEBELMER). Musketry & Training reconnaissances, working carried out by all Coys in the daylight. Casualties Nil	[initials]

A7092. Wt. W12839/M1293 750,000. 1/17. D. D & L. Ltd. Forms/C2118/14.

Instructions regarding War Diaries and Intelligence Summaries are contained in F. S. Regs., Part II. and the Staff Manual respectively. Title pages will be prepared in manuscript.

WAR DIARY
~~or~~
~~INTELLIGENCE SUMMARY.~~
(*Erase heading not required.*)

Army Form C. 2118.

Place	Date	Hour	Summary of Events and Information	Remarks and references to Appendices
Q19.c.5.8 Sht 57d SE	14.6.18 Friday		Battalion in Reserve to 113 Bde – Usual Training carried out in addition to working parties found for wiring &c. Improvised Baths were erected and much appreciated by the participants. Message received during night of 14/15 June from 3rd Army that enemy would attack from ALBERT to ARRAS on 15th inst. Necessary precautions immediately taken and all concerned, warned. Casualties: Nil	[illegible]
do.	15.6.18 Saturday		Battalion in Reserve to 113 Bde:– Usual Training carried out in addition to working parties found for wiring &c. Baths at FORCEVILLE were allotted to this unit & much appreciated. Day passed off quietly, the enemy making no attack, as was expected. Casualties 2 ORs Killed	[illegible]
do.	16.6.18 Sunday.		Battalion in Reserve to 113 Bde. Work and Training as on previous days. The Regt Canteen established near Bn Hqrs with a good stock of Oranges, Smokes, Biscuits. Excellent business done, Canteen sold out in about 2 hrs, and everyone satisfied with efforts made to supply the almost necessary luxuries. The day was marked by very fine weather & quietness. Casualties Nil	[illegible]

A7092/. Wt. W12839/M1293 750,000. 1/17. D. D & I. Ltd. Forms/C2118/14.

Instructions regarding War Diaries and Intelligence Summaries are contained in F. S. Regs., Part II. and the Staff Manual respectively. Title pages will be prepared in manuscript.

WAR DIARY

or

~~INTELLIGENCE SUMMARY.~~

(Erase heading not required.)

Army Form C. 2118.

Place	Date	Hour	Summary of Events and Information	Remarks and references to Appendices
Q19.c.5.8 Sht 57d SE	17.6.18 Monday		Battalion in Reserve to 113th Inf Bde. Training carried out during morning. Following work executed during the day. One Platoon of 'B' Coy wiring and 2 Officers + 100 O.Rs. reported to O.C. Special Coy R.Es. (No 3) for Ammunition Carrying. This party did no work owing to ammunition not arriving. A few light shells fell near Bn H.Qrs but caused no casualties. Casualties Nil	
Q19.c.5.8 Sht 57d SE	18.6.18 Tuesday		Battalion in Reserve to 113 Inf Bde. The morning was set apart for training to those who were not on fatigue the previous night. The following working parties were found: One Platoon of B Coy wiring. 2 Officers + 100 O.Rs. carrying T.M. Ammunition under O.C. No 3 Special Coy R.Es. 4 Officers + 200 O.Rs. carrying Ammunition under O.C. 113 L.T.M Battery. Casualties Nil	
Q19.c.5.4 Sht 57d SE	19.6.18 Wednesday		Battalion in Reserve to 113th Inf Bde. No work carried out during the morning owing to the fatigue parties as found on previous night not returning to their Billets until 3.30 am. Training under Coy. Commanders carried out in the afternoon but was interfered with by wet weather which also prevented wiring in latter portion of day. Casualties Nil.	

Instructions regarding War Diaries and Intelligence Summaries are contained in F. S. Regs., Part II. and the Staff Manual respectively. Title pages will be prepared in manuscript.

WAR DIARY
or
~~INTELLIGENCE~~ SUMMARY.
(Erase heading not required.)

Army Form C. 2118.

Place	Date	Hour	Summary of Events and Information	Remarks and references to Appendices
Q19.c.5.8. Sht 57d S.E.	20.6.18 Thursday		Battalion in Reserve to 113th Inf Bde – Usual training. Lewis classes formed under Bn. L.G.O. Instruction in the use of new Rifle Grenade Discharger was given to majority of NCOs in each Coy. Signallers & Runners paraded under Intelligence Officer for map reading &c. Demonstration in use of new ~~[illegible]~~ message carrying rocket. About 100 O.R. were employed in working & wiring. No enemy activity on Bn. area Casualties Nil.	
Q19.c.5.8. Sht 57d S.E.	21.6.18 Friday		Battalion in Reserve to 113 Inf Bde:– Usual training carried out. Work & wiring Parties found by the Bn. to extent of 1 Officer & 130 O.Rs. & 3 Officers & 80 O.Rs. respectively. Slight shelling of vicinity of 'D' Coys trenches, otherwise very quiet. Casualties One O.R. wounded	
Q19.c.5.8. Sht 57d S.E.	22.6.18 Saturday		Battalion in Reserve to 113 Inf Bde:– Training and work were the ~~[illegible]~~ orders of the day. Coys. not finding working parties were employed in improving their shelters & trenches under Coy Commanders supervision. Runners, Signallers, Snipers and Stretcher Bearers paraded under their respective Commanders for instruction. Casualties Nil	

A7092). Wt. W12839/M1293 750,000. 1/17. D. D & L. Ltd. Forms/C2118/14.

Instructions regarding War Diaries and Intelligence Summaries are contained in F. S. Regs., Part II. and the Staff Manual respectively. Title pages will be prepared in manuscript.

WAR DIARY or INTELLIGENCE SUMMARY.

(Erase heading not required.)

Army Form C. 2118.

Place	Date	Hour	Summary of Events and Information	Remarks and references to Appendices
Q19 c.5.8 Sht 57d SE	23.6.18 SUNDAY		During night of 22/23 June the 115 Bde took over Command of LEFT MESNIL SECTOR this unit reverting to its former command and occupying same position i.e. Reserve Bn. Various working Parties were found which left about 30% excluding Runners, Snipers &c for training. This was carried out, the usual programme being augmented by the erection of a Range which was utilized. Casualties Nil	[initials]
Q19 c.5.8 Sht 57d SE	24.6.18 MONDAY		Bn in Reserve LEFT MESNIL SECTOR. The usual training and work. Range again made use of. Casualties Nil	[initials]
Q19 c.5.8 Sht 57d SE	25.6.18 TUESDAY		Bn in Reserve LEFT MESNIL SECTOR. Training & work as on previous day plus a few extra fatigue Parties demanded by Brigade. The new dugouts at Bn. Headqrs. received some shelling during the morning but caused no casualties or damage. Casualties Nil	[initials]
Q19 c.5.8 Sht 57d SE	26.6.18 WEDNESDAY		Bn in Reserve LEFT MESNIL SECTOR. Very quiet day. Nothing unusual to record excepting the large numbers of aeroplanes in the vicinity of the Line during the evening. Work and training as on previous day. Casualties Nil	[initials]

(A7092). Wt. W12839/M1293. 750,000. 1/17. D. D. & L., Ltd. Forms/C.2118/14.

Instructions regarding War Diaries and Intelligence Summaries are contained in F. S. Regs., Part II. and the Staff Manual respectively. Title pages will be prepared in manuscript.

WAR DIARY
or
INTELLIGENCE SUMMARY.
(Erase heading not required.)

Army Form C. 2118.

Place	Date	Hour	Summary of Events and Information	Remarks and references to Appendices
Q.19.c.5.8 Sht 57d. SE	27.6.18 THURSDAY		Battalion in Reserve LEFT MESNIL SECTOR. Baths at FORCEVILLE allotted to this Unit today and utilised. During the morning an hours training was carried out by those unable to Bath. Afternoon was spent in resting, chiefly, preparatory to relief of 17 R.W.F. in Front Line. The Battn. moved off at 9.30pm to relieve 17. Bn. R.W.F in Front Line of LEFT MESNIL SECTOR. Relief was completed without a casualty and O.K. reported about 12 midnight. Whilst in Reserve on night of 26/27th June the enemy shelled Bn Hqrs with 4.2s & 5.9s causing no material damage but wounding 2 Other Ranks. Casualties 2 O.Rs. wounded.	
Q.28.a.7.7.	28.6.18 FRIDAY		Battalion in FRONT LINE, LEFT MESNIL SECTOR. Great enemy artillery activity throughout the day but, luckily, causing few casualties. Our Artillery retaliated vigorously and compelled the Hun to adopt a more quiet attitude. Very little work & no wiring carried out owing to shortage of material. A Patrol of 6 Other Ranks under the Command of 2Lt. R.M. Morgan left our lines at 12 midnight & returned at 2am. on 29th having been unsuccessful in its endeavours to catch an enemy patrol. During night 28/29th June the disposition of the Battalion was altered to allow for withdrawal of one Bde from Divisional Front. This was successfully completed and dispositions of Coys were as follows:- LEFT FRONT COY – 'A' : RIGHT FRONT COY – 'D' : SUPPORT COY – 'C' 'B' Coy being under Command of 17. R.W.F. Casualties:- One Other Rank killed & four wounded	

(A7092). Wt. W12839/M1293. 750,000. 1/17. D. D. & L., Ltd. Forms/C.2118/14.

Army Form C. 2118.

WAR DIARY
or
INTELLIGENCE SUMMARY.
(Erase heading not required.)

Instructions regarding War Diaries and Intelligence Summaries are contained in F. S. Regs., Part II. and the Staff Manual respectively. Title pages will be prepared in manuscript.

Place	Date	Hour	Summary of Events and Information	Remarks and references to Appendices
Q28 a. 7.7. Sht 57d SE.	29.6.18 ~~MONDAY~~ SATURDAY		Battalion in FRONT LINE. LEFT MESNIL SECTOR With the exception of slight indiscriminate shelling by the enemy, the morning passed away quietly. Enemy Aeroplanes shewed a little more activity + "dash" than usual, but were effectively kept at a respectable distance by our A A's + L. Guns. During the afternoon and evening excepting two short bursts of Artillery fire by the enemy, it was quiet. A Patrol of 6 O Ranks under 2Lt G.W. Rayner left our line 10/30pm. having for its object the capture of enemy sentry, as on previous night + to ascertain result of Shoot by 6" Newtons on enemy wire. Enemy Sentry was not at his post and consequently, identification were not secured, however the wire was examined + found to be badly damaged. Casualties 2 O.Rs wounded	WD
Q28 a. 7.7. Sht 57d SE.	30.6.18 SUNDAY		Battalion in FRONT LINE. LEFT MESNIL SECTOR. The enemy artillery was fairly active against our forward trenches during morning and afternoon. In the evening two heavy bursts of 77 m.m shells were again directed against our trenches but caused no casualties. Our Artillery and Trench Mortars were very active + inactive respectively, the former continuing a steady fire throughout the day and the latter firing for 30 minutes only. Our aircraft were easily superior throughout the day, making constant patrols over enemy's lines. Enemy Aircraft energetic during morning only. The usual patrol of 6 Other Ranks under 2Lt B. J Haworth left our	WD

Army Form C. 2118.

Instructions regarding War Diaries and Intelligence Summaries are contained in F. S. Regs., Part II. and the Staff Manual respectively. Title pages will be prepared in manuscript.

WAR DIARY
~~or~~
~~INTELLIGENCE SUMMARY.~~

(Erase heading not required.)

Place	Date	Hour	Summary of Events and Information	Remarks and references to Appendices
	30.6.18 SUNDAY (contd).		line at 10.35 pm but beyond making a good reconnaissance of disused trench, were unsuccessful. They returned at 12.15am having had no casualties. Casualties One O.R. Killed	
			July 12th 1918. [signature] Major Commanding 10th Bn. S.W.B.	

(A7092). Wt. W12839/M1293 750,000. 1/17. D. D. & L., Ltd. Forms/C.2118/14.

Army Form C. 2118.

Instructions regarding War Diaries and Intelligence Summaries are contained in F. S. Regs., Part II. and the Staff Manual respectively. Title pages will be prepared in manuscript.

July 1918

WAR DIARY
or
INTELLIGENCE SUMMARY.
(Erase heading not required.)

10th Batt South Wales Borderers

Place	Date	Hour	Summary of Events and Information	Remarks and references to Appendices
Q 3 a [illegible] Sheet 57d SE.	1/7/18 MONDAY		Battalion in FRONT LINE – LEFT MESNIL SECTOR. Enemy artillery very active on the front of division on our right during night in retaliation for minor operation carried out by them. The fire did not extend to our front except for occasional light "strafes" on our front area during night and at Stand To in the morning. Remainder of day was very quiet until dark at night when the battalion was relieved by the 14th RWF – the 113th brigade relieving the 115th – During the relief a raid was made by the enemy on the front of the 2nd RWF on our immediate right – the accompanying strafe causing some casualties to our right company – "D" Company. The remainder of the relief was carried out quietly, and the battalion marched to FORCEVILLE – relief being complete at 2 am. Headquarters were established at P21d 50 70 Sheet 57d SE. Casualties 1 OR Killed 3 OR Wounded	[illegible]
P21d 50 70 Sheet 57d SE	2/7/18 TUESDAY		Battalion in reserve at FORCEVILLE – together with the remainder of the brigade. The day was spent in cleaning up and usual inspections held – the remainder of the day the men had a rest. They are billeted in trenches immediately outside village – the Company HQ being located in tents and houses nearby. A tragedy occurred at our [illegible] HQ at LEALVILLERS early in the morning of the 2nd July. The HQ was shelled and direct hits were obtained on the house where HQ were located – with the result that 2 officers & 8 OR were killed & 2 officers and 8 OR wounded. The names of the officers were – Capt A J Evans & Capt W L G Foster killed and Lt E A Travers & Lt & QM R M Whitehill – wounded. Casualties 2 off 8 OR killed 2 off 8 OR wounded	[illegible]

(A7092). Wt. W12839/M1293. 750,000. 2/17. D. D. & L., Ltd. Forms/C.2118/14.

Instructions regarding War Diaries and Intelligence Summaries are contained in F. S. Regs., Part II. and the Staff Manual respectively. Title pages will be prepared in manuscript.

WAR DIARY
or
INTELLIGENCE SUMMARY.
(Erase heading not required.)

Army Form C. 2118.

Place	Date	Hour	Summary of Events and Information	Remarks and references to Appendices
P 21 d 50.70 Sheet 57d SE	3/7/18 WEDNESDAY		Battalion in reserve at FORCEVILLE. The day was passed very quietly, only a small amount of training being carried out. The Commanding Officer (Major W.J. Monteith) inspected the battalion in the morning after the strengths of the various units had been readjusted on the lines of the new organization. During the afternoon musketry training was carried out. At 3.30pm the funeral of the Officers & men killed at and near [illegible] yesterday took place in the cemetery at [illegible]. The Divisional Chaplain (Rev [illegible] MC) officiated and the service was attended by a number of officers & men of the battalion. The Last Post was sounded by the battalion buglers.	[illegible]
P 21 d 50.70 Sheet 57d SE	4/7/18 THURSDAY		Battalion in reserve at FORCEVILLE. The day was passed very quietly – practically the whole battalion being on working parties digging [illegible] in the vicinity during morning. The Divisional Band arrived & played to the battalion during afternoon & evening & was much appreciated by all ranks.	[illegible]
P 21 d 50.70 Sheet 57d SE	5/7/18 FRIDAY		Battalion in reserve at FORCEVILLE. The day was passed very quietly – the whole battalion having baths & clean change of clothing, afterwards being inspected by M.O. The remainder of the day was spent in training & firing practice on the range with the exception of C Company who were on working party cable burying at P 26 b 8 2. Major Bowen returned from hospital today & took over command of the battalion from Major Monteith.	[illegible]

(A7092). Wt. W12839/M1293. 750,000. 1/17. D. D. & L., Ltd. Forms/C.2118/14.

Army Form C. 2118.

WAR DIARY
or
INTELLIGENCE SUMMARY.
(*Erase heading not required.*)

Instructions regarding War Diaries and Intelligence Summaries are contained in F. S. Regs., Part II. and the Staff Manual respectively. Title pages will be prepared in manuscript.

Place	Date	Hour	Summary of Events and Information	Remarks and references to Appendices
[illegible] Sheet 57d SE	10/7/18 WEDNESDAY		Battalion in front line – RIGHT MESNIL SECTOR The battalion relieved the 16th R.W. Fusiliers on the night of 10th July in the above sector. There was nothing unusual occurred and the relief was carried out quite satisfactorily, being completed at 3-15am. Nothing of importance occurred during remainder of day. Casualties – Nil	[initials]
6.28 central Sheet 57d SE.	11/7/18 THURSDAY		Battalion in front line – RIGHT MESNIL SECTOR The day passed very quietly – nothing of importance happening. During the night our 18 pounder guns were firing short and a few shells fell about our front line, with the result that one of our men was killed and two were wounded. A patrol left BRACKEN TRENCH for reconnoitring purposes, consisting of 1 officer & 4 O.Rs. After going about 15 yards from our trench, they came across a Bosche patrol which had got through our outpost line. A fight ensued and a stick bomb thrown by the enemy patrol wounded our officer and three men. The Bosche patrol then retired before assistance could be brought. Killed – One man. Casualties Wounded – 1 Officer (2/Lt Ellis) 5 O.R.	[initials]

(A7092). Wt. W12839/M1293. 750,000. 1/17. D. D. & L., Ltd. Forms/C.2118/14.

Instructions regarding War Diaries and Intelligence Summaries are contained in F. S. Regs., Part II. and the Staff Manual respectively. Title pages will be prepared in manuscript.

WAR DIARY
or
INTELLIGENCE SUMMARY.
(Erase heading not required.)

Army Form C. 2118.

Place	Date	Hour	Summary of Events and Information	Remarks and references to Appendices
P 21 d 50 70 Sheet 57 D SE	6/7/18 SATURDAY		Battalion in reserve at FORCEVILLE. Nothing of special interest happened today. Practically the whole of the battalion being on working parties digging trenches in the vicinity. A small amount of training was carried out during early part of evening. Four new officers joined the battalion, their names being: 2/Lt. R.P. Thomas, 2/Lts Thomas, Nelson & Simpson. Major Montelle rejoined Battle Surplus.	[illegible]
P 21 d 50 70 Sheet 57 D SE	7/7/18 SUNDAY		Battalion in reserve at FORCEVILLE. The various denominations attended Church Parade in the morning; the remainder of the day the troops had a rest. "B" Company attended on the range in the afternoon for firing practice.	[illegible]
P 21 d 50 70 Sheet 57 D SE	8/7/18 MONDAY		Battalion in reserve at FORCEVILLE. Nothing of special interest happened today. One of our stretcher-bearers was slightly wounded by shell during the night. The Battalion found working parties digging trenches in the vicinity. Training in Musketry was carried out in the evening. Capt. J.W. Hughes C.F. joined the Battalion today. The Senior Officers & Coy Officers reconnoitred the front line in MESNIL Right Sub-sector.	[illegible]
P 21 d 50 70 Sheet 57 D SE			Battalion in reserve at FORCEVILLE. The whole Batt. was out under Brigade Instructions in the vicinity during the morning. There was a [illegible] G.O.C. inspection in the afternoon. The Batt. relieved the [illegible] in the Right Sub Sector.	[illegible]

(A7092). Wt. W12839/M1293. 750,000. 1/17. D. D. & L., Ltd. Forms/C.2118/14.

Army Form C. 2118.

WAR DIARY
or
INTELLIGENCE SUMMARY.
(Erase heading not required.)

Instructions regarding War Diaries and Intelligence Summaries are contained in F. S. Regs., Part II. and the Staff Manual respectively. Title pages will be prepared in manuscript.

Place	Date	Hour	Summary of Events and Information	Remarks and references to Appendices
C.38 central SHEET 57D SE	12/7/18 FRIDAY		Battalion in front line – RIGHT MESNIL SECTOR. The day again passed quietly. A feature of the first four days of the tour of duty, was the appearance of an enemy aeroplane at "Stand to" each morning and at dusk each evening. The machine always came over flying very low and generally fired his machine gun into our lines, until our Lewis Guns & rifles opened out rapid fire when he reached the vicinity of BHQ, when he retired quickly back to his own lines. The enemy was slightly more active than usual with his artillery & TM's. Two patrols left our lines after dark for reconnaissance duty. Casualties 3 OR wounded.	[initials]
SHEET 57d SE C.28 central	13/7/18 SATURDAY		Battalion in front line – RIGHT MESNIL SECTOR. There is nothing of special interest to report. The day passing quietly. Two patrols left our lines at night – one for reconnaissance & another for fighting, whose duty it was to lay in wait for any approaching enemy. They remained out for 2½ hours & then withdrew, none of the enemy having been seen. The other patrol did some good work & was complimented by Brigade. Casualties Nil	[initials]

(A7092). Wt. W12839/M1293. 750,000. 1/17. D. D. & L., Ltd. Forms/C.2118/14.

Instructions regarding War Diaries and Intelligence Summaries are contained in F. S. Regs., Part II. and the Staff Manual respectively. Title pages will be prepared in manuscript.

WAR DIARY
or
INTELLIGENCE SUMMARY.
(Erase heading not required.)

Army Form C. 2118.

Place	Date	Hour	Summary of Events and Information	Remarks and references to Appendices
C.28 central. SHEET 57D SE	14/7/18 SUNDAY		Battalion in front line. RIGHT MESNIL SECTOR. A very quiet day on the whole. During the day, our snipers, who, by the way, had done some splendid work up to date, reported having killed a Boche who was seen between our front line OP and the enemy post. The enemy opened MG fire on the spot where the man was hit, but despite this, Pt Bassett crawled out to obtain indentification, but failed to find anything on his person with the exception of a revolver which he brought back to our lines. Casualties. 6 OR.	[illegible]
C.28 central SHEET 57D SE	15.7.18 MONDAY		Battalion in front line. RIGHT MESNIL SECTOR. Another very quiet day was spent – hostile fire being much below normal. Between 3am & 4am considerable amount of gas shelling was directed on AUCHONVILLERS ROAD on our left, but did not affect us. Two reconnoitring patrols left our lines during the night to obtain information about a suspected enemy post. The patrols reported post held by night. Casualties 1 OR wounded (at duty)	[illegible]
C.28 central SHEET 57D SE	16.7.18 TUESDAY		Battalion in front line – RIGHT MESNIL SECTOR. Very quiet during day but in the evening enemy artillery livened up, lightly shelling our front support posts. During the night an inter company relief took place – A Company relieving C Company in left front sector – D company relieving B company in right front sector. Relief reported complete 12.30 am. Casualties 3 OR wounded.	[illegible]

(A7092). Wt. W12839/M1293 75,000. 1/17. D. D. & L., Ltd. Forms/C.2118/14.

Instructions regarding War Diaries and Intelligence Summaries are contained in F. S. Regs., Part II. and the Staff Manual respectively. Title pages will be prepared in manuscript.

WAR DIARY
or
INTELLIGENCE SUMMARY.
(Erase heading not required.)

Army Form C. 2118.

Place	Date	Hour	Summary of Events and Information	Remarks and references to Appendices
C 28 cent. SHEET 57D SE	17-7-18 WEDNESDAY		Battalion in front line – RIGHT MESNIL SECTOR. Our guns of all calibres were very active during the day shelling bridges which the enemy were trying to erect over the ANCRE. Our fire was very effective, direct hits being obtained on bridges. Our 6" NEWTONS also joined in & did effectively on some huts which were being used as MG nests by enemy. Between 9pm & 11pm the enemy opened out heavy fire with 4.2 & 5.9s on all our lines, only causing a few slight casualties. The C.O. (Major Bowen) who was standing outside BHQ watching the strafe, was slightly hit in the arm. He remained at duty during the night, but was evacuated the following morning. Three patrols left our lines during night. Casualties 1 off wounded, 3 OR	[initials]
C 28 central SHEET 57D SE	18-7-18 THURSDAY		Battalion in front line – RIGHT MESNIL SECTOR. Another very quiet day was spent chiefly engaged in showing the sector to officers of relieving division (17th Division). Major Monteith came up from Battle Surplus & assumed command of the battalion. During the night a divisional relief took place, the battalion being relieved by 9th Batt. Duke of Wellington's. The relief passed off quietly & was reported complete on the morning of the 19th. Earlier in the evening a party of the enemy, while attempting a silent raid on one of our posts, came across one of our snipers in NO MANS LAND whom they overpowered & took prisoner. Casualties 1 OR missing, 1 wounded	[initials]

(A7092). Wt. W12839/M1293. 75,000. 1/17. D. D. & L., Ltd. Forms/C.2118/14.

Instructions regarding War Diaries and Intelligence Summaries are contained in F. S. Regs., Part II. and the Staff Manual respectively. Title pages will be prepared in manuscript.

WAR DIARY
or
INTELLIGENCE SUMMARY.
(Erase heading not required.)

Army Form C. 2118.

Place	Date	Hour	Summary of Events and Information	Remarks and references to Appendices
T.10.c.90.75 SHEET 57d SW.	19.7.18 FRIDAY.		After relief in front line the battalion [illegible] by companies to the transport lines between HEALVILLERS & TOUTENCOURT where they had breakfast & rested until 11 a.m. after which the companies marched independently to HERISSART, where they were all billeted. Battalion HQ was established at T.10.c.90.75. The remainder of the day was devoted to rest. Three new officers joined the battalion today, their names being 2 Lts. Forbes, Anderson & Ache.	[illegible]
T.10.c.90.75 SHEET 57d SW.	20.7.18 SATURDAY		Battalion in reserve at HERISSART. The day was spent in cleaning up & [illegible] inspections were held in the afternoon to find deficiencies of Kit, clothing etc. The Commanding Officer & one officer per company were away on reconnaissance of the battle positions which the Brigade would take up in case of enemy attack	[illegible]
T.10.c.90.75 SHEET 57d SW.	21.7.18 SUNDAY.		Battalion in reserve at HERISSART. Church parades took place at [illegible] for the various denominations. After which two companies went on the range from 9 a.m. to 1 p.m. for firing practice & general musketry training. The remaining two companies being on the range from 2 p.m. until 6 p.m. Some of the officers were again out with the CO on reconnaissance. Everybody is fixed up very comfortably, most of the battalion being in same camp as occupied before going into line for last tour of duty. A few bombs were dropped near our transport lines during night, one being a few yards from tent occupied by T.O. but no damage was done as tent was empty at the time.	[illegible]

(A7092). Wt. W12839/M1293. 750,000. 1/17. D. D. & L., Ltd. Forms/C.2118/14.

Army Form C. 2118.

Instructions regarding War Diaries and Intelligence Summaries are contained in F. S. Regs., Part II. and the Staff Manual respectively. Title pages will be prepared in manuscript.

WAR DIARY
or
~~INTELLIGENCE~~ SUMMARY.

(*Erase heading not required.*)

Place	Date	Hour	Summary of Events and Information	Remarks and references to Appendices
57 D.C. 90.95 Sheet 57d SW	22.7.18 MONDAY		Battalion in reserve at HERISSART. The day was spent in pretty hard training both morning & afternoon, the usual squad drill, extended order drill, musketry, &c. being carried out. In the evening a football match took place between the Signallers & Transport & a very good game was witnessed. The final score was a win for the Signallers by one goal to nil. The Commanding Officer again took some of the company officers on reconnaissance.	[illegible]
D.C. 90.75 Sheet 57d SW	23.7.18 TUESDAY		Battalion in reserve at HERISSART. Usual training programme carried out in the first part of the morning, but owing to heavy rainstorms, the various companies had to return to billets & the remainder of the training hours were spent in indoor instruction on Lewis Gunnery & lectures on various subjects.	[illegible]
D.C. 90.75 Sheet 57d SW	24.7.18 WEDNESDAY		Battalion in reserve at HERISSART. Usual training again carried out — companies alternately doing musketry & range firing & ordinary training. Lectures were given for a short time in the evening by company officers. Everything was very quiet & nothing of special interest occurred.	[illegible]

(A7092). Wt. W12839/M1293. 750,000. 1/17. D. D. & L., Ltd. Forms/C.2118/14.

Instructions regarding War Diaries and Intelligence Summaries are contained in F. S. Regs., Part II. and the Staff Manual respectively. Title pages will be prepared in manuscript.

WAR DIARY
or
INTELLIGENCE SUMMARY.
(Erase heading not required.)

Army Form C. 2118.

Place	Date	Hour	Summary of Events and Information	Remarks and references to Appendices
T10C 90.75 Sheet 57D SE	25/7/18 THURSDAY		Battalion in reserve in HERISSART. The training this morning consisted of a battalion Route March and a small tactical scheme, this change in the ordinary routine was much appreciated by all ranks. In the afternoon there was a lecture on GAS by the Divisional Gas Officer. In the evening, the Battalion Sports took place and were a great success. The Sports Officer was able to pick out the best runners etc for the Brigade Sports which take place on Monday. The Divisional Band was present & gave us many delightful overtures.	[illegible]
T10.C 90.75 Sheet 57D SE	26/7/18 FRIDAY		Battalion in reserve in HERISSART. Ordinary training programme again continued, companies carrying out firing practice on range etc. Day was stormy unsettled & the rain rather interfered with the training. Nothing of special interest to report.	[illegible]
T10C 90.75 Sheet 57D SE	27/7/18 SATURDAY		Battalion in reserve in HERISSART. The ordinary routine of training was again carried on & some companies on the range and the others practising live bombing in the [illegible] AREA. The Corps Commander was due to inspect the Battalion at range practice but owing to violent rainstorms the inspection was cancelled and the afternoon was spent in drying the clothing of the men. In the evening [illegible] concert was held in the SCHOOL ROOM at HERISSART and [illegible]	[illegible]

(A7092). Wt. W12839/M1293. 750,000. 1/17. D. D. & L., Ltd. Forms/C.2118/14.

Instructions regarding War Diaries and Intelligence Summaries are contained in F. S. Regs., Part II. and the Staff Manual respectively. Title pages will be prepared in manuscript.

WAR DIARY
or
INTELLIGENCE SUMMARY.
(*Erase heading not required.*)

Army Form C. 2118.

Place	Date	Hour	Summary of Events and Information	Remarks and references to Appendices
T 10 C 90 95 SHEET 57D SW	28/7/18 SUNDAY		Battalion in reserve in HERISSART. The day was exceedingly quiet – the various denominations attending church parades. Afterwards the battalion had to carry out a certain amount of firing practice on the range until 1 pm when all training finished for the day and the men had a good rest. In the evening a battalion concert organised by the C of E Padre, Rev C. J. Augler was held in the SCHOOLROOM and was much appreciated by all ranks. Major A. R. [illegible] MC on arrival took over command of the battalion from today.	
T 10 C 90 95 SHEET 57D SW	29/7/18 MONDAY		Battalion in reserve in HERISSART. Today was a general holiday throughout the brigade on the occasion of the Brigade Sports being held. The men had entered for the various competitions in large numbers, and won several [illegible] of the important ones. The weather conditions were perfect and everybody had a very pleasant afternoon. The drums of the [illegible] attended and played excellently. The cookers were taken up to the ground and tea was served to the men.	

Instructions regarding War Diaries and Intelligence Summaries are contained in F. S. Regs., Part II. and the Staff Manual respectively. Title pages will be prepared in manuscript.

WAR DIARY
or
INTELLIGENCE SUMMARY.
(Erase heading not required.)

Army Form C. 2118.

Place	Date	Hour	Summary of Events and Information	Remarks and references to Appendices
P.7.d.45.32 SHEET 57d SE	30.7.18 TUESDAY		Battalion in reserve in ACHEUX The battalion moved today to reserve in ACHEUX in conjunction with the remainder of the 113th Brigade. The morning was spent in cleaning up & general organisation for the move. The [illegible] left MENISSART at 1pm and arrived at its destination at 5pm, after a march, which though not very far, was very fatiguing owing to the extreme heat. Battalion HQrs was established at P.7.d.45.32. Three companies were billeted in tents & bivouacs in ACHEUX WOOD and the remaining company in barns in the village. The [illegible] relieved was the 14th Batt., Royal [illegible]	[initials]
P.7.d.45.32 SHEET 57d SE	31.7.18 WEDNESDAY		Battalion in reserve in ACHEUX The morning was spent in cleaning up of equipment &c and generally making ourselves comfortable. One officer from each company proceeded on reconnaissance of the PURPLE & BROWN LINES. In the afternoon, the battalion was inspected by the Commanding Officer. During the night, the village & vicinity was visited by enemy aeroplanes which dropped some bombs but caused no casualties.	[initials]

[signature] Major

(A7092). Wt. W12839/M1293. 750,000. 1/17. D. D. & L., Ltd. Forms/C.2118/14.

Instructions regarding War Diaries and Intelligence Summaries are contained in F. S. Regs., Part II. and the Staff Manual respectively. Title pages will be prepared in manuscript.

WAR DIARY
or
~~INTELLIGENCE SUMMARY.~~

(*Erase heading not required.*)

10th S.W.B.

Army Form C. 2118.

WR 32

Place	Date	Hour	Summary of Events and Information	Remarks and references to Appendices
T.10.C.90.75 SHEET 57D S.W.	1st/8/18 THURSDAY		Battalion in reserve in ACHEUX. The day was spent in training – also most of the battalion had baths in the village. In the morning, the companies carried out "company in attack" training, and in the evening, the whole battalion took part in a practice attack in front of the village. Major Bowen (C.O.) returned from hospital, but left again for Divl. Rest Station owing to his wound not having properly healed	WMcE
T.10.C.90.75 SHEET 57D S.W.	2/8/18 FRIDAY		Battalion in reserve in ACHEUX. The training programme was continued during day, but was rather hampered owing to heavy rainstorms. In the early morning, the whole battalion paraded – two companies giving a demonstration & practising "company in attack" training – two companies witnessing the demonstration & were inspected by the Commanding Officer. Owing to rain, the remainder of the morning was spent in instruction in billets. In the afternoon, the C.O. gave a lecture on "Attack Formations" to all officers & NCOs – after which, the whole battalion again paraded for another practice attack on the same ground as yesterday.	WMcE
T.10.C.90.75 SHEET 57D S.W.	3/8/18 SATURDAY		Battalion in reserve in ACHEUX. The morning was set apart for the actual practise attack by the whole battalion which was to be witnessed by the Divisional Commander, General Cubitt. The battalion paraded at 7am for inspection &c, after which, we were to carry out the attack, but owing to heavy rain, the whole affair was cancelled. In the afternoon, the Divisional Sports took place at TOUTENCOURT, & the battalion, though not very successful, did its utmost to uphold its traditions.	WMcE

(A7092). Wt. W12839/M1293. 750,000. 1/17. D. D. & L., Ltd. Forms/C.2118/14.

Instructions regarding War Diaries and Intelligence Summaries are contained in F. S. Regs., Part II. and the Staff Manual respectively. Title pages will be prepared in manuscript.

WAR DIARY
or
~~INTELLIGENCE SUMMARY.~~
(Erase heading not required.)

Army Form C. 2118.

Place	Date	Hour	Summary of Events and Information	Remarks and references to Appendices
T.10.C.90.75. SHEET 57D S.W.	4/8/18 SUNDAY		Battalion in reserve in ACHEUX. Practically the whole battalion was out on working parties in the Brown line near BEAUSSART. The men were given task work and everybody had finished about 12.30 pm, when they marched back to billets. In the afternoon, the Divisional Horse Show & Steeplechases took place at TOUTENCOURT, where a very fine show was witnessed. Lorries were provided for the men of the battalion. 2/Lt [illegible] joined the battalion & was posted to C Coy.	WMcE
T.10.C.90.75 SHEET 57d SW	5/8/18 MONDAY		Battalion in reserve in ACHEUX. The morning was spent in company training until 12.30 pm. The battalion had received orders to move, so the afternoon was given over to preparation. At 9.30 pm, the battalion marched to the new position in the Purple System in the vicinity of SENLIS, where we relieved the 10th Battn. West Yorks. Regt., relief being complete at 1 am. HQ were established at V.12.C.40.05. The 1/Battle Surplus left for VALHEUREUX previous to our marching away.	WMcE
V.12.C.40.05 SHEET 57D SE	6/8/18 TUESDAY		Battalion in reserve to 115th Brigade in AVELUY RIGHT SECTOR. The men are billeted in the trenches of the PURPLE SYSTEM. The day passed very quietly and was spent in draining the trenches, which were very wet owing to rain, and generally making things as comfortable as possible. There was practically no enemy activity – in consequence of his having had to retire over the ANCRE on our immediate front. CASUALTIES. 1 Man wounded.	WMcE

(A7092). Wt. W12839/M1293. 750,000. 1/17. D. D. & L., Ltd. Forms/C.2118/14.

Army Form C. 2118.

WAR DIARY
or
INTELLIGENCE SUMMARY.
(*Erase heading not required.*)

Instructions regarding War Diaries and Intelligence Summaries are contained in F. S. Regs., Part II. and the Staff Manual respectively. Title pages will be prepared in manuscript.

Place	Date	Hour	Summary of Events and Information	Remarks and references to Appendices
V.12.C.40.05 SHEET 57D SE	7/8/18 WEDNESDAY		Battalion in reserve - AVELUY RIGHT SECTOR. The day again passed quietly - the enemy displaying very little activity. The men were on various working parties - some making concrete emplacements - but chiefly improving their trenches & making more dugouts & accomodation generally. The Brigadier General Commanding inspected the Battalion area in the morning & was very pleased with the work carried out. On the night of the 7/8th, there was a heavy bombardment by our guns on our immediate right to support the divisions of the 4th Army who successfully attacked early in the morning of the 8th in the vicinity of MORLANCOURT. CASUALTIES NIL	[initials]
V.12.C.40.05 SHEET 57D SE	8/8/18 THURSDAY		Battalion in reserve - AVELUY RIGHT SECTOR. The activity today was much above normal, all our batteries in the vicinity bombarding the enemy's trenches & communications incessantly throughout the day & night. There was practically no retaliatory fire, but two shells unfortunately landed direct on our right & right centre companies lines causing casualties. As far as the battalion was concerned the day was again spent in general trench improvements, salvage work etc. The night of the 8/9th was again marked by lively artillery activity on our part. Casualties. 2 OR Killed 2 OR wounded.	[initials]
V.12.C.40.05 SHEET 57D SE	9/8/18 FRIDAY		Battalion in reserve - AVELUY RIGHT SECTOR. The day was generally quieter than previous day - with the exception of our own artillery who kept up harassing fire throughout day & night. The enemy's attitude was again passive & there was practically no retaliation for our fire. The battalion was again engaged on work in the battalion area, making general improvements to trenches etc. In the evening there was a heavy bombardment away to our right - and we were able to see our troops attacking.	[initials]

(A7092). Wt. W12839/M1293. 750,000. 1/17. D. D. & L., Ltd. Forms/C.2118/14.

Instructions regarding War Diaries and Intelligence Summaries are contained in F. S. Regs., Part II. and the Staff Manual respectively. Title pages will be prepared in manuscript.

WAR DIARY
or
INTELLIGENCE SUMMARY.

(Erase heading not required.)

Army Form C. 2118.

Place	Date	Hour	Summary of Events and Information	Remarks and references to Appendices
T.10.C.40.05 SHEET 57D. SE	10/8/18 SATURDAY		Battalion in 1st support – AVELUY RIGHT SECTOR. The day again passed very quietly – the enemy's attitude being almost absolutely inactive on our front. The battalion was again employed on work improving the trenches in the area in the morning and afternoon, and at night 200 men were engaged on front line work, connecting up the new posts in the ANCRE VALLEY &c. The party was rather badly "strafed" by shell fire, but sustained no casualties. Casualties Nil.	
T.10C.40.05 SHEET 57D SE.	11/8/18 SUNDAY		Battalion in support – AVELUY RIGHT SECTOR. The enemy was more active today – several counter battery strafes taking place. The day was spent with the usual working parties. In the evening a battalion relief took place, and this battalion went into support to the 17th R.W.F., who relieved the 2nd R.W.F. in the front line. Owing to a change in brigade dispositions, this only necessitated moving four platoons forward of our original line and B.H.Q remained in same place. About 8 pm, in the evening, a chance shell wounded 3 of our runners. About 11 pm, the enemy commenced to bombard B.H.Q. with heavy shells, and one of the first happened to drop amongst a party of "C" Company who were outside, causing 6 casualties, one of whom died before we could evacuate him. Casualties 1 Killed, 8 wounded	
T.10C.40.05 SHEET 57D SE.	12/8/18 MONDAY		Battalion in support – AVELUY RIGHT SECTOR. The day passed fairly quietly – though the fire of the enemy was fairly active. Several large parties from the battalion being engaged on front line working parties on the night 11th/12th & did not return until about 5 am. During the night, the enemy sent over about 200 gas shells in the area, but we only sustained two slight gas casualties. Casualties 2 O.R. slightly gassed.	

(A7092). Wt. W12839/M1293 75,000. 1/17. D. D. & L., Ltd. Forms/C.2118/14.

Instructions regarding War Diaries and Intelligence Summaries are contained in F. S. Regs., Part II. and the Staff Manual respectively. Title pages will be prepared in manuscript.

WAR DIARY
or
INTELLIGENCE SUMMARY.
(*Erase heading not required.*)

Army Form C. 2118.

Place	Date	Hour	Summary of Events and Information	Remarks and references to Appendices
T.10C.40.05 SHEET 57D SE	13/8/18 TUESDAY		Battalion in support - RIGHT AVELUY SECTOR. Another quiet day was spent - the activity on both sides being below normal. The enemy again carried out some counter battery work in vicinity of BHQ. The battalion was again engaged on various working parties under RE's. At night the enemy again bombarded the area with Gas shells but we sustained no casualties. Casualties 2 O.R. slightly wounded	
T.10C.40.05 SHEET 57D SE	14/8/18 WEDNESDAY		Battalion in support - AVELUY RIGHT SECTOR. The day was quiet and uneventful - there being nothing of special interest to record. The usual working parties were carried out and some of the companies had baths near SENLIS. Our artillery was fairly active during day & night with harassing fire on enemy communications - though they were unable to fire on his forward positions owing to the uncertainty of the exact location of the line to which he had retired east of the ANCRE. Casualties Nil.	
T.10C.40.05 SHEET 57D SE	15/8/18 THURSDAY		Battalion in support - AVELUY RIGHT SECTOR. The day was again passed quietly. Two companies of the battalion - "A" & "B" - received orders to take over from the 14th RWF in the PURPLE LINE - LEFT BRIGADE SECTOR owing to a change in the dispositions of the Division - thus leaving our present line held by remaining two companies. The new position was duly reconnoitred by company officers, but the relief was postponed at the last moment. The remainder of the battalion carried out the usual work programme. Casualties Nil.	

(A7092). Wt. W12839/M1293. 75,000. 1/17. D. D. & L., Ltd. Forms/C.2118/14.

Army Form C. 2118.

Instructions regarding War Diaries and Intelligence Summaries are contained in F. S. Regs., Part II. and the Staff Manual respectively. Title pages will be prepared in manuscript.

WAR DIARY
or
INTELLIGENCE SUMMARY.

(Erase heading not required.)

Place	Date	Hour	Summary of Events and Information	Remarks and references to Appendices
T.10.C.40.05. SHEET 57D SE	16/8/18 FRIDAY.		Battalion in support – AVELUY RIGHT SECTOR. The relief, which was cancelled yesterday, took place today. The two remaining companies of the battalion extended their sectors – "A" + "B" companies moving off about 2pm. While on the way to new locality, the enemy heavily bombarded some of our batteries, by which the companies happened to be passing, but they were able to get under cover and we only sustained two casualties. Relief was complete at 5pm. Capt Hornsby was appointed O.C. Detachment with H.Q at P.36.a.2.8. Casualties. 2 O.R. wounded.	
T.10.C.40.05 SHEET 57D SE	17/8/18 SATURDAY		Battalion in support – 2 Companies AVELUY RIGHT – 2 companies AVELUY LEFT. The day was passed quietly, the usual work programme being again continued. The Commanding Officer and other officers + NCOs. of "A" + "B" companies proceeded to front area AVELUY LEFT SECTOR for reconnoitring purposes. The attitude of the enemy was passive though our guns were busy carrying out harassing fire. Casualties. Nil.	
T.10.C.40.05 SHEET 57D SE	18/8/18 SUNDAY.		Battalion in support – 2 companies AVELUY RIGHT – 2 companies AVELUY LEFT. Received orders to move to front line – AVELUY LEFT SECTOR. The 17th RWF took over our lines + H.Q at T.10.C.40.05. "C" + "D" companies moved over to relieve the detachment under Capt Hornsby, which, after relief in PURPLE SYSTEM, moved up to forward area, taking over the line from 2nd Battn, 318th American Inf. Regiment – relief being complete at 12 midnight. B.H.Q. were established at Q.34.a.1.3. The relief took place quite quietly with the exception of two O.R. being wounded by a gas shell. Casualties. 2 O.R. wounded.	

A7092). Wt. W12839/M1293 750,000. 1/17. D. D & L Ltd. Forms/C2118/14.

Instructions regarding War Diaries and Intelligence Summaries are contained in F. S. Regs., Part II. and the Staff Manual respectively. Title pages will be prepared in manuscript.

WAR DIARY
or
INTELLIGENCE SUMMARY.
(Erase heading not required.)

Army Form C. 2118.

Place	Date	Hour	Summary of Events and Information	Remarks and references to Appendices
Q.34-a.1.3	19. 8. 18. MONDAY		Battalion in Front Line - AVELUY LEFT SECTOR. The day was passed very quietly. The enemy shelled at intervals with Gas shells. No casualties occurred.	WMS
Q.34-a.1.3.	20. 8. 18. TUESDAY		Battalion in Front Line - AVELUY LEFT SECTOR. The day was passed quietly. The enemy shelled during the night with gas shells. The Battn were relieved by 14th Welsh and moved to BOUZINCOURT. Relief carried out without incident.	WMS
BOUZINCOURT	21. 8. 18		The day was spent in cleaning up and making up deficiencies.	WMS
BOUZINCOURT	22. 8. 18		The Battalion were employed on working parties.	WMS

A7092 Wt. W128 9/M1293 750,000. 1/17. D. D & I. Ltd. Forms/C2118/14.

Instructions regarding War Diaries and Intelligence Summaries are contained in F. S. Regs., Part II. and the Staff Manual respectively. Title pages will be prepared in manuscript.

WAR DIARY
or
INTELLIGENCE SUMMARY.
(Erase heading not required.)

Army Form C. 2118.

Place	Date	Hour	Summary of Events and Information	Remarks and references to Appendices
BOUZINCOURT	23. 8. 18. FRIDAY		Battalion in reserve. Companies on working parties. Orders for Bn to take over line on E. side of Ancre for attack at 1 am on 24th:- Left BOUZINCOURT at 9.30 pm and arrived in assembly position at 12.30 am. Battalion crossed river by trench board Bridge, in single file. The enemy shelled same at 12 midnight, Killing Lieut Thomas and having a direct hit on a 'B' Company L.G. team. Battalion formed up for attack, A & D Coys in front waves, B & C Coys in support. No rest was possible as Battn were required to attack as soon as it arrived in position.	WMG
	24. 8. 18. SATURDAY		Attacked at 1.0 am on trenches just East of ANCRE, our objective being LA BOISELLE, with the 10th S.W.B on left, 14th R.W.F on right and 2nd R.W.F in Support. All enemy resistance was broken down and our Coys swept forward, halting on what Coy Commanders thought to be objective. It was then quite dark, this with heavy mists from Ancre made operations very difficult, and it was afterwards found that Bde was 1000 yds short of its proper line, & that an enemy M.G. nest was posted on LA BOISELLE ridge and made advance impossible. Orders to attack at 4 pm were cancelled at 3 pm: at 5 pm orders were received that 115 Bde would outflank LA BOISELLE on the North & 113 Bde on the South,- the two Brigades finding touch at MAMETZ. The Battn withdrew from its position at 5 pm and carried through a highly successful operation, arriving at MAMETZ at 5.30 am after an all night march. Only 3 casualties occurred which were inflicted by our Artillery. The Battalion passed through	WMG

A7092 Wt. W128 9/M1293 750,000. 1/17. D. D & L. Ltd. Forms/C2118/14.

Instructions regarding War Diaries and Intelligence Summaries are contained in F. S. Regs., Part II. and the Staff Manual respectively. Title pages will be prepared in manuscript.

WAR DIARY
or
INTELLIGENCE SUMMARY.
(Erase heading not required.)

Army Form C. 2118.

Place	Date	Hour	Summary of Events and Information	Remarks and references to Appendices
MAMETZ	24. 8. 18. SATURDAY		Continued. CONTALMAISON en route. It was afterwards found to contain 200 of the enemy hidden in cellars. This night march was carried out without halt or hitch, the men behaving finely. The Lucas lamps were used to great advantage in keeping touch. The arrival of the Battalion at MAMETZ was greeted by a hail of MG bullets but enemy withdrew into woods very rapidly, & Battn was able to take up allotted positions without much trouble. The transport were bombed when bringing up rations and 2/Lieut Hughes & 1 CQMS killed 2 CQMS wounded. 2/Lieut R.J. Haworth took over duties as Transport Officer.	
BAZENTIN-LE-PETIT	25. 8. 18. SUNDAY		Battalion holding Front Line BAZENTIN-LE-PETIT. B & D Coys in Front Line, A & C Coys in Support. The morning passed quietly; during the afternoon orders were received for Battn to take LONGUEVALLE, zero hour at 5.0 pm. Battn 'stood to' and waited for final orders. This was cancelled at 5.20 pm. The Battn 'stood down' and took advantage of the lull to obtain a much needed rest. Water brought up by T.O. was welcomed; this being the first supply since attack started.	
BAZENTIN-LE-PETIT.	26. 8. 18. MONDAY		Battalion holding Front Line BAZENTIN-LE-PETIT. 'A & C' Coys went forward at dawn to act as left flank guard to 114 Bde. The enemy made a fierce fight but Capt Hornby & Capt Hoffmeister shewed the greatest skill & manoeuvred their Coys with great dash. 'A' Coy led and captured 4 MGs & 30 prisoners, 'C' Coy followed through them and took high ground commanding High Wood. B & D Coys were then ordered forward & passed on to ridge with	

A7092 Wt. W128 9/M1293. 750,000. 1/17. D. D & L. Ltd. Forms/C2118/14.

Instructions regarding War Diaries and Intelligence Summaries are contained in F. S. Regs., Part II. and the Staff Manual respectively. Title pages will be prepared in manuscript.

WAR DIARY
or
INTELLIGENCE SUMMARY.
(Erase heading not required.)

Army Form C. 2118.

Place	Date	Hour	Summary of Events and Information	Remarks and references to Appendices
	26. 8. 18 MONDAY Continued		great dash. By noon all Coys were in the Line occupying frontage of 2000 Yds having advanced 3000 yds. Casualties estimated at 50 OR. 2/Lt. Carfull wounded. The attack made by A & B. Coys opened way for advance of the 17th Division on left flank and very materially helped 113 Bde attack. Colonel Cockburn, C.O. 2/R.W.F. wounded.	WMS
NEAR LONGUEVALLE	27. 8. 18. TUESDAY		Battalion holding Front Line from HIGH WOOD to LONGUEVALLE. At about 3.0 pm, enemy counter-attacked along edge DELVILLE WOOD. Enemy succeeded in getting M.G. into position on right flank and enfilading 'C' Coy who were Right Coy. causing about 15 casualties. Right flank curved back to form defensive flank & held up enemy. An American forced to served in German army gave himself up & volunteered valuable information as to enemy dispositions.	WMS
	28 8 18. WEDNESDAY		Battalion formed up in the morning near HIGH WOOD, in rear of 17 R.W.F, to pass through 113 Bde, who were attacking through DELVILLE & LONGUEVALLE. This attack had initial success but enemy guns came into action from high ground East and held up our men. 10th S.W.B. caught in this fire scattered into shell holes, - owing to a misunderstanding A & B. Coys went forward with 113 Bde and were practically in Front Line. They were withdrawn at dusk into trenches South of HIGH WOOD.	WMS
	29. 8. 18. THURSDAY		The Battalion rested in trenches south of HIGH WOOD. C & D Coys in dug-outs in the wood. Capt. Hoffmeister evacuated sick leaving 2/Lieut Simpson in charge of 'C' Company.	WMS

A7092. Wt. W125.9/M1293. 750,000. 1/17. D. D & L. Ltd. Forms/C2118/14.

Instructions regarding War Diaries and Intelligence Summaries are contained in F. S. Regs., Part II. and the Staff Manual respectively. Title pages will be prepared in manuscript.

WAR DIARY
or
INTELLIGENCE SUMMARY.
(Erase heading not required.)

Army Form C. 2118.

Place	Date	Hour	Summary of Events and Information	Remarks and references to Appendices
	30. 8. 18. FRIDAY.		At 3.30 am Battalion left trenches E of High Wood with 2/RWF on right. The enemy had withdrawn during the night. Captured 6 prisoners. The Bn advanced 300 yds and then pushed on to LES BOEUFS. Lieut. Loxton leading the battle patrol ran into an ambush and was wounded. He was seen being carried back by the enemy; his body was found next day behind the then German Line. Our advance was held up by M.G. East of LES BOEUFS. The men are tired but very high morale. Lieut Schofield evacuated Gassed. 6 Officers arrived with draft of 120 O.R. 2/Lieuts Roberts & Ellis rejoined from Courses.	MMcG
LES BOEUFS	31. 8. 18. SATURDAY		All Coys. spent a good day in LES BOEUFS. B.Coy. very comfortable, situated in deep dugouts. Advance temporarily held up by M.G. nest E of village. 2/Lieut Jewell killed by Shell. Only a few casualties amongst Other Ranks. Men rested and moral very high. 2/Lieut Roberts took over duties of Intelligence Officer.	MMcG

A R Lyke Major,
Comdg. 10th Bn South Wales Borderers.

A7092 Wt. W12S 9/M1293 750,000. 1/17. D. D & L. Ltd. Forms/C2118/14.

AUGUST

Instructions regarding War Diaries and Intelligence Summaries are contained in F. S. Regs., Part II. and the Staff Manual respectively. Title pages will be prepared in manuscript.

WAR DIARY
or
INTELLIGENCE SUMMARY.

(*Erase heading not required.*)

10 SWB

98 33

Army Form C. 2118.

115/18

Place	Date	Hour	Summary of Events and Information	Remarks and references to Appendices
	23.8.18	11am	Orders came to take over a line on E side of the Ancre for an attack at 1am on the 24th. Left BOUZINCOURT at 9.30 pm. Bn crossed the river Ancre by a trench board bridge in single file and arrived in assembly position by 12.30 am. Lt Thomas and members of a B Coy Lewis Gun team were killed. Bn formed up for the attack A & D in front waves, B & C in support. No rest was possible as the Battalion was required to attack as soon as they reached their assembly position.	
	24.8.18	1am	Attacked at 1am trenches just east of the ANCRE, objective LA BOISELLE, 10th SWB on left, 17th RWF on right, 2nd RWF in support. All enemy resistance was overcome and our Coys swept forward halting on what Coys thought was their objective. It was then quite dark, and the heavy mists arising from the Ancre made operations very difficult and it was afterwards found that they had halted 1000 yds short of their objective and that an enemy M.G. nest was sited on the LA BOISELLE ridge and made advance impossible. Orders to attack at 7am were cancelled at 3am. At 2pm orders were received that 115th Bde would outflank LA BOISELLE from the north and the 113 Bde from the south, both Bdes to find touch at MAMETZ. Bn withdrew from its positions at 5 pm and carried out a highly successful operation arriving at MAMETZ at 6.30 am after an all night march. Bn only had three casualties. Bn passed through Contalmaison en route and it was afterwards found to contain 200 Boche hidden in cellars. This night march was carried out without halt or hitch, the men behaving finely. The Lucas lamps were used to great advantage for keeping in touch. The arrival of the Bn in MAMETZ was greeted with a hail of M.G. bullets but the enemy withdrew rapidly into the woods and the Bn was able to take up allotted positions without much trouble. 2/Lt Hughes was killed bringing up rations. Transport was bombed and 2 G.S. mules killed 1 wounded. 2/Lt Haworth took over duties of T.O.	
	25.8.18		B & D in front line in BAZENTIN-LE-PETIT. A & C in support, morning passed quietly. During afternoon orders received for Bn to take LONGUEVAL Ridge at 6 pm. Bn "stood to" to wait for final orders – cancellation of orders came at 5.20 pm. Bn "stood down" and took advantage of the lull to obtain a much needed rest. Water was brought up by T.O., very welcome first supply since attack started.	
	26.8.18		A & C Coys went forward from BAZENTIN to act as flank guard to 114 Bde at dawn. Enemy fought fiercely but Capts Hornsby & Hoplister showed the greatest skill and manoeuvred their Coys with great dash. A Coy led and captured 4 M.G. and 30 prisoners. C Coy followed through and took the high ground commanding HIGH WOOD. B and D Coys were then ordered forward and pressed on the ridge with great dash. By now all Coys were in the line occupying a frontage of 2000 yds having advanced 3000 yds. Casualties [illegible] 2/Lt Careful wounded	

A7092. Wt. W12839/M1293 750,000. 1/17. D. D & I. Ltd. Forms/C2118/14.

Army Form C. 2118.

Instructions regarding War Diaries and Intelligence Summaries are contained in F. S. Regs., Part II. and the Staff Manual respectively. Title pages will be prepared in manuscript.

WAR DIARY
or
~~INTELLIGENCE SUMMARY.~~

(Erase heading not required.)

Place	Date	Hour	Summary of Events and Information	Remarks and references to Appendices
	27.8.16		Bn in front line from HIGH WOOD to LONGUEVAL at about 3 pm the enemy counter attacked along ridge over DELVILLE Wood Enemy succeeded in MG on right flank of C Coy enfilading them causing 15 casualties. Right flank curved back to form defensive flank and held up the enemy. An American forced to serve in the German army gave himself up and volunteered very valuable information as to enemy dispositions.	
	28.8.16		Bn formed up in the morning near High Wood in rear of 17th RWF to pass through 113 Bde, who were attacking through DELVILLE & LONGUEVAL – this attack had initial success but enemy guns came into action from high ground east and held up the attack 10th SWB came under fire and took up position in shell-holes owing to a misunderstanding A & B Coys went forward with 113 Bde but were withdrawn at dusk into positions south of HIGH WOOD	
	29.8.16		Battalion rested in trenches South of High Wood C & D Coys in dugouts in the Wood Capt Hoffmeister evacuated to hospital leaving 2/Lt Simpson in charge of C Coy	
	30.8.16		At 3.30 am Bn left trenches E of HIGH WOOD. 10th SWB on left, 2nd RWF on the right 6 prisoners Enemy had withdrawn during the night Bn advanced 3000 yds and then pushed on to LES BOEUFS Lt LOXTON leading the scouts was ambushed and wounded he was seen being carried back by the enemy his body was found next day behind the then German line Advance held up by MG fire east of LESBOEUFS men tired but moral very high Lt Schofield evacuated gassed.	
	31.8.16		6 new officers joined Bn with draft of 120 men All Coys spent a good day in LESBOEUFS B Coy very comfortable in deep dugouts Advance temporarily held up by MG nest east of village 2Lt Jewell killed by a shell only a few casualties	
	~~1.9.16~~		~~2nd & 17 RWF attacked from LESBOEUFS at 5.30 am attack went well but left flank was unguarded~~	

A7092/. Wt. W12839/M1293 750,000. 1/17. D. D & I Ltd. Forms/C2118/14.

SEPT. 10th S.W. Borderers

Instructions regarding War Diaries and Intelligence Summaries are contained in F. S. Regs., Part II. and the Staff Manual respectively. Title pages will be prepared in manuscript.

WAR DIARY
or
INTELLIGENCE SUMMARY.
(Erase heading not required.)

Army Form C. 2118.

Place	Date	Hour	Summary of Events and Information	Remarks and references to Appendices
	1.9.18	5.30am	2nd & 17th RWF attacked from LESBOEUFS at 5.30 am 10th SWB in support attack went ~~[illegible]~~ well but left flank was left unguarded Boche countered and made situation rather uncomfortable. A & B Coys went up to support left flank and did splendidly 2/Lt Ashe charged 100 of the enemy with 8 men and 20 of the 17th Division, he took 8 MGs and 81 prisoners. Flank thus secured and line established. Work of these two Coys saved a very critical situation. 2Lt Excell wounded after doing some very fine work	
	2.9.18		Spent the early morning getting into positions for advance on MESNIL under cover of 113 Bde. A & C in front B & D in rear. 5 pm formed up for attack from Sailly to MESNIL. Enemy allowed reconnoitring officers to go forward to point of assembly when Bn followed he opened out heavy MG fire on 2nd RWF on right 10th SWB on left. Capt Hornsby killed, Capt Lloyd, Lts Anderson, Davies, Francey wounded. about 50 casualties in the ranks. have formed east of Sailly for the night. Boche withdrawal reported by 10th SWB at 7am.	
	3.9.18		Bn Advanced and occupied trenches south of MESNIL-EN-ARROUAISE 10th SWB on left, 17th RWF on the right, Slight Boche barrage C Coy had 10 casualties. 114 Bde went through and advanced to the line of the CANAL DU NORD	
	4.9.18		Occupying same trenches waiting for the Equancourt - NURLU line to fall when we are to pass through 114 Bde. No action. At 9pm enemy shelled B Coy trenches with 5.9 HE Gas Shells causing 5 casualties and 26 gassed. Strength of Bn 320. 4 new officers joined - Lts Jones, Wakefield, Bundy, Urquhart. Bn enjoyed nights rest although it was exceedingly cold. Lt Haworth took command of A Coy on return of 2/Lt Powell from leave	
	5.9.18		Bn prepared to pass through 114 Bde but no advance materialised owing to stiff enemy resistance to 114 Bde. Unit was relieved by 15th DLI of the 21st Division. and moved into bivouacs at LESBOEUFS. Bn was on the offensive for 13 Days and during operations lost Capt Hornsby Lts Thomas Hughes Jewell Loxton killed and Capts Lloyd, Lts Careful Excell, Anderson Davies and Francey wounded Lt Schofield ~~[illegible]~~ gassed 294 OR casualties. Total advance 24 Kilos	
	6.9.18 to 9.9.18		In rest at LESBOEUFS training & reorganizing	

A7092. Wt. W12839/M1293 750,000. 1/17. D. D & L. Ltd. Forms/C2118/14.

Army Form C. 2118.

WAR DIARY
or
INTELLIGENCE SUMMARY.
(Erase heading not required.)

Instructions regarding War Diaries and Intelligence Summaries are contained in F. S. Regs., Part II. and the Staff Manual respectively. Title pages will be prepared in manuscript.

Place	Date	Hour	Summary of Events and Information	Remarks and references to Appendices
	10.9.18		Marched from LESBOEUFS to LECHELLE Lt Col A L BOWEN commanding	
	11.9.18		Moved up into line in the GOUZEAUCOURT Sector: Orders to attack at dawn. Relieved 6th Dorsets	
	12.9.18	5.25	At 5.25 am C Coy under 2/Lt Simpson and two sections of A Coy attacked AFRICAN TRENCH in conjunction with NEW ZEALAND Division on the left. Very strong resistance encountered from the JAEGER DIVISION. A party of men under 2/Lt Bundy entered the German line but were heavily counter attacked and driven out when 2/Lt Bundy was wounded. Our casualties about 50. Endeavours were made four times during the afternoon to advance our line but owing to very strong hostile resistance each attempt was unsuccessful. The following Coy Commanders were killed during the first attack – Lts W E Williams, T S Selby MC and G. Simpson & 2/Lt Bundy and Williams were wounded. Total casualties suffered in BD 79	
	13.9.18		Quiet day spent, and men resting. C Coy were withdrawn to positions held before attack	
	14.9.18 and 15.9.18		With the exception of desultory shelling, sector was fairly quiet	
	16.9.18		Very heavy enemy barrage put down on our lines but no attack followed. Unit was relieved at 11 pm by two Coys of 13th RNF and two Coys of 13th Welsh	
	17.9.18		After relief proceeded to new area near Canal Du Nord. Men billeted in old trenches	
	18.9.18	6 am	Moved forward in Corps Reserve to support an attack by 3rd & 4th Armies. Had no casualties going up, for enemy retaliation was very light. Occupied trenches south of FINS – GOUZEAUCOURT road. At 5 pm BD was attached to 114 Bde and moved forward into AFRICAN TRENCH and HEATHER TRENCH in close support of the front Battalions of 114 Bde. The right of the attack reached final objective but left were held up.	
	19.9.18		Relieved the 113 Bde in the line from RUE ENTER to AFRICAN TRENCH. Lt Col Bowen sent forward and formed a defensive flank. B Coy performing this task.	
	20.9.18		Quiet during the day but enemy shelled heavily before dusk. Relieved by 1st Dawson and proceeded to LECHELLE	

Instructions regarding War Diaries and Intelligence Summaries are contained in F. S. Regs., Part II. and the Staff Manual respectively. Title pages will be prepared in manuscript.

WAR DIARY
or
INTELLIGENCE SUMMARY.
(*Erase heading not required.*)

Army Form C. 2118.

Place	Date	Hour	Summary of Events and Information	Remarks and references to Appendices
LECHELLE	21.9.18		Bn had a good rest moved from here to LE TRANSLOY by route march starting at 2 30 pm	
	22.9.18 23 " " 24 " " 25 " " 26 " " 27 " "		Reorganizing, training and resting at LE TRANSLOY	
	28.9.18		Left LE TRANSLOY by motor bus and proceeded to SOREL le GRAND. Bn billeted in Nissen huts. Waiting to move forward should the attack be very successful	
	29.9.18		Did not move but Battalion is placed under one hours notice. Day spent in training	
	30.9.18		Still in SOREL le GRAND. Training and organizing for further efforts. All men are being trained in the use of German Bombs. The victories from all fronts are (~~[illegible]~~) raising the moral of the men to a very high degree. although during September the Bn has not advanced so much as in August it has given the Boshe no rest when in action.	

[signature]
Lieut Colonel
Commanding 10th Bn S. W. B.

(A7092). Wt. W12839/M1293. 75,000. 1/17. D. D. & L., Ltd. Forms/C.2118/14.

Instructions regarding War Diaries and Intelligence Summaries are contained in F. S. Regs., Part II. and the Staff Manual respectively. Title pages will be prepared in manuscript.

Vol 34 Army Form C. 2118.

115/38

WAR DIARY
or
~~INTELLIGENCE SUMMARY.~~
(Erase heading not required.)

Place	Date	Hour	10th Bn. South Wales Borderers Summary of Events and Information October 1918.	Remarks and references to Appendices
SOREL-LE GRAND V.24.b.8.8 57c. S.E. 1/20000	1/10/18		The Battalion at SOREL-LE-GRAND. The day was spent in re-fitting and training, Platoon drill, Physical training and instruction in use of German Hand Grenades being the main subjects.	
SOREL-LE GRAND. V.24.b.8.8. 57c. S.E. 1/20000.	2.10.18		The Battalion at SOREL-LE-GRAND. The following training was carried out:- Physical training, Rifle Grenade Firing, throwing German Hand Grenades, Platoon and Company in attack.	
SOREL-LE GRAND. V.24.b.8.8. 57c. S.E. 1/20000	3.10.18		The Battalion at SOREL-LE-GRAND. The Battalion, having received orders to move, marched off in S.E. direction through HEUDICOURT, passed S. of EPEHY and halted N. of RONSSOY where Battalion was accommodated in a trench for the night.	
LEMPIRE. E10 + 16. Sht. 62.c 1/40000.	4.10.18		The Battalion at LEMPIRE. Orders were received to move to BONY and the Battalion marched off at 06.15 by Platoons at 150x distance. During the march the captured HINDENBURG LINE was crossed. The Battalion arrived at BONY about 12.00 hrs and pending further orders rested in the HINDENBURG SUPPORT TRENCH. The Officers reconnoitred the front held by the 50th Div. Upon completion of reconnaissance, the Battalion moved through BONY, GOUY and LE CATELET en route for the line which was eventually taken over from units of 50th Div in the LE CATELET - NAUROY Line	

D. D. & L., London, E.C. (A8091) Wt. W1771/M2031 750,000 5/17 Sch. 52 Forms C2118/14.

Instructions regarding War Diaries and Intelligence Summaries are contained in F. S. Regs., Part II. and the Staff Manual respectively. Title pages will be prepared in manuscript.

WAR DIARY

or

~~INTELLIGENCE SUMMARY.~~

(Erase heading not required.)

Army Form C. 2118.

Place	Date	Hour	Summary of Events and Information	Remarks and references to Appendices
LE CATELET - NAUREY LINE	5.10.18		The Battalion relieved a Battalion of the Royal Munster Fusiliers in the LE CATELET - NAUREY LINE. The Battalion advanced with C & D Coys in the vanguard and B & A Coys in close support. The advanced troops came in contact with enemy Infantry at a point 300 yds. S.E. of AUBENCHEUL-AUX-BOIS. Here the enemy made a stand using his Machine Guns and artillery freely, therefore, it was decided to halt and consolidate the ground gained.	
near AUBENCHEUL-AUX-BOIS. APPROX:- T.19 b. Sht. 57. B. S. W	6.10.18		The 17th Bn. R.W.F. having occupied AUBENCHEUL-AUX-BOIS during the night, this unit moved forward in the direction of VILLERS OUTREAUX; two platoons being sent forward to occupy a Sunken Road S.W. of VILLERS OUTREAUX and a Quarry E. of AUBENCHEUL. This was successfully accomplished and in the night a platoon was pushed forward to a sunken portion of Road on the right, contact being maintained on right and left with Royal Munster Fusiliers and 17th Bn. RWF respectively. This position was consolidated and during the night patrols were sent out who, after a careful reconnaissance, reported the enemy position as being very strongly held by Machine Guns and fortified by all means used in modern warfare, the barbed wire being very conspicuous in its numerous belts of thickness not hitherto encountered in such a quantity	

D. D. & L., London, E.C. (A8001) Wt. W1771/M2031 750,000 5/17 Sch. 52 Forms C2118/14

Army Form C. 2118.

Instructions regarding War Diaries and Intelligence Summaries are contained in F. S. Regs., Part II. and the Staff Manual respectively. Title pages will be prepared in manuscript.

WAR DIARY
or
~~INTELLIGENCE SUMMARY.~~

(Erase heading not required.)

Place	Date	Hour	Summary of Events and Information	Remarks and references to Appendices
near VILLERS OUTREAUX approx. T25. Sht 57B. S.W.	7.10.18		Battalion near VILLERS OUTREAUX. The enemy Artillery and machine Gun fire on Battn front was fairly heavy. The Royal Munster Fusiliers on the right attacked VILLERS FARM at dawn but failed to take it. The Battalion was ordered to move into assembly position preparatory to attacking the ground E. of VILLERS OUTREAUX in a N.E. direction. The Battalion moved off at 8.30 pm. and successfully assembled in its position by 00.55 hrs 8th October.	
near VILLERS OUTREAUX approx. T20 + 26. Sht 57.B S.W.	8.10.18.		Battalion near VILLERS OUTREAUX. The Battalion attacked in a N.E. direction, the object being to cut off VILLERS OUTREAUX from the EAST. ZERO HOUR - 01.00 hrs. A & B Coys were the leading Companies with C & D in close support. Almost immediately after the attack commenced, our troops were obstructed by a formidable belt of Barbed Wire. This obstacle was brilliantly surmounted by the dash and high morale of our Officers and men with the result that the objective was partially gained. Groups of men who had lost direction owing to the darkness were collected by the Officers and taken back to re-organise. Later in the day, these men were taken forward to the objective which the remainder of the Battalion had reached. Major. J.S.H. Monteith was in Command of the of our troops who had successfully reached the objective on first occasion. On arrival of the remainder, the whole Battalion was re-organised, meanwhile the 114th Inf Brigade had leap-frogged, passing through our Battalion and attacking the WALINCOURT LINE, capturing MALINCOURT and passing through the WALINCOURT LINE with but very little opposition from the enemy. At 16.00 hrs the Battn	

(A8001) Wt. W1771/M2031 750,000 5/17 Sch. 52 Forms/C2118/14 D. D. & L. London, E.C.

Army Form C. 2118.

Instructions regarding War Diaries and Intelligence Summaries are contained in F. S. Regs., Part II. and the Staff Manual respectively. Title pages will be prepared in manuscript.

WAR DIARY

~~or~~

~~INTELLIGENCE SUMMARY.~~

(Erase heading not required.)

Place	Date	Hour	Summary of Events and Information	Remarks and references to Appendices
near VILLERS OUTREAUX approx T.20 + 26. Sht 57.B.S.W.	8.10.18 (contd).		moved off by Companies in artillery formation in a N.E. direction. On arrival at a point about one mile S.E. of MALINCOURT, the Battalion halted and dug in, staying there for the night.	
approx U 13. Sht 57.B.S.W.	9.10.18		The Battalion one mile S.E. of MILANCOURT. The 33rd Division, having passed through our Division in pursuit of the enemy, our Division were thus placed in Support with orders to move at one hour's notice. No orders being received during the day, the Battalion spent the night in the same position.	
near MILANCOURT approx. U.13. Sht 57 B.S.W.	10.10.18		The Battalion one mile S.E of MILANCOURT. Orders having been received to advance the Battalion passed the Starting Point at 15.30 hrs en route for CLARY. On arrival at this village it was noted that many French civilians had defied the German order to evacuate. The civilians gave our troops a very enthusiastic reception, the tricolours being very conspicuous. Billets were occupied in CLARY at which place our troops stayed for the night	
CLARY O.17. Sht 57. B.S.W.	11.10.18		The Battalion at CLARY. The Battalion spent the day in this village, chiefly resting. In the presence of our Brig.-General (Brig.-Gen. H. de Pree) Lt. Col. Ash-Bowen (under whose command the Battalion had been during the recent operations) addressed each Coy. separately thanking all ranks for their great and untiring efforts which were rewarded by the capture of ground to a depth of 12 miles held by the enemy since 1914.	

D. D. & L., London, E.C. (A8001) Wt. W1771/M2031 750,000 5/17 Sch. 52 Forms/C2118/14

Instructions regarding War Diaries and Intelligence Summaries are contained in F. S. Regs., Part II. and the Staff Manual respectively. Title pages will be prepared in manuscript.

WAR DIARY
or
INTELLIGENCE SUMMARY.
(*Erase heading not required.*)

Army Form C. 2118.

Place	Date	Hour	Summary of Events and Information	Remarks and references to Appendices
CLARY O.17. Sht 57B S.W	12.10.18		The Battalion at CLARY.	
	–		The Battalion left CLARY at 10.45 hrs for TROISVILLE, passing BERTRY en route. On arrival at TROISVILLE at 12.30 hrs, an alarm Post was fixed upon and all concerned warned. The Battalion then entered billets at TROISVILLE at which place the night was spent.	
			It may be here stated in a brief summary of our operations from the 1st inst that the results achieved were greater than had ever before been the case with this unit. Apart from huge military stores and material captured from the enemy, the enemy's best fortifications were wrested from him. This include the much vaunted HINDENBURG LINE the invincibility of which he had openly boasted to the world. Artillery pieces and numerous Machine Guns were also captured. The prisoners captured shewed good morale throughout the operations. The total number captured by this unit cannot be determined owing to the liquid state of the battle area, prisoners being passed to rear Units as soon as captured. The loss of the undermentioned Officers and 196 O.Rs as killed and wounded is deeply regretted but sacrifices were willingly given in the true British spirit and perhaps, the happiest period of the advance occurred when the French civilians were released from the enemy's unscrupulous treatment.	
			Lt Col. A.J. Bowen and all Officers & O.Rs of the Battalion were highly praised by the Divisional Commander for brilliant leadership & spirit of determination shewn, particularly on the attack on VILLERS OUTREAUX which was successfully taken	

D. D. & L., London, E.C. (A8004) Wt. W1771/M2031 750,000 5/17 Sch. 52 Forms C2118/14

Army Form C. 2118.

Instructions regarding War Diaries and Intelligence Summaries are contained in F. S. Regs., Part II. and the Staff Manual respectively. Title pages will be prepared in manuscript.

WAR DIARY
or
INTELLIGENCE SUMMARY.
(Erase heading not required.)

Place	Date	Hour	Summary of Events and Information	Remarks and references to Appendices
CLARY. O.17. Sht 57B. S.W.	12.10.18 (contd)		only after very trying difficulties both for the Leaders and the men (the most trying being the re-organizing of the Battalion during the attack on this village) had been overcome. The Officer casualties above referred to are Capt. J.A. Jones. Killed in Action Lieut R.H. Jones. Killed in Action 2Lt. D. Jones. Killed in Action Capt. J.F. England Wounded in Action 2Lt W.J. Roberts. MC. Wounded in Action 2Lt G.W. Rayner Wounded in Action 2Lt J.W. Capp. Wounded in Action 2Lt J.S. Wanson Wounded in Action 2Lt. J.G. Williams Wounded in Action.	
TROISVILLE Sht 57B N.E	13.10.18		The Battalion at TROISVILLE at 16.45 hrs, the Battalion proceeded to the Line, relieving a unit of the 33rd Div. in Sector of 1½ miles N.E of LE CATEAU. This was completed successfully, whereupon, the Commanding Officer, Major A.R. Sykes M.C., re-organised his front, placing A & D Coys in front line holding the Bridge Heads crossing the River SELLE. B & C Coys were placed in Support and Reserve respectively. The re-organization was successfully carried out, there being no casualties. The 2nd R.W.F were on our RIGHT and the 57th Bde on our LEFT.	

D. D. & L., London, E.C. (A8001) Wt. W1771/M2031 750,000 5/17 Sch. 52 Forms/C2118/14

Instructions regarding War Diaries and Intelligence Summaries are contained in F. S. Regs., Part II. and the Staff Manual respectively. Title pages will be prepared in manuscript.

Army Form C. 2118.

WAR DIARY
or
~~INTELLIGENCE SUMMARY.~~

(*Erase heading not required.*)

Place	Date	Hour	Summary of Events and Information	Remarks and references to Appendices
K 19. b. 2. 9. Sht. 57. B.	14.10.18		The Battalion in the Line. There was no change on the Battalion Front during the night, with the exception of constant shelling of Battalion Headquarters which was situate at VAMBOURLIEUX FARM, the day passed away without incident of importance. In the afternoon the 51st Brigade on our left reported the evacuation by the enemy of NEUVILLY and BRIASTRE. "C" & "B" companies worked under the direction of the C.R.E. during the night, digging trenches.	
K. 19. b. 2. 9 Sht. 57. B	15.10.18		The Battalion in the Line. Patrols reported the enemy as holding the Railway Embankment opposite our sector, in strength, being plentifully supplied with machine guns which are particularly active at night. The day passed away normally, Battalion Headquarters being the enemy's chief objective; this he shelled persistently with 77 & 10.5 m.m shells. The Brigade on our left were relieved during the night with the result that a Battalion of the East Yorks linked up on our left flank.	
K 19. b. 2. 9. Sht. 57. B.	16.10.18		The Battalion in the Line. Apart from the shelling of Battn Hdqrs with 77 m.m. & 15 cm. shells, the enemy was quieter than usual. During the day, Inter Coy reliefs were carried out successfully, "B" Coy. relieving "D" and "C" Coy relieving "A". "B" & "C" Companies becoming Right and Left Front Companies respectively and "D" and "A" Companies Support and Reserve, respectively.	

D. D. & L., London, E.C. (A8004) Wt. W1771/M2031 750,000 5/17 Sch. 52 Forms/C2118/14

Army Form C. 2118.

Instructions regarding War Diaries and Intelligence Summaries are contained in F. S. Regs., Part II. and the Staff Manual respectively. Title pages will be prepared in manuscript.

WAR DIARY

~~or~~

~~INTELLIGENCE SUMMARY.~~

(*Erase heading not required.*)

Place	Date	Hour	Summary of Events and Information	Remarks and references to Appendices
K19.b.2.9 Sht 57B.	17.10.18		The Battalion in the Line. At 01.00 hrs the Special "N" Coy. R.E. discharged Gas Projectors against the enemy opposite our sector. The enemy retaliated by Gas shelling our forward Companies which fire he maintained until 05.30 hrs, otherwise the forward Companies had a quiet day. Battalion Headqrs was heavily shelled between 13.00 & 13.30 hrs with all calibre shell resulting in our [illegible] (Lt & Qm G.J. Cottell) being wounded. At 21.50 hrs a fighting Patrol of one officer & 30 ORs crossed the river Selle with object of searching the ground N. of the Railway for enemy posts and to clear them. They encountered a German post but the enemy shewed no fight but instead flight. 2Lt Hicks who was commanding the patrol secured further and valuable information concerning the enemy's defences after which he rejoined the Battalion with his men, having done exceedingly well. The patrol suffered no casualties.	
K19.b.2.9 Sht 57B	18.10.18		The Battalion in the Line. From 05.00 to 06.30 hrs the enemy again bombarded Bn. Hqrs. The forward area was very heavily shelled with shells of all calibres during the same hours, also his M. Guns were particularly active at Dawn. At 01.45 hrs 2Lt R.S. Granger and 10 ORs crossed the River SELLE to observe any enemy patrols or parties moving about in area opposite our left front Coy. No enemy patrols were encountered and patrol safely returned to our lines without any casualties at 03.00 hrs. At 05.00 hrs, a fighting patrol of 31 ORs under 2Lt Rudkins command crossed the river SELLE with the object of holding the QUARRY K15.b.40.90 until relieved by a platoon of 14th Welch Regt (which Battn was relieving our Unit at 18.00 hrs). They reached the QUARRY and found it occupied by the enemy with a M.G. crew. The patrol, after a careful reconnaissance attacked the garrison of the QUARRY with bombs succeeding in killing the garrison after which the objective was consolidated with 4 posts being established around same.	

D. D. & L., London, E.C. (A8094) Wt. W1771/M2031 750,000 5/17 Sch. 52 Forms/C2118/14

Instructions regarding War Diaries and Intelligence Summaries are contained in F. S. Regs., Part II. and the Staff Manual respectively. Title pages will be prepared in manuscript.

WAR DIARY
or
~~INTELLIGENCE SUMMARY.~~
(*Erase heading not required.*)

Army Form C. 2118.

Place	Date	Hour	Summary of Events and Information	Remarks and references to Appendices
			after being in this position for about 20 minutes, the enemy heavily counter-attacked, wounding 2/Lt Rathus and 5 ORs. Owing to the danger of being cut off, our party withdrew from its position. The Battalion was relieved during the night by 14th Bn. Welch Regt after which Billets in TROISVILLE were occupied	
TROISVILLE Sht 57.B.	19.10.18		The Battalion in TROISVILLE. The Brig.-General inspected 'B' Echelon during the day. Baths at BERTRY were utilized and much appreciated. Remainder of day was spent in refitting. A few shells fell in TROISVILLE during the day but no casualties were caused.	
TROISVILLE Sht 57. B.	20.10.18		The Battalion in TROISVILLE. The 113 & 114 Inf. Brigades having had a successful attack, this unit was not called upon. The enemy shelled the Billets in a desultory fashion throughout the day, otherwise nothing to report. Major. A.R. Sykes M.C. (2nd in Command) awarded Distinguished Service Order and 20529 Sgt. J. I. Pollock + 48179 Pte W.H. Rigby awarded M.M.	?
TROISVILLES. Sht 57.B	21.10.18		The Battalion in TROISVILLE. Moved off at 1330 hours to relieve a Battalion of 113 Inf Bde. Relief successfully carried out, Bn HdQrs being established at K.15.a.20.90 Sht 57.B, with C.B.A Coys as Left, Centre, Right Coys respectively and 'D' Coy in Support. Patrols were sent out and touch maintained with the enemy whose activity did not interfere with our work.	

D. D. & L. London, E.C. (A8001) Wt. W1771/M2031 750,000 5/17 Sch. 52 Forms C2118/14

Instructions regarding War Diaries and Intelligence Summaries are contained in F. S. Regs., Part II. and the Staff Manual respectively. Title pages will be prepared in manuscript.

WAR DIARY

~~or INTELLIGENCE SUMMARY.~~

(Erase heading not required.)

Army Form C. 2118.

Place	Date	Hour	Summary of Events and Information	Remarks and references to Appendices
K 16.a.20.90. Sht 57.B.NE	22.10.18.		Battalion in the Line Our patrols located many enemy M.Gs during the morning. During the act of establishing a POST at K17.C.0.3 2Lt Kane was killed by a sniper. The Railway Embankment and SELLE VALLEY were heavily bombarded by the enemy, all types and sizes of shells being used. A Bn of the A&SH relieved the Bn during the night after which Billets in TROISVILLE were occupied.	
FOREST Sht 57.B.NE	23.10.18		Battalion in TROISVILLE Moved off at 06.00 hrs for village of FOREST where in Billets were occupied for the day.	
FOREST Sht 57.B.NE	24.10.18		Battalion in FOREST. Day was spent in resting.	
FOREST. Sht 57.B.N.E	25.10.18		Battalion in FOREST. Nothing to record. Day spent in Resting.	
FOREST. Sht 57.B.NE	26.10.18		Battalion in FOREST. The Battalion moved into Brigade Reserve NE of ENGLEFONTAINE.	
F.5.a.1.9. (51a N.E)	27.10.18.		Battalion in Brigade Reserve NE of ENGLEFONTAINE. Very heavy shelling by the enemy - plenty of gas shells being used.	

D. D. & L., London, E.C. (A8001) Wt. W1771/M2031 750,000 5/17 Sch. 52 Forms C2118/14

Instructions regarding War Diaries and Intelligence Summaries are contained in F. S. Regs., Part II. and the Staff Manual respectively. Title pages will be prepared in manuscript.

WAR DIARY
or
INTELLIGENCE SUMMARY.

(Erase heading not required.)

Army Form C. 2118.

Place	Date	Hour	Summary of Events and Information	Remarks and references to Appendices
F.5.a.1.9. (Sheet 51a NE)	28/10/18.		Battalion still in Brigade Reserve. Battn H.Q in cellar at F.5.a.1.9. (51a NE) The enemy shelled very heavily at intervals during the day, using a large amount of gas shells.	
F.5.a.1.9. (Sheet 51a NE)	29/10/18		Battalion still in Brigade Reserve. The Battalion was relieved by the 13th R Bn Welsh Regt and then marched to billets at FOREST, arriving at 2030 hours.	
FOREST (Sheet 57b NE)	30/10/18		Battalion in FOREST. The morning was spent in cleaning up & refitting, the remainder of the day spent resting.	
FOREST (Sheet 57b NE)	31/10/18		Battalion in FOREST. Training, during the morning, was carried out by Coys under Coy Commanders. The afternoon was devoted to Recreational training. The Battalion had baths during the day.	

31/10/18.

C A Bowen
Lieut Colonel
Commanding 10th Bn South Wales Borderers.

(A7092). Wt. W12839/M1293. 75,000. 1/17. D. D. & L., Ltd. Forms/C.2118/14.

38/115

Army Form C. 2118.

WAR DIARY
or
~~INTELLIGENCE SUMMARY~~.

(Erase heading not required.)

Instructions regarding War Diaries and Intelligence Summaries are contained in F. S. Regs., Part II. and the Staff Manual respectively. Title pages will be prepared in manuscript.

VR 35

10th Battn South Wales Borderers

Place	Date	Hour	Summary of Events and Information	Remarks and references to Appendices
FOREST (Sheet 57b. NE)	FRIDAY 1/11/18.		Battalion in billets in FOREST Training was carried out during the morning. The afternoon was devoted to recreational training.	[illegible]
FOREST (Sheet 57b NE)	SATURDAY 2/11/18		Battalion in billets at FOREST. The Coys were at the disposal of Company Commanders, preparing for the Line during the morning. The 115th Infantry Brigade relieved 114th Infantry Brigade in Front Line; 10th Battn. South Wales Borderers relieving 15th Battalion Welsh Regt. Battn. HQ being at F.6.c.1.3. Casualties:- 2/Lieut. H. Slawson Wounded, 6 Other Ranks Wounded.	[illegible]
F.6.c.1.3. (Sheet 51a NE)	3/11/18 SUNDAY		Battalion in Front Line. The enemy was very active with his artillery during the day. Our artillery kept up harassing fire on enemy positions during the day. Casualties 2 OR wounded.	[illegible]
F.6.c.1.3. (Sheet 51a NE)	4/11/18 MONDAY		Battalion in Front Line. The 38th Division attacked MORMAL FOREST east of ENGLEFONTAINE. ORDER OF BATTLE 114th Bde in Reserve 113th Bde in Support 115th Bde in Line. Dispositions of 115th Inf Bde. 2ND R.W.F. on Right 10th S.W.B. on Centre 17th R.W.F on Left	[illegible]

A7092 Wt. W128.9/M1293 750,000. 1/17. D. D & L. Ltd. Forms/C2118/14.

Army Form C. 2118.

Instructions regarding War Diaries and Intelligence Summaries are contained in F. S. Regs., Part II. and the Staff Manual respectively. Title pages will be prepared in manuscript.

WAR DIARY
or
~~INTELLIGENCE SUMMARY.~~

(Erase heading not required.)

Place	Date	Hour	Summary of Events and Information	Remarks and references to Appendices
F.6.c.1.3 (Sheet 51a NE)	MONDAY 4/11/18 Contd.		The 10th Bn SWB attacked in the following order 'A' Coy. on right, with 'C' Coy in Support, 'B' Coy. on left with D. Coy in Support. The attack was assisted by two tanks and an artillery & Trench Mortar barrage. The final objective of the Battalion which lay 800 yards inside the FOREST was reached at 7.15 am (one hour after ZERO) in conjunction with the 2nd & 17th RWF. The opposition offered by elements of the 16th & 58th German Infantry Divisions was very weak and easily overcome. One hour after reaching the objective the 113th Inf Brigade passed through the 115th Infantry Brigade and continued the advance. After spending the rest of the day consolidating the Battalion moved into billets at ENGLEFONTAINE for the night. The total Battalion Casualties numbered 42. Included in this number the Battalion had the misfortune to lose Captain W.G. Williams wounded, 2/Lieut H.T. Jones Killed, and Lieut L.S Cassell, MORC, USA medical officer attached, Killed.	
ENGLEFONTAINE (Sheet 51a NE)	TUESDAY 5/11/18		The Battalion were still in billets in ENGLEFONTAINE The day was spent in cleaning, refitting and resting. Draft of 11 O.R, all casuals joined the Battn.	[illegible]
ENGLEFONTAINE (Sheet 51a NE)	WEDNESDAY 6/11/18		The Battalion still in billets in ENGLEFONTAINE. The Battalion moved into bivouacs near LOCQUIGNOL. The accomodation was poor & the men got very little rest owing to very heavy rain.	[illegible]

A7092 Wt. W12S 9/M1293 750,000. 1/17. D. D & L. Ltd. Forms/C2118/14.

Army Form C. 2118.

Instructions regarding War Diaries and Intelligence Summaries are contained in F. S. Regs., Part II. and the Staff Manual respectively. Title pages will be prepared in manuscript.

WAR DIARY
or
~~INTELLIGENCE~~ SUMMARY.

(Erase heading not required.)

Place	Date	Hour	Summary of Events and Information	Remarks and references to Appendices
LOGQUIGNOL	THURSDAY 7/11/18.		The Battalion were in bivouacs and moved in the morning to billets in S'ARBARAS and then again to very good billets at AULNOYE. The 38th Division take over the front ~~from~~ 33rd Division. The 115th Infantry Brigade being in reserve.	[illegible]
AULNOYE	FRIDAY 8/11/18.		The Battalion were in billets in AULNOYE. One hours notice was given the Battn to take up position between AULNOYE and POT DE VIN. The Battn moved off at 5.30 am and arrived in position by 07.00 hours. Battn returned to billets in AULNOYE at 12.30 hours Remainder of the day was spent in resting.	[illegible]
AULNOYE	SATURDAY 9/11/18.		The Battalion were in billets in AULNOYE. The day was spent in cleaning, refitting etc. Battn paraded for Church Parade at 14.30 hours.	[illegible]
AULNOYE	SUNDAY 10/11/18.		Battalion in billets in AULNOYE. The Battalion paraded at 09.15 hours for Brigade Route March to POT de VIN, Dress full marching order. On return to billets men rested; Battalion paraded for Church Parade at 14.30 hours. Dress Belt & Side arms.	[illegible]
AULNOYE	MONDAY 11/11/18.		Battalion in billets at AULNOYE Training was carried out by Coys as follows:- 09.00 - 10.00 hours Physical Training Steady drill & L.G. Instruction. The C.O. inspected the smoke kits of the Battalion at 11.15 hours. The afternoon was spent Cleaning & Refitting, etc. The enemy signed an Armistice Lasting for 36 days which was effective from 11.00 hours. The Band of the 33rd Battn M.G.C. marched through the streets of the village playing all kinds of national anthems. In the evening they	[illegible]

A7092 Wt. W128.9/M1293 750,000. 1/17. D. D & L. Ltd. Forms/C2118/14.

Army Form C. 2118.

Instructions regarding War Diaries and Intelligence Summaries are contained in F. S. Regs., Part II. and the Staff Manual respectively. Title pages will be prepared in manuscript.

WAR DIARY
or
~~INTELLIGENCE SUMMARY~~.

(Erase heading not required.)

Place	Date	Hour	Summary of Events and Information	Remarks and references to Appendices
AULNOYE	MONDAY 11/11/18.		again paraded & marched, through the village with an escort of men with lighted torches, to the square where a large beacon was lit in honour of this occasion. The morale of the troops was of the very best.	[illegible]
AULNOYE	TUESDAY 12/11/18.		Battalion resting in billets in AULNOYE. The Companies were at the disposal of Coy Commanders for General cleaning up during the morning. The Battalion had baths during the day. 1 Officer & 200 OR were on working party salving coal from wood dumps at AULNOYE Station, from 14 00 hours to 16.30 hours.	[illegible]
AULNOYE	WEDNESDAY 13/11/18.		Battalion in billets in AULNOYE. The Coys were at the disposal of Coy Commanders. Armourer Sergt inspected the rifles of the Battalion during the morning. 1 Officer & 200 OR were on working party salving coal from coal dumps at AULNOYE Station, from 14 00 - 16.30 hours.	[illegible]
AULNOYE	THURSDAY 14/11/18.		Battalion still in AULNOYE. The C.O. inspected the Battalion during the morning. dress:- full marching order with Lewis Guns. The Armourer Sergt. repaired rifles of Battn during morning. A Rugby match was played against 17th R.W.F. and naturally the Battn. team won. Lieut. Mr W.H. Lancaster joined the Battn.	[illegible]

Instructions regarding War Diaries and Intelligence Summaries are contained in F. S. Regs., Part II. and the Staff Manual respectively. Title pages will be prepared in manuscript.

WAR DIARY
or
~~INTELLIGENCE SUMMARY.~~

(Erase heading not required.)

Army Form C. 2118.

Place	Date	Hour	Summary of Events and Information	Remarks and references to Appendices
AULNOYE	FRIDAY 15/11/18		Battalion in billets in AULNOYE. The Battn. paraded for a Bde Route march at 09.00 hours. Route:- LA TOQUE – POT DE VIN Cross roads (D.9.a) – road junction V.24.a) – BACHANT cross roads (U.18.d) – AULNOYE Station. The afternoon was spent in recreation, football etc.	[illegible]
AULNOYE	SATURDAY 16/11/18.		Battalion in billets in AULNOYE. The Battn paraded for Physical Training from 09.00 – 10.00 hours. The C.O. inspected billets, kits, etc. during the remainder of the morning. In the afternoon the Battalion played a rugby football match against 2nd Bn R.W.F. and the Battn team again won.	[illegible]
AULNOYE	SUNDAY 17/11/18.		Battalion in billets in AULNOYE. A Thanksgiving Service was held which was attended by the G.O.C. Division at 11.00 hours. After the Service the Battn. marched past the G.O.C. Captain J.R. England awarded M.C. for action at VILLERS OUTREAUX. 21315 Pte R. Evans awarded the D.C.M. also.	[illegible]
AULNOYE	MONDAY 18/11/18.		Battalion in billets in AULNOYE. Training was carried out by Coys from 09.00 – 12.00 hours. Afternoon was spent in recreation, football etc. 44464 Cpl. Parker and 44287 L/Cpl Apps S.G. awarded Military Medal for action on MORMAL FOREST, 4/11/18.	[illegible]

Army Form C. 2118.

Instructions regarding War Diaries and Intelligence Summaries are contained in F. S. Regs., Part II. and the Staff Manual respectively. Title pages will be prepared in manuscript.

WAR DIARY
or
~~INTELLIGENCE SUMMARY~~.
(Erase heading not required.)

Place	Date	Hour	Summary of Events and Information	Remarks and references to Appendices
AULNOYE	TUESDAY 19/11/18.		Battalion in billets in AULNOYE The Brigade route marched during the morning; football etc during afternoon. Draft of 17 OR. and 2/Lieut S. Hicks joined unit.	[illegible initials]
AULNOYE	WEDNESDAY 20/11/18		Battalion in billets in AULNOYE. Training was carried out during the morning from 09.00-12.15 hours. NCO's paraded under R.S.M. for instruction in Guard & Sentry duties. [illegible] Cpl. Dover G.G. awarded Bar to Military Medal for action on MORMAL FOREST 4/11/18.	[illegible initials]
AULNOYE	THURSDAY 21/11/18.		Battalion in billets in AULNOYE. The Brigade Route marched during the morning; football, etc. played during the afternoon.	[illegible initials]
AULNOYE	FRIDAY 22/11/18.		Battalion in billets in AULNOYE. Training was carried out; R.S.M. instructed Coys in Arms Drill during the morning. The Battn were to play a Rugby match against 17th R.W.F. but owing the latter failing to get a team, the fixture was cancelled.	[illegible initials]
AULNOYE	SATURDAY 23/11/18.		Battalion in billets in AULNOYE The G.O.C. Division presented medal ribbons to the Brigade. The Battalion paraded outside billets, and marched to Brigade parade ground where the presentation took place. Weather very good but a little cold. Afternoon spent in recreation.	[illegible initials]

A7092 Wt. W128.9/M1293 750,000. 1/17. D. D & L. Ltd. Forms/C2118/14.

Instructions regarding War Diaries and Intelligence Summaries are contained in F. S. Regs., Part II. and the Staff Manual respectively. Title pages will be prepared in manuscript.

WAR DIARY
or
INTELLIGENCE SUMMARY.
(Erase heading not required.)

Army Form C. 2118.

Place	Date	Hour	Summary of Events and Information	Remarks and references to Appendices
AULNOYE	24/11/18 SUNDAY		Battalion in billets at AULNOYE. Battalion attended Church parade at 11-00 hours A Thanksgiving service for Non-Conformists was held, which was attended by the G.O.C. Division at 09-45 hours	[illegible]
AULNOYE	25/11/18 MONDAY		Battalion in billets in AULNOYE. Training was carried out from 09-00 hours to 12-15 hours An inspection of billets was carried out commencing at 10-00 hours Classes in "Practice & theory of Banking", "Gardening", "English", "Arithmetic" and "Music" commenced A Rugby football match was played with the 2nd R.W.F. which resulted in a win for the Battalion	[illegible]
AULNOYE	TUESDAY 26/11/18		Battalion in billets in AULNOYE The Brigade Route-marched during the morning. The Brigade Recreation Room was opened from 18-00 hours.	[illegible]
AULNOYE	WEDNESDAY 27/11/18		Battalion in billets in AULNOYE The Battalion carried out training from 09-00 to 12-45 hours An association Football Match was played between 2nd R.W.F. and the Battalion, which resulted in a win for the Battalion. Score 10/[illegible]. 11 goals 2nd R.W.F. - Nil. There was also a cross country run. Sgt Parry first	[illegible]
AULNOYE	THURSDAY 28/11/18		Battalion in billets in AULNOYE. Training in the morning was carried out from 09.00 to 12.45 hours. In the afternoon the battalion cross-country running team won a Brigade competition by 80 clear points, Pte Henderson running first in the Brigade Weather very wet.	[illegible]

Army Form C. 2118.

WAR DIARY

or

~~INTELLIGENCE SUMMARY.~~

(Erase heading not required.)

Instructions regarding War Diaries and Intelligence Summaries are contained in F. S. Regs., Part II. and the Staff Manual respectively. Title pages will be prepared in manuscript.

Place	Date	Hour	Summary of Events and Information	Remarks and references to Appendices
AULNOYE	FRIDAY. 29-11-18		Battalion in billets at Aulnoye. Morning was spent in training from 09.00 – 12.15 hours. Owing to heavy rain several billets had to be changed. The afternoon was as usual spent in recreation as far as weather conditions permitted.	[initials]
AULNOYE	SATURDAY 30-11-18.		Battalion in billets at Aulnoye. Lt. Col. A. L. Bowen inspected small kit of the battalion at 11.00 hours in billets. The afternoon was spent in recreation Battalion "Association" team played Brigade H. Qrs., and won	[initials]

30/11/18.

C. A. Bowen [signature]

Lieut. Colonel.

Commanding 10th Bn. South Wales Borderers

A7092 Wt. W128.9/M1293. 750,000. 1/17. D. D & I. Ltd. Forms/C2118/14.

Instructions regarding War Diaries and Intelligence Summaries are contained in F. S. Regs., Part II. and the Staff Manual respectively. Title pages will be prepared in manuscript.

10TH BN SOUTH WALES BORDERERS.

WAR DIARY or ~~INTELLIGENCE~~ SUMMARY.

(Erase heading not required.)

Army Form C. 2118.

DECEMBER 1918

VIII 36

Place	Date	Hour	Summary of Events and Information — Map Ref. Sheet.	Remarks and references to Appendices
AULNOYE.	1-12-18.		Battalion in billets at Aulnoye. Lieut-Colonel C. O. HARVEY DSO. assumed command of the battalion from this date. Major A. BOWEN, 2nd in command. The morning was spent in Physical training and Drill. Lewis Gun classes paraded under L.G.O. Signallers under Signal sargeant. In addition educational classes were attended. The afternoon was spent in recreation.	[illegible]
AULNOYE	2-12-18.		Battalion in billets at Aulnoye The battalion paraded at 0945 hrs. and marched to near PETIT-MAUBERGE where His Majesty The King was expected. As His Majesties car appeared the whole Brigade cheered so heartily that the King stopped his car and spoke to the brigade staff and officers Commanding Units. He then proceeded on foot past the whole brigade lined along the road. Everyone was delighted ~~to~~ see His Majesty looking so well. The battalion as usual spent the afternoon on the recreation field where "Soccer" football seemed to predominate. First meeting of sargeants' mess held.	[illegible]
AULNOYE	3-12-18.		Battalion at Aulnoye. The morning was spent in the usual training, and when ~~[illegible]~~ rain interfered, lectures were held. Educational Classes were also attended by a big number of officers and men	[illegible]

A7092 Wt. W125 9/M1293 750,000. 1/17. D. D & L. Ltd. Forms/C2118/14.

Army Form C. 2118.

WAR DIARY
or
~~INTELLIGENCE SUMMARY~~.
(Erase heading not required.)

Instructions regarding War Diaries and Intelligence Summaries are contained in F. S. Regs., Part II. and the Staff Manual respectively. Title pages will be prepared in manuscript.

Place	Date	Hour	Summary of Events and Information	Remarks and references to Appendices
AULNOYE	4.12.18		Battalion in billets at AULNOYE. A Brigade route march had to be postponed owing to wet weather, and lectures in billets took place under Company Commanders orders. Sport, in the afternoon, had also to be put off.	WMS
AULNOYE	5.12.18		Battalion in AULNOYE. In the morning a Brigade route march took place. The Battn passed the starting point at 09.45 hours and arrived back to billets at 13.30 hours. when a feet inspection took place. A small draft of miners left for England. The afternoon was spent in sport Lieut. S. L. Hordle, 2/Lieut W. L. Wakefield, and 20. OR rejoined Battn.	WMS
AULNOYE	6.12.18		Battalion in AULNOYE. In the morning the Battalion carried out a programme of training consisting of Physical Training and drill. Classes were held under the L.G.O and Signal Sergeant. In the afternoon a football programme was arranged between Coys. A. Coy v. C. Coy B. Coy. v. D. Coy.	WMS

A7092 Wt. W128 9/M1293 750,000. 1/17. D. D & L. Ltd. Forms/C2118/14.

Instructions regarding War Diaries and Intelligence Summaries are contained in F. S. Regs., Part II. and the Staff Manual respectively. Title pages will be prepared in manuscript.

WAR DIARY
or
~~INTELLIGENCE SUMMARY.~~

(*Erase heading not required.*)

Army Form C. 2118.

Place	Date	Hour	Summary of Events and Information	Remarks and references to Appendices
AULNOYE	7.	12.18.	Battalion in billets in AULNOYE. The Battalion paraded for Commanding Officer's Inspection on Football Field, V.29.b.3.3 at 09.30 hours. Dress:- Full marching order. After the Inspection battalion drill was carried out. 11.00–12.30 hours:- Kit and billet inspections by Coy. Officers, and fitting of equipment. Recreational training was carried out during the afternoon. Boxing contests were held in Boxing Hall, at 14.00 hours.	
AULNOYE	8.	12.18.	Battalion in billets in AULNOYE. The Battalion paraded for Divine Service at 11.00 hours. The C.O. inspected the Lewis Guns of the Battalion at 09.45 hours also the billets of the Battalion at 12.00 hours.	
AULNOYE	9.	12.18.	Battalion in billets in AULNOYE. During the morning training was carried out, consisting of Physical Training, musketry and Company Drill. Lewis Gun classes continued under L.G.O. The C.O. inspected the Signalling Equipment. Recreational training was carried out during the afternoon; educational classes were held during the day. No 20408 C.S.M. J. WILLIAMS. D.C.M., M.M. awarded the VICTORIA CROSS for action at VILLERS OUTREAUX, 8.10.18.	

A7092 Wt. W128 9/M1293 750,000 1/17. D. D & I. Ltd. Forms/C2118/14.

Instructions regarding War Diaries and Intelligence Summaries are contained in F. S. Regs., Part II. and the Staff Manual respectively. Title pages will be prepared in manuscript.

WAR DIARY
or
~~INTELLIGENCE SUMMARY.~~
(Erase heading not required.)

Army Form C. 2118.

Place	Date	Hour	Summary of Events and Information	Remarks and references to Appendices
AULNOYE	10	12.18.	Battalion in billets at AULNOYE The Battalion paraded for route march at 09.00 hours on Battalion alarm Post. An officers class, under Major A.R. SYKES, DSO, MC. was held during the morning. Educational Classes were carried out during the afternoon. Lieut B. J. Howarth proceeded to M.T. School, WISSANT.	WMG
AULNOYE	11.	12.18	Battalion in billets in AULNOYE. Training was carried out during the morning, 50% of NCO's were under Major A.R. Sykes D.S.O, MC. for instruction from 09.00 – 10.45 hours. The C.O. inspected the Transport of the Battalion on Football Field, U.29.d.3.3 at 10.30 hours. The replay of Div. Rugby Football Championship was played, resulting in a draw. The Battn. Reading room opened for men of the Battalion. Educational classes were carried out during the evening.	WMG
AULNOYE	12.	12.18.	Battalion in billets in AULNOYE. Training was carried out during the morning consisting of drill and Physical Training. 50% of NCO's were under Major Sykes for instruction from 09.00 – 10.45 hours, the remainder from 11.00 – 12.30 hours. Recreational training was carried out during afternoon. Billet Wardens and 2 pioneers proceeded to new area. Educational Classes were held during afternoon. Major A.R. Bowen awarded D.S.O, Captain E.P. Enright awarded M.C. also Lieut A.J. Canton, No. 22297 Sergt. W. Leclare and 33306 Pte James awarded D.C.M.	WMG

A7092 Wt. W128_9/M1293 750,000. 1/17. D. D & L. Ltd. Forms/C2118/14.

Instructions regarding War Diaries and Intelligence Summaries are contained in F. S. Regs., Part II. and the Staff Manual respectively. Title pages will be prepared in manuscript.

WAR DIARY

or

~~INTELLIGENCE SUMMARY.~~

(Erase heading not required.)

Army Form C. 2118.

Place	Date	Hour	Summary of Events and Information	Remarks and references to Appendices
AULNOYE	13.12.18		Battalion in billets in AULNOYE. The Battalion paraded for route march at 09.00 hours. Dress:- Full Marching Order, less Jerkins & Steel helmets. Available transport also paraded. After the march an inspection of feet was held. Educational Classes were held during the afternoon. Div. Rugby Football Championship was replayed again and resulted in a win for the RAMC. RAMC - 3 pts, 14th Bn ~~Welsh~~ Welsh Regt NIL.	
AULNOYE	14.12.18.		Battalion in billets in AULNOYE. The Battalion paraded at 09.15 hours for Inspection by the Commanding Officer, Dress:- Musketry order. 10.00 - 10.45 hours - Battalion Drill. 11.00 - 12.00 hours. - Inspection of billets by Commanding Officers. Educational classes were carried out as usual.	
AULNOYE	15.12.18.		Battalion in billets in AULNOYE. The Battalion paraded for Divine Service at 10.45 hours.	
AULNOYE	16.12.18		Battalion in billets in AULNOYE. Training was carried out consisting of Coy. Drill, Bayonet Fighting &c. 2 Officers & 50% NCOs paraded under Major A. L. Bowen D.S.O. for Platoon Coy. and communication Drill from 09.00 - 10.30 hours; the remaining Officers and NCOs parade as above from 11.00 - 12.30 hours. The R.S.M. lectured all NCOs on Battalion Drill & ceremonial Drill. Educational classes were carried out during the day.	

Army Form C. 2118.

Instructions regarding War Diaries and Intelligence Summaries are contained in F. S. Regs., Part II. and the Staff Manual respectively. Title pages will be prepared in manuscript.

WAR DIARY
or
~~INTELLIGENCE SUMMARY.~~

(*Erase heading not required.*)

Place	Date	Hour	Summary of Events and Information	Remarks and references to Appendices
AULNOYE	17.12.18.		Battalion in billets in AULNOYE. Training consisting of P.T., Coy. Drill, musketry, was carried out during the morning. L.G. and signal classes were carried out under L.G.O and Signal Instructor respectively. Officers and NCO's were under Major A.L. Bowen for Battn drill and communication drill. A Battalion whist Drive was held which resulted in an enjoyable evening for all who participated.	
AULNOYE	18.12.18.		Battalion in billets in AULNOYE. Training consisting of P.T., Coy. Drill were carried out during the morning. 10 men per Coy. paraded for Lewis Gun Instruction under LGO. Battn and Coy. signallers paraded under Corpl. Williams. The RSM. lectured all Officers and NCO's on Battalion Drill. Educational Classes were held during the day. Draft of 11 OR arrived and posted to 'C' Coy	
AULNOYE	19.12.18.		Battalion in billets in AULNOYE. Training was carried out consisting of P.T., Coy. Drill, and boxing under Capt. Cobb. Recreational training was carried out during the afternoon. Educational Classes were held during the day. Inter-Coy. league matches (association football) were played during the afternoon.	

A7092 Wt. W125 9/M1293. 750,000. 1/17. D. D & I. Ltd. Forms/C2118/14.

Army Form C. 2118.

Instructions regarding War Diaries and Intelligence Summaries are contained in F. S. Regs., Part II. and the Staff Manual respectively. Title pages will be prepared in manuscript.

WAR DIARY
or
~~INTELLIGENCE SUMMARY.~~

(Erase heading not required.)

Place	Date	Hour	Summary of Events and Information	Remarks and references to Appendices
AULNOYE	20.12.18.		Battalion in billets in AULNOYE. The Battalion were to have route marched during the morning but owing to heavy rain, the march was cancelled until 13.55 hours. Lewis gun and Signal Classes were carried out in the vicinity of billets. The C.O. held a kit inspection in billets commencing at 11.30 hours. A feet inspection was held after the route march.	WMD
AULNOYE	21.12.18.		Battalion in billets in AULNOYE. Companies were at the disposal of Coy Commanders during the morning. Lewis Gun classes were carried on under Lieut Clayton D.B. The G.O.C. inspected the Transport at 11.45 hours. Half of the Battalion had baths during the day. Educational classes were carried out as usual during the day.	WMD
AULNOYE	22.12.18		Battalion in billets in AULNOYE. The Battn paraded for Divine Service at 10.45 hours. The C.O. inspected the equipment of the employed men at 10.00 hours. The remainder of the Battn bathed from 08.00 hours to 10.00 hours.	WMD
AULNOYE	23.12.18		Battalion in billets in AULNOYE. The Battn paraded for Brigade Route March in following order:— Drums, B. C. D. A. Headquarter details paraded with their Coys. Dress: full marching order. The Bn passed starting point at 09.15 hours. On return to billets a feet inspection was held. The afternoon was devoted to recreational training, comprising of boxing, tug of war, & football.	WMD

A7092 Wt. W128 9/M1293 750,000. 1/17. D. D & L. Ltd. Forms/C2118/14.

Army Form C. 2118.

Instructions regarding War Diaries and Intelligence Summaries are contained in F. S. Regs., Part II. and the Staff Manual respectively. Title pages will be prepared in manuscript.

WAR DIARY

or

~~INTELLIGENCE SUMMARY~~.

(Erase heading not required.)

Place	Date	Hour	Summary of Events and Information	Remarks and references to Appendices
AULNOYE	23.12.18 Continued.		Major A.R. Sykes inspected the Battalion transport at 09.00 hours, in full marching order. Educational classes were carried out from 17.00 – 18.00 hours. Draft of 52 O.R. joined Battalion.	[initials]
AULNOYE	24.12.18.		Battalion in billets in AULNOYE. Companies were at the disposal of Coy Commanders, during the morning. Recreational training was carried out during afternoon. The Bde Tug of War competitions were cancelled owing to the bad state of the ground. A whist drive was held in Bn Recreational Hut at 17.30 hours	[initials]
AULNOYE	25.12.18.		Battalion in billets in AULNOYE. The Battn paraded for Divine Service at 09.30 hours, dress - belt & sidearms. The Battn had Xmas Dinner in the Battn Recreation Hut, and everyone thoroughly enjoyed same. The G.O.C. was present and wished all ranks a merry Xmas; all ranks gave three hearty cheers. The Commanding Officer gave a speech and drank the health of all, wishing them a merry Xmas & a Bright & prosperous New Year. All ranks again gave three hearty cheers. Three cheers were given for Coy Sergt. Major J. Williams V.C., everybody regretting that he was not present. All ranks spent the remainder of the Day as they pleased.	[initials]
AULNOYE	26.12.18		Battalion in billets in AULNOYE. Only recreational training was carried out, comprising of Boxing cross country running and Football. The Officers played the NCOs football and succeeded in winning to the tune of 5 goals to one.	[initials]

A7092 Wt. W128 9/M1293 750,000. 1/17. D. D & L. Ltd. Forms/C2118/14.

Instructions regarding War Diaries and Intelligence Summaries are contained in F. S. Regs., Part II. and the Staff Manual respectively. Title pages will be prepared in manuscript.

WAR DIARY
or
~~INTELLIGENCE SUMMARY.~~
(Erase heading not required.)

Army Form C. 2118.

Place	Date	Hour	Summary of Events and Information	Remarks and references to Appendices
AULNOYE	26. 12. 18 Continued		The Tug of War competitions took place during the afternoon, our team losing to 17th R.W.F. quite easily, owing to the team being on an average 1 stone per man lighter. The 2nd RWF pulled Bde HQ and won. The Divisional Eisteddfod proved an enjoyable evening for all who attended.	hmd
AULNOYE	27. 12. 18		Battalion in billets in AULNOYE. The Battn paraded for Bde Route March at 09.23 hours in the order - Band, 'C', 'D', Drums, A.B. Dress - Full marching order. Route:- Concrete Bridge - POT DE VIN - road junction - PETIT MAUBEUGE. Recreational training was carried out during the afternoon.	hmd
AULNOYE	28. 12. 18.		Battalion in billets in AULNOYE. Training consisting of physical training, arms drill was carried out from 09.15 hours to 11.00 hours. The remainder of the day was devoted to cleaning up Battalion area prior to moving.	hmd
AULNOYE	29. 12. 18		Battalion in AULNOYE. The 38th Division commenced to move to QUERRIEU AREA. The Battalion paraded on Battn Alarm post at 09.12 hours in full marching order for march to ENGLEFONTAINE. Order of march:- Band, D, A, Drums, B, C. The Battn passed the starting point at 09.22 hours and were all in billets by 13.15 hours at ENGLEFONTAINE.	hmd

A7092 Wt. W128 9/M1293. 750,000. 1/17. D. D & I. Ltd. Forms/C2118/14.

Army Form C. 2118.

Instructions regarding War Diaries and Intelligence Summaries are contained in F. S. Regs., Part II. and the Staff Manual respectively. Title pages will be prepared in manuscript.

WAR DIARY
or
~~INTELLIGENCE~~ SUMMARY.

(Erase heading not required.)

Place	Date	Hour	Summary of Events and Information	Remarks and references to Appendices
ENGLEFONTAINE	30/12/18.		Battalion in billets in ENGLEFONTAINE. The Battalion paraded at 08.55 hours on ENGLEFONTAINE – HECQ road for march to INCHY in following order:- Drums, HQ. A. B, Band, C, D. Coys. Battalion passed starting point, Xroads S end of ENGLEFONTAINE, at 09.10 hours and arrived in billets at INCHY by 13.30 hours. The remainder of the day was spent resting.	[illegible]
INCHY.	31/12/18.		Battalion in billets in INCHY. The Battalion paraded at 07.30 hours in full marching plus one blanket for journey to GLISY. The Battn embussed at 08.00 hours, and arrived at GLISY at 16.00 hours.	[illegible]

31/12/18.

W Hawes Lieut Colonel
Comdg 10th Bn S. W. B.

A7092 Wt. W128.9/M1293. 750,000. 1/17. D. D & I. Ltd. Forms/C2118/14.

38

Instructions regarding War Diaries and Intelligence Summaries are contained in F. S. Regs., Part II. and the Staff Manual respectively. Title pages will be prepared in manuscript.

WAR DIARY
or
~~INTELLIGENCE SUMMARY.~~

(Erase heading not required.)

10 SWB

January 1919

37

Army Form C. 2118.

Place	Date	Hour	Summary of Events and Information 10th Battalion South Wales Borderers	Remarks and references to Appendices
GLISY.	1/1/19.		The Battalion billeted in Camp, 400x S. of GLISY. (Ref. 1/100,000 AMIENS) The Battalion spent the Day cleaning up equipment and improving the Camp.	
GLISY.	2/1/19.		The Battalion in Camp near GLISY. Physical Training was carried out by all Coys from 09.15 - 10.15 hours. The Battalion formed up for Bn Drill at 11.15 hours. Dress:- Drill Order. The remainder of the Day was spent improving the Camp.	
GLISY	3/1/19.		The Battalion in Camp near GLISY. Training consisting of physical training & Company Drill was carried out from 09.30 - 10.30 hours. Blankets of the Bn were inspected under Coy. arrangements at 12.00 hours. The afternoon was devoted to improvement of billets.	
GLISY.	4/1/19.		The Battalion in Camp near GLISY. Training was carried out during the morning consisting of Coy. Drill, Guard and Sentry Drill, 2 officers per Company and all NCOs were under the RSM for instruction in Guard & Sentry duties from 11.00 - 12.30. Lewis Gunners were at the disposal of L.G.O. for cleaning of guns from 09.30 - 12.00 hours. The Commanding Officer inspected the Draft of 10 O.R., which joined Bn. night of 3/1/19., at 10.30 hours. Recreational Training was carried out from 14.00 - 16.00 hours.	

D. D. & L., London, E.C.
(A8001) Wt. W1771/M2031 750,000 5/17 Sch. 52 Forms C2118/14

Army Form C. 2118.

WAR DIARY
or
~~INTELLIGENCE SUMMARY.~~
(*Erase heading not required.*)

Instructions regarding War Diaries and Intelligence Summaries are contained in F. S. Regs., Part II. and the Staff Manual respectively. Title pages will be prepared in manuscript.

January 1919.

Place	Date	Hour	Summary of Events and Information	Remarks and references to Appendices
GLISY	5/1/19.		The Battalion in Camp near GLISY. The Battalion paraded for Divine Service at 10.10 hours in the order: Band, A B C D Coys. Dress – Belt and sidearms. R.C's paraded at 10.45 hours for Mass in Church GLISY at 11.00 hours. Nonconformists paraded at 09.15 hours for Service in Schoolroom GLISY at 09.30 hours. 11 OR. were despatched to Corps Concentration Camp for Demobilization.	
GLISY	6/1/19.		The Battalion in Camp near GLISY. The Battalion paraded for Battalion Drill on Battalion parade ground at 08.45 hours. Physical Training was carried out from 10.00 – 10.30 hours. From 11.00 – 11.45 hours, Companies carried out Company Drill. The remainder of the morning was devoted to cleaning up of Company Lines and equipment. Recreational training was carried out from 14.00 to 16.00 hours.	
GLISY	7/1/19.		The Battalion in Camp near GLISY. Training consisting of Battalion Drill, was carried out from 08.45 – 09.30 hours. All Lewis Gunners paraded under L.G.O. for instruction from 10.00 – 12.00. Signallers paraded under Sergeant Whill for instruction. All Officers less H.Q. paraded for Ceremonial Drill under the R.S.M. at 10.00 hrs. The remainder of the Battn. from 10.00 – 12.00 were employed under 2/Lieut. C.E. Parkhouse for work on improving cookhouses, and banking up earth round huts of the Officers' Mess. All mounted Officers paraded under Major J.H.J. Montcith, mounted at 11.15 hours. Recreational training was carried out from 14.00 – 16.00 hours.	

D. D. & L., London, E.C. (A8001) Wt. W1771/M2031 750,000 5/17 Sch. 52 Forms C2118/14

Instructions regarding War Diaries and Intelligence Summaries are contained in F. S. Regs., Part II. and the Staff Manual respectively. Title pages will be prepared in manuscript.

WAR DIARY
or
~~INTELLIGENCE SUMMARY.~~
(Erase heading not required.)

Army Form C. 2118.

Place	Date	Hour	Summary of Events and Information	Remarks and references to Appendices
GLISY	8/1/19		Battalion in Camp near GLISY The Battalion paraded at 09.05 hours on the Battalion parade ground for Brigade Route March, in close column of Companies. Dress:- Full Marching Order.	
GLISY	9/1/19		Battalion in Camp near GLISY. The Battalion parade for Commanding Officers Inspection at 09.30 hours. Dress:- Full Marching Order. Recreational Training was carried out during the afternoon.	
GLISY	10/1/19.		Battalion in Camp near GLISY. The Battalion paraded for Inspection by the G.O.C. 115 Bde at 09.20 hours on the Battalion Parade Ground. Dress - Full marching Order.	
GLISY	11/1/19.		Battalion in Camp near GLISY. The Battalion were under training, consisting of Company Drill, from 09.30-10.00 hours. From 10.45 hours they were employed on a general fatigue. H.Q. C. & D. Coys bathed from 12.30-17.00 hours. Voluntary educational classes were held, subjects, book keeping & Shorthand from 17.30 to 18.30 hours. 6 OR. proceeded to Corps Concentration Camps for demobilization.	

A7092 Wt. W128 9/M1293 750,000. 1/17. D. D & L. Ltd. Forms/C2118/14.

Army Form C. 2118.

WAR DIARY
or
~~INTELLIGENCE SUMMARY.~~
(Erase heading not required.)

Instructions regarding War Diaries and Intelligence Summaries are contained in F. S. Regs., Part II. and the Staff Manual respectively. Title pages will be prepared in manuscript.

Place	Date	Hour	Summary of Events and Information	Remarks and references to Appendices
GLISY.	12/1/19.		Battalion in Camp near GLISY. 'A' Coy 'B' Coy and H.Q. paraded at 09.50 hours for divine Service; 'C' Coy D Coy paraded at 10.20 hours. The Services were held in B Coy dining Hut. The Band attended both Services. All Nonconformists paraded at 09.15 hours, for Divine Service at 09.30 hours. All R.C's paraded at 10.45 hours for Mass at 11-00 hours in Church, GLISY. Dress for all denominations:- Belt + Sidearms. Voluntary Services were held in the evening. 8 O.R. proceeded to Corps Concentration Camp for Demobilization.	
GLISY.	13/1/19.		Battalion in Camp near GLISY. The Battalion paraded in Mass on Battalion parade ground for Route March, at 09.15 hours. Dress:- Fighting Order. 9 O.R. proceeded to Corps Concentration Camp for Demobilization.	
GLISY	14/1/19.		Battalion in Camp near GLISY. Educational Classes for the Battn were held during the morning. Physical Training was carried out by Coys when not at above Classes. Recreational Training was carried out from 14.00 – 15.30 hours. 8 O.R. proceeded to Corps Concentration Camp for Demobilization.	
GLISY.	15/1/19.		Battalion in Camp near GLISY. Battalion paraded in mass on Battn parade ground, Dress:- Musketry Order. The Cross Country team went for a run during the morning. Recreational Training was carried out during afternoon.	

Instructions regarding War Diaries and Intelligence Summaries are contained in F. S. Regs., Part II. and the Staff Manual respectively. Title pages will be prepared in manuscript.

WAR DIARY
or
INTELLIGENCE SUMMARY.
(Erase heading not required.)

Army Form C. 2118.

Place	Date	Hour	Summary of Events and Information	Remarks and references to Appendices
GLISY.	16/1/19.		Battalion in Camp near GLISY. Companies carried out Physical Training as follows:- A & D Coys from 09.00 – 10.00 hours, B & C Coys from 10.00 – 11.00 hours. Educational Classes were held from 09.00 – 11.00, in general [illegible] subjects. Recreational Training was carried out from 14.00 – 16.00 hours. The following officers & O.R. attended the presentation and consecration of the Kings Colours which was ~~[illegible]~~ presented to the Battalion. Lieut Colonel C.D. Harvey D.S.O., Captain W.M. Evans D.S.O., Major A.R. Sykes [illegible], Major W.H. Monteith, Captain A.W. Preston, Captain C.E. Morgan, Captain E.P. Enright, Lieut M.A. Langmaster M.C. The Colour party being Lieut D.R. Clayton, C.Sgt. Brice, C.Sgt. Power & L/Cpl. Ridley.	
GLISY.	17/1/19.		Battalion in Camp near GLISY. The Battalion paraded on the Parade Ground in Review Order at 09.30 hours to receive the Colours. The Colour Party consisted of Lieut J.R. Graves, C.Sgt. Click, C.Sgt. Power, L/Cpl. Ridley. The remainder of the morning was spent in Educational Classes & Physical Training. Recreational Training was carried out during the afternoon.	

A7092 Wt. W128/9/M1293. 750,000. 1/17. D. D & L. Ltd. Forms/C2118/14.

Instructions regarding War Diaries and Intelligence Summaries are contained in F. S. Regs., Part II. and the Staff Manual respectively. Title pages will be prepared in manuscript.

WAR DIARY
or
~~INTELLIGENCE SUMMARY.~~
(Erase heading not required.)

Army Form C. 2118.

Place	Date	Hour	Summary of Events and Information	Remarks and references to Appendices
GLISY.	18/1/19.		The Battalion in Camp near GLISY. The Commanding Officer inspected the kits of the men of the Battalion in their huts commencing at 11.00 hours. Recreational Training was carried out during the afternoon.	
GLISY.	19/1/19.		The Battalion in Camp near GLISY. Parade Services were held at 10.45 hours & 11.20 hours. C & D Coys. paraded on Bn. Parade Ground for the first Service, A & B Coy and H.Q. for the 2nd Service. Services were also held for Nonconformists & Roman Catholics. Cross country runners went for a practice run during the morning. 2/Lieut A. Anderson rejoined Bn & was posted D Coy.	
GLISY.	20/1/19.		Battalion in Camp near GLISY. The Battalion paraded in Mass on Battalion Parade Ground at 09.15 hours for route march. Dress:- Musketry order. Route:- GLISY – N.26.c.6.3 – T.2.a.3.2. – T.2.a.5.1 – ST NICHOLAS – BOVES – S.12.b.4.8. S.6.b.9.8. – M.29.d.1.6. – Road East & West through M.30 – GLISY. (Ref. Sheet 62 D) 1 N.C.O. & 10 men per Coy were employed on improving the Camp, from 08.30 hours. Voluntary Educational Classes were held from 14.30 to 18.30 hours.	

A7092 Wt. W128.9/M1293. 750,000. 1/17. D. D & L. Ltd. Forms/C2118/14.

Army Form C. 2118.

Instructions regarding War Diaries and Intelligence Summaries are contained in F. S. Regs., Part II. and the Staff Manual respectively. Title pages will be prepared in manuscript.

WAR DIARY
or
INTELLIGENCE SUMMARY.
(Erase heading not required.)

Place	Date	Hour	Summary of Events and Information	Remarks and references to Appendices
GLISY.	21/1/19.		Battalion in Camp near GLISY. The Battalion had baths from 08.00 hours to 15.00 hours. When not bathing Coys were employed on working parties in the Camp. Cross Country runners paraded for a cross country run at 10.00 hours. Captain W. Phennah M.C. gave a lecture on "Gardening" in B. Coy Recreational Hut at 11.30 hours, 12 men per Coy attended. The Cadre personnel paraded for C.O's Inspection at 09.30 hours.	
GLISY	22/1/19.		Battalion in Camp near GLISY. One N.C.O. + 12 men per Coy paraded at 08.30 hours outside Orderly Room for work under 2/Lt C.E. D. Parkhouse. The remainder of Batt'n paraded for Physical Training under C.S.M. Clarke from 0900 to 10.00 hours. All subaltern officers attended. From 10.30 to 12.30 hours - Compulsory Classes were held. The Cross Country runners paraded at 1000 hours for Cross Country run	
GLISY.	23/1/19.		Battalion in Camp near GLISY. The whole Battalion were employed on working parties in the Camp from 09.00 to 12.30 hours. The Medical Officer gave a lecture to all Coys on "Venereal Diseases" at 14.15 hours in B Coy Recreation Hut. All officers attended. As usual the cross country runners paraded at 10.00 hours.	

A7092 Wt. W128 9/M1293 750,000. 1/17. D. D & I. Ltd. Forms/C2118/14.

Army Form C. 2118.

Instructions regarding War Diaries and Intelligence Summaries are contained in F. S. Regs., Part II. and the Staff Manual respectively. Title pages will be prepared in manuscript.

WAR DIARY
or
INTELLIGENCE SUMMARY.
(Erase heading not required.)

Place	Date	Hour	Summary of Events and Information	Remarks and references to Appendices
GLISY.	24/1/19.		Battalion in Camp near GLISY. The whole Battn, with the exception of 1 NCO. and 14 OR on work, paraded on the Battalion Parade Ground for a cross country run at 09.15 hours Dress:- Clean fatigue less tunics & puttees. Length of course 3½ miles. Compulsory educational classes were held from 10.30 to 12.30 hours. Subjects, French, arithmetic, mechanics, French (officers) English Geography, English, Shorthand (elementary).	
GLISY	25/1/19.		Battalion in Camp near GLISY. The Battalion paraded in mass on Battalion parade Ground at 09.15 hours for route march. Dress:- Fighting Order. Route:- X. roads N.20.c.9.1. - GLISY. - LAMOTTE - Rd junction N.1.d.9.7 - BARNEY CROSS ROADS - CAMON - LONGEAU - GLISY. Recreational training was carried out from 14-00 to 1600 hours. A Battn bicycle race was held for runners & Signallers at 15.15 hours. Prize:- 20 francs. 40432 Pte Baker G was the winner.	
GLISY.	26/1/19.		Battalion in Camp near GLISY. Parade Services were held at 09.30 & 11.00 hours for C of E. and R.C. respectively. Non-conformist Service was also held at 09.30 hrs All Cross Country runners went for a practise run at 10.00 hrs under 2/Lt W.G. GRAY Lt NEWH LANCASTER M.C & 11 ORs Proceeded for Demobilization	

A7092 Wt. W128 9/M1293 750,000. 1/17. D. D & L. Ltd. Forms/C2118/14.

Instructions regarding War Diaries and Intelligence Summaries are contained in F. S. Regs., Part II. and the Staff Manual respectively. Title pages will be prepared in manuscript.

WAR DIARY
or
INTELLIGENCE SUMMARY.
(*Erase heading not required.*)

Army Form C. 2118.

Place	Date	Hour	Summary of Events and Information	Remarks and references to Appendices
GLISY	27.1.19		Battalion in camp near GLISY. All ranks of the Battn paraded at 09.15 hrs in close column of Coys for Muster Roll Call – Dress Clean Fatigue A lecture was delivered by R.S.M NORMAN CA to Bn (who paraded as strong as possible) at 10.45 to 12.30 hrs. Subject:- "EXTENSION OF SERVICE". Compulsory educational Classes were held. Work under Bn Works Officer 2/Lt. Parkhouse was carried out. Battn Cross Country Runners went for a practice run at 10.00 hrs under 2/Lt. W. G. GRAY. 2Lt A.O. Jones & 11 ORs proceeded for Demobilization.	
GLISY	28.1.19.		Battalion in camp near GLISY. Compulsory educational classes were held from 09.15 to 11.20 hrs Work under Bn Works Officer was carried out. All ranks excluding Coy Cooks & 1 Orderly man per Coy paraded for a lecture delivered by the Commanding Officer Lt. Col C.A. Harmey D.S.O. at 12.00 hrs Subject "EXTENSION OF SERVICE". Twenty one Cross Country Runners (including Capt W. M. EVANS D.C.O. & 2/Lt GRAY) representing Battalion proceeded to QUERRIEU by Lorry to take part in Divisional Competition Ten other Ranks proceeded for Demobilization	

A7092. Wt. W128 9/M1293. 750,000. 1/17. D. D. & L. Ltd. Forms/C2118/14.

Instructions regarding War Diaries and Intelligence Summaries are contained in F. S. Regs., Part II. and the Staff Manual respectively. Title pages will be prepared in manuscript.

WAR DIARY
or
INTELLIGENCE SUMMARY.
(Erase heading not required.)

Army Form C. 2118.

Place	Date	Hour	Summary of Events and Information	Remarks and references to Appendices
GLISY	29.1.19		Battalion in Camp near GLISY. The Battn paraded at 09.15 hrs in close column of Coys under R.S.M. Norman for Arms Drill. From 10.30 to 12.30. Compulsory Educational Classes were held. Four NCOs & Thirty two men worked on Camp under Bn Work Officer. Each Coy established themselves in 3 huts. 13 ORs proceeded for Demobilization.	
GLISY	30.1.19		All Coys paraded for P.T. under S.M.I Clarke A.G.S. at 09.15 hrs. Compulsory educational Classes were held. Work under Bn Works Officer was carried out. An inspection of Sports Kit was held. Battn emblems were sewn on tunics of all Ranks.	
GLISY	31.1.19		Battalion in Camp near GLISY. Work under Bn Works Officer was carried out. 2/Lt W. G. GRAY assumed command of B Coy	

W Cobb.
Captain
for Lt Col
Commdg 10 S W B

3.2.19

A7092 Wt. W125,9/M1293 750,000. 1/17. D. D & L. Ltd. Forms/C2118/14.

Army Form C. 2118.

38

Instructions regarding War Diaries and Intelligence Summaries are contained in F. S. Regs., Part II. and the Staff Manual respectively. Title pages will be prepared in manuscript.

WAR DIARY
or
~~INTELLIGENCE SUMMARY.~~
(Erase heading not required.)

10th Battn South Wales Borderers

FEBRUARY. 1919.

Place	Date	Hour	Summary of Events and Information (Map ref:- AMIENS. 1/100,000.)	Remarks and references to Appendices
GLISY.	1.2.19		Battalion billeted in Camp near GLISY. The Commanding Officer inspected the Battalion at 11.00 hours, and then each Company lines. One NCO and 10 men were on work under the Battalion Works Officer from 08.30 hours to 12.30 hours and then again at 13.45 hours. Captain E. P. Enright MC appointed Educational Officer vice Captain R. M. Morgan to UK for Demobilization.	[initials]
GLISY	2.2.19		Battalion Billeted in Camp near GLISY. The Battalion paraded for Divine Service at 09.45 hours on the Battalion Parade Ground. Service was held in the Battalion Recreation Hut. Dress:- Belt & Sidearms. Nonconformists paraded at 11.00 and Roman Catholics at 10.45 for Divine Service. Dress:- Belt & Sidearms.	[initials]
GLISY	3.2.19		Battalion billeted in Camp near GLISY. Training consisting of P.T. was carried out from 09.15 to 10.30 hours. Compulsory educational classes were held from 10.30 to 12.30 hours. Companies bathed during the day.	[initials]
GLISY.	4.2.19		Battalion billeted in Camp near GLISY. Physical Training was carried out from 09.15 to 10.30 hours, under Sergeant Powell. Educational Classes were held from 10.30 to 12.30 hours. Captain W. J. Cobb MC, 2/Lieut. S. Hicks & A. G. McPherson rejoined from Course. Headquarter details bathed at 09.00 hours.	[initials]

A7092 Wt. W128_9/M1293 750,000. 1/17. D. D. & L. Ltd. Forms/C2118/14.

Army Form C. 2118.

Instructions regarding War Diaries and Intelligence Summaries are contained in F. S. Regs., Part II. and the Staff Manual respectively. Title pages will be prepared in manuscript.

WAR DIARY

or

~~INTELLIGENCE SUMMARY.~~

(Erase heading not required.)

Place	Date	Hour	Summary of Events and Information	Remarks and references to Appendices
GLISY	5.2.19		The Battalion billeted in Camp near GLISY. The Band & Drums paraded for Inspection by the Adjutant at 09.15 hours. Dress:- Drill Order. The Battalion paraded on the Battalion parade Ground for guard and sentry drill under the R.S.M, from 09.15 - 10.00 hours. Physical Training under Coy. arrangements was carried out from 10.15 - 10.45 hours. All Coys were lectured at 11.15 hours on the Army Order XIV - Armies of Occupation.	[illegible]
GLISY.	6.2.19		The Battalion billeted in Camp near GLISY. Training consisting of P.T. was carried out from 09.15 - 10.00 hours, under Coy arrangements. Compulsory Educational Classes were held from 11-00 to 12.30 hours. The Commanding Officer inspected the huts at 10.45 hours; all men were standing by their kits in Musketry Order. A Whist Drive was held in Battalion Recreation Hut at 18.30 hours, and a supper provided. All ranks thoroughly enjoyed themselves.	[illegible]
GLISY	7.2.19		The Battalion billeted in Camp near GLISY. H.R.H. The Prince of Wales visited the Battalion at 11.00 hours, and chatted with officers & men. He inspected the Cookhouses, Recreation Hut & the men's huts. The Officers & men cheered heartily as the Prince got into his Car to go.	[illegible]

A7092 Wt. W128.9/M1293 750,000. 1/17. D. D & L. Ltd. Forms/C2118/14.

Instructions regarding War Diaries and Intelligence Summaries are contained in F. S. Regs., Part II. and the Staff Manual respectively. Title pages will be prepared in manuscript.

WAR DIARY

or

~~INTELLIGENCE SUMMARY.~~

(Erase heading not required.)

Army Form C. 2118.

Place	Date	Hour	Summary of Events and Information	Remarks and references to Appendices
GLISY.	8.2.19		The Battalion in Camp near GLISY. Training consisting of P.T and football was carried out from 09.15 to 10.15 hours. The remainder of the morning was devoted to Educational Classes, consisting of English, French, Geography & History. The C.O. inspected the Transport at 09.45 hours in full marching order.	
GLISY.	9.2.19.		The Battalion in Camp near GLISY. The Battalion paraded for Divine Service at 09.45 hours on Battn. Parade Ground. Dress - Belt & Sidearms. The Service was held in the Bn Recreation Hut at 10.00 hours. Nonconformists and Roman Catholics attended services at 11.00 hours. A Voluntary C of E Service was held in the evening at 18.30 hours in the Bn Recreation Hut.	
GLISY	10/2/19		Morning was spent in PT and Education. afternoon - all men turned out for football. In spite of snow - the games were greatly enjoyed Bn still take great interest in "Supper Bar" instituted in the Bn Recreation Hut. Capt. W.T. Sweleigh rejoined Bn from leave in U.K.	WMG

A7092 Wt. W128 9/M1293 750,000. 1/17. D. D & L. Ltd. Forms/C2118/14.

Army Form C. 2118.

Instructions regarding War Diaries and Intelligence Summaries are contained in F. S. Regs., Part II. and the Staff Manual respectively. Title pages will be prepared in manuscript.

WAR DIARY
or
INTELLIGENCE SUMMARY.
(Erase heading not required.)

Place	Date	Hour	Summary of Events and Information	Remarks and references to Appendices
GLISY	11/2/19		Bn paraded for Route March. mustered 103 O.R. – very fresh morning. Roads rather slippery, made going rather difficult. Band & bugles amalgamate to form Bugle Band – greatly appreciated by civilians through which Bn passed. Bn practised in Judging Distance & Observation: Col C D Harvey took several snaps of the Battn on line of March. Afternoon spent in Boxing – Major A L Bowen re-joined Bn from leave in U.K.	WmE
GLISY	12/2/19		Morning – PT and Education: During afternoon Major General Commanding 38th Div made farewell speech to Officers & O.R. warned for Army of Occupation – 9 Officers 116 O.R. on parade. 2/Lt C F Tudge rejoined from leave	WmE
GLISY	13/2/19		Morning spent in PT. Fitting of Equipment & Education. During afternoon the Company played football on the ice ponds Thoroughly enjoyed. Capt Gwynright M.C. proceeded to U K as Conducting Officer. 2/Lt Powell left Bn to proceed on leave to UK 2/Lt Stricke takes up duties as T.O vice 2/Lt Powell	WmE

A7092 Wt. W128_9/M1293 750,000. 1/17. D. D & L. Ltd. Forms/C2118/14.

Instructions regarding War Diaries and Intelligence Summaries are contained in F. S. Regs., Part II. and the Staff Manual respectively. Title pages will be prepared in manuscript.

WAR DIARY
or
INTELLIGENCE SUMMARY.
(Erase heading not required.)

Army Form C. 2118.

Place	Date	Hour	Summary of Events and Information	Remarks and references to Appendices
GLISY.	14/2/19	–	Usual programme for morning Training. Afternoon spent in football – Thaw set in – Band gave its last performance at Officers Mess – comprised of six bandsmen only.	WMG
GLISY	15/2/19	–	Morning devoted to P.T. Arms drill & Education. 2/Lt Wakefield returned from draft. conducting to UK. The Company was paid during the afternoon.	WMG
GLISY.	16/2/19	–	Usual Sunday services were held – There were no Other parades	WMG
GLISY	17/2/19		Bn paraded for Route March to QUERRIEU, to see a Shield made by Divisional R.E. All the Battle honours of the Division from Aug. 21. 1918 were carved across the top – and underneath, the shoulderstraps of all the German Divisions (54 in all) that the Divn fought, from 21 Aug. 18 to 11/11/18. It was made of wood which was used by the Division to cross the ANCRE and SELLE. Only Two men fell out on the way to QUERRIEU + two men on the way back – As the march was 18 miles	WMG

A7092 Wt. W128 9/M1293 750,000. 1/17. D. D & L. Ltd. Forms/C2118/14.

Army Form C. 2118.

Instructions regarding War Diaries and Intelligence Summaries are contained in F. S. Regs., Part II. and the Staff Manual respectively. Title pages will be prepared in manuscript.

WAR DIARY
or
INTELLIGENCE SUMMARY.
(Erase heading not required.)

Place	Date	Hour	Summary of Events and Information	Remarks and references to Appendices
GLISY	17/2/19		this was thought very creditable. Bn had lunch in grounds of 38th Div. H.Q. Arrived back at Camp 16.20 hours – when dinners were served. At 1800 hours, a concert was held in Recreation Hut ~~at which~~ Colonel Harvey took the Chair. A very varied & interesting programme winding up with a playlet "The Cure" by the Bn MO (LT. T.L. CRAWHALL) was highly appreciated by ~~the~~ all ranks.	[initials]
GLISY	18/2/19		Morning Programme – 0900 – 0945 Cleaning up equipment; 0945 – 10.30 Arms Drill under RSM; 1100 – 12.30 Education. During afternoon Officers played remainder of Bn at Association. A very good game resulted in O.R. winning 1 goal to Nil.	[initials]
GLISY	19/2/19		Usual morning programme. A Rugby Match between 21st and 38th Divisions at ALLONVILLE resulted in a win for 38th Div – 32 points to Nil. During afternoon men played football.	[initials]

A7092 Wt. W128.9/M1293 750,000. 1/17. D. D & L Ltd. Forms/C2118/14.

Army Form C. 2118.

Instructions regarding War Diaries and Intelligence Summaries are contained in F. S. Regs., Part II. and the Staff Manual respectively. Title pages will be prepared in manuscript.

WAR DIARY
or
INTELLIGENCE SUMMARY.
(Erase heading not required.)

Place	Date	Hour	Summary of Events and Information	Remarks and references to Appendices
20/2/1919 GLISY.			Usual morning programme. Afternoon – inter platoon games. Men not playing, worked on old Coy lines – & fitting with stoves, &c. 2/Lt A Anderson left for dispersal station – also Sgt Watkins (bandmaster) Sgt-Drummer Brayley took over duties of Bandmaster.	WMG
21/GLISY	21/2/19		Morning spent in P.T. Arms Drill and Education. Rain prevented "Sports" during the afternoon. At 1800 hours, a concert was held in Bn Recreation Hut – Capt W.T. Cobb took the chair. Programme consisted of 2 playlets (I) "A Daughter of Thieves" and (II) "The Cure" by Lt T L Crawhall, Bn MO, were well presented, and highly enjoyed. Characters – (I) Major A.L. Bowen DSO, Capt J. Morris MC (TMB), Lt T.L. Crawhall MO (II) Capt. J.W. Hughes. CF, Lt T. L. Crawhall, 2/Lt J.M. Lloyd, 2/Lt S Hicks Pianoforte Solos, Violin solos, songs, exhibition club swinging	WMG

A7092 Wt. W128 9/M1293 750,000. 1/17. D. D & L. Ltd. Forms/C2118/14.

Instructions regarding War Diaries and Intelligence Summaries are contained in F. S. Regs., Part II. and the Staff Manual respectively. Title pages will be prepared in manuscript.

WAR DIARY
or
INTELLIGENCE SUMMARY.
(Erase heading not required.)

Army Form C. 2118.

Place	Date	Hour	Summary of Events and Information	Remarks and references to Appendices
GLISY	21/2/19		and a humorous sketch, by 6 O.R. of the Bn, were added & formed a very excellent programme. Brigadier General de Pree (115 Bde) Col Beasley (17th RWF) Col Sproule (131 F.A) and Major de Rivemont (2 RWF) attended & were afterwards ~~the~~ entertained as Bn guests, at dinner.	WMG
GLISY	22/2/19		0915 – 0945 P.T. 1000 – 1100 Handling of Arms 1115 – 1230 Education The Officers played the men at Association football during the afternoon, winning a very hard game by two goals to one.	WMG
GLISY	23/2/19		A United Service was held in Bn Recreation Hut at 1000 hrs. During the afternoon, the band of 2/ RWF numbering 47 played in GLISY Village from 1430 to 1600 hours. 2/Lt. W. L. Wakefield evacuated to F.A.	WMG.

A7092 Wt. W128 9/M1293 750,000. 1/17. D. D & L. Ltd. Forms/C2118/14.

Instructions regarding War Diaries and Intelligence Summaries are contained in F. S. Regs., Part II. and the Staff Manual respectively. Title pages will be prepared in manuscript.

WAR DIARY
or
INTELLIGENCE SUMMARY.
(Erase heading not required.)

Army Form C. 2118.

Place	Date	Hour	Summary of Events and Information	Remarks and references to Appendices
GLISY.	24/2/19	–	Mornings programme. 0915 – 0945. P.T. 1000 – 1045. Musketry J. D. Rapid aiming, firing & loading 1100 – 1145 Arms Drill 1145 – 1245. Education During the afternoon, men played football. At 14.10 fire alarm was sounded, for practice purposes.	WMG
GLISY	25/2/19		Battalion Route-marched through St NICHOLAS BOVES, CAGNY, LONGEAU and GLISY. Starting 0915, and arriving back at 12.30. Dress Fighting Order. Warning orders for Men due to proceed to Army of Occupation received.	WMG
GLISY.	26/2/19		0915 – 0945 P.T. 1000 – 1045 Kit Inspection. 1100 – 1215. Education. (Gardening Class). Remainder of day devoted to preparing rolls &c for draft proceeding to join 1st & 2nd 8th Gds.	WMG

A7092 Wt. W128.9/M1293. 750,000. 1/17. D. D & L. Ltd. Forms/C2118/14.

Instructions regarding War Diaries and Intelligence Summaries are contained in F. S. Regs., Part II. and the Staff Manual respectively. Title pages will be prepared in manuscript.

WAR DIARY
or
INTELLIGENCE SUMMARY.
(Erase heading not required.)

Army Form C. 2118.

Place	Date	Hour	Summary of Events and Information	Remarks and references to Appendices
GLISY.	27/2/19		Draft of 9 Officers and 106 O.R. left the unit at 0800 hours for Army of Occupation. Men were paraded in Recreation Hut, prior to starting and Col Harvey and Major A.L. Bowen addressed them, and thanked them for all they had done in the Battalion. They were then conveyed by lorry to CANDAS. To 1st Bn S.W.B. – Capt W.T. Cobb MC, 2/Lt W.T. Deleigh, 2/Lt S. Hicks, 2/Lt A.J. McPherson To 2nd S.W.B. – 2/Lt M.G. Jones, 2/Lt J.M. Lloyd, 2/Lt C.F. Tudge, 2/Lt T.J. Trebble, 2/Lt W.G. Gray This left Bn with 9 Officers, 81 O.R. Remainder of day was devoted to cleaning up Camp, reorganising unit and "closing up" into new billets.	WMG
GLISY	28/2/19		No men for parades. Details fell in for Education 10.30 – 1200, combining with 115 L.T.M.B. 2/Lt W.R. WAKEFIELD reported back from Hospital. C.D. Harvey Lt Col Cmdg 10/S.W.B.	WMG

A7092 Wt. W128.9/M1293 750,000. 1/17. D. D & L. Ltd. Forms/C2118/14.

Instructions regarding War Diaries and Intelligence Summaries are contained in F. S. Regs., Part II. and the Staff Manual respectively. Title pages will be prepared in manuscript.

WAR DIARY
or
INTELLIGENCE SUMMARY.
(Erase heading not required.)

Army Form C. 2118.

10 SWB

Vol 39

Place	Date	Hour	Summary of Events and Information	Remarks and references to Appendices
GLISY	1/3/19	-	Medical Officer lectured "details" on Influenza 1100 hrs - 1230. 2/Lt Greaves conducted draft for dispersal, which included a/RSM Norman, Sgt-Dr Drayley and L/Cpl Hunt and Cpl Beavan. Bn accounts audited - President - Major AL Bowen DSO Members { Capt WM Evans Lt D P Clayton Summer Time came into use at 2300hrs (old time)	WME
GLISY	2/3/19		A United Service was held in Battalion Recreation at 1000 hours. Audit Board assembled at 1100 hours and carried on with the Battalion Accounts. Band of 2RWF played in GLISY VILLAGE from 1600 - 1700 hours. All Officers attending were afterwards entertained by 115 Bde HQ to tea.	WME
GLISY	3/3/19	0900 hours.	Promulgation in case of Pte Bailey T. 48455. Absenting himself without leave.	
		0915 "	Summary of Evidence taken, in case of No 51883 Pte MILLEN.	WME

A7092. Wt. W128 9/M1293 750,000. 1/17. D. D & L. Ltd. Forms/C2118/14.

Instructions regarding War Diaries and Intelligence Summaries are contained in F. S. Regs., Part II. and the Staff Manual respectively. Title pages will be prepared in manuscript.

WAR DIARY
or
INTELLIGENCE SUMMARY.

(Erase heading not required.)

Army Form C. 2118.

Place	Date	Hour	Summary of Events and Information	Remarks and references to Appendices
3/3/19 GLISY			1100 hrs. Inspection of Small kit by Commanding Officer. Football match, versus 38th D.A.C postponed owing to weather conditions.	WMG
GLISY 4/3/	4/3/19		Education Class 1100 - 1230. During the afternoon, the Bn team played against 38th Div Ammunition Column; at association football. After a very interesting game the DAC won 3 goals to 2. Band of No 223 P.of.W. Coy played at Officers Mess during the evening and gave very interesting and varied programme.	WMG
GLISY	5/3/19		Education Class 1100 - 1230. 2/Lt S.P. Powell returned from leave, and resumed duties as Transport Officer. Mobilisation equipment was checked under Unit arrangement.	WMG

A7092 Wt. W128 9/M1293 750,000. 1/17. D. D & L. Ltd. Forms/C2118/14.

Instructions regarding War Diaries and Intelligence Summaries are contained in F. S. Regs., Part II. and the Staff Manual respectively. Title pages will be prepared in manuscript.

WAR DIARY
or
INTELLIGENCE SUMMARY.

(Erase heading not required.)

Army Form C. 2118.

Place	Date	Hour	Summary of Events and Information	Remarks and references to Appendices
GLISY.	6/3/19		Rides 0900 to 1000 hours. Education 1100 – 12 30. Pte Grimmer, Officers Mess Cook, demobilised — Units strength 10 Offrs 58 O.R. 10 Mules proceeded to 49 M.V.S. for demobilisation.	[illegible]
GLISY	7/3/19		Education 1100 – 1230 hours. Nothing of other interest	[illegible]
GLISY.	8/3/19		Education. 1100 – 1230 hours. 1400 hours Fire Picquet paraded for inspection. 2/Lt S J. Powell left, with party of 11 O.R., for as Conducting Officer. Major A G Bowen appointed O/C Wagon Park –	[illegible]
GLISY	9/3/19		United Service in Recreation Room at 1000 hours. At 18:30 2/Lt C.S. Millard read a very interesting paper in Recreation Hut on "The Principles of the Sermon on the Mount"	[illegible]

A7092 Wt. W128 9/M1293 750,000. 1/17. D. D & L. Ltd. Forms/C2118/14.

Army Form C. 2118.

Instructions regarding War Diaries and Intelligence Summaries are contained in F. S. Regs., Part II. and the Staff Manual respectively. Title pages will be prepared in manuscript.

WAR DIARY
or
INTELLIGENCE SUMMARY.
(Erase heading not required.)

Place	Date	Hour	Summary of Events and Information	Remarks and references to Appendices
GLISY	10/3/19		Education 1100-1230 hrs. Col Harvey attended Conference at Divisional H.Q. QUERRIEU on "Arms, Equipment + Stores"	WMG
GLISY	11/3/19		Education 1100-12.30 hours. During the afternoon an Association Match was played between 38th DAC. and 16th SWB. former winning by 3 goals to one after a hard game.	WMG
GLISY	12/3/19		Education 1100 - 12.30 hours. Capt T Morris MC. and the 9 personnel of unit attached 115th TMB rejoined unit - Capt Morris appointed O/C A Coy. 1415 hours. M.O inoculated 'volunteers' against influenza.	WMG
GLISY	13/3/19		Education 1100 - 12.30 hrs. Capt Horner, U.S.A. late M.O. of the Unit paid Bn a visit.	WMG

A7092. Wt. W128.9/M1293. 750,000. 1/17. D. D & L. Ltd. Forms/C2118/14.

Army Form C. 2118.

WAR DIARY
or
INTELLIGENCE SUMMARY.
(Erase heading not required.)

Instructions regarding War Diaries and Intelligence Summaries are contained in F. S. Regs., Part II. and the Staff Manual respectively. Title pages will be prepared in manuscript.

Place	Date	Hour	Summary of Events and Information	Remarks and references to Appendices
GLISY.	14/3/19	–	Education Class 1100 – 1230 hours. Lt Col Harvey left unit to proceed on leave to UK. Major Bowen assumed Command of the Bn: Duties of O/C Wagon Park taken over by Brigade Transport Officer.	WmE
GLISY	15/3/19		Bn bathed from 0900 hrs – 1000 hrs at GLISY BATHS. Usual Education Classes were held & men were then paid. Nothing of interest otherwise.	WmE
GLISY	16/3/19		United Service in Recreation Hut at 1000 hours. 2/Lt. C B Millard proceeded as Draft Conducting Officer to Dispersal Station.	WmE
GLISY.	17/3/19.		Usual Education Classes. Lt. T L Crawhall left unit for Army of Occupation.	WmE

A7092 Wt. W128 9/M1293 750,000. 1/17. D. D & L. Ltd. Forms/C2118/14.

Instructions regarding War Diaries and Intelligence Summaries are contained in F. S. Regs., Part II. and the Staff Manual respectively. Title pages will be prepared in manuscript.

WAR DIARY
or
INTELLIGENCE SUMMARY.
(Erase heading not required.)

Army Form C. 2118.

Place	Date	Hour	Summary of Events and Information	Remarks and references to Appendices
GLISY.	18/3/19	–	Usual Education Classes.	WmG
GLISY	19/3/19		Education 11.00 – 12.30 hours. Men spent afternoon playing football.	WmG.
GLISY	20/3/19		Education 11.00 – 12.30. 10/SWB played 38th DAC at Association football at 14.30. This resulted in a draw of 1 goal each, after a very interesting game. Capt JR Morris MC proceeded to join 51st SWB Battalion, in Army of Occupation	WmG.
GLISY.	21/3/19		Baths at GLISY 0900 – 1000 hrs.	WmG
GLISY	22/3/19		Battalion moved from GLISY to Hut Camp at BLANGY-TRONVILLE, where Divisional Infantry Cadres were concentrating. Move completed by 1300 hours. A Brigade Officers Mess was formed, each Bn advancing 200 francs for initial outlay. All leave & demobilisation suspended owing to threatened Strikes in England.	WmG

(A7092). Wt. W12839/M1293. 750,000. 1/17. D. D. & L., Ltd. Forms/C.2118/14.

Army Form C. 2118.

WAR DIARY
or
INTELLIGENCE SUMMARY.
(Erase heading not required.)

Instructions regarding War Diaries and Intelligence Summaries are contained in F. S. Regs., Part II. and the Staff Manual respectively. Title pages will be prepared in manuscript.

Place	Date	Hour	Summary of Events and Information	Remarks and references to Appendices
~~GEISY~~ BLANGY TRONVILLE	23/3/19		Battn settled in new Camp. 113 Bde & 115 Bde held combined C of E Service in Recreation Hut 17th RWF. A Chaplain of 113 Bde took the Service. Capt J W Hughes evacuated to 131 F.A.	WMG
BLANGY TRONVILLE.	24/3/19		No 51863 Pte W.H. Millen tried by F G.C.M. - Charge "Desertion" Demobilisation & leave re-opened	WMG
BLANGY TRONVILLE.	25-3-19		Captn: W. M. Evans proceeded to U.K. on leave. Men making themselves comfortable in billets.	W.L.W
BLANGY TRONVILLE.	26-3-19		Men making themselves comfortable in billets and cleaning their equipment. 12.15 hrs. Promulgation in case of No 51863 Pte W Millen "Deserting His Majesties Forces")	W.L.W

(A7092). Wt. W12839/M1293. 750,000. 1/17. D. D. & L., Ltd. Forms/C.2118/14.

Army Form C. 2118.

WAR DIARY
or
INTELLIGENCE SUMMARY.
(Erase heading not required.)

Instructions regarding War Diaries and Intelligence Summaries are contained in F. S. Regs., Part II. and the Staff Manual respectively. Title pages will be prepared in manuscript.

Place	Date	Hour	Summary of Events and Information	Remarks and references to Appendices
BLANGY TRONVILLE	27.3.19		Very rough weather and exceedingly cold Major A.L. Bowen D.S.O. attended "Court of Enquiry" at Glisy	W.L.W.
BLANGY TRONVILLE	28.3.19		Education 11.00 — 12.30 hrs Brigadier General H. De-Pree, inspected the camp Grand concert 18.00 hrs in the recreation room 2nd R.W.F	W.L.W.
BLANGY TRONVILLE	29.3.19		Lieut. D.P. Clayton proceeded on leave to U.K Lieut. J.P. Enright rejoined from leave Rev. J.W. Hughes rejoined from Field Ambulance.	W.L.W.
BLANGY TRONVILLE	30.3.19		Lieut. J.B. Greaves rejoined from leave. 'Church of England' service 11.00 hrs recreation hut 2nd R.W.F	W.L.W.
BLANGY TRONVILLE	31.3.19		Usual Education Classes	W.L.W.

A. Bowen Major
Comdg 10th Batt. R.W.F.

(A7092). Wt. W12839/M1293. 750,000. 1/17. D. D. & L., Ltd. Forms/C.2118/14.

Instructions regarding War Diaries and Intelligence Summaries are contained in F. S. Regs., Part II. and the Staff Manual respectively. Title pages will be prepared in manuscript.

WAR DIARY
or
INTELLIGENCE SUMMARY.
(Erase heading not required.)

Army Form C. 2118.

10S W B

APRIL

Place	Date	Hour	Summary of Events and Information	Remarks and references to Appendices
BLANGY TRONVILLE	1-4-19		Education classes 11.00 — 12.30 hrs 1st round of Divisional football competition 113 Bde 1 goal – 121 Bde Field Artillery Bde 115 Bde 1 goal – D.A.C. 6 goals.	[illegible]
BLANGY TRONVILLE	2-4-19		Education classes 11-00 – 12.30 hrs 114 Brigade [illegible] R.E. [illegible] [illegible] [illegible] [illegible]	[illegible]
BLANGY TRONVILLE	3-4-19		Baths at Blangy 10.00 to 12 hrs. Education classes 11.00 to 12.30 hrs.	[illegible]
BLANGY TRONVILLE	4-4-19		Education Classes 11.00 to 12.30 hrs. 115 v 113 Rugger match. Concert arranged by 115 Bde at 14 hrs.	[illegible]
BLANGY TRONVILLE	5-4-19		Education Classes 11-00 to 12.30 hours 113 Bde v R.E. 2nd Round Divisional Competition – Result 113 Bde 3 goals. R.E. 2 goals	[illegible]
BLANGY TRONVILLE	6-4-19		Church Services were held as times as under: C. of E. in 2nd RWF Recreation Hut at 11-00 hours Nonconformists in 17th RWF — " — at 10.00 hours Roman Catholics at Church, Blangy Tronville at 10.00 hours. An association Football match 115 Bde v 13th Welsh was played resulting in a win for the former of 1–0 goals. Lieut J.B. Greaves proceeded to Dispersal Area for Demobilization	[illegible]

(A7092). Wt. W12839/M1293. 750,000. 1/17. D. D. & L., Ltd. Forms/C.2118/14.

Instructions regarding War Diaries and Intelligence Summaries are contained in F. S. Regs., Part II. and the Staff Manual respectively. Title pages will be prepared in manuscript.

WAR DIARY
or
INTELLIGENCE SUMMARY.
(Erase heading not required.)

Army Form C. 2118.

Place	Date	Hour	Summary of Events and Information	Remarks and references to Appendices
BLANGY TRONVILLE	7/4/19		The Battalion paraded for route march consisting of all Divisional Infantry Cadres at 09.30 hours and returned to Camp at 12.45 hours. Route:- Ref. Amiens Sheet 1/100,000 Cross roads ¼ mile W of 1st B in BLANGY – lane ½ mile South of BLANGY village – road junction ½ mile NE of first E in B. DE GENTELLES – cross roads at last S in ST NICHOLAS – cross roads ½ mile N of N in ST NICHOLAS – to Blangy [illegible].	WMG
BLANGY TRONVILLE	8/4/19		Educational Classes were held between 11-00 and 12.30 hours. Rifles were inspected at 14.00 hours. Recreational Training was carried out during the afternoons.	WMG
Blangy Tronville	9/4/19		Education Classes were held between 11.00 & 12.30 hours. All Blankets were shaken at 14.00 hours. Lieut. Millard rejoined Battn from Conducting Duties.	WMG
Blangy Tronville	10/4/19		Education Classes were held between 11-00 & 12.30 hours.	WMG
Blangy Tronville	11/4/19		Education was carried out under Bde arrangements. Captain [illegible] Bde Educational Officer taking Battn between 11.00 – 12.30 hours.	WMG
Blangy Tronville	12/4/19		Education Classes were held from 11-00 – 12.30 hours	WMG

(A7092). Wt. W12839/M1293. 750,000. 1/17. D. D. & L., Ltd. Forms/C.2118/14.

Instructions regarding War Diaries and Intelligence Summaries are contained in F. S. Regs., Part II. and the Staff Manual respectively. Title pages will be prepared in manuscript.

WAR DIARY
or
INTELLIGENCE SUMMARY.
(Erase heading not required.)

Army Form C. 2118.

Place	Date	Hour	Summary of Events and Information	Remarks and references to Appendices
Blangy-Tronville	13/4/19		Church Services for all denominations were held in the Camp. The Bath paraded for C. of E. Service at 10.50 hours which was held in the 2nd RWF Recreation Hut.	
Blangy-Tronville	14/4/19		The Battalion took part in a route march of all Divisional Cadres parading on the Bde. Parade Ground at 09.30 hours, and returning to Camp by 12.30 hours. Route:- Villers Bretonneux by main road.	
Blangy-Tronville	15/4/19		Education Classes were held under Brigade arrangements from 11.00 - 12.30 hrs. The Battalion paraded for a rifle and equipment inspection at 14-00 hours, by the Adjutant. The final of the Div. Cadre football competition was played, commencing at 14.45 hours resulting in a draw of nil goals 113 Inf Bde v D.A.C.	
Blangy-Tronville	16/4/19		Education Classes were carried out from 11.00 - 12.30 under Bde. arrangements. Lieut Colonel C.D. Harvey DSO rejoined Battalion from Leave.	
Blangy-Tronville	17/4/19		The Battalion paraded for Lecture on Venereal Disease by the MO at 10.50 hours held in 115th Brigade Recreation Hut. Education Classes were held from 11.30 - 12.30 hours The replay of Div. Cadre Football Competition resulted in a draw of Nil goals.	

(A7092). Wt. W12839/M1293. 750,000. 1/17. D. D. & L., Ltd. Forms/C.2118/14.

Instructions regarding War Diaries and Intelligence Summaries are contained in F. S. Regs., Part II. and the Staff Manual respectively. Title pages will be prepared in manuscript.

WAR DIARY
or
INTELLIGENCE SUMMARY.
(Erase heading not required.)

Army Form C. 2118.

Place	Date	Hour	Summary of Events and Information	Remarks and references to Appendices
Blangy-Tronville	18/4/19		Church Services were held as under, during the morning. C. of E. 11.00 hours 114 Bde Recreation Hut. Nonconformists 11.00 hours 114 Bde Recreation Hut Roman Catholics 10.00 hours Church GLISY.	WMG.
Blangy-Tronville	19/4/19		Education Classes were held during the morning from 11.00 - 12.30 hours. The Div Cadre Football Competition final was again replayed at GLISY, kicked off at 14.45 hours, resulting in the D.A.C. 1 goal. 113 Bde. Nil.	WMG
Blangy-Tronville	20/4/19		The Battalion paraded by their respective denominations for Church Parade, as under, C. of E. 11.00 hours 114 Bde Recreation Hut Nonconformists 10.00 hours " " Roman Catholics 10.00 hours Church GLISY.	WMG
Blangy-Tronville	21/4/19		Education Classes were held during the morning between 11.00 - 12.30 hours.	WMG
Blangy-Tronville	22/4/19		Education Classes were held during the morning between 11.00 & 12.30 hours The Commanding Officer inspected the Kits of the Battn at 10.30 hours.	WMG
Blangy-Tronville	23/4/19.		Education Classes were held during the morning between 11.00 & 12.30 hours Physical Training was carried out from 10.00 - 10.45 hours. under Sergt Cox. Lieut D.P. Clayton rejoined Battalion from Leave.	WMG
Blangy-Tronville	24/4/19		Physical Training was carried out between 10.00 & 10.45 hours under Sergt. Cox Education Classes were held during morning from 11.00 to 11.45 hours.	WMG

(A7092). Wt. W12839/M1293. 750,000. 1/17. D. D. & L., Ltd. Forms/C.2118/14.

Instructions regarding War Diaries and Intelligence Summaries are contained in F. S. Regs., Part II. and the Staff Manual respectively. Title pages will be prepared in manuscript.

WAR DIARY
or
INTELLIGENCE SUMMARY.
(Erase heading not required.)

Army Form C. 2118.

Place	Date	Hour	Summary of Events and Information	Remarks and references to Appendices
Blangy-Tronville	25/4/19		Physical Training comprising chiefly of football was carried out from 10/9.45 hours. Education Classes were held from 11.00 to 11-45 hours	[initials]
Blangy Tronville	26/4/19		Physical Training was carried out from 09.15 - 10.00 hours. The Adjutant inspected the rifles of all men at 10.30 hours. Education was held from 11.00 - 12.30 hours.	[initials]
Blangy-Tronville	27/4/19.		Services as under were attended by denominations of this Battalion. Church of England . 11.00 hours 114 Bde Recreation Hut Nonconformists . 10.00 -"- -"- -"- -"- Roman Catholics . 10:00 -- Parish Church Blangy Tronville.	[initials]
Blangy-Tronville	28/4/19.		Educational Classes were held during morning from 11-00 - 12 30 hours. owing to a severe ~~snow~~ storm the Physical Training was not carried out. Captain W.H. Evans DSO rejoined from Leave.	[initials]
Blangy-Tronville	29/4/19.		Educational Classes were held from 11-00 - 12 30 hours. a party of 1 officer and 8. O.R. had a lorry ride to the devastated area, to see 15" German Gun. Lieut & Qm. J. Golden rejoined from Leave	[initials]
Blangy-Tronville	30/4/19		A fatigue party of 1 NCO. & 7 men were employed in chopping and sawing wood from 09.30 hours to 12.30 hours.	[initials]

30/4/19.

W. Hawes [signature] Lieut Colonel
Commanding 10th Bn S. W. B.

(A7092). Wt. W12839/M1293. 750,000. 1/17. D. D. & L., Ltd. Forms/C.2118/14.

Instructions regarding War Diaries and Intelligence Summaries are contained in F. S. Regs., Part II. and the Staff Manual respectively. Title pages will be prepared in manuscript.

WAR DIARY
or
INTELLIGENCE SUMMARY.
(Erase heading not required.)

Army Form C. 2118.

38

10 SWB

MAY 1919

41

Place	Date	Hour	Summary of Events and Information	Remarks and references to Appendices
BLANGY-TRONVILLE	1/5/19		Baths at Glisy allotted to unit from 0930 to 1015 hours. Education Class under Capt Phennah 1100 - 12.15. Promulgation of Sentence in case of 48182 ~~Pte~~ LCpl Baxter at 12.30 hrs Weather still very unfavourable. Bde Sports postponed till 6/5/19	Censor WMG
BLANGY TRONVILLE	2/5/19		Weather interfered with Recreational Training. 1100 - 1215 Education.	WMG
BLANGY TRONVILLE	3/5/19		0900 - All blankets shaken 1000 - 1045. Football. 1100 - 1200 Education 1200 Pay. At 1700 hours the 2/RWF played a combined 10/SWB + 17th RWF team, game resulting in a win for the allies by one goal to nil. "Cadre" reduced from 4 Officers + 46 OR to 3 Officers + 36	WMG
BLANGY TRONVILLE	4/5/19		1000. Nonconformist Service. 1100 C of E Service. Band of 2/RWF attended. At 1800 hours the 38th Divl Orchestra gave a concert in 114 Bde Recreation Room; well attended - and highly appreciated	[illegible]

(A7092). Wt. W12839/M1293. 750,000. 1/17. D. D. & L., Ltd. Forms/C.2118/14.

Army Form C. 2118.

Instructions regarding War Diaries and Intelligence Summaries are contained in F. S. Regs., Part II. and the Staff Manual respectively. Title pages will be prepared in manuscript.

WAR DIARY
or
INTELLIGENCE SUMMARY.
(Erase heading not required.)

Place	Date	Hour	Summary of Events and Information	Remarks and references to Appendices
BLANGY TRONVILLE	5/5/19		Morning spent preparing ground for Brigade Sports on 6th Lt-Col Harvey proceeded on Special Leave to U.K.	WMG
BLANGY TRONVILLE	6/5/19		115 Bde Sports held on football field opposite Camp, commencing at 1400 hours. Band of 2/RWF was in attendance. There was keen competition, the jumping, relay race & 100x being especially good.	WMG
BLANGY TRONVILLE	7/5/19		All huts scrubbed. 1100 hrs - 1200 education 113 Bde Sports held during afternoon. Lt Dr Clayton proceeded on 7 days Special Leave to U.K.	WMG
BLANGY TRONVILLE	8/5/19		38th Div R.A Sports at Glisy	WMG
BLANGY TRONVILLE	9/5/19		Inspection of Rifles &c. 114 Bde Sports held during afternoon.	WMG
BLANGY TRONVILLE	10/5/19		Party of 7 visited devastated area and German 15" How. near VILLERS BRETTONEUX - Education & pay parade, from 1100hrs - 12.30	WMG

(A7092). Wt. W12839/M1293. 750,000. 1/17. D. D. & L., Ltd. Forms/C.2118/14.

Instructions regarding War Diaries and Intelligence Summaries are contained in F. S. Regs., Part II. and the Staff Manual respectively. Title pages will be prepared in manuscript.

WAR DIARY
or
INTELLIGENCE SUMMARY.
(Erase heading not required.)

Army Form C. 2118.

Place	Date	Hour	Summary of Events and Information	Remarks and references to Appendices
~~11/5/~~ BLANGY TRONVILLE.	11/5/19		Usual Sunday Services.	WmG
BLANGY TRONVILLE	12/5/19		Morning spent in cleaning up lines. Wood fatigues. First notification of departure on 16th received: All personnel on Leave wired ~~for~~ to return.	WmG
BLANGY TRONVILLE.	13/5/19		All available men employed loading Mobilisation Stores, on to Wagons at GLISY. Task completed by 16.20 hours, ~~the~~ dinners were served on return to Camp.	WmG
BLANGY TRONVILLE	14/5/19		All huts thoroughly scrubbed out during the morning. Heats in "Relay Race" & Boat Race within the Brigade were run off at 10.00 hours - resulting in wins for 17th R.F. and 2nd R.F. respectively. Winners thus qualify as Brigade Representatives in Division Sports. 10/8 R.D. teams ran 2nd in both races.	WmG

(A7092). Wt. W12839/M1293. 750,000. 1/17. D. D. & L., Ltd. Forms/C.2118/14.

Army Form C. 2118.

Instructions regarding War Diaries and Intelligence Summaries are contained in F. S. Regs., Part II. and the Staff Manual respectively. Title pages will be prepared in manuscript.

WAR DIARY
or
INTELLIGENCE SUMMARY.

(Erase heading not required.)

Place	Date	Hour	Summary of Events and Information	Remarks and references to Appendices
15/5/19 Blangy Tronville			Kits of all Cadre personnel were inspected prior to its proceeding for demobilization. Div Sports were held in the afternoon on the Battalion Sports ground.	D.P.C.
16/5/19 Blangy Tronville			The Cadre personnel left Blangy Camp for LONGEAU (entraining station) entraining there at about 15.00. The train left at 19.50 hours. Captain W.M. Evans DSO proceeded to Dispersal Area for demobilization.	D.P.C.
17/5/19. Havre.			The train arrived in HAVRE about 06.30 hours but was put on a siding and did not leave there until about 11.00 hours; personnel then detrained and unloaded all the wagons etc from the train. After this the wagons were drawn by specially provided teams to the Quay and the personnel taken by motor lorries to No 2 Embarkation Camp. Baths & delousing of personnel was carried out during the afternoon	D.P.C.
18/5/19. Havre.			All personnel were confined to Camp during the day, awaiting orders.	D.P.C.
19/5/19 Havre.			All personnel were confined to Camp awaiting orders.	D.P.C.
20/5/19.			All personnel were confined to camp expecting orders which were eventually received at about 07.30 hours, for embarkation.	D.P.C.
21/5/19.			A loading party left the camp for the Quay by the 11.30 train from Harfleur. The remainder of the Cadre personnel left Camp at 14.30 hours and embarked at about 17.30 hours, arriving at Southampton 03.00 hours 22/5/19, but did not disembark until 07.30 hours.	D.P.C.

D. P. [illegible] Lieut Colonel
Comdg 10th Bn South Wales Borderers.

(A7092). Wt. W12839/M1293. 750,000. 1/17. D. D. & L., Ltd. Forms/C.2118/14.

www.ingramcontent.com/pod-product-compliance
Lightning Source LLC
Chambersburg PA
CBHW080823010526
44111CB00015B/2597
9781474518802